The Semblance of Subjectivity

The Semblance of Subjectivity

Essays in Adorno's Aesthetic Theory

edited by Tom Huhn and Lambert Zuidervaart

The MIT Press
Cambridge, Massachusetts
London, England

©1997 Massachusetts Institute of Technology

This book was set in New Baskerville by Omegatype Typography.

Printed and bound in the United States of America.

Library of Congress Cataloging-in-Publication Data

The semblence of subjectivity : essays in Adorno's Aesthetic theory /
    edited by Tom Huhn and Lambert Zuidervaart.
        p.   cm. — (Studies in contemporary German social thought)
    Includes bibliographical references and index.
    ISBN 0-262-08257-8 (hard : alk. paper)
    1. Adorno, Theodor W., 1903–1969. Ästhetische Theorie.
2. Aesthetics, Modern—20th century.   I. Huhn, Tom.
II. Zuidervaart, Lambert.   III. Series.
B3199.A33A8133   1997
111'.85—dc21   96-37741
                                                              CIP

For Joyce Alene Recker and Nancy R. Steele

Contents

Contents

Acknowledgments

Many colleagues and friends have had a hand, and sometimes two, in helping to bring this collection together. We would like to thank Herb Arnold, Matt Beaverson, Jordan Greenberg, Noah Isenberg, Erhard Konerding, Bob Hullot-Kentor, Gabi Marcus, Jan Miel, Andy Szegedy-Maszak, Paul Schwaber, and David Weisberg.

We are also grateful to Tom McCarthy and Larry Cohen of The MIT Press for their diligent, persistent support of this project, and to Carol Roberts for her very fine copyediting.

Three of the essays included here were originally published in German: Martin Jay's essay appeared in *Auge und Affekt: Wahrnehmung und Interaktion,* edited by Gertrud Koch, Frankfurt: Fischer Verlag, 1995. Rolf Tiedemann's essay appeared as "Begriff, Bild, Name; Über Adorno's Utopie der Erkenntnis," in *Frankfurter Adorno Blätter II,* Herausgegeben vom Theodor W. Adorno Archiv, Munich: edition text + kritik, 1993, pp. 92–111. Rüdiger Bubner's essay appeared in his *Ästhetische Erfahrung,* Frankfurt: Suhrkamp, 1989.

Portions of Lambert Zuidervaart's essay will appear as an entry on Adorno in *The Encyclopedia of Aesthetics,* edited by Michael Kelly, and are included here with permission from the editor and Oxford University Press.

In regard to citations, for a full list of abbreviations used for Adorno's works, see the opening pages of the bibliography. If a parenthetical citation includes two sets of page numbers separated by a slash, the first refers to the German and the second to the published English translation. Unless otherwise indicated, a single parenthetical citation refers to the English translation.

1
Introduction

Lambert Zuidervaart

Even at its highest elevations, art is semblance; but art receives this...from what lacks semblance.... Indelible from resistance to the fungible world... is the resistance of the eye that does not want the world's colors to die. In semblance nonsemblance is promised.

—*Adorno,* Negative Dialectics

Nearly three decades have passed since the death of Theodor W. Adorno in 1969 and the posthumous publication of his *Aesthetic Theory* one year later. Not until the third decade, however, have his aesthetic writings begun to receive sustained attention in the English-speaking world.[1] Indeed, the reception of Adorno's aesthetics in Anglo-American philosophy has barely begun, despite the many translations of his writings[2] and the abundance of secondary literature from scholars in history, literature, music, cultural studies, religion, and the social sciences.[3] In philosophy, and especially among Anglo-American philosophers, there has not been a serious engagement with Adorno's *Aesthetic Theory* on the scale, say, of the attention given Hans-Georg Gadamer's *Truth and Method.* If, in Peter Hohendahl's word's, Adorno has "turned...into a classic" since the mid-1980s,[4] it is as a most peculiar classic, one whose last major book and its central philosophical claims are, for the most part, ignored in the English-speaking world.

Many factors might account for this, not the least of which is the Habermasian turn in Critical Theory away from Adorno's traditional, albeit explosive, subject/object paradigm toward a theory of communicative and intersubjective rationality. The rise of poststructuralism and postmodernism has also made Adorno's dialectical method and paradoxical modernism seem outmoded. Then, too, the theme of a possible "end" of philosophy does not bode well for an author who unrelentingly rewrites the philosophical tradition. Add to this some unreliable translations, analytical philosophy's avoidance of difficult German thinkers, and the long ascendancy of Martin Heidegger among Continental philosophers, and the relative neglect of Adorno's aesthetics becomes understandable.

Yet there have been few philosophers as well versed in contemporary art, especially music, as he, and even fewer aestheticians who have written so much of interest to the social sciences. And, as Fredric Jameson observes, over against post-Marxists who would consign Adorno's negative dialectic to the dustbin of intellectual history, the postmodern era makes it inappropriate to assume that anything is outmoded just because it has fallen out of fashion.[5] Perhaps as aesthetics itself becomes ever more interdisciplinary, shading into cultural theory, Adorno's *Aesthetic Theory* will receive the attention it so clearly deserves.

Cultural Critique

The essays in this volume demonstrate both the complexity and the significance of this last of Adorno's *Hauptwerke*. Not only does *Aesthetic Theory* reconfigure the insights developed in his many volumes on modern music, literature, and culture, but also it shows the relevance of his more strictly philosophical and sociological writings for aesthetics and cultural theory. Conversely, *Aesthetic Theory* also suggests the force and importance of philosophical aesthetics for fields of philosophy and the social sciences in which discourse about the arts and aesthetic phenomena is often ignored—epistemology, ethics, and social theory, to name a few. Three topics are of particular relevance to contemporary scholarship and cultural critique: (1) the culture industry, (2) autonomy in the arts, and (3) the aesthetics of nature.

Adorno's critique of the culture industry arises in part from his debate with Walter Benjamin in the 1930s over the implications of film and radio for the democratization of culture. Whereas Benjamin had suggested that film has a progressive impact on ordinary experience and can serve to politicize the masses, Adorno's 1938 essay "On the Fetish-Character in Music and the Regression of Listening" argues that the broadcast and recording industries resist musical innovation, turn commercial success into a fetish, and promote the regression of both musical and political consciousness.

In "The Culture Industry," a chapter in *Dialectic of Enlightenment* (1944), Adorno's argument expands to include all mass media. Under capitalist conditions, he says, artworks and other cultural artifacts are commodities produced in the manner described by Karl Marx. According to Marx, commodities are products whose use value, their ability to satisfy human wants, is dominated by their exchange value, their ability to command other products in exchange. Capitalist commodity production obscures the fact that human labor power is the source of value and that laborers must be exploited in order to generate the surplus value from which capitalists make their profit.

Building on this Marxian analysis and on Georg Lukács's theory of "reification," Adorno argues that a new level of sophistication and obfuscation characterizes commodity production in advanced capitalism and covertly guides the culture industry. Under such conditions, cultural artifacts are mass-produced without regard for their use value, and their exchange value is presented *as* use value, as something to be enjoyed for its own sake. The culture industry pushes people to consume films, recordings, broadcast concerts, and the like, not in order to appreciate their filmic or musical qualities but in order to make them a commercial success, a "hit" or a "star," to which the consumer willingly contributes. Twentieth-century capitalism has become, as it were, a self-celebrating system within which the culture industry proves indispensable. Consequently, concerns about artistic quality become harder to raise, and the "masses," whose exploited labor keeps the system going, become less conscious of their genuine and unfulfilled needs. Both of these consequences, together with the "standardization" of culture in the service of economic and political power, provide the target for Adorno's critique of the culture industry.

Critics of Adorno frequently describe his approach as elitist and monolithic. His published essays on jazz, for example, have been accused of failing to comprehend the ways in which African-American music has arisen from conditions of oppression and served emancipatory purposes.[6] Even if such criticisms have some merit, however, the central theoretical claims in his critique remain relevant at a time when new mergers and globalization have swept the entertainment, telecommunications, and information industries. Apart from a theory of their economic underpinnings and cultural impact, such trends cannot be properly understood or evaluated.

According to Adorno, the emergence of advanced capitalism, with its ever-tighter fusion of state and economic power, does not leave the arts unaffected. Where these do not provide fodder for the cultural-industrial apparatus, they become all the more alienated from mainstream society. Increased alienation does not lessen their social significance, however, for it gives them the distance needed for social critique and utopian projection. Moreover, the alienation of the arts from society is itself socially produced. Arts that resist the culture industry are, in a phrase from *Aesthetic Theory*, "the social antithesis of society" (AT 19/11).[7]

Adorno's account of artistic autonomy is highly complex. On the one hand, the independence of the arts from religious, political, and other social structures, as institutionalized and theorized in Western societies, creates a space where societal wounds can be exposed and alternative arrangements imagined. On the other hand, because such independence itself depends on the division of labor, class conflict, and dominance in society of the capitalist "exchange principle," the space of exposure and imagination serves to shore up the societal system even as that space becomes internally problematic and externally irrelevant. As Adorno puts it at the beginning of *Aesthetic Theory*, referring to the modern art movements, absolute freedom in art stands in a contradiction with the abiding unfreedom of society as a whole. Yet it is only because of autonomy that certain works of art can achieve a critical and utopian "truth content" (*Wahrheitsgehalt*), in whose absence a fundamental transformation of society would be even more difficult to envision.

This complex position puts Adorno at odds not only with formalist approaches, which either assume or ignore art's social significance, but also with the socialist realism of Marxist-Leninism and the political commitment (*engagement*) promoted by Sartre, Brecht, and much of the New Left. The controversial claim in his 1962 essay "Commitment" must be situated in that polemical field: "This is not the time for political works of art; rather, politics has migrated into the autonomous work of art, and it has penetrated most deeply into works that present themselves as politically dead."[8]

Both societal structures and cultural contexts have shifted in the intervening years. The rise of new social movements, such as feminism, the ecology movement, and gay and lesbian liberation, have helped turn the focus of cultural theory from autonomous works to emancipatory practices; postmodernism has challenged the normative assumptions built into modernist legitimations of high art; and the institutions of the artworld—museums, publishers, symphony orchestras, and so on—have increasingly acknowledged and exploited their symbiotic relations with corporations, foundations, and the culture industry. Such developments cast doubt on the validity of Adorno's dialectical autonomism.

At the same time, however, concerns about the need for artistic autonomy have arisen within the new social movements, particularly in response to moralistic and antimodern pressures from a revitalized Right, and the increasing dependence of arts organizations on business strategies and corporate generosity has raised questions about the future of alternative modes of artistic expression. Although Adorno's approach needs to be rethought in this environment, it nevertheless provides a crucial counterweight to prevailing assumptions about the social significance of the arts and their institutional frames.

Adorno himself was a master "rethinker." Much of *Aesthetic Theory* can be read as a modernist reconceptualizing of philosophical aesthetics, especially the writings of Immanuel Kant and G. W. F. Hegel. Nowhere is this project more provocative than in Adorno's return to an aesthetics of nature. On the one hand, Adorno rejects Hegel's dismissal of natural beauty as inferior to the humanly produced beauty of art. On the other hand, he also rejects Kant's reduction of natural beauty to an indefinite object of taste. Yet he also refuses either to celebrate natural beauty as such or to define its independent nature. Rather, he sketches a genealogy of the modern discourse of "natural beauty" and from this identifies the referent in question as the trace of the nonidentical, which art seeks to rescue, with unavoidably mixed results.

Initially, such an approach does not seem promising for the recently developed field of environmental aesthetics. Adorno does not so much theorize the aesthetic dimension of nature and daily life as challenge the assumption that these "have" an "aesthetic dimension." What is important about Adorno's approach, however, is his insistence that such matters are socially constructed within a political and economic system and that any discourse of "natural beauty" must be linked to contemporary artistic practices.

More specifically, Adorno describes natural beauty as the trace of the nonidentical in things under the spell of universal identity. Amid its social construction as a category of alterity, that which is experienced as natural beauty reminds us that not everything is exchange value, not everything submits to the control of instrumental reason, not everything fits the grid of our definitions and categories. Contrary to Hegel, natural beauty is not deficient because it is indeterminant, but rather natural beauty is indeterminant because discursive thought is deficient. Among the various ways in which Western societies "relate" to "nature," only art has the capacity to preserve this trace of indeterminacy while giving it definite contours. In that capacity, art not only challenges the dominance of exchange value and instrumental rationality but also raises the trace of the nonidentical into a hint of reconciliation between nature and culture, a reconciliation that would presuppose an end to class domination in society.

Adorno's account of natural beauty envisions and articulates a continual reversal of the subject/object relation, such that the supposedly rational and controlling subject becomes an accomplice of the object, and the supposedly controlled and meaningless object begins to speak for itself. For Adorno, such a reversal, common in modern art, holds open the possibility that the alienation of subject and object, a central fissure within the dialectic of enlightenment, can be transcended, not only in art but also in other modes of social labor. In other words, a reconciliation between culture and nature, together with the lessening of social domination, is not out of the question. This is the underlying issue that an Adornoesque "environmental aesthetic" would have to address.

Semblance and Subjectivity

Closely related to the figure of art's "rescuing" natural beauty from sheer indeterminacy are Adorno's notions of "mimesis" and "expression" in art, which he usually pairs with "rationality" and "semblance" as their dialectical counterparts. Mimesis, a truly protean concept, refers to an archaic openness to the other, to the disparate and diffuse and contrary. Such openness lives on in artworks whose form accommodates the conflicting impulses of their content. Successful artworks embody a mimetic rationality and thereby provide a crucial alternative to the control and reduction characterizing the instrumental rationality that prevails under capitalism. Similarly, expression refers to a capacity to register that which impresses itself on human experience despite the various control mechanisms set up by society and the psyche. In artworks, such a capacity is mediated by the mimetic behavior that goes into artists' productive activity. The more expressive artworks become, the more their semblance of self-sufficiency is shaken, even though this semblance is required if they are to be expressions of something more than what society and the individual psyche permit.

The centrality of such themes in Adorno's thought and their relevance for contemporary scholarship have led the editors to organize this volume of essays on *Aesthetic Theory* around Adorno's concepts of semblance and subjectivity. Whereas the concept of semblance or illusion (*Schein*) points to Adorno's links with Marx, Nietzsche, and Freud, the so-called masters of suspicion, the concept of subjectivity (*das Subjekt*) recalls his lifelong struggle with a philosophy of consciousness stemming from Kant, Hegel, and Lukács. Adorno's elaboration of these two concepts takes many a dialectical twist. The arts, despite their being suspected of illusion since Plato's *Republic*, turn out in Adorno's account of modernism to have an unusually sophisticated capacity to critique illusion, including their own. But those cultural phenomena that purport to be "realistic," whether the sciences as construed by logical positivism or "popular" culture as manufactured by the entertainment industry, turn out to occupy the height of pretense. So, too, those "objects" that traditional philosophy has considered irrational or heteronomous, whether nature, the body, or the subconscious, emerge in Adorno's philosophy as repressed voices of the rational, and the autonomous subjectivity that was supposed to secure a humane existence, whether Kant's transcendental ego, Hegel's absolute spirit, or Lukács's proletarian class consciousness, turns out to be socially constituted within a dialectic of domination.

The preface to *Negative Dialectics* presents Adorno's philosophical project as an extended and immanent critique of autonomous subjectivity. He has set out "to use the strength of the subject to break through the fallacy [*Trug*] of constitutive subjectivity."[9] The breakthrough Adorno envisions pertains not only to the epistemic subject of foundationalist epistemologies but also to the moral and cultural subjectivities promoted by Kant and Hegel as well as the collective historical and political agencies affirmed by Marx and Lukács. Unlike linguistic deconstruction and poststructural debunking, however, this breakthrough deliberately calls on the very subjectivity whose pretensions to autonomy it exposes.

Adorno's project amounts to a critique *of* the semblance *of* subjectivity. In each instance, the "of" must be read as both subjective and objective. The critique takes aim at semblance, but it must occur within and by way of semblance. Subjectivity is a semblance, but one such that no semblance (and hence no critique) could occur in the absence of subjectivity. The full complexity of Adorno's project begins to emerge when one adds the thought, familiar from Marx's critique of ideology, Hegel's phenomenology of spirit, and Kant's dialectic of transcendental illusions, that the semblance in question is necessary, being both unavoidable and instructive. When it comes to semblance and subjectivity, the one cannot be had without the other, and although each must be criticized, no critique can dispense with either one, for each holds potentials that exceed its constricted shape in contemporary society.

Adorno construes modern art as a societal semblance, perhaps not the only such semblance, but certainly one whose history makes it especially disturbing as well as especially instructive. On the one hand, modern art participates in the technological fetishism, social blindness, and historical desperation that characterize advanced capitalist societies. On the other hand, modern art also challenges advanced capitalism's instrumentalized relationship to nature, its administrative neutralization of oppositional forces, and its short-sighted blockage of a more humane future. And modern art's ability to engage in such societal critique depends on its participating in precisely those patterns that it exposes. For a philosophy aiming to criticize the same patterns, modern art is a necessary illusion, a societally unavoidable and instructive semblance.

Modern art is also a semblance of subjectivity, in both senses of that phrase: the production and reception of modern art requires the very subjectivity to whose pretensions and failures it attests. Moreover, in simultaneously engaging and unmasking subjectivity, modern art gives expression to those repressed voices whose liberated and pluralistic chorus would mark collective subjectivity, were the logic of domination surpassed. In this more utopian sense, too, modern art is doubly a semblance of subjectivity: a negative image of a different collective future, but one whose capacity to project what is possible stems from hidden layers of contemporary experience.

Earlier, the critique of semblance was said to occur within and by way of semblance. *Aesthetic Theory* is just such a critique with regard to modern art. Not only does it require modern art in order to occur, but also Adorno's critique is itself, and regards itself as being, a necessary illusion, a semblance of subjectivity. In his final work, in all its incompleteness, one hears a theoretical articulation of the many deflations and projections of subjectivity already voiced in modern art. "One hears" and wonders whether, in order to "hear" something beyond the fetishism and blindness and desperation of advanced capitalist societies, "one" must already participate in a subjectivity whose social constitution breaks the mold of domination.

Conceptual Constellations

Crucial to the pursuit of such speculations, as prompted by Adorno's critique of the semblance of subjectivity, is his dialectical transformation of concepts that have guided philosophical aesthetics in the past. What Adorno provides, as the essays in this volume demonstrate, is a way of reconceptualizing philosophical insights that restores their critical and speculative sharpness in a society that blunts both critique and speculation. The paradoxical genius of *Aesthetic Theory* is that it turns traditional concepts into a theoretical cutting edge. Of particular importance, and closely tied to the concepts of semblance and subjectivity, are the notions of mimesis and autonomy, both of which might seem strangely outmoded in the 1990s.

Concerning the first of these notions, Martin Jay notes both post-structuralism's apparent hostility to mimesis as "an ideologically suspect recirculation of the readymade" (pp. 29–30) and the Frankfurt School's apparent esteem for mimesis as a counterweight to the modern dominance of instrumental reason. Comparing Adorno's conception of mimesis with that of the poststructuralist Philippe Lacoue-Labarthe, however, Jay finds the view on each side to be more complex and less separate than initial impressions might suggest.

According to Jay, Adorno understands mimesis in terms of a receptive assimilation of subject to object, unlike instrumental reason's coercive subsumption of the object. Far from constituting a mere opposite, mimesis provides an alternative mode of rationality, one that is crucial to modern art and that points to the possibility of a more fully rational society. Adorno tries to incorporate such mimetic rationality into his own writing, most notably by employing parataxis, as discussed in his important essay on Hölderlin.[10]

Significantly, it is Hölderlin who provides Lacoue-Labarthe with a wedge against the representational mimesis through which both traditional tragedy and ontotheological philosophy transfigure the negative into something positive. By exposing the gaps, the play, the unsettledness at work between an original and its imitation, Hölderlin's dramas show mimesis to be paradoxical. Like Adorno, Lacoue-Labarthe connects the paradoxes of mimesis with the antinomies of semblance or illusion. And, again like Adorno, he contrasts a fragmentary and unending mimesis with the forced and totalized reconciliation of "copy" and "original" (mimetology) promoted by the "Nazi myth."

Jay turns next to sensual elements in the two authors' accounts. Whereas Lacoue-Labarthe, like Jacques Derrida, rejects the privileging of vision in speculative mimetology and contrasts this with a presensual and rhythmic repetition of a nonexistent original, Adorno regards visuality (*Anschaulichkeit*) as necessary to the dialectic of mimesis and rationality, and he distrusts the destructive force of rhythmic repetition, for example, in the music of Igor Stravinsky. The key to this contrast might lie in Adorno's hope for a meaningful future, which could strike Lacoue-Labarthe as speculative and conciliatory.

Jay concludes that mimesis is a "polysemic, even catachrestic" concept whose valence depends on how it gets linked with rationality. Although poststructuralists oppose "mimetology" for its "deadening logic" of visual replication and favor mimesis as "an infinite oscillation between original and copy" (p. 46), Adorno opposes the subordination of mimesis to instrumental reason, and he favors a corrective interaction between mimesis and rationality, especially in modern art. Either way, a certain kind of mimesis can serve to decenter the strong constitutive subject that both Lacoue-Labarthe and Adorno see as a problematic legacy of traditional philosophy.

Like Martin Jay, Shierry Weber Nicholsen regards Adorno's elusive and pervasive conception of mimesis as categorially central and formally constitutive to his *Aesthetic Theory*. She claims that it derives, to a significant degree, from Walter Benjamin's writings about language. Adorno and Benjamin share a notion of philosophical form that emerges from their shared conception of mimesis.

In philosophical and literary texts from the early 1930s, Benjamin portrays mimesis as an original human capacity to both produce and perceive resemblances, and he suggests that this capacity has migrated into language as an "archive of nonsensuous similarity" (*Reflections*, p. 336). Like Benjamin, Nicholsen says, Adorno regards mimesis as a human capacity to assimilate self to other that has migrated elsewhere, namely, into art. *Aesthetic Theory* considers mimesis to be crucial for appropriate performance and reception of the work of art. To understand a work, both the performer and the recipient must devotedly trace the work's internal articulations. Yet, at the same time, one must take reflective distance from the work. It is in the tension between mimetic tracing and critical thought that the enigmatic quality of art emerges and philosophical reflection takes wing.

Next Nicholsen uncovers a clue to Adorno's account of art's enigmatic quality in Benjamin's conception of aura. In "The Stocking," from *Berlin Childhood*, Benjamin's childhood delight at extracting "the Dowry" from "the Pouch" formed by rolled-up socks becomes a metaphor for the interpreter's problematic attempt to extract truth from texts. It is the mixture of continuity and discontinuity between interpreter and text that makes up a text's enigmatic quality. More precisely, the enigmatic quality is the object's capacity to return our gaze while it participates in a dark web of similarities with other objects. It is their aura.

As Nicholsen shows, Adorno's *Aesthetic Theory* translates Benjamin's notion of aura into a complex account of the "languages" of nature, art, and philosophical aesthetics. What links all three languages is the enigmatic quality generated by mimesis. Natural beauty is enigmatic because, in its individuality, independence, and transience, it defies conceptualization and calls for "unconscious apperception." Art is enigmatic because it tries to capture the fleeting and mute expression of natural beauty, but in the nondiscursive "language" of expressive artistic form. Philosophical discourse about art is enigmatic because it tries to give discursive expression to art's opaque but highly articulate attempt to let natural beauty speak. Despite the increase in a certain kind of rationality from one field to the next, all three confound the expectations of ordinary discourse and overturn the priority of subject over object. In each case, mimesis is the key.

Indeed, mimesis is the key to *Aesthetic Theory*'s own form, Nicholsen concludes. Using images from Benjamin's description of language as an archive of nonsensuous similarity, she suggests that, like Benjamin's unfinished *Passagenwerk* (*Arcades Project*), Adorno's text is a "constellation" of concepts across which "flames" of resemblance flash and at whose blank center lies the undefined notion of mimesis. Instead of gathering quotations, as Benjamin planned to do, Adorno gathers concepts from previous theories and sets them into new and explosive relationships. The sentences bearing the flames created by historical recontextualization are linked but not locked. Or, to use another image also suggested by Benjamin, *Aesthetic Theory* is a weaving of "unbroken, proliferating arabesques," in which each sequence of sentences interlaces many others. Combining these images, Nicholsen pictures the book as multiple constellations, interlaced, its nodes being faceted jewels, flashing at one moment and gone the next. Like the art it speaks about, then, Adorno's text calls for unusually concentrated mimesis on the part of its readers.

Another side to the relationship between Adorno and Benjamin surfaces in their diverse links with surrealism, as explored in the essay by Richard Wolin. Benjamin's elective affinity for surrealism begins with "protosurrealist stirrings" in his youthful critique of neo-Kantianism and culminates in the monumental and uncompleted *Passagenwerk.* What attracts Benjamin to surrealism, says Wolin, is his search for a suprarational mode of experience and his concept of constellation as a montagelike juxtaposition of phenomena that would let their truth emerge, even if only for a messianic moment.

Wolin singles out four aspects of surrealism as having special appeal for Benjamin. One is the potential of montage for avoiding the staleness and abstraction of conventional philosophical practices. Another is surrealism's immersion in the details of everyday life, similar to Benjamin's "micrological" emphasis on particularity. A third aspect is the surrealist attack on aestheticism in favor of integrating art and life. Finally, and perhaps most important, surrealists privilege dreams, which in Benjamin become repositories of humanity's repressed desires. His *Passagenwerk* aims to provide a montagelike interpretation and remembrance of nineteenth-century Europe's collective dream life in order to release utopian desires from their systematic imprisonment in bourgeois cultural commodities.

As is well known, Adorno expressed sharp criticisms not only of Benjamin's methodology but also of the surrealism that partially inspired it. According to Adorno's 1956 essay "Looking Back on Surrealism," surrealist montage in the visual arts tends to absorb the fragments of everyday life without mediation, hence without critique of a societal system that fosters the same sort of reification. Moreover, the surrealist appropriation of dream life fetishizes the manifest content of dreams and, in the absence of analytic interpretation, promotes regression to unreflective fixations. Earlier, Adorno had also criticized two of Benjamin's *Passagenwerk*-related studies for their lack of mediation and their problematic privileging of dreams.

In Wolin's judgment, Adorno is right to challenge Benjamin's attempt to make utopian purses from the ears of fetishized commodities, but wrong to use surrealists' theoretical pronouncements as the measure of their artistic productions. Moreover, Adorno's sympathies for surrealism actually exceed his negative evaluations, and his emphasis on constructing conceptual constellations resembles the surrealist technique of montage, with a similar aim of resisting linear thought. Already in the 1956 essay, Adorno credits surrealism with countering the tendency in the movement of Neue Sachlichkeit to deny the havoc wreaked by advanced capitalism. Later, in *Aesthetic Theory*, Adorno finds even more to endorse: surrealism highlights spontaneity, exposes the chaos within a supposedly rational society, and shows just how rigid and brittle the current societal order is. Adorno also praises the technique of montage for changing conventional modes of perception and challenging the affirmative character of late romantic art. He is especially appreciative of later surrealism, once it moves beyond aggressive protest and incorporates its resistance to bourgeois aestheticism into a new mode of nonrepresentational painting. Despite his criticisms, then, Adorno sees surrealism as contributing what Wolin describes as "deaestheticized" and hence authentically modern works of art: works that shed "the aura of affirmation" and embody "the moment of refusal or negativity" (p. 119).

Rolf Tiedemann demonstrates that a "utopia of knowledge" guides all of Adorno's work and that without it both Adorno's aesthetics and his critiques of society and philosophy would lose their point. This utopian horizon places Adorno at odds with contemporary German intellectuals who call for crude thinking (Botho Strauss) and celebrate posthistory (many postmodernists). Like Ernst Bloch, Adorno holds that historical labor is necessary for the arrival of a "true society," and existing traces of utopia are needed in order to keep open the possibility of something different from the current societal whole, which is false.

According to Jürgen Habermas, Adorno's conception of utopia as a reconciled condition in which the alien is not annexed can be translated into the ideal of noncoercive communication. Tiedemann, however, argues that such a translation overlooks Adorno's grounds for holding to the utopian idea of universal reconciliation. Adorno anchors this idea not in language as communication but in language as an autonomous expression of that which cannot be communicated. His conception of utopia derives from the idea of a language in which word and thing unite without loss.

Philosophical language cannot remain unaffected by such a conception. Adorno's negative dialectic acknowledges the abstraction built into the conceptual language of philosophy, even as he critiques such abstraction and confronts it with the idea of the nonconceptual—that which is fully concrete, nonidentical, and unintentional. Tiedemann says that Adorno tries to circumvent the limitations of abstract philosophical language through the interpretation of images. It was in conversation with Benjamin that Adorno developed a theory of dialectical images, according to which historical material can be made to produce a critical consciousness of capitalist society. In these kaleidoscopic constellations, the philosopher can grasp whatever escapes the net of conceptual abstraction. Such an approach allows for considerable fantasy and spontaneity. It does not hesitate to learn from artworks that mobilize a different potential for knowledge than that of ordinary language and systematic philosophy. In a sense, the philosophical reader of dialectical images is a composer of concepts.

Built into this understanding of philosophy as interpretation is a somewhat mystical view of language, inherited from Benjamin, according to which things possess their own language. Accordingly, Adorno's philosophy can be described as an attempt at answering the language of things and conjuring a unity from the alienated and abstracted features of reified phenomena. The communication Adorno sought would occur between object and subject, not simply among human beings: "the condition Adorno has in mind aims for nothing less than reconciling human beings with nature, of which reconciling human beings with one another would be a part" (p. 138).

Adorno's utopia of knowledge is the name that cannot be named, even though it can be approximated through the effort to unmask false names, an effort at once conceptual and resistant to conceptual limitations. A refusal to accept death propels all of Adorno's thinking—always, however, with a view to sociohistorical conditions. Only for the sake of real historical transformation does Adorno hold fast to the prospect of utopia, seeking its traces in a society that continually betrays it.

Not all of Adorno's readers share the sympathies of Jay, Nicholsen, Wolin, and Tiedemann toward his conception and pursuit of mimetic rationality. In fact, Rüdiger Bubner challenges what he takes to be the central idea of Adorno's philosophy, namely, that theory itself must become aesthetic. Beginning with Adorno's 1931 inaugural lecture, "The Actuality of Philosophy," Bubner explores the reasons Adorno resisted philosophy's traditional project of establishing first principles. This resistance culminates in a text called *Aesthetic Theory*, whose main concern, says Bubner, is how philosophy and art can converge.

Adorno's primary reason for refusing to specify first principles is historical: the project is a relic of idealism's illusory belief in philosophy's purity and autonomy. What gives this reason initial weight, according to Bubner, is Adorno's own ungrounded first principle pertaining to the historical development of capitalist society. Adorno posits that the ideology of invariability has come to pervade society's every nook and cranny, making it imperative for philosophy to insist that truth is historical. Hence, says Bubner, every philosophical truth claim must recant its own insight, and for this a different type of language is required, namely, the language of art.

Bubner charges Adorno's historical diagnosis with making everything appear reified, including theory itself. It thereby paralyzes Adorno's own theory, blocking the free use of traditional philosophical methods and preventing serious engagement with the objects of inquiry. Moreover, Adorno's own starting point—a negative account of historical development—remains outside the discussion. Along with Max Horkheimer in *Dialectic of Enlightenment*, Adorno turns the critique of enlightenment back on itself, in order to show how theory's claim to autonomy is itself a manifestation of the myth that the project of enlightenment seeks to supplant. "Myth" points to an irrational principle or condition that no amount of enlightenment can overcome, since myth forms the basis of historical development. Over against the dialectic of myth and enlightenment, Adorno posits what Bubner describes as "a vaguely defined ideal of an *eschatological reconciliation*," and this ideal can be experienced only in the "pseudoreality" or "illusion" created by art (p. 157).

For Adorno, art that is progressive provides knowledge as a negation of contemporary society. But in order to interpret art in this way,
says Bubner, the art critic must draw on historical, philosophical, and
sociological knowledge that is extraneous to the aesthetic structure
of specific artworks and therefore, in Bubner's opinion, extraneous
to art as such. Adorno can posit art and philosophy's convergence in
knowledge only by assuming that societal reality and progressive art
follow their own internal laws and directly oppose each other. Bubner calls this assumption the ungrounded dogma of contradiction.
Adorno's aesthetic theory stands and falls, he says, with its need to
occupy a vantage point external to both art and society, "a *third position*, totally removed from ideology" (p. 161).

Adorno's thesis about convergence is complicated further by his
appeal to the concepts of mimesis and the work of art. According to
Bubner, Adorno's philosophy both opposes the traditional concept
of mimesis and tries to incorporate a mimetic procedure that assimilates theory to its object. Bubner regards Adorno's argument for this
revised concept of mimesis as unpersuasive. Equally problematic is
Adorno's paradoxical reliance on the concept of the work of art even
while he demonstrates the concept's demise in modern art. Rather
than providing grounds for continuing to employ this category,
Adorno builds the paradox into his own interpretations of particular
pieces of music and literature.

What Bubner finds especially problematic is the role Adorno's theory assigns to aesthetic experience. Because art is defined as a societal critique that makes up for theory's limitations, the results of
encounters with artistic phenomena are prescribed in advance, and
"there is no longer...a need for individual aesthetic experience"
(p. 168). This alleged indifference to aesthetic experience arises,
says Bubner, from Adorno's inversion of Hegel's dialectic of limits.
Adorno agrees with Hegel that a limit can never be drawn from only
one side. Whereas Hegel uses this insight to argue for art's subordination to philosophy, Adorno uses it to postulate art as that autonomous sphere whose cognitive capacity sets limits to philosophy. In
Bubner's view, however, only philosophy can stipulate such a definition of art, and thus Adorno's philosophy surreptitiously places itself

in the superior position of calling on art to save philosophy from its own limitations. Such machinations undermine both aesthetic experience and the theoretical character of philosophy itself: *"The aestheticizing of theory impoverishes a theory of the aesthetic"* (p. 172).

In contrast to Bubner, who worries about the implications of *Aesthetic Theory* for traditional philosophy, J. M. Bernstein finds promise in Adorno's aesthetics for the development of a materialist ethics. To show this, Bernstein explores the connection between Adorno's "Meditations on Metaphysics" in *Negative Dialectics* and the "rescue of semblance" thematized in *Aesthetic Theory*. Like Hegel, Adorno aims to articulate the experience of modern diremptions between science and art, concept and object, and universal and particular. His philosophy cannot be positive in a Hegelian sense, however, because experience itself has withered: individual subjects no longer directly experience the diremptions that nevertheless rake furrows into their backs. The question haunting Adorno's philosophy, says Bernstein, is whether the "wound that eviscerates life...has become so routine that it has become our second nature" (p. 183).

This question drives Adorno's search for metaphysical experience in *Negative Dialectics,* where he argues that, after Auschwitz, traditional metaphysical reflections about transcendence can be neither perpetuated nor avoided. Neither enlightened moralities, with their emphasis on societal immanence, nor traditional metaphysics, with its inability to express human suffering, can transcend rationalized immanence without losing touch with the bodily sensation of moral abhorrence at unspeakable agony.

Bernstein claims that Adorno derives his concept of metaphysical experience from a materialist rereading of Kant's moral theology. Adorno credits Kant with recognizing that it must be possible to overcome the separation between the good and the right if moral pursuits are to make sense. To secure a connection, and to ward off despair, Kant postulates an "intelligible world" where happiness would be proportionate to virtue. Because this notion is incoherent even on Kantian grounds, however, Adorno reconfigures it into a space between the real and the imaginary. What occupies this space, this gap between what understanding can grasp and what it can only declare logically possible, is the necessary semblance.

The rescue of necessary semblance is the task of Adorno's aesthet-ics. Driven by the unthinkability of despair, Adorno's rescue aims at an experience of the possible that exceeds what is currently consid-ered to be possible, and he finds this in autonomous and modernist works of art. According to Bernstein's reading of *Aesthetic Theory*, such works suggest four claims to be heeded by, and by way of, philo-sophical aesthetics: (1) that particular things can resist subsumption and yet yield meaning; (2) that human happiness is promised, in a negative fashion, as an immanent possibility; (3) that claims about what is possible can arise outside philosophy proper and become es-sential for philosophy; and (4) that all such claims, though objective, may nevertheless be sheer illusion, depending on what is done in re-sponse to such claims. Like Walter Benjamin, then, Adorno regards modernist works of art as sensuous particulars that provide us with experience of a world that is constituted by the absence of experi-ence. For Adorno, this capacity enables artworks to advance claims on behalf of sensuous particularity that resist the reigning universal-ity, and thereby to elicit experience that provides a materialist "moral image of the world" (p. 202).

Building on Benjamin's account of aura, *Aesthetic Theory* suggests that aesthetic perception breathes the aura of an artwork not by pro-jection onto the object but by assimilation to it. And this process is as-sisted by modernist works, which in their abstraction and negativity resist projection. By resisting subjective projection, such works con-tinue the modern disenchantment of the world. But by resisting the disqualification of so-called secondary qualities, modernist works also challenge the limitations of instrumental rationality. The inde-pendence of modernist works allows them to engage subjectivity on terms other than those typically prescribed and thereby to invoke the promise of happiness.

Hence, says Bernstein, to undergo aesthetic experience is "to ex-perience the possibility of experience in its robust sense" and thus to attain "the moral image of the world—in semblance" (p. 208). Aes-thetic experience, feeding on the immanence of the artwork, can dis-close a transcendence "toward a future habitation of this world," "a transfigured world in which happiness and virtue would be recon-ciled" (p. 208). Without such a speculative thought prompted by the rescue of artistic semblance, morality would lapse into either cynicism or despair.

Whereas Bubner and Bernstein examine Adorno's rescue of *artistic* semblance, with contrasting results, Heinz Paetzold considers the implications of Adorno's conception of *natural* beauty for what some philosophers label environmental ethics and environmental aesthetics. Paetzold locates Adorno's legacy in the link he maintains between philosophy of art and the aesthetics of nature. Although Adorno accepts the turn toward philosophy of art in Friedrich Schelling and Hegel, he rejects the suppression of nature that accompanies this turn. On the one hand, Adorno emphasizes the historically mediated character of natural beauty. On the other hand, he portrays art as an attempt to redeem the utopian reconciliation promised by natural beauty. Artworks and natural beauty alike "represent models of experience that transcend the totality of the principle of exchange and commodity production" (p. 219). In this they resist the logic of instrumental reason and provide traces of the nonidentical, whose meaning cannot be subjectively imposed. As Paetzold puts it, "the images that natural beauty stimulates are fueled with the images that explicitly modern works of art provide" (p. 221).

Paetzold's essay develops a conversation between Adorno and Gernot Böhme and Martin Seel, two German theorists who have recently developed an aesthetics of nature. Böhme argues for a contemporary philosophy of nature that not only recognizes the fundamental interconnectedness of nature and the human world but also incorporates the new emphasis on organic processes of communication and information in the natural sciences. Given such a philosophy, the aesthetics of nature should start from our bodily awareness (*Befindlichkeit*) of the ways in which natural things present themselves (*Aussichheraustreten*). This will lead to a new notion of semblance, one that appreciates the ephemeral, as well as to a reevaluation of the art of gardening, with its implicit critique of traditional oppositions between nature and culture.

While Böhme's approach emphasizes the philosophy of nature, Seel enters environmental aesthetics from the field of ethics, primarily the ethics of individual conduct, and only secondarily the ethics of social responsibility. Seel distinguishes three types of aesthetic attitude toward nature: sensuous contemplation, orientation, and imagination. Each attitude can support individual well-being, whether by helping to "put the many outlooks on life into perspective" or by intensifying "existential feelings and ideas" or by offering "new visions of the world" (p. 229). Such attitudes also play into our experience of art. And, in the intersubjective dimension, the aesthetic experience of nature can motivate a care of nature and can help people take distance from established viewpoints.

Although Paetzold agrees with much of what Böhme and Seel propose, he criticizes both for failing to take contemporary modes of artistic production into account. Unlike Böhme, for example, Paetzold upholds Adorno's insight that works of art, with their capacity to wrest technology from subservience to capitalistic social domination, are crucial to an aesthetic awareness of nature that would support "a decisive shift in humanity's social condition" (p. 227). Nevertheless, Paetzold appreciates Böhme's emphasis on the ephemeral, in contrast with the traditional attempt, perhaps continued by Adorno, to overcome the provisional character of the semblance by way of the idea. According to Paetzold, many contemporary art productions, such as Joseph Beuys's "social sculpture" and various site-specific works, highlight the ephemeral, a point ignored by Martin Seel, with his emphasis on the supposed permanence of artworks. Adorno can still teach us to examine how contemporary artworks challenge the dominant patterns of technology and social domination, even as he reminds us that the path between the aesthetics of art and the aesthetics of nature is a two-way street.

This reminder and its implications for social critique bring to mind Immanuel Kant's description of beauty as "the symbol of morality." The connection is not accidental, according to Tom Huhn. Huhn reads Adorno's *Aesthetic Theory* as a complex transposition of themes from Kant's *Critique of Judgment*. What links the two texts, across the two centuries separating them, is a recognition of the "social opacity of the aesthetic." Whereas Kant locates such opacity in aesthetic judgments concerning natural beauty, Adorno finds its site in the work of art.

The key to this relocation lies in Kant's account of the sublime, as interpreted by Adorno and reinterpreted by Huhn. According to

Huhn, Kant depicts aesthetic judgments about natural beauty as both achieving universality and occluding the universality achieved. Taste posits intersubjectivity but neither renders intersubjectivity objective nor recognizes it—hence the social opacity of the aesthetic, sealing the failure of human freedom to come to fruition in nature. As if to compensate for such failure, the Kantian sublime becomes a placeholder for the promise that human freedom will be actualized.

What Kant does not recognize, and what Adorno shows, is that, by resisting the "imperious subjectivity" announced in Kantian sublimity, art has become the site of the sublime, precisely insofar as it eschews any imitation of nature. On the one hand, art embodies the increasing reification of the subjective. On the other hand, art accomplishes a much more complex mediation of the particular and the universal than was possible in the Kantian account of beauty. Insofar as art achieves autonomy, it functions, in Huhn's words, as "the default sphere" for "failed dreams... of human emancipation" but also as an "active, independent agency" to keep such dreams alive (p. 243).

According to Huhn, Adorno reads Kant's account of the sublime as a symptom of what ails taste: sublimity's disregard for nature and its celebration of human power simply radicalize the effacement of nature already achieved in the exercise of taste, for which natural objects serve as mere occasions. Yet the sublime continues the quest for human freedom, as does art, once the domination and impotence in the sublime becomes apparent.

Adorno credits the artwork with achieving the objectivity denied to taste. Such objectivity is not one of static permanence: it resides in the transient process of the artwork as an "afterimage." It is an objectivity not resulting from subjective effort but rather testifying to the failure of subjectivity to achieve freedom. The modern artwork becomes "the objective counterimage of subjectivity" (p. 250), and in this counterimage resides a hope, albeit faint and dissonant, for that emancipation missed in natural beauty and the sublime. Modern art poses the question whether subjectivity can recover opportunities it prematurely cast aside.

Huhn elaborates this question by considering Adorno's account of technique in art. Like Kant, who describes artistic beauty as a transformation of instrumental rationality, Adorno regards artistic technique as a "dialectical overcoming of technology" (p. 251). Through artistic technique, the inexorable logic of means and end can be pushed into a pure expression of nature as that which exceeds and resists subjectivity's technological grasp. Like natural beauty in a Kantian frame, however, technique occludes its own social character, for we consider it an individual achievement. Still, the dogged pursuit of technique in modern art results in transient works whose alterity gives expression to something other than ourselves—perhaps the others we have yet to become.

The tenuous autonomy of such artworks provides another window into Adorno's complex Kantianism concerning subjectivity and its discontents. In an essay very much in the spirit of Adorno, Gregg Horowitz explores the theme of art's relationship to history. Arguing against historicist attempts to use nonaesthetic factors to explain the development of art, Horowitz proposes a concept of autonomy more Kantian than Hegelian in its inspiration. He reads Hegel as needing to retrieve art for history precisely because of the autonomy art had achieved, as witnessed in Kant's *Critique of Judgment*. Indeed, the idea of a history for art arises only as a consequence of art's autonomy, itself a historical phenomenon. This approach continues Adorno's opposition to historicist explanations for failing to grasp the historical character of their own project as well as of art's autonomy.

According to Horowitz, Kant's account of art as autonomous requires the production of artifacts that appear to be produced without purpose. Contrary to a romantic interpretation, this paradoxical demand does not mean that the artist should flaunt all the rules. Rather, the artist should work up his or her materials in such a way that these no longer appear to be a constraint. For that to occur, however, the mechanism of the natural world from which come stone and pigment and the like must indeed be a constraint. As Horowitz puts it, Kant regards art as "the labor of remaking the world of mechanism as a world that need not be the realm of necessity" (p. 273). By having the look of free labor, of unnecessary work, the artwork appears, like nature, to lack external determination—it has the look of autonomy.

This look is *not* one of freedom. Rather, according to Horowitz's reading of Kant, "autonomous art looks like the failure of freedom" (p. 274). In order to appear unconstrained and incompatible with the world of external determination, the work must show what does not constrain it and hence must seem bound to the very world the work appears to negate. From such appearances arise historicizing attempts to reconnect art with its context. But in imputing to historical understanding the freedom from external determination that autonomous art necessarily fails to achieve, historicist contextualizers from Hegel to Arthur Danto deploy a conception of history that feeds on art's failed freedom.

That imputation and its related thesis about the death of art are deeply problematic. It is precisely the failure of art to free itself from nature that keeps it alive, unreconciled, ever battling the world of external determination—a process Horowitz reads as "the specifically human story of perpetual self-creation in time through nonreconciliation" (p. 277). By contrast, the historicist attempt to reduce art to extra-aesthetic factors from a vantage point detached from such factors amounts to a capitulation, in the name of freedom, to things as they are and a denial of history as future-oriented self-creation.

What is needed, instead of historicist reduction and resignation, is a critical history of art. Such a historiography, as Horowitz envisions it, would be fully attuned to the objective contradiction between art and its history, oriented by the modernist idea of autonomy rather than the romantic idea of freedom, and alive to the protest in modern art against false reconciliation.

Other Adorno scholars do not embrace the modernist idea of autonomy, however. This is particularly so for feminist critics of the Frankfurt School, such as Sabine Wilke and Heidi Schlipphacke. Wilke and Schlipphacke develop a feminist critique of Adorno's construction of subjectivity. Far from being a gender-neutral category, they argue, this construction relies on stereotypical projections of male and female subjectivity, and such projections inform the theoretical apparatus and aesthetic judgments in *Aesthetic Theory*.

While acknowledging Adorno's insight into the reification of the body in Western civilization, Wilke and Schlipphacke show that *Dialectic of Enlightenment* remains bound to an "androcentric model of male bourgeois subjectivity" (p. 288). This is particularly apparent from the book's discussion of female figures in the tale of Odysseus—the Sirens, the lotus-eaters, and Circe. Horkheimer and Adorno do not problematize stereotypes of female sexuality; instead, their critique of instrumental reason reinforces such stereotypes and reinscribes women in the web of patriarchy. By failing to theorize the role of gender politics in the logic of domination, Horkheimer and Adorno cast the female subject as serving the development of male bourgeois subjectivity and as standing in for proscribed and impotent forms of sensuality.

Turning to *Aesthetic Theory*, Wilke and Schlipphacke trace the dialectic of aesthetic autonomy whereby art comes into its own as an agency of negatively utopian critique. According to Adorno, they say, art becomes autonomous by transfiguring corporeal sensuality into the "pleasure" of dissonance and its negation. Adorno links the repressed bodily nature of art, still evident in cuisine, pornography, and the circus, with female subjectivity, and he compares properly aesthetic experience with the male orgasm.

Unfortunately, such unacknowledged genderizing of art and aesthetic experience comports all too well with the way in which Adorno evaluates works by specific artists, the authors claim. Not only does his rare mention of female artists, such as Hedwig Courts-Mahler and Selma Lagerlöf, place their work in a stereotypically negative light, but also he tends to use the work of "softer" male artists like Stefan George, Oscar Wilde, and Frédéric Chopin as whipping boys whose "decorative" and "aristocratic" art cannot hold a candle to the "substantial" and "serious" work of, say, Franz Kafka, Samuel Beckett, and Arnold Schoenberg. Adorno's scorn for purportedly effeminate and childish art is even more pronounced in his essays on jazz and on Hugo von Hofmannsthal in *Prisms*. In his aesthetic judgments, as in his theoretical account, Adorno fails to problematize the repression of the female body that he nevertheless detects in the development of autonomous art.

Yet there are readers for whom such failures might be compensated in part by the incomparable pungency of Adorno's aesthetic writings. Adorno's interpretations of Kafka, Beckett, and Schoenberg would appear to such readers as just the antidote needed to counter a hypercommercialized culture industry. In fact, the concluding essay, by Robert Hullot-Kentor, portrays Adorno's work as a "philosophy of dissonance" resembling Schoenberg's music, to which Adorno devoted some of his own most intransigent writing.

What propels Adorno's formidable texts, Hullot-Kentor claims, is a need to maintain critical consciousness over against mass culture. Adorno heard a similar opposition in Schoenberg's music. Both of them would have been appalled by a recent conference on Schoenberg called "Constructive Dissonance," for it is precisely the tendency to sentimentalize, homogenize, and neutralize, whether in hyped-up popular music or in glossy symphony concerts, that both Adorno and Schoenberg resist.

Adorno regards Schoenberg as the key figure in the movement of music away from commercial neutralization through an internal critique of music's own illusory character. Modern music, like modern drama and modern visual art, sets itself against fictional representation of the world in order to let the world's essence come to expression. For Adorno, Hullot-Kentor writes, the musical breakthrough in this direction occurs when Schoenberg bids farewell to tonality in favor of expression that is tied to freely manipulated musical materials. Schoenberg discovered how musical expression could be made binding rather than fictive, namely, by employing dissonance as the principle of musical structure. In Schoenberg's music, Adorno detects the possibility of "a transformed subjectivity," one that does not dominate its object but "gives it binding expression" (p. 318). And with this possibility, Hullot-Kentor suggests, Adorno also finds room for a revolution in the course of history.

The shape of that room and its location remain a conundrum not only of Adorno's thought but also of progressive politics at the close of the twentieth century. What Adorno and the authors in this volume have shown is that aesthetic theory is less marginal to such concerns than its apparent obsolescence might suggest. There can be no horizon for dramatic historical change unless people can imagine and enact something other than the prevailing modes of reality and reason. And for such imagination and such enactment, there must be semblances of subjectivity.

Notes

The epigraph is from Theodor W. Adorno, *Negative Dialektik* (1966, 1967), *Gesammelte Schriften*, vol. 6 (Frankfurt am Main: Suhrkamp, 1973), pp. 396–97; *Negative Dialectics*, trans. E. B. Ashton (New York: Seabury Press, 1973), pp. 404–5. Translation modified. Hereafter cited as ND, thus: ND 396–97/404–5.

Introduction

1. The following books dealing with Adorno's aesthetics have appeared in English since 1990: Fredric Jameson, *Late Marxism: Adorno, or, The Persistence of the Dialectic* (New York: Verso, 1990); Karla L. Schultz, *Mimesis on the Move: Theodor W. Adorno's Concept of Imitation* (New York: Peter Lang, 1990); Lambert Zuidervaart, *Adorno's Aesthetic Theory: The Redemption of Illusion* (Cambridge, Mass.: MIT Press, 1991); David Roberts, *Art and Enlightenment: Aesthetic Theory after Adorno* (Lincoln: University of Nebraska Press, 1991); Albrecht Wellmer, *The Persistence of Modernity: Essays on Aesthetics, Ethics, and Postmodernism*, trans. David Midgley (Cambridge, Mass.: MIT Press, 1991); J. M. Bernstein, *The Fate of Art: Aesthetic Alienation from Kant to Derrida and Adorno* (University Park: Pennsylvania State University Press, 1992); Max Paddison, *Adorno's Aesthetics of Music* (New York: Cambridge University Press, 1993); Peter Uwe Hohendahl, *Prismatic Thought: Theodor W. Adorno* (Lincoln: University of Nebraska Press, 1995); Shierry Weber Nicholsen, *Exact Imagination, Late Work: On Adorno's Aesthetics* (Cambridge, Mass.: MIT Press, forthcoming).

2. Interest in Adorno's aesthetics has been sparked by recent translations of his writings on modern music, literature, and the mass media. Robert Hullot-Kentor's retranslation of *Aesthetic Theory* (Minneapolis: University of Minnesota Press, 1996) should heighten the level of scholarly engagement with this seminal text. Other translations to have appeared since 1990 include *Notes to Literature*, 2 vols. (New York: Columbia University Press, 1991, 1992): *The Culture Industry: Selected Essays on Mass Culture* (London: Routledge, 1991); *Alban Berg: Master of the Smallest Link* (New York: Cambridge University Press, 1991); *Quasi una fantasia: Essays on Modern Music* (New York: Verso, 1992); *Hegel: Three Studies* (Cambridge, Mass.: MIT Press, 1993); *The Stars Down to Earth and Other Essays on the Irrational in Culture* (New York: Routledge, 1994); and *Keywords* (New York: Columbia University Press, forthcoming). *The Correspondence of Walter Benjamin, 1910–1940*, edited and annotated by Gershom Scholem and Theodor W. Adorno, has been published by the University of Chicago Press (1994).

3. Other recent books containing discussions of Adorno's aesthetics include Terry Eagleton, *The Ideology of the Aesthetic* (Oxford: Basil Blackwell, 1990); Ronald Roblin, ed., *The Aesthetics of the Critical Theorists: Studies on Benjamin, Adorno, Marcuse, and Habermas* (Lewiston, N.Y.: Edwin Mellen Press, 1990); Rose Rosengard Subotnik, *Developing Variations: Style and Ideology in Western Music* (Minneapolis: University of Minnesota Press, 1991); Willem van Reijen et al., *Adorno: An Introduction*, trans. Dieter Engelbrecht (Philadelphia: Pennbridge Books, 1992); Richard Wolin, *The Terms of Cultural Criticism: The Frankfurt School, Existentialism, Poststructuralism* (New York: Columbia University Press, 1992); Rolf Wiggershaus, *The Frankfurt School: Its History, Theories, and Political Significance*, trans. Michael Robertson (Cambridge, Mass.: MIT Press, 1994); Richard Wolin, *Walter Benjamin: An Aesthetic of Redemption*, 2d ed. (Berkeley: University of California Press, 1994); and Martin Jay, *The Dialectical Imagination*, 2d ed. (Berkeley: University of California Press, 1996). Mention should also be made of a special issue on Adorno in *New German Critique* (no. 56, spring–summer 1992). A book not strictly on Adorno's aesthetics but nonetheless germane to this anthology is by Asha Varadharajan, *Exotic Parodies: Subjectivity in Adorno, Said, and Spivak* (Minneapolis: University of Minnesota Press, 1995).

4. Hohendahl, *Prismatic Thought*, p. 243.

5. "[W]here … it is asserted … that this or that mode of looking at things is now definitively outmoded, we may confidently expect the putatively extinct specimens to reappear in the lists in the near future." Jameson, *Late Marxism*, p. 241.

Lambert Zuidervaart

6. J. Bradford Robinson attempts to lay such charges to rest in "The Jazz Essays of Adorno: Some Thoughts on Jazz Reception in Weimar Germany," *Popular Music* 13 (January 1994): 1–25.

7. Throughout this volume, the abbreviation "AT" will indicate Adorno's *Aesthetic Theory*. Where double pagination is given, the first number refers to Theodor W. Adorno, *Ästhetische Theorie*, ed. Gretel Adorno and Rolf Tiedemann, *Gesammelte Schriften*, vol. 7 (Frankfurt am Main: Suhrkamp, 1970; 2d ed., 1972); the second number refers to *Aesthetic Theory*, trans. C. Lenhardt (London: Routledge & Kegan Paul, 1984). Single pagination refers to the Lenhardt translation. Individual authors sometimes modify this translation or substitute their own. Other abbreviations for Adorno's books and the editions used can be found in the bibliography.

8. In *Notes to Literature*, vol. 2, ed. Rolf Tiedemann, trans. Shierry Weber Nicholsen (New York: Columbia University Press, 1992), pp. 93–94.

9. ND 10/xx.

10. Theodor W. Adorno, "Parataxis: On Hölderlin's Late Poetry," in *Notes to Literature*, vol. 2, pp. 108–49.

2

Mimesis and Mimetology: Adorno and Lacoue-Labarthe

Martin Jay

Mimesis, Roland Barthes insists in *S/Z*, produced a sickening feeling in his stomach, a kind of nausea that came from its conservative reproduction of already existing signs.[1] For the resolutely antirepresentational Barthes, any straightforward imitation of the external world, any aesthetic practice based on reference and repetition rather than the free play of signs, was inherently inadequate. A semiotic approach, he argues, must attend to the semantic play in the system, which undoes the closed economy of mimetic imitation. Likewise, in "The Double Session," Jacques Derrida disapprovingly asked if traditional literary criticism, with its search for univocal hidden meanings and the thematic kernels of texts, was not "a part of what we have called the *ontological* interpretation of mimesis or of metaphysical mimetologism?"[2] For Gilles Deleuze and Félix Guattari, mimesis is "radically false," a part of the paranoid order of spatial stasis they call the "copy" as opposed to the liberated, nomadic space of the "map."[3] Jean-François Lyotard identified mimesis with the "masters' law" and praised Diogenes' "cynical body" for defying it.[4] And Paul de Man dismisses mimesis as merely one literary trope among others, a trope, moreover, whose alleged naturalness needs to be deconstructed, for "what we call ideology is precisely the confusion of linguistic with natural reality, of reference with phenomenalism."[5]

For these theorists, and for many others normally labeled, for better or worse, poststructuralist, a conventional aesthetic privileging of mimesis or what is taken to be its synonym, imitation, is an ideologically suspect recirculation of the readymade, a false belief in the fixity of meaning and the possibility of achieving full presence, a language game that fails to see itself as such. Lacan's warnings against the mis-recognitions of the mirror stage would be yet another instance of this critique. Whereas in the much older Platonic critique of mimesis its danger was understood to be the undermining of a stable notion of truth, which is threatened by duplicitous copies of mere appear-ances, here it is precisely the opposite worry that is at work: the anxi-ety that mimesis means privileging an allegedly "true" original over its infinite duplications.[6] Or rather, at least in the case of Derrida, it involves that worry *and* its apparent contrary: that the mimetic "dou-ble" may itself be taken as self-sufficient, needing no external refer-ent at all. That assumption, which underlies certain modernist aesthetic practices, implies a no less dubious belief in the full onto-logical presence of the simulacrum itself.

In apparent contrast, the competing intellectual tradition known as the Frankfurt School found much in mimesis to praise. Although no less suspicious than poststructuralism of the naive referentialism of naturalist and realist aesthetics, Critical Theory valued mimesis as a valuable resource in its struggle to counter the reigning power of instrumental rationality in the modern world. Drawing on Walter Benjamin's suggestive ruminations of 1933, "On the Mimetic Faculty" and "The Doctrine of the Similar,"[7] and Roger Caillois's 1938 book *Le mythe et l'homme*,[8] Max Horkheimer and Theodor W. Adorno mourned the loss or withering of a primal and inherently benign hu-man capacity to imitate nature as the dialectic of enlightenment fol-lowed its fateful course.[9] Although they recognized the sinister potential of mimetic behavior when combined with the instrumental rationality it generally opposed—a potential realized precisely in the mocking Nazi mimicry of the Jews and duplicated in the culture in-dustry at its most repressive—by and large, mimesis served as an hon-orific term in their vocabulary.[10] In his *Aesthetic Theory*, Adorno could thus call the mimetic behavior that is precariously preserved in art "a receptacle for all that has been violently lopped off from and re-pressed in man by centuries of civilization, during which human be-ings were forcibly subjected to suffering" and "the endeavour to recover the bliss of a world that is gone."[11]

Not surprisingly, a significant secondary literature has arisen around the enigmatic concept of mimesis in Critical Theory, especially in the thought of Adorno, which one commentator has gone so far as to call the "obscure operator" of his entire system and another has called "a foundational concept never defined nor argued, but always alluded to, by name, as though it had preexisted all the texts."[12] Commentators have carefully unraveled its overdetermined origins in anthropological theories of shamanism and sympathetic magic, zoological analyses of animal mimicry, psychological theories of compulsive repetition, and aesthetic ideas of representation. However, no one, to my knowledge, has attempted the formidable task of thinking about Adorno's positive evocation of mimesis in the light of more recent poststructuralist commentary on the same theme.[13]

Such a task becomes all the more intriguing when we realize that several thinkers in the poststructuralist camp are less unequivocally hostile to mimesis than the picture painted above would suggest. That is, despite the animadversions against naive referentiality in the work of theorists like de Man, Lyotard, and Barthes, mimesis in a more complicated sense has played a positive role in certain poststructuralist theory. A case can be made, in fact, for the Derrida of "The Double Session,"[14] but it is in the work of Philippe Lacoue-Labarthe in particular that the most profound poststructuralist meditation on the implications of the concept can be found. After a brief sketch of Adorno's complicated use of the term, I want to pass on to how mimesis figures in Lacoue-Labarthe's work, most notably the texts recently collected in *Typography*.[15] By then comparing the two, I hope to provide a new perspective on the significance of this extraordinarily vexed term.

I

A first approximation of Adorno's use of mimesis, whether in aesthetic, philosophical, anthropological, or psychological contexts, would necessarily stress its relational character, its way of bridging but not collapsing differences. These differences are not, however, simply between a representation and what is represented, as the dominant tradition of thought about mimesis assumes, nor between one producing subject and another (the genius, say, imitating divine creation), as a subordinate tradition assumes.[16] The crucial difference is rather between what are traditionally called subjects and objects (or at least the "other" of subjects) in the world. Conceptual thought can be understood as an act of aggression perpetrated by a dominating subject on a world assumed to be external to it; it subsumes particulars under universals, violently reducing their uniqueness to typifications or exemplars of a general or essential principle. Mimesis, in contrast, involves a more sympathetic, compassionate, and noncoercive relationship of affinity between nonidentical particulars, which do not then become reified into two poles of a subject/object dualism. Rather than producing hierarchical subsumption under a subjectively generated category, it preserves the rough equality of the object and subject involved.

More precisely, it assimilates the latter to the former in such a way that the unposited, unintended object implicitly predominates, thwarting the imperialist gesture of subjective control and constitution that is the hallmark of philosophical idealism. "Mimetic behaviour," Adorno insists, "does not imitate something but assimilates itself to that something."[17] The word "imitation" (*Nachahmung*), he implies, suggests too active a role for the subject, whose making alone cannot be the source of the meaning it finds in the mimetic relation with the other.[18] Instead, Adorno prefers the verb *anschmiegen* (to snuggle up or mold to) to stress a relationship of contiguity.[19] In a way, he is returning to the original Greek use of the term, for example, in the Delian hymns or Pindar, when "mimesis" meant the expression of an inner state through cultic rituals rather than the reproduction of external reality, rituals that included music, dance, and mime.[20] Although in these instances, "mimesis" meant an outward expression of something inward rather than a relation between subject and external object, in both cases, the mode was more like benign assimilation than domination.

In more passively assimilating itself to the other, the subject of mimesis also preserves the sensuous, somatic element that the abstractions of idealist reason factor out of cognition or sublate into a higher rationality. Precisely which senses are most involved I will examine shortly, but for now suffice it to say that mimesis necessarily entails a crucial role for the body in the interaction between self and world. Equally important, it is the body as both the source of pleasure and the locus of pain.

Yet mimesis, as Adorno develops it, is not to be understood as the simple opposite of reason, as it sometimes has been.[21] It is closer to what Habermas once called a "placeholder" for a "primordial reason," which, however, cannot be satisfactorily theorized without betraying its preconceptual status.[22] As Adorno explains in *Aesthetic Theory*,

The continued existence of mimesis, understood as the nonconceptual affinity of a subjective creation with its objective and unposited other, defines art as a form of cognition and to that extent as "rational". . . . What the stubborn persistence of aesthetic mimesis proves is not that there is an innate play instinct, as some ideologues would have us believe, but that to this day rationality has never been fully realized, rationality understood in the sense of an agency in the service of mankind and of human potentials, perhaps even of "humanized nature" (Marx).[23]

Although initially manifest in the context of what Sir James Fraser calls "sympathetic magic," mimesis should thus not be reduced to "the superstitious belief in the ability to have a direct impact on things."[24] Nor is it simply an appreciation of the uncanny similitudes that supposedly already exist in nature, those wondrous astrological, physiognomic, or graphological correspondences, the "secret language of things" that Benjamin in his more antimodern moods finds so intriguing. In aesthetic mimesis in particular, what is preserved— as well as transformed—is the sedimented "material" of past artistic endeavors, which suggest a historical and natural "other" worthy of assimilation. Moreover, mimesis partakes of nonmagical forms of knowing, in part through its preservation of some of the cognitive power of intuition, as opposed to conceptual appropriation, the intuition Kant sees as a hallmark of aesthetic experience.[25]

Its nonmagical status also follows from the complicated relationship mimesis has to expression, by which Adorno means something more than revealing the psychological interiority of the individual artist. Instead, what is expressed is a dissonant resistance to the harmonizing impulses of affirmative art, a resistance that is grounded in a remembrance of the sedimented suffering of the past and the continuing suffering of the present—the suffering of the object as well as the subject, of what might be called "nature" as well as humankind.[26] "Expression in art is mimetic," Adorno claims, "just as the expression of living creatures is the expression of suffering."[27] Mimesis is thus a check to the ideological overcoming of real pain in the idealist art of consolation or the realist art of reconciliation.[28] Hence mimesis remains vital to the uncompromisingly dissonant modernist art, for example, that of Beckett or Kafka, Adorno so vigorously championed (for reasons that were thus diametrically opposed to Barthes's semiotic celebration of the alleged free play of signifiers).[29]

Perhaps most important, the rational moment of mimesis paradoxically follows from its own need to be supplemented by—or, rather, placed in a force field with—precisely that very conceptuality it seems to spurn. In aesthetic experience, Adorno insists, mimesis is never sufficient unto itself, but always needs to be juxtaposed in a constellation with the constructive impulse of "spirit."[30] "In art," he writes, "mimesis is both inferior and superior to spirit: it is contrary to spirit and yet the cause of spirit's being kindled. In artworks spirit has become the principle of construction. For spirit to live up to its telos means that it must well up from the mimetic impulses, constructing them by assimilation rather than external decree."[31] Spirit and mimesis, construction and expression, thus exist in a creative tension in works of art, a tension that should be preserved. Although they infiltrate each other—"To represent the mimesis it supplanted," Adorno wrote in *Negative Dialectics,* "the concept has no other way than to adopt something mimetic in its own conduct, without abandoning itself"[32]—the two cannot be simply identified at some higher level of unity.

Precisely because works of art preserve rather than falsely reconcile such tensions, they also stage what might be called a negative dialectic of imitation in relation to what exists outside their apparently self-enclosed boundaries. Adorno presents this negative dialectic as an unavoidable antinomy. On the one hand, works of art—or at least modernist ones that take seriously the "art for art's sake" credo—strive for autotelic self-sufficiency, which allows Adorno to say that "the mimesis of works of art is their resemblance to themselves."[33] As Lambert Zuidervaart points out, this claim implicitly answers the Platonic fear that art is duplicitous because it fails to imitate a higher reality; for Adorno instead, "similarity with itself separates the artwork from a false reality, where nothing is really real because everything obeys the law of exchange."[34] That is, by refusing to imitate, or be assimilated entirely to, a bad external reality—by paradoxically honoring, one might say, the Jewish taboo on graven images—works of art hold out the hope for a more benign version of mimesis in a future world beyond domination and reification.

On the other hand, the actual failure of such works to achieve absolute self-identity, a failure produced, inter alia, by their always being made for those who enjoy, exchange, or consume them, bears witness to the still-unredeemed quality of life in the social world. That imperfection necessarily infiltrates the work and mocks the illusory claim to completion. As such, it also bears witness to bodily pain, the unhealed wounds of damaged life that are indirectly represented in the artwork's dissonant fissures. The very illusory quality of art, its deceitful claim to present the absolute in sensuous terms, is thus at once a protest against the inadequacies of the world it refuses to imitate and an expression of the inability to transcend those inadequacies through aesthetic means alone.

Adorno, to be sure, was aware that the delicate balance he admired in certain modernist works was threatened by the increasing hegemony of spirit and construction, understood in essentially instrumental rationalist terms, over mimesis or expression. The withering away of the sensuous moment in late modernist art meant that all that was being imitated was the reified social relations of the administered world, a conclusion he amplified in his critique of Schoenberg's move from atonalism to the twelve-tone row.[35] Its effects were felt outside the realm of art as well, Adorno insists, for "the contemporary loss of any subjective capacity for experience is most likely identical with the tenacious repression of mimesis today."[36] And when the repressed does return, Adorno laments, it often does so in the distorted form of a sadistic mimicry that shows its subordination to the ends of instrumental, dominating rationality.

To combat that repression is no easy task, but one modest effort is discerned by Fredric Jameson in Adorno's own, idiosyncratic prose style. Without ever reducing philosophy to a variant of literature,

Adorno seeks to subvert the dominating, homogenizing power of conceptual thinking by introducing a mimetic element in his own writing. According to Jameson, this moment appears in those moves in Adorno's prose that can be called narrative. That is, his writing stages the conflicts and tensions of a story over time, with various theoretical terms and philosophical arguments playing the roles of actors, a procedure that tacitly undercuts the atemporal impulse of conceptual reason. "This micro-work of the sentence on the isolated concept," Jameson writes, "is, then, what undermines its apparent rational autonomy and pre-forms it...for its multiple positions in the larger movement of the constellation or the 'model.' The mimetic or the narrative may be thought to be a kind of homeopathic strategy in which, by revealing the primal movement of domination hidden away within abstract thought, the venom of abstraction is neutralized, allowing some potential or utopian truth-content to come into its own."[37]

Whether or not the term "narrative" is fully appropriate here—it may suggest too linear an emplotment to capture the chiasmic logic Jameson himself recognizes as Adorno's main trope—the importance of Adorno's stylistic mimesis of mimesis is worth taking seriously, for it goes beyond a mere external staging of dialectical conflicts. Perhaps a more fruitful way to bring it to the surface would be to follow Adorno's own praise for the stylistic device that he finds best resists conceptual synthesis: paratactic rather than hypotactic syntax.[38] By resisting the imperative to arrange ideas hierarchically, parataxis both undercuts the mediating logic of conceptual subordination and bears witness to the crisis of meaningful experience (*Erfahrung* in Benjamin's well-known sense, rather than *Erlebnis*) in the modern world.

In his discussion of Hölderlin, Adorno acknowledges, to be sure, that language, unlike music, cannot avoid some conceptual homogenizing: "by virtue of its significative element, the opposite pole to its mimetic-expressive element, language is chained to the form of judgment and proposition and thereby to the synthetic form of the concept. In poetry, unlike music, a conceptual synthesis turns against its medium; it becomes a constitutive dissociation."[39] In the later poetry of Hölderlin, this dissociation is especially "striking—artificial disturbances that evade the logical hierarchy of subordinating syntax."[40]

But precisely because he remains true to the unsublatable tension between the synthetic and the dissociative impulses in language—to what we have seen Adorno call elsewhere the spiritual/constructive and the mimetic/expressive moments in art—Hölderlin produces an aesthetic instantiation of negative dialectics. As such, he resists the mythologizing reading based solely on the putative content of the poems that Heidegger wants to force on him as the simple antithesis of idealism, the gnomic prophet of prereflective Being. The same resistance might be discerned in Adorno's own writing, which never one-sidedly pits mimesis or sympathetic magic against conceptual rationality, synthetic domination, or theoretical reflection in a nondialectical opposition.

II

To invoke Adorno's admiration for, and arguably mimetic appropriation of, Hölderlin's paratactic style provides a convenient bridge to Lacoue-Labarthe, who finds in Hölderlin—albeit more so in the dramatic works like *The Death of Empedocles* and the translations of Sophocles than in the later poetry—a profound lesson on the same issues. In "The Caesura of the Speculative," one of the central essays in *Typography,* Lacoue-Labarthe, in fact, approvingly cites Adorno's text, claiming that its author is justified in "comparing the 'parataxis' characteristic of Hölderlin's late style with the writing of Beethoven's last quartets."[41]

Lacoue-Labarthe's target in this piece is what he sees as the speculative dialectic at work in both tragedy, understood in a certain way, and absolute idealism, a speculative dialectic he identifies with what Heidegger calls "the ontotheological in its fully accomplished form."[42] He finds, underlying that dialectic, "the guiding thread of a primary and constant preoccupation, of a single question—none other than that of *mimesis,* at whatever level one chooses to examine it (whether it be that of 'imitation,' in the sense of the 'imitation of the Ancients,' of mimesis as a mode of *poiesis,* i.e., Aristotelian mimesis, or even—and this does not fail to enter into play—of mimesis in the sense of 'mimetism' or *imitatio*)."[43] According to Lacoue-Labarthe, only mimesis provides the means to transfigure negativity into positive being through representation; only mimesis allows the tragic pleasure that overcomes a visceral feeling of horror at the terrible events reproduced. This economy of specular transfiguration is precisely what underlies idealist philosophy as well, indeed philosophy in general. As such, it is the basis of what Derrida calls a "mimetologism," the imitation of the same in a closed system of ultimate higher reconciliation, a system in which what is mimetically re-presented is the putative unity of the logos itself, a logos that is identified with the truth.[44]

Lacoue-Labarthe is careful to deny that Hölderlin consciously transcends this economy, at least at the level of his own theoretical understanding, which is "speculative through and through."[45] Indeed, he implies that a complete extrication from the mimetological, speculative economy would be impossible.[46] But what Hölderlin's work does accomplish is a kind of internal dislocation of it, an exposure of a caesura in its smoothly working operation (as in the alexandrine), like the pause in poetic meter. And he does so by regressing behind Aristotle's affirmative understanding of mimetic representation to reveal what "*haunts* Plato under the name of mimesis and against which Plato fights with all of his philosophical determination until he finds a way of arresting it and fixing its concept."[47] Rather than expelling the troubling implications of the mimetic duplication of the same—an expulsion Lacoue-Labarthe calls the speculative "denegation" of mimesis—Hölderlin allows it to fester in the midst of his own tragic dramas, producing a kind of endless oscillation between proximity and distance that denies sublation and reconciliation and that cannot rest content at either pole.

More precisely, the dialectical structure of speculative recuperation and the infinite oscillation coexist in an uneasy equilibrium, the melodic and the rhythmic impulses of the work never coming together completely. The caesura in the work is thus mimetic representation itself, the space between the original and its duplicate, the hiatus rather than either pole. For this reason, Lacoue-Labarthe is able to conclude, with an implicit nod to Benjamin, that Hölderlin's dramas come closer to the baroque *Trauerspiel* than to classical Greek tragedy.[48] Whereas the structure of speculative dialectics that underlies the latter is like the completed work of mourning, which in German is *Trauerarbeit*, the *Trauerspiel* keeps the "play" of mourning going forever without any final reconciliation or working through, keeping, that is, the "play" in the system from achieving any terminal stasis.[49]

If it follows any logic, it is that of paradox, which Lacoue-Labarthe dubs "hyperbologic." Expatiating in the other essays in his collection on its meaning, Lacoue-Labarthe points to the ambivalence at work even in Aristotle's notion of mimesis, at once a duplication or copy of what already exists and a supplement or addition to fill the lack in what exists. Whereas the former is reproductive, the latter is productive. Whereas the former assumes nature is sufficient unto itself, the latter implies the need for a substitution. The paradox follows from the fact that mimetic substitution means both the need to imitate what already exists and the realization that what exists is itself insufficient and must be supplemented by the imitation.

As Diderot shows in his discussion of actors who can imitate the identity of a character precisely because they themselves lack all fixed character, the result undercuts the notion of a proper, self-possessed identity. "The paradox," Lacoue-Labarthe writes, "states a *law of impropriety*, which is also the very law of mimesis: only the 'man without qualities,' the being without properties or specificity, the subjectless subject (absent from himself, distracted from himself, deprived of self) is able to present or produce in general."[50] Plato also grasps this paradox but denounces the hypocrisy he sees as its issue, whereas Diderot—and Lacoue-Labarthe—appreciate it precisely for its destabilizing effect, its active unsettling of reified selfhood (indeed even of the fragile notion of the self that underpins Adorno's notion of mimesis as the expression of suffering).

Significantly, Lacoue-Labarthe connects the hyperbologic of the mimetic paradox to that of semblance or illusion (*Schein*) in general, a category Adorno also privileges in his writings on aesthetics.[51] "The division between appearance and reality, presence and absence, the same and the other, or identity and difference," Lacoue-Labarthe argues, "grounds (and . . . constantly unsteadies) mimesis. At whatever level one takes it—in the copy or the reproduction, the art of the actor, mimetism, disguise, dialogic writing—the rule is always the same: the more it resembles, the more it differs."[52] For Adorno as well, it is aesthetic illusion that resists mimetological closure, or what he calls the "general mimetic abandonment to reification, which is the principle of death."[53] Even certain variants of modernist art had succumbed to that principle through a simple presentation of external reality without aesthetic transfiguration into illusion: "Ever since the beginning of modernism art has absorbed objects from outside," Adorno remarks, "leaving them as they are without assimilating them (e.g., montage). This indicates a surrender by mimesis to its antagonist, a trend which is caused by the pressure reality exerts on art."[54] Lacoue-Labarthe's hostility to the ideology of the genuine or authentic original, which mimesis merely duplicates, is thus explicitly shared by Adorno, who warns in *Minima Moralia* against "the concept of genuineness as such. In it dwells the notion of the supremacy of the original over the derived. This notion, however, is always linked with social legitimation. All ruling strata claim to be the oldest settlers, autochthonous."[55]

Perhaps more than Lacoue-Labarthe though, Adorno is willing to retain an emphatic notion of truth in relation to works of art, for "the definition of art in terms of illusion is only half correct: art is true to the degree to which it is an illusion of the nonillusory (*Schein des Scheinlosen*). In the last analysis, to experience art is to recognize that its truth content is not null and void."[56] But it was precisely Adorno's point—and here he tacitly anticipates Lacoue-Labarthe's defense of the hyperbologic paradox—that such truth is manifest only in the nonsublatable, negative dialectic of illusion and nonillusion itself. As such, it could be understood as comparable to a permanent allegory without symbolic reconciliation.[57]

Significantly, it is the yearning for totalized reconciliation that Lacoue-Labarthe, in an essay jointly written with Jean-Luc Nancy, claims was at the root of "the Nazi myth."[58] Myth, they claimed, "is *the* mimetic instrument par excellence,"[59] because it seeks absolute identification through typified existence (real "experience" through the realization of racial types). Although arguing that the Germans' need for mimetic mythologizing was stronger than elsewhere, because their imitation of the Greeks was itself an imitation of an earlier French mimesis of the ancients, they darkly conclude, in a way reminiscent of Horkheimer and Adorno's *Dialectic of Enlightenment,* that "this logic, with its double trait of the mimetic will-to-identity and the self-fulfillment of form, belongs profoundly to the mood or

character of the West in general, and more precisely, to the fundamental tendency of the *subject,* in the metaphysical sense of the
word."[60] Like the Frankfurt School theorists, they acknowledge the
complicity of mimesis in one of its guises—in their case, that of the
nonallegorical search for perfect identity, in that of Horkheimer
and Adorno, the "organized control of mimesis"[61] by instrumental
rationality—in the realization of nightmare politics. Even the
Heidegger from whom Lacoue-Labarthe and Nancy had learned so
much is not exempt from this critique: "an unacknowledged mimetology seems to overdetermine the thought of Heidegger politically," Lacoue-Labarthe admits, after the growing scandal about
Heidegger's politics in the 1980s.[62]

The victims of Nazism, in contrast, are those who adhere to a nonmimetological variant of mimesis, which resists mythic closure. "All in
all," writes Lacoue-Labarthe in his book *Heidegger, Art and Politics,* "the
Jews are infinitely mimetic beings, or in other words, the site of an *endless mimesis,* which is both interminable and inorganic, producing no
art and achieving no appropriation."[63] Although the claim that Jews
have never produced art may seem perverse (as well as inaccurate), it
is meant in a flattering way to the extent that "art" suggests symbolic
sublimation of the unreconciled fissures of existence. Horkheimer
and Adorno make a similar claim in *Dialectic of Enlightenment,* when
they argue that for all the Jews' complicity in the millennia-long process of dominating nature, "they did not eliminate adaptation to nature, but converted it into a series of duties in the form of ritual. They
have retained the aspect of expiation, but have avoided the reversion
to mythology which symbolism implies."[64]

III

Much more could be done to tease out the telling similarities between Adorno's and Lacoue-Labarthe's general notions of mimesis,
but I want to turn now to the specific issue of the sensual element in
their accounts. In the essay just discussed, "The Nazi Myth," Lacoue-
Labarthe and Nancy claim that the Aryan type is the product of "a
construction and conformation of the world according to a vision,
an image, the image of the creator of forms.... [T]he *anschauen—*

'seeing' as vision and intuition piercing to the heart of the things and *forming* being itself, the 'seeing' of an active, practical, operative dream—is the heart of the 'mythicotypical' process."[65] Privileging vision, in other words, is understood to be in the service of the speculative, theatrical, theoretical version of mimesis, which elsewhere Lacoue-Labarthe damns as mimetological.[66]

A similar argument informs his consideration of the psychoanalytic theory of the self in "The Echo of the Subject," included in *Typography*. Its targets are Lacan's privileging of vision in the mirror stage and in the Imaginary and René Girard's notion of mimetic rivalry, both of which depend on a conceptualization of the subject in narcissistic terms. Preferring a notion of aural to visual mimesis—the Greek nymph Echo to that of her love object, Narcissus—he turns to the analyst Theodor Reik's discussion of voice and rhythm, in *The Haunting Melody*, for help in constructing a nonidentical, uncanny version of the self. He calls it "allobiographical"—"the 'novel' of an other (be it a double)"[67]—rather than autobiographical. Such a self, he claims, is not based on specular reflection, on the imitation of the same, but rather on the *unheimliche*, rhythmic repetition of an original that never existed in itself, a perpetual spacing without end. Rhythm, in fact, "establishes the break between the visible and the audible, the temporal and the spatial (but also the inscribed and the fictive), thus resisting the hold of such partitions and bearing a relation to *archi-écriture* in the Derridean sense of the term."[68] As such, perhaps it remains, as Derrida himself says in his introduction to *Typography*, "outside the order of the sensible. It belongs to no sense."[69] And, I might add, it rejects the Platonic realm of pure intelligibility as well.

Although one might discern a certain similarity between this argument and Benjamin's faith in "nonsensuous correspondences"—for example, those between heavenly constellations of stars and human destiny claimed by astrology—as the basis of a benign notion of mimesis, for Adorno, such a parallel is harder to discern. Despite his oft-proclaimed embrace of the Jewish taboo on graven images and his recognition that, of all the senses, smell is perhaps the most mimetic, Adorno never completely denigrated visuality per se or sought a realm prior to both the senses and intelligibility.[70] As Gertrud Koch and Miriam Hansen have recently shown, even when it came to the mass cultural phenomenon known as film, Adorno could posit an emancipatory potential in the medium itself.[71] However much Hollywood films are part of the ideological culture industry, the cinematic mimesis of expressive bodies suggests a prelinguistic experience prior to the conscious articulations of the ego.

In *Aesthetic Theory*, Adorno specifically defends the importance of a visual moment in art, which is another way to say the intuitive as opposed to the purely conceptual: "the desideratum of visuality [*Anschaulichkeit*] seeks to preserve the mimetic moment of art."[72] But rather than fetishizing that moment into the essence of art per se or rigidly opposing sensuality to spirituality, Adorno also argues that "mimesis only goes on living through its antithesis, which is rational control by artworks over all that is heterogeneous to them. . . . Art is a vision of the nonvisual; it is similar to a concept without actually being one."[73] Once again, it is the constellation of mimesis and rationality, expression and spirit, that defines the unsublated aesthetic prefiguration of the utopia that Adorno refuses to abandon.

Perhaps because of that refusal, Adorno never finds rhythmic repetition without end, that infinite spacing and perpetual deferral so characteristic of deconstruction, as unambiguously congenial as did Lacoue-Labarthe. One of the central charges against Stravinsky in Adorno's celebrated invidious comparison of his music with Schoenberg's was directed precisely against the Russian composer's overreliance on rhythmic composition: "even in those cases where the Schoenberg school operates with such rhythms, they are for the most part charged with melodic and contrapuntal content, while the rhythmic proportions which in Stravinsky dominate the musical foreground are employed solely in the sense of shock effects."[74] These shocks are simply absorbed by the numbed and overpowered musical subject, who no longer expresses the suffering of modern life, let alone has the will to resist it. Unlike Lacoue-Labarthe, Adorno never relegates to the margins of his analysis the expressive moment of mimesis, which reveals the body—natural as well as human—in pain.

Adorno's suspicion of the value of rhythmic repetition derives, it might be speculated, from the link he sees between it and what Freud had understood as the functioning of the death drive. In fact, as Josef Früchtl rightly argues, the ambivalence toward mimesis that can at times be detected in Adorno may be explained in part by his recognition that reconciliation and destruction are closely intertwined.[75] That is, the radically antinarrative structure of the death drive, its compulsion to repeat in the service of restoring a state of undifferentiated stasis that can, however, never be realized short of actual death, lends to nonmimetological mimesis a melancholic tone that antiutopian poststructuralists like Lacoue-Labarthe find congenial, but which Adorno does not.

Adorno, however much he may have been a practitioner of a "melancholy science," never gleefully embraces the masochistic self-shattering that defenders of the repetition compulsion claim is a release from the ideological mystifications of subjecthood.[76] He understands that the radical reduction of ego strength through the mimetic duplication of the inorganic world—what Caillois calls psychasthenia, in his study of insect mimicry—could also mean the triumph of reification. As his frequent denunciations of surrealism demonstrate, Adorno remains suspicious of an aesthetic that is based on the uncanny evocation of compulsive beauty by a depersonalized subject who ultimately reveals itself as "inanimate and virtually dead."[77] Although Jameson may overstate the case by saying that it is narration itself that Adorno hoped mimesis would rescue in its conflict with conceptuality, it is nonetheless true that he never damns narrative coherence tout court as merely another version of the speculative suppression of nonidentity that is, in Derrida's terms, a version of mimetologism. He does, to be sure, acknowledge that any attempt to restore it, under the present circumstances, is necessarily ideological—telling a story could only be based on the very continuity of experience (*Erfahrung*) that had been lost in the modern world—but he does not rule out the possibility of a future in which it might once again be meaningful.[78]

It is perhaps such historical hopes, which despite everything Adorno never lost, that most distinguish his meditations on this theme from those of Lacoue-Labarthe, who seems to defend an endlessly oscillating mimesis that is based on a paradoxical hyperbologic that steadfastly resists ontological stability, subjective integrity, and speculative representation, all of which are seen as evidence of mimetological closure. In contrast, Adorno places mimesis, also understood as susceptible to, but not identical with, mimetology, in a tense constellation with its apparent opposites: rationality, spirit, narrative coherence, and subjective construction. Neither *Trauerarbeit*, in the sense of a fully triumphal mastery of otherness through a higher level sublimation like that of classical tragedy, nor *Trauerspiel*, in the sense of a perpetually melancholic resistance to any closure, defines his delicately nuanced position. Instead, Adorno practices a *trauerliche Wissenschaft*, a "melancholy science," in which the noun is no less important than the adjective. As a result, mimesis may be a necessary element in his utopian vision, but it is by no means sufficient unto itself.

IV

What have we learned by this comparison between the uses of mimesis in Adorno and Lacoue-Labarthe? First, it is clear that the most interesting contemporary debate over mimesis has little to do with the issue of referential representation versus the autoreferentiality of sign systems. Nor can it be reduced to a mere synonym for imitation. Despite the easy dismissal of mimesis by the thinkers cited at the beginning of this paper, it survives in important and unexpectedly similar ways in both poststructuralism and Critical Theory.

Second, it is no less obvious that the word itself is polysemic, even catachrestic, with meanings that carry with them the residues of their separate origins in anthropological, psychological, aesthetic, philosophical, and zoological discourses. So, too, the value of the "original" model to be mimetically duplicated—variously identified with nature as a nonsubjective other, the active producer of that nature, the cultural tradition of the ancients, or the reified relations of the modern world—inevitably inflects the judgment about the process itself. If, then, there is an economy of mimesis, what Derrida calls an economimesis, it is difficult to reduce it to a circulation or equilibrium of identical acceptations.[79] Instead, the term changes its meaning and often its evaluative charge depending on the context in which it appears. It is for this reason that even mimicry, which often seems to be related to the mocking and demeaning imitation of victims, can turn around and become a tool of resistance, as postcolonial theorists like Homi

Bhabha and postmodernist feminist artists like Cindy Sherman have recently demonstrated.[80]

Third, that context often involves the complex relation between mimesis and rationality or conceptuality. What the poststructuralists call mimetology involves subordinating mimesis to a deadening logic of sameness or sublation, a theoretical/theatrical logic based on visual reproduction, which they see as typical of the Western ontotheological project in general. Mimesis understood as rhythmic repetition without closure, an infinite oscillation between original and copy, is posited as the—to be sure, never fully successful—hyperbological antidote to mimetology, as the uncanny caesura in a speculative system that seeks to stifle its playful uncertainties.

In the case of Adorno, mimesis becomes problematic when it is in league not with reason per se but with the instrumental rationality of the modern world. Then what it imitates is the *nature morte* of a world of reified relations, in which the suffering of both humans and nature is no longer expressed. But as his discussion of the interaction between mimesis and rationality in art indicates, Adorno feels that both are necessary to avoid surrendering to the potential in mimesis alone to ape the repetitive rhythms of the death drive. Despite his occasional adoption of a rhetoric of nostalgia for a lost paradise of mimetic affinities, Adorno posits a constellation in which reason and mimesis each make up for the deficiencies of the other.

Finally, we have seen that both Adorno and Lacoue-Labarthe share an appreciation for the function mimesis can play in decentering the strong constitutive subject, opening a place for otherness and nonidentity and enabling a nondominating relationship between the human and the nonhuman. Although Adorno never goes as far as Lacoue-Labarthe in marginalizing the suffering subject or advocating the surrender of its ego strength, he recognizes that such a subject has to be put in a constellation with the other victims of domination rather than given absolute pride of place. What in Roland Barthes produces feelings of nausea, in Lyotard a denunciation of the "master's law," and in Deleuze and Guattari a nomadic flight from paranoid despotism turns out in the two theorists I have examined to be a potential source of healing and solace. Which of these opposing attitudes we should ourselves imitate is a conclusion I let each reader draw for himself or herself. Unlike concepts that coerce, mimetic affinities should, after all, operate only through sympathetic attractions whose power cannot be imposed by theorists from the outside.

Notes

1. Roland Barthes, *S/Z* (Paris: Seuil, 1970), p. 145.

2. Jacques Derrida, "The Double Session," in *Dissemination,* trans. Barbara Johnson (Chicago: University of Chicago Press, 1981), p. 245.

3. Gilles Deleuze and Félix Guattari, *Mille plateaux* (Paris: Les Editions de Minuit, 1980), p. 144.

4. Jean-François Lyotard, "On the Strength of the Weak," in Lyotard, *Toward the Postmodern,* ed. Robert Harvey and Mark S. Roberts (Atlantic Highlands, N. J.: Humanities Press, 1993), p. 69.

5. Paul de Man, *The Resistance to Theory* (Minneapolis: University of Minnesota Press, 1986), p. 11.

6. For a useful comparison of the Platonic with the poststructuralist complaints against mimesis, see Christopher Prendergast, *The Order of Mimesis: Balzac, Stendhal, Nerval, Flaubert* (New York: Cambridge University Press, 1986), chap. 1.

7. Walter Benjamin, "On the Mimetic Faculty," in *Reflections: Essays, Aphorisms, Autobiographical Writings,* ed. Peter Demetz, trans. Edmund Jephcott (New York: Harcourt Brace Jovanovich, 1978); "Doctrine of the Similar," *New German Critique* 17 (spring 1979): 65–69.

8. Roger Caillois, *Le mythe et l'homme* (Paris: Gallimard, 1938); see also his "Mimicry and Legendary Psychasthenia," *October* 31 (winter 1984): 17–32.

9. Max Horkheimer and Theodor W. Adorno, *Dialectic of Enlightenment,* trans. John Cumming (New York: Seabury Press, 1972), for example, pp. 180–81, 227.

10. In *Dialectic of Enlightenment,* however, the ambiguities of mimesis are perhaps more explicitly stressed than in later works like *Aesthetic Theory.* For a discussion that contends that Adorno understands the impossibility of disentangling the reductive from the emancipatory moments in mimesis, see Alexander García Düttmann, *Das Gedächtnis des Denkens: Versuch über Heidegger und Adorno* (Frankfurt: Suhrkamp, 1991).

11. Theodor W. Adorno, *Aesthetic Theory,* trans. C. Lenhardt, ed. Gretel Adorno and Rolf Tiedemann (London: Routledge & Kegan Paul, 1984), pp. 453, 465. Herbert Marcuse, however, was less convinced. In *The Aesthetic Dimension: Toward a Critique of Marxist Aesthetics* (Boston: Beacon Press, 1978), he writes, "the realm of freedom lies beyond mimesis.... Mimesis remains re-presentation of reality. This bondage resists the utopian quality of art" (p. 47). But he also acknowledges the role of aesthetic mimesis in preserving the memory of past happiness (p. 67). In the later Critical Theory

of Jürgen Habermas, mimesis plays a much more marginal role, and, when it appears, it is usually assimilated into his communicative notion of intersubjective rationality. See, for example, his remark in "Questions and Counter-Questions," in *Habermas and Modernity*, ed. Richard J. Bernstein (Cambridge, Mass.: MIT Press, 1985), that "modern art harbors a utopia that becomes a reality to the degree that the mimetic powers sublimated in the work of art find resonance in the mimetic relations of a balanced and undistorted intersubjectivity of everyday life" (p. 202).

12. Michael Taussig, *Mimesis and Alterity: A Particular History of the Senses* (New York: Routledge, 1993), p. 45; Fredric Jameson, *Late Marxism: Adorno, or, The Persistence of the Dialectic* (New York: Verso, 1990), p. 64; for other discussions, see Martin Lüdke, *Anmerkungen zu einer "Logik des Zerfalls": Adorno—Beckett* (Frankfurt: Suhrkamp, 1981), chap. 5; Michael Cahn, "Subversive Mimesis: Theodor W. Adorno and the Modern Impasse of Critique," in *Mimesis in Contemporary Theory: An Interdisciplinary Approach*, ed. Mihai Spariosu (Philadelphia: John Benjamins, 1984); Karla L. Schultz, *Mimesis on the Move: Theodor W. Adorno's Concept of Imitation* (New York: Peter Lang, 1990); and, most notably, Josef Früchtl, *Mimesis: Konstellation eines Zentralbegriffs bei Adorno* (Würzberg: Königshausen & Neumann, 1986).

13. A partial exception is Früchtl, who devotes some interesting pages to Julia Kristeva's relation to Adorno. See his *Mimesis*, p. 181.

14. See, for example, David Carroll, *Paraesthetics: Foucault, Lyotard, Derrida* (New York: Methuen, 1987), pp. 101–5.

15. Philippe Lacoue-Labarthe, *Typography: Mimesis, Philosophy, Politics*, ed. Christopher Fynsk, introduction by Jacques Derrida (Cambridge, Mass.: Harvard University Press, 1989). The texts, translated by various hands, were chosen from his collections, *Le sujet de la philosophie: Typographies I* (Paris: Aubier-Flammarion, 1979) and *L'imitation des modernes: Typographies II* (Paris: Galilee, 1986); and from *Mimesis: Des articulations* (Paris: Aubier-Flammarion, 1975).

16. This second tradition is Kantian. See the critical discussion in Derrida, "Econo-mimesis," *Diacritics* 11 (1981): 9.

17. Adorno, *Aesthetic Theory*, p. 162.

18. It is for this reason that Adorno explicitly repudiates the *verum-factum* principle adopted by Hegelian Marxists like Lukács. For a discussion, see my "Vico and Western Marxism," *Fin-de-Siècle Socialism and Other Essays* (New York: Routledge, 1988). W. Martin Lüdke points out that, for Adorno, a more primitive adaptation to nature, which can be called mimicry, becomes true mimesis only when it turns into a conscious and intentional doubling of nature (*Anmerkungen zu einer "Logik des Zerfall,"* p. 58). This is true, it seems to me, only if the constructive impulse of this doubling is not understood to outweigh the assimilative.

19. For a discussion, see Cahn, "Subversive Mimesis," p. 6, n. 44.

20. W. Tatarkiewicz, "Mimesis," *Dictionary of the History of Ideas*, vol. 3 (New York: Scribner, 1973), p. 226.

21. For example, by David Roberts, who claims that "Adorno's *utopia* of reconciliation in turn may be seen as the rational veneer for a profoundly arational *mysticism* of

redemptive mimesis beyond and behind all civilization." *Art and Enlightenment: Aesthetic Theory after Adorno* (Lincoln: University of Nebraska Press, 1991), p. 70.

22. Jürgen Habermas, *The Theory of Communicative Action*, vol. 1, trans. Thomas McCarthy (Boston: Beacon Press, 1984), p. 382. His attempt, like that of Albrecht Wellmer, in *Zur Dialektik von Moderne und Postmoderne: Vernunftkritik nach Adorno* (Frankfurt: Suhrkamp, 1985), to relocate mimesis within an intersubjective, communicative sphere has been criticized by Früchtl, *Mimesis*, p. 190. Interestingly, it was conservative theorists like David Hume and Edmund Burke who first pointed to the positive role of mimesis in sociability. See the discussion in Terry Eagleton, *The Ideology of the Aesthetic* (Oxford: Basil Blackwell, 1990), p. 53. Imitation was also privileged by Gabriel Tarde and then criticized by Emile Durkheim in his classic study *Suicide.*

23. Adorno, *Aesthetic Theory,* pp. 80, and 453.

24. Ibid., p. 453. A major weakness of Taussig's *Mimesis and Alterity* is its failure to make this distinction. See my review in *Visual Anthropology Review* 9, no. 2 (fall 1993).

25. For a helpful comparison of Adorno and Kant on this issue, see J. M. Bernstein, *The Fate of Art: Aesthetic Alienation from Kant to Derrida and Adorno* (University Park: Pennsylvania State University Press, 1992), pp. 201–6.

26. García Düttmann argues that in *Dialectic of Enlightenment,* the name "nature" stands metonymically for the relations with the other (p. 118). If so, it would be important to recognize that it includes what in French is nicely differentiated as *l'autre* and *l'autrui,* the objective and subjective "other."

27. Adorno, *Aesthetic Theory,* p. 162. Although the suffering of mute nature is expressed in mimesis, it takes human intervention to enable its appearance (an argument that in some ways parallels Heidegger's description of the relationship between *Dasein,* the being that cares for Being, and *Sein*).

28. According to Adorno, "Realism, which does not grasp subjective experience, to say nothing of going beyond it, only mimics reconciliation." "Trying to Understand *Endgame*," in *Notes to Literature,* 2 vols., ed. Rolf Tiedemann, trans. Shierry Weber Nicholsen (New York: Columbia University Press, 1991), vol. 1, p. 250.

29. Here the effects of Benjamin's antistructuralist linguistics on Adorno can be discerned, for Benjamin saw the Saussurean insistence on the absolute arbitrariness of the sign as evidence of the fall of language from its prelapsarian state, in which a mimetic relationship between names and things prevailed. For a helpful account of the differences between Benjaminian and structuralist linguistics, see Irving Wohlfarth, "On Some Jewish Motifs in Benjamin," in *The Problems of Modernity: Adorno and Benjamin,* ed. Andrew Benjamin (New York: Routledge, 1989). For a suggestive gloss on Adorno's "mimetic" relationship to Benjamin, which goes beyond simple imitation through "influence," see Jameson, *Late Marxism,* p. 52. He argues, in fact, that on the question of mimesis itself, the two were by no means as unified as is often assumed (p. 256).

30. For a lucid account of Adorno's argument about the dialectic of mimesis and rationality, see Peter Osborne, "Adorno and the Metaphysics of Modernism: The Problem of a 'Postmodern' Art," in *The Problems of Modernity: Adorno and Benjamin,* pp. 29–32.

31. Adorno, *Aesthetic Theory*, p. 174.

32. Theodor W. Adorno, *Negative Dialectics*, trans. E. B. Ashton (New York: Seabury Press, 1973), p. 14.

33. Adorno, *Aesthetic Theory*, p. 153.

34. Lambert Zuidervaart, *Adorno's Aesthetic Theory: The Redemption of Illusion* (Cambridge, Mass.: MIT Press, 1991), p. 181.

35. Theodor W. Adorno, *Philosophy of Modern Music*, trans. Anne G. Mitchell and Wesley V. Blomster (New York: Seabury Press, 1973), p. 64.

36. Adorno, *Aesthetic Theory*, p. 455.

37. Jameson, *Late Marxism*, p. 68. For another consideration of the relation between mimesis and narrative, see Prendergast, *The Order of Mimesis*, pp. 216–72.

38. Still another possibility would be to follow his discussion of hieroglyphic writing and *écriture* in mass culture and modernist art, as Miriam Hansen has suggested in "Mass Culture as Hieroglyphic Writing: Adorno, Derrida, Kracauer," *New German Critique* 56 (spring/summer 1992): 43–73.

39. Adorno, "Parataxis: On Hölderlin's Late Poetry," in *Notes to Literature*, vol. 2, trans. Shierry Weber Nicholsen (New York: Columbia University Press, 1992), p. 130.

40. Ibid., p. 131.

41. Lacoue-Labarthe, *Typography*, p. 226. The comparison was made in Adorno, "Parataxis: Hölderlin's Late Poetry," p. 133. Lacoue-Labarthe's most extensive discussion of Adorno comes in a later piece, "The Caesura of Religion," in *Opera through Other Eyes*, ed. David J. Levin (Stanford: Stanford University Press, 1994), pp. 45–77, which is a critique of Adorno's essay on Schoenberg's *Moses und Aron*, "Sakrales Fragment." Here he chastises Adorno for finding a redemptive moment in the music of the opera, which Lacoue-Labarthe claims reflects a failure to recognize the importance of the libretto in producing a sublime rather than redeemed work.

42. Lacoue-Labarthe, *Typography*, p. 208.

43. Ibid., p. 214. Unlike Adorno, Lacoue-Labarthe emphasizes the importance of imitating the ancients, as opposed to imitating nature, which emerged into prominence in the Renaissance. As Tartarkiewicz points out, "The watchword of *imitating antiquity* appeared as early as the fifteenth century and by the end of the seventeenth century it supplanted almost completely the idea of *imitating nature*. This was the greatest revolution in the concept of imitation. It changed the classical theory of art into an academic one. A compromise formula was devised for the principle of imitation; nature should be imitated but in the way it was imitated by the Ancients." "Mimesis," p. 229.

44. Derrida, like Adorno, generally denies the identity of mimesis and straightforward imitation. See his remarks in "The Double Session," p. 183. He is, however, far more eager than Adorno to uncouple mimesis from any notion of truth, defined either as unveiling (*alëtheia*) or agreement (*homoiösis* or *adaequatio*). See "The Double Session," pp. 192, 207.

45. Lacoue-Labarthe, *Typography*, p. 224.

46. As does Derrida in "The Double Session," p. 207.

47. Lacoue-Labarthe, *Typography*, p. 227.

48. Benjamin cites Hölderlin's Sophocles translations as evidence of a belated "baroque" confusion of *Trauerspiel* and Greek tragedy. See *The Origin of German Tragic Drama*, trans. John Osborne (London: NLB, 1977), p. 189. For a useful discussion of the more totalizing and harmonizing version of the baroque against which Benjamin and Lacoue-Labarthe warned, that of Hugo von Hofmannstahl and the Salzburg Festival, see Michael P. Steinberg, *The Meaning of the Salzburg Festival: Austria as Theater and Ideology, 1890–1938* (Ithaca, N. Y.: Cornell University Press, 1990), pp. 223–41. Steinberg borrows Adorno's distinction between theater and drama from *In Search of Wagner* to set the ideological totalization of Hofmannstahl's baroque against Benjamin's critical version.

49. As Derrida puts it, in his introduction, "Desistance," in *Typography*, "A *Trauerspiel* plays at mourning, it doubles the *work* of mourning: the speculative, dialectic, opposition, identification, nostalgic interiorization, even the double bind of imitation. But it doesn't avoid it" (p. 42).

50. Lacoue-Labarthe, *Typography*, pp. 258–59.

51. For a helpful account of Adorno's thoughts on semblance, see Zuidervaart, *Adorno's Aesthetic Theory*, chap. 8.

52. Lacoue-Labarthe, *Typography*, p. 260.

53. Adorno, *Aesthetic Theory*, p. 193.

54. Ibid.

55. Theodor W. Adorno, *Minima Moralia: Reflections from Damaged Life*, trans. E. F. N. Jephcott (London: NLB, 1974), p. 155.

56. Adorno, *Aesthetic Theory*, pp. 191–92. In his introduction to *Typography*, Derrida introduces the term "desistance" to signify Lacoue-Labarthe's playing with the relationship between mimesis and truth: "Mimesis 'precedes' truth in a certain sense; by destabilizing it in advance, it introduces a desire for *homoiösis* [adequation, similitude, resemblance] and makes it possible, perhaps, to account for it, as for everything, that might be its effect, up to and including what is called the subject" (p. 27).

57. For another way to approach the allegorical implications of this argument, see Terry Eagleton, who writes of Adorno's appropriation of Benjamin's notion of nonsensuous correspondences: "One might even name this mimesis *allegory*, that figurative mode which relates through difference, preserving the relative autonomy of a set of signifying units while suggesting an affinity with some other range of signifiers." *The Ideology of the Aesthetic*, p. 356.

58. Philippe Lacoue-Labarthe and Jean-Luc Nancy, "The Nazi Myth," *Critical Inquiry* 16, no. 2 (winter 1990): 291–312.

59. Ibid., p. 298. For a critical gloss on this claim, see Jean-François Lyotard, *The Differend: Phrases in Dispute*, trans. Georges Van Den Abbeele (Minneapolis: University of Minnesota Press, 1988), p. 152.

60. Ibid., p. 312. It is also evident, Lacoue-Labarthe claims in "Transcendence Ends in Politics," *Typography* (p. 297), in Heidegger's pre-*Kehre* work, whose mimetological flaws help explain his political "error." For a critique of this argument, which sees it as a subtle way to exonerate the later Heidegger, see Richard Wolin, "French Heidegger Wars," in *The Heidegger Controversy: A Critical Reader*, ed. Richard Wolin (New York: Columbia University Press, 1991), pp. 294–304.

61. Horkheimer and Adorno, *Dialectic of Enlightenment*, p. 180.

62. Lacoue-Labarthe, "Transcendence Ends in Politics," *Typography*, p. 300.

63. Lacoue-Labarthe, *Heidegger, Art and Politics: The Fiction of the Political*, trans. Chris Turner (Oxford: Basil Blackwell, 1990), p. 96.

64. Horkheimer and Adorno, *Dialectic of Enlightenment*, p. 186.

65. Lacoue-Labarthe and Nancy, "The Nazi Myth," p. 311.

66. Lacoue-Labarthe's critique of ocularcentrism is typical of many other recent French thinkers, as I have tried to demonstrate in *Downcast Eyes: The Denigration of Vision in Twentieth-Century French Thought* (Berkeley: University of California Press, 1993). See the similar discussion of sight in Derrida, "Economimesis," where the privileging of vision is related directly to the symbolic recuperation he identifies with mourning, because vision is less directly affected by the unsublatable object than other senses are (p. 19). He claims that the disgust associated with vomit resists such a mourning process, because it produces objects that cannot be reabsorbed or symbolically represented. Derrida, to be sure, also strongly attacks hearing when it is a matter of hearing oneself speak, which implies autoaffection.

67. Lacoue-Labarthe, *Typography*, p. 179.

68. Ibid., p. 199.

69. Derrida, introduction to *Typography*, p. 33.

70. In fact, in *Dialectic of Enlightenment*, he and Horkheimer include the prohibition on images among the ways in which rulers prevented the subjugated masses from reverting to mimetic behavior (pp. 180–1). They do, to be sure, claim in that text that the sense of smell is superior in terms of the ability to assimilate to the other—"when we see we remain what we are; but when we smell we are taken over by otherness" (p. 184)—but visuality plays a more critical role as the source of mimetic resistance to conceptuality in *Aesthetic Theory*.

71. Gertrud Koch, "Mimesis and *Bilderverbot*," *Screen* 34, no. 3 (autumn, 1993): 211–22; Hansen, "Mass Culture as Hieroglyphic Writing."

72. Adorno, *Aesthetic Theory*, p. 141. For a discussion of the value of visuality in Adorno and its relation to Benjamin's notion of "dialectical images," see Susan Buck-

Morss, *The Origin of Negative Dialectics: Theodor W. Adorno, Walter Benjamin, and the Frankfurt Institute* (New York: Free Press, 1977), pp. 102–110.

73. Ibid., pp. 141–42.

74. Adorno, *Philosophy of Modern Music*, p. 155.

75. Früchtl, *Mimesis*, p. 260.

76. See, for example, Leo Bersani, *The Freudian Body: Psychoanalysis and Art* (New York: Columbia University Press, 1986), chap. 3.

77. Theodor W. Adorno, "Looking Back on Surrealism," in *The Idea of the Modern in Literature and the Arts*, ed. Irving Howe (New York: Horizon Press, 1967), p. 223. For a recent account of surrealism that thematizes its debts to the uncanny and the compulsive repetitions of the death drive, see Hal Foster, *Compulsive Beauty* (Cambridge, Mass.: MIT Press, 1993).

78. See, in particular, Theodor W. Adorno, "The Position of the Narrator in the Contemporary Novel," *Notes to Literature*, vol. 1.

79. In "Economimesis," Derrida, borrowing Bataille's distinction, argues that it is neither a "restricted economy" of circulation nor a "general economy" of waste but something other (p. 4).

80. Homi Bhabha, "Of Mimicry and Man: The Ambivalence of Colonial Discourse," *October* 28 (1984): 125–33; for a discussion of Sherman and mimicry, see Craig Owens, *Beyond Recognition: Representation, Power, and Culture*, ed. Scott Bryson, Barbara Kruger, Lynne Tillman, and Jane Weinstock (Berkeley: University of California Press, 1992), pp. 83–85. Both are indebted to Lacan's discussion of mimicry in *The Four Fundamental Concepts of Psycho-analysis*, ed. Jacques-Alain Miller, trans. Alan Sheridan (New York: Norton, 1978), pp. 97–100.

3

Aesthetic Theory's Mimesis of Walter Benjamin

Shierry Weber Nicholsen

[T]o grasp Benjamin's "influence" on Adorno, as . . . a liberation by mimesis and as the practical demonstration of the possibility of another kind of writing—which is . . . to say: another kind of thinking.
—*Fredric Jameson,* Late Marxism

Until recently, perhaps, mimesis would not have struck us as a central concept in Adorno's *Aesthetic Theory*. Untutored, we have associated mimesis with premodernist, representational art and its theories and have been preoccupied with deconstructing representations. Auerbach has been out of fashion.[1] And yet, as Fredric Jameson has noted in *Late Marxism*, his book on Adorno, mimesis is omnipresent in *Aesthetic Theory*, foundational but strikingly undefined even for a theorist who opposes all definition.[2] In fact, as I try to show here, mimesis is the hidden face of a figure whose explicit face is sometimes enigma, sometimes language, a figure in which subject and object, psyche and matter are both continuous and discontinuous, and to pursue the elusive mimesis is to begin to illuminate the whole conceptual design and form of *Aesthetic Theory*.

To mention mimesis in conjunction with language is to point to Walter Benjamin and his writings on the mimetic faculty, which he claimed had come in the course of history to be housed in language. Mimesis figures much more prominently and evocatively in Benjamin's work—where it is explicitly tied not only to his theories of language in their theological or mystical aspect but to his interest in occult experience in general as well as to his more familiar physiognomic approach to the reading of historical phenomena—than it does in the controlled and consistent presentation of *Aesthetic Theory,* which, however outrageous it may seem to Anglo-American philosophers, nevertheless confines itself to Adorno's reconfiguring of concepts from previous aesthetic theories in a way that initially conceals differences in emphasis among them.[3] Benjamin deals explicitly with mimesis in an important text, "On the Mimetic Faculty," and its earlier version, "Doctrine of the Similar," which were written in the early 1930s and are linked in their content with other important works from that period. In this essay, I take Benjamin's more explicit statements about mimesis, and the writings in which he embodies their implications, as a guide in reconstructing the nature and function of Adorno's concept of mimesis in *Aesthetic Theory.* This inquiry will lead us into both Benjamin's and Adorno's notions of experience, language, and configurational or constellational form. In doing so, it will shed light on the relationship between Benjamin's and Adorno's thought in a more general sense, a relationship that, as Pierre Missac has pointed out, has hardly received the focused critical attention it deserves.[4] And because I try to show that the very notion of philosophical form in the two thinkers emerges from their conception of mimesis, Jameson's provocative suggestion that Benjamin's "influence" on Adorno should be seen as a "liberation by mimesis," opening the possibility of another kind of thinking and writing, is doubly to the point.

I   Approaching Mimesis: Benjamin's "On the Mimetic Faculty" and "Doctrine of the Similar"

[Benjamin's] idiosyncratic notion of language as "nonrepresentational mimesis."
—*Jameson,* Late Marxism

Let me set the stage for Benjamin's texts by pointing out some dimensions of the question of mimesis. If we think of mimesis as imitation or representation, we may easily proceed to think about copies and replicas and more generally about visual representations and likenesses. Although, in the case of copies, we may speak dismissively of "mere imitation," the question is not so simple. We may ask, for instance, what kinds of "things" may be represented and in what form? Must a visual representation, for instance, be an imitation of a visual phenomenon? What is the nature of the sameness or similarity or resemblance of the imitation to what it imitates? By what process is that similarity grasped and embodied? In the most general form of the question, what is the nature of the link with otherness that is both presupposed and created by imitation?

Alternatively, we may ask about the purpose or function of imitation. This question can lead to considerations of power and to notions of magic and ritual. We may understand imitation as a means of connecting with and controlling, or being transformed by, the power and the order inherent in the other. As several writers have recently noted, this kind of magical imitation, as opposed to "mere" imitation, might take the form of sympathetic magic, based on similarity and akin to Roman Jakobson's notion of the paradigmatic or metaphorical axis of language, or of contagious magic, based on combination and contiguity and akin to the syntagmatic or metonymic axis of language.[5] Indeed, it is from the direction of such considerations that Benjamin approaches mimesis in "On the Mimetic Faculty" and "Doctrine of the Similar."

In those texts, Benjamin's remarks on mimesis focus not on works of art but on the human mimetic faculty—the capacity to both produce and perceive resemblances. Indeed, for Benjamin, the crucial arena within which the mimetic faculty is exercised is the human being and human experience itself; the human being's "gift of seeing resemblances is nothing other than a rudiment of the powerful compulsion in former times to become and behave like something else."[6] This perspective on mimesis is linked with Benjamin's interest in occult experience, which signifies for him an identification of perception with its objects, a kind of continuity or affinity between subject and object, psyche and matter, macrocosm and microcosm. He notes that it is the process of producing similarities, rather than the similarities themselves, that will best help us understand this dimension of experience (*New German Critique* 17:65). Benjamin sees this mimetic capacity at work in an archaic period in which cosmic order was perceived, through forms of divination that were forms of "reading," as a system of correspondences, in which—as astrology tells us—the human being participated fully, both embodying and perceiving these correspondences.

Benjamin sets his remarks on the mimetic faculty in a historical framework. He argues that the mimetic faculty has not withered in the course of history, as one might suppose from the disappearance of magic, ritual, and forms of divination, but rather has migrated from a more direct perception and reading of correspondences into language: "It is now language which represents the medium in which objects meet and enter into relationship with each other, no longer directly, as once in the mind of the augur or priest, but in their essences, in their most volatile and delicate substance, even in their aromata. In other words: it is to writing and language that clairvoyance has, over the course of history, yielded its old powers" (*New German Critique* 17:68). Language, Benjamin says in a striking phrase from "On the Mimetic Faculty," is an "archive of nonsensuous similarity" (*Reflections*, 336).

The question of what Benjamin might mean by the phrase "nonsensuous similarity" and the implications of the notion that the mimetic faculty has migrated into language will be central to my inquiry here. For the moment, let me simply note some of the phrases and images with which he begins to elaborate this idea in "On the Mimetic Faculty." First, Benjamin makes it clear that he means something beyond onomatopoeia, which would represent a sensuous rather than a nonsensuous similarity. To suggest what this further something might be, he presents the image of a set of words in various languages arrayed around the thing they all mean—a configuration, in other words. Further, he proposes that language incorporates nonsensuous similarities in written script as well as in the spoken language and that this is the basis for the graphologists' reading of handwriting. Finally, in an extremely evocative phrase that has resonances in the "Theses on the Philosophy of History" and elsewhere, Benjamin compares the mimetic element in language to a flame that manifests itself through a bearer, the "semiotic," or communicative, aspect of language, and that flashes up briefly and then is gone.[7]

The child and childhood experience play an important and explicit role in Benjamin's discussion of the mimetic faculty. Ontogeny recapitulates phylogeny, and in the child's imitative play we see the mimetic faculty at work. Further, this play shows us how mimesis builds on similarities between the human and the nonhuman, between consciousness and matter or the order of nature. As Benjamin points out, children by no means confine their imitations to other human beings: "The child plays at being not only a shopkeeper or teacher but also a windmill and a train" (*Reflections*, 333). In fact, it is in connection with the astrological view of the child that Benjamin introduces the notion of nonsensuous similarity. For if the ancients considered the cosmic processes capable of being imitated, "it is not difficult to imagine that the newborn child was thought to be in full possession of [the mimetic] gift, and in particular to be perfectly molded on the structure of cosmic being" (*Reflections*, 334). The similarity between child and cosmos, in other words, is the initial exemplar of nonsensuous similarity.

"On the Mimetic Faculty" and "Doctrine of the Similar" are wild texts, exciting and evocative but enigmatic. The importance of the child in them, however, points us to another of Benjamin's texts from the same period, *A Berlin Childhood ca. 1900,* a set of miniatures, some of which read like glosses on Benjamin's texts on mimesis. Although I cannot do justice here to all that this rich and complex text could do to illuminate Benjamin's concept of mimesis, let me point out some of the miniatures most relevant here, and the themes they develop about mimesis. "Hiding Places," for instance, shows the child's compulsion to imitate the objects around him and how that compulsion is intertwined with archaic forces. It highlights the way the self jeopardizes its autonomous existence by assimilating itself to the other. The self identified with the world of matter is in danger of being irretrievably lost: "In the same way one who is hanged becomes aware only then of what rope and wood are." The child hiding under a wooden table becomes a wooden idol in a temple and must free himself with a "shriek of self-liberation."[8] "The Mummerehlen" implicates language in this dialectic of disguise and entrapment: "I learned to disguise myself in words." Words mediate the loss of self as a loss of one's own image. They could make him like things, Benjamin says, "but never like my own image." He was "disfigured by likeness" to everything that surrounded him (*Gesammelte Schriften* 7.1, 417).

A *Berlin Childhood* also links childhood mimesis to Benjamin's *Passagenwerk*, or *Arcades Project*, the project of "reading" the nineteenth century in cultural artifacts. The miniature "Loggias," which Benjamin intended as the signature piece for the work, shows the child molded not so much by cosmic or astrological as by historical or cultural forces: "The rhythm of streetcars and carpet-beating rocked me in my sleep. It was the mold in which my dreams took shape." This historical molding, too, is a kind of entrapment. The child remains enclosed in the loggias, under the sway of the city-god Berlin, "as in a mausoleum long intended for him" (*Gesammelte Schriften* 7.1, 386–88). This is the dark side of childhood mimesis. It helps us to understand why Benjamin saw his *Passagenwerk* as an attempt to awaken from the nineteenth century.

A *Berlin Childhood* gives body to some of the enigmatic phrasings of Benjamin's texts on mimesis. Configured quite differently, the lines of thought Benjamin introduces have an important presence in Adorno's *Aesthetic Theory*, as we will now see.

II Mimesis in Adorno's *Aesthetic Theory*: Experience and Enigma

[T]he peculiar status of *mimesis* in Adorno—a foundational concept never defined nor argued but always alluded to, by name, as though it had preexisted all the texts.

—*Jameson*, Late Marxism

Initially, it is not so obvious that Adorno's use of mimesis can be understood via Benjamin's. With Adorno we find ourselves in a different context—aesthetic theory, as opposed to the theory of mimesis as such, or the philosophy of language, or narratives of experience. Even Jameson, who draws attention to the importance of mimesis in Adorno, considers that Adorno's use of the concept "has very little in common with Benjamin's." He compares the status of mimesis in Adorno's work instead with that of the aura in Benjamin's work, adding that Benjamin's notion of the aura "otherwise has nothing to do with" mimesis in Adorno.[9] In fact, though, as we will see, not only is

Adorno's notion of mimesis closely related to Benjamin's, the concept of the aura is implicated in that of mimesis.

Mimesis does indeed have a peculiar status in *Aesthetic Theory*. It becomes articulated only by appearing in contexts in which other aesthetic concepts are more explicitly thematized. Even a small selection of the contexts in which the term "mimesis" appears in *Aesthetic Theory* demonstrates the great diversity of those contexts. But this very diversity offers us a configuration in which we can begin to see the dimensions of Adorno's notion of mimesis and the ways in which it is indeed illuminated by Benjamin's interpretation of the concept. I begin, then, with a display of some of the contexts in which the term "mimesis" appears in *Aesthetic Theory*:[10]

Art is a refuge for mimetic behavior. (86/79)

Mimetic behavior does not imitate something but assimilates itself to [*sich selbst gleichmacht*] that something. (169/162)

The idea that only like can know like ... distinguishes the knowledge that is art from conceptual knowledge: what is essentially mimetic calls for mimetic behavior. (190/183)

The most drastic form in which the mimetic faculty manifests itself in the practice of artistic representation is as an imitation of the dynamic curve of the work being performed. (189/182)

The mimesis of works of art is their resemblance to themselves. (159/153)

The mimetic moment that is indispensable to art may well be universal in its substance, but it can be attained only by way of the irreducible particularity of individual subjects. (68/61)

Expression in art is mimetic, just as the expression of living creatures is the expression of pain. (169/162)

Construction is not a corrective to expression, or a way of securing it through objectification; rather it has to emerge unplanned, as it were, from mimetic impulses. (72/65)

There is something of the dowser in art's immanent process. Following the hand in the direction in which it is being pulled: this is mimesis as the full execution of objectivity. (175/168)

The process that every work of art is, is dug to its depths by the irreconcilability of two moments: regression to literal magic on the one hand, and cession of the mimetic impulse to a thinglike rationality on the other. (87/81)

Through spiritualization, works of art attain the mimetic features that the primary tendency of their spirit is to suppress. (275/264)

Shierry Weber Nicholsen

The continued existence of mimesis, the nonconceptual affinity of a subjective creation to its nonposited other, defines art as a form of cognition and to that extent as "rational." (86–87/80)

Mimesis... is called forth by the complexity of the technical procedure, whose immanent rationality seems, however, to work against expression. (174/167)

The tension between an objectifying technique and the mimetic nature of artworks is played out in the effort to salvage permanently what is fleeting and transitory, as something immune from reification and paired with it. (325–26/312)

Works of modern art abandon themselves mimetically to reification, which for them is the principle of death. (201/193)

The mimetic impulses that move the work of art, that are integrated within it and disintegrate it in turn, represent nonlinguistic expression. (274/263)

In nonintentional language, mimetic impulses are passed on to the whole, which synthesizes them. (274/263)

The efforts of prose writers since Joyce... might be explained as attempts to transform communicative language into a mimetic language. (171/164)

This display renders visible the main contours of Adorno's notion of mimesis. First, like Benjamin, Adorno thinks of mimesis as an assimilation of the self to the other, thus a kind of enactment—mimetic behavior. Second, like Benjamin, Adorno posits a historical trajectory in which mimetic behavior migrates out of an archaic context, although in *Aesthetic Theory* he takes art rather than language to be its refuge. Third, in the sphere of art and aesthetics, Adorno conceives mimesis both as the activity of assimilating the self to the other—this is the link with expression—and as the affinity of the creation, the work of art, with objectivity. He is interested in the work as well as in the subject's mimetic activity. Fourth, mimesis in art is inherently engaged in a dialectic with reason in its various aspects—as cognition, construction, technique, spiritualization, objectification, and so on. Finally, the mimetic impulse finds expression in the "languagelike" character of art.

In what follows, I will not set out to explore all these diverse faces of Adorno's conception of mimesis. Indeed, I suspect that, in pursuing any of these paths, we will cross the others and that all roads lead from mimesis to language, as in Benjamin's "On the Mimetic Faculty."

Here, however, I follow the path indicated by Benjamin and begin with the subject's mimetic behavior as exercised in both perceiving and producing resemblances, and specifically with Adorno's conception of the part mimesis plays in understanding the work of art, for it is there that we see most vividly Adorno's notion of mimesis as enactment.

"Only like can know like . . .: what is essentially mimetic calls for mimetic behavior" (*Aesthetic Theory*, 190/183). As I indicated above, Adorno follows Benjamin in locating mimesis within the subject's experience, both the experience of producing and the experience of perceiving resemblances—experience as evidenced in behavior. This experience, Adorno indicates, is necessarily that of a specific individual, but, as he rightly insists, this does not mean that his theory is psychologistic. Rather, Adorno is interested in the objective aspects of that subjective experience. Indeed, as we have seen, the mimetic experience is precisely one of assimilating the self to the other through mimetic behavior.

It is in Adorno's description of aesthetic receptivity, or understanding, that we can best see this notion at work. For Adorno, understanding a work of art is not a matter of conceptual analysis. Rather, the prototype for aesthetic understanding is the performance of a dramatic script or, by analogy, a musical composition. The performer's activity is a mimetic one: the performer actually creates an imitation of the work that is noted in the score by recreating its every detail (no matter that there is no "original" work but only a score and its many imitations or reproductions). Hence, as Adorno says, "imitation of the dynamic curve of the work being performed" is the "most drastic" manifestation of the mimetic faculty in the practice of artistic representation (189/182). This does not apply to music or drama alone, however; every work of art can be seen as a dynamic totality that requires a kind of performance or reenactment by the listener or viewer. The work itself is analogous to a musical score. The recipient—listener, viewer, reader—follows along or mimes the internal trajectories of the work at hand, tracing its internal articulations down to the finest nuance, just as, more crudely, the mimicking child mimes various aspects of a train or a windmill. A work is certainly different from a person, and yet the act of aesthetic understanding is an act whereby the self is assimilated to the other; the subject virtually embodies, in a quasi-sensuous mode, the work, which is the other. This is the case whether the mimicking takes the form of an audible performance or is a silent internal tracing of the work's articulations.

This notion of an active experiential reproduction of the work by its receiver is expounded in many places in Adorno's aesthetic writings.[11] But in *Aesthetic Theory* Adorno lays equal weight on the respects in which this kind of nonconceptual mimetic reenactment is not adequate for an understanding of art as such—or indeed, for an understanding of any single work of art, for each work seems also to say something about art as such. Mimetic aesthetic experience must be supplemented by philosophical reflection; in a different tonality, this is the need for the shriek of self-liberation that we saw in the *Berlin Childhood*, a response to the limiting and entrapping potential of mimesis.

It is the enigmatic face of the work of art, the enigmatic gaze it directs at us, that incites this philosophical reflection. The notion of art's enigmatic quality—or its picture-puzzle or rebuslike quality, in an image more familiar from Benjamin's work than from Adorno's— is crucial to Adorno's concept of art and inseparable from the notion of the work of art as mimetic and requiring or inciting mimetic behavior in the viewer or listener. First of all, the work is enigmatic because it is mimetic rather than conceptual. Being nonconceptual, it cannot be unenigmatic, because it cannot have a discursive meaning. Further, the work is enigmatic because, as the mimetic has migrated from ritual into art, it has lost its purpose; art has become, in Kant's phrase, purposive but without purpose. As Adorno says, art cannot answer the question, "What are you for?"

Full understanding of art would not imply dissolving the enigmatic quality, which is intrinsic to it, but rather understanding *that* art is enigmatic and reflecting on the meaning of its enigmatic quality. But this cannot be done through the mimetic experiencing of the work of art. The enigmatic quality implies otherness as well as affinity. It requires distance if it is to be perceived. The experiential understanding of art that is gained through mimetic assimilation to the work does not have this kind of distance; it is trapped inside the work, so to speak, and accordingly cannot do full justice to it: "When one is inside works of art, reenacting them, the enigmatic quality makes itself invisible" (183/176). Or, in an even blunter formulation, "The musician who understand his score follows the most minute movements in it, but in a certain sense he does not know what he is playing" (189/182).

If the skilled interpreter is likely to miss the enigmatic quality, what does enable us to perceive it? Adorno suggests that we can begin to get a sense of it by thinking of the person without aesthetic sensibility, to whom the work may seem simply unintelligible, offering no point of access: "The enigmatic quality of art can be given direct confirmation by the so-called unmusical person who does not understand 'the language of music,' hears only galimatias, and asks himself what all these noises are supposed to mean" (183/177). In this context, Adorno ends by defining the enigmatic quality as the difference between what such a person hears and what a knowledgeable listener hears. Enigma is, as it were, the difference between what is experienced from completely outside the work of art and what is experienced from completely inside it. Thus, when Adorno says that artworks' demand to be understood in terms of their substance "is tied to specific experience of the works but can be fulfilled only in and through theory that actively reflects experience" (185/179), he is not talking about two separate mental activities, experience and theoretical reflection. Rather, he is attempting to specify a reflection that takes place on and perhaps within that enigmatic zone of difference, a zone of experience in which the enactment and assimilation of the other that constitute mimesis are inseparable from—but also distinct from—the rationality of philosophical reflection. This is not a zone or a kind of reflection in which "subject" (the one reflecting) knows "object" (the work of art, or the mimetic experience of it). Rather, the enigmatic quality, too, and the experience of it seem to be characterized by the kind of resemblance that is the hallmark of mimesis, a resemblance that implies continuity and affinity, as well as discontinuity, between subject and object.

For Adorno, as for Benjamin, rationality is inseparable from language, and in order to investigate further the dialectic of mimesis and rationality that is so apparent in the passages from *Aesthetic Theory* displayed above, as well as the question of the kind of reflection the enigmatic quality incites, we will need to explore the relationship between mimesis and language.[12] The enigmatic or rebuslike face of art, which is nonconceptual but languagelike, can serve as our point of departure for this next step, and here again Benjamin can serve as our guide. Our path will lead us to language by way of his conception of the aura. The questions of resemblance as both similarity and difference and of the continuity and affinity between subject and object will continue to be central to our exploration.

III   Enigma and Aura: Matter in a State of Resemblance

The beautiful may require the servile imitation of what is undefinable in things.

—*Paul Valéry, quoted in Benjamin's "On Some Motifs in Baudelaire"*

Enigma, especially in the form of the picture puzzle or rebus (*Rätselbild, Vexierbild*), is a familiar notion in Benjamin's work, and in his work as in Adorno's it is associated with the complex of ideas clustered around mimesis. In "Doctrine of the Similar," Benjamin mentions the "images, or more precisely, picture puzzles" in handwriting as one of the places in language to which mimesis has emigrated. The enigma or picture puzzle, then, appears to be one of the forms in which nonsensuous similarity appears.

How can we elucidate this notion of a "picture puzzle" in its relevance for Benjamin's conception of mimesis? Once again, one of the miniatures from the *Berlin Childhood* affords us a starting point. This one is entitled "The Stocking" ["Der Strumpf"]. It describes a childhood game in which the child unrolls a rolled-up pair of socks:

The first cabinet that opened when I wanted it to was the bureau. I had only to pull on the knob and the door clicked open for me. Among the underclothing stored there was the thing that made the bureau an adventure. I had to make a path to the farthest corner; there I found my stockings piled, rolled up in the old-fashioned way. Each pair looked like a small pouch. Nothing gave me more pleasure than plunging my hand as deep as possible into the inside of that pouch. I did not do so for the sake of the warmth. It was "the Dowry" [*das Mitgebrachte*], which I held in my hand in the rolled-up interior, that drew me into its depths. When I had got my hand around it and confirmed my possession of the soft woolen mass to the best of my ability, the second part of the game, which brought the revelation, began. For now I began working "the Dowry" out of its woolen pouch. I drew it closer and closer to me until the amazing event occurred: I had extracted "the Dowry," but "the Pouch" in which it had lain no longer existed. I could not test this process often enough. It taught me that form and content, the veil and what it hides, are one and the same. It led me to extricate the truth from literature as cautiously as the child's hand brought the stocking out of "the Pouch." (*Gesammelte Schriften* 7.1, 416–17)

This miniature seems to consist of a narrative followed by an interpretation of its meaning ("It taught me..."), its message. The message seems to concern the enigmatic quality of art and to offer a very clear statement: the pouch, which seemed to hide, veil, or contain the precious internal gift, or "dowry," was in fact one and the same with it; in other words, one cannot extract a "truth" from literature without at the same time destroying the literary covering. But of course this clear division into narrative and message is inconsistent with the purported message itself, which says that the one cannot be extracted from the other. A puzzling picture indeed! The text in fact poses a riddle that is not capable of this kind of solution. Note that the "amazing event," the moment in which dowry and pouch fuse into one and the same third thing, the stocking, occurs in a flash that is absent from the narrative itself, a flash that no doubt is the moment of continuity and discontinuity between the narrative and the message, the moment that both confirms and explodes the illusions of possession and revelation. And note that the child must repeat the process over and over again, beginning with an excursion into the depths and the interior, and ending with a purported message that fails to capture the mysterious combination of continuity and discontinuity that is the essence of the picture puzzle, that both is and is about enigma. Similarly, the reader will recall, for Adorno enigma marked the point of continuity and discontinuity between the subject's experience of the work and its nonconceptual or mimetic aspect.

This enigmatic mixture of continuity and discontinuity is at the heart of Benjamin's notion of mimesis. What are similarity and resemblance—which for Benjamin are the essence of mimesis—but that mixture, "the same and not the same"? Another of Benjamin's central texts from this period, his essay "The Image of Proust," sheds further light on this connection and demonstrates the relationship in Benjamin's work between the mimetic and the aesthetic. Benjamin tells us that Proust's "impassioned cult of similarity" and his homesickness for "the world distorted in a state of resemblance" to which the *mémoire involontaire* provides access are indicators of the hegemony of the dreamworld, in which "everything that happens appears not in identical but in similar guise, opaquely similar one to another."[13] (And Benjamin offers the stocking game we saw earlier as an image of this dreamworld of opaque similarity.) "The world distorted in a state of resemblance": this is not a matter of individual acts of imitation but rather a tissue of reality in which the glue of coherence is resemblance. But it is a world in which enigma and distortion are pervasive, for the resemblances are always opaque. Like the "third thing" in the stocking game, they can never be separated and laid bare. It is a pervasive mimesis, in other words, that constitutes this world of the special images of Proust's *mémoire involontaire.*

The relationship of that world to the consciousness that perceives it is a relationship of mutual gazing. In his essay on Baudelaire, Benjamin quotes Paul Valéry on the dreamworld: "In dreams... there is an equation. The things I see see me just as much as I see them."[14] The notion of the object returning our gaze links the Proustian dreamworld with the domain of the aura, which Benjamin here calls "the associations which, at home in the *mémoire involontaire,* tend to cluster around the object of a perception" (*Illuminations,* 186). "To perceive the aura of an object," he says, is "to invest it with the ability to look at us in return" (*Illuminations,* 188). The aura of an object thus indicates its continuity with the whole tissue of opaque similarities that is the "world distorted in a state of resemblance."

With the aura, we have entered the domain of the aesthetic, and Benjamin makes it clear that beauty, too, is none other than this same cluster of opaque resemblances, gazing at us from across the depths of memory. "One would define beauty," he says, commenting on Goethe's notion of correspondences, "as the object of experience in the state of resemblance. This definition would probably coincide with Valéry's formulation: 'beauty may require the servile imitation of what is indefinable in objects'" (*Illuminations,* 199, n. 13). (We will see shortly how Adorno uses this same quotation from Valéry to similar effect.) Beauty, then, is the opaque similarity between the work and the object of experience as perceived in the state of resemblance. Beauty is the signal that the work as an object participates in the state of resemblance; the aura that is the hallmark of beauty is precisely a reflection of the web of similarities that characterizes that state. Beauty is mimesis of the indefinable in objects because the indefinable is precisely their participation in the enigmatic coherence of opaque similarities.

Language and words, too, can become part of this state of resemblance; they, too, can be defined in terms of a cluster of associations in the gaze that looks back at us from across a distance. "Words too can have an aura of their own," says Benjamin, and he quotes Karl Kraus: "The closer one looks at a word, the greater the distance from which it looks back" (*Illuminations*, 200, n. 17). And not only "The Mummerehlen" but other miniatures in the *Berlin Childhood* as well provide examples of the auratic yet distorting mimetic capacities of words.[15] Whereas in "On the Mimetic Faculty" Benjamin indicates that mimesis had migrated into language, here it seems that language participates in the "world in a state of resemblance" governed by mimesis, the world of aesthetic experience. Language is thus capable both of being absorbed into that world and of absorbing that world into itself. The enigmatic relationship of language and mimesis bears further exploration. First, however, I return to *Aesthetic Theory* to examine Adorno's conceptions of enigma and mimesis in the light of what we have just seen.

IV   The Mute Languages of Nature and Art

As indeterminate, and hostile to definition, natural beauty is undefinable.... [T]he beautiful in nature flashes out, only to disappear immediately when one tries to pin it down. Art does not imitate nature . . . but rather natural beauty as such.... "The beautiful may require the servile imitation of what is undefinable in things" [Valéry].
—*Aesthetic Theory*, 113/107

In Benjamin's essays on Proust and Baudelaire, we saw how mimesis as resemblance is intertwined with the notion of an indeterminate cluster of associations from the depths, and how that clustering is experienced as aura, as the return of our gaze by its objects. For Benjamin, language is one more phenomenon that both leads into those depths and participates in the phenomenon of the auratic gaze. It is as though there were a state of resemblance as such, a mimetic state in which nature—or the cosmos, or the world of matter—and consciousness are on the same footing. A quality of depth, distance, and otherness is built into that state, even at the same time as that state is undoing the separateness of consciousness. This is its enigmatic quality.

Benjamin's reflections on the "world in a state of resemblance" might be thought of as an extended meditation on similarity and on the relationships that characterize the state of resemblance. What we find in *Aesthetic Theory*, in contrast, is not a meditation on resemblance so much as a focus on the question of what is imitated and what form the imitation takes. One of Adorno's answers to that question—the one I want to pursue here—is a discourse on nature and language.

"Art does not imitate nature, nor even individual natural beauty, but rather natural beauty as such" (113/107), says Adorno in an important assertion about mimesis in art. What does it mean to imitate natural beauty as such? Natural beauty, Adorno says, is indeterminable, undefinable; it cannot be conceptualized. This is so because of its particularity, its individuality: "Natural beauty cannot be defined by means of general concepts, because the very substance of the category lies in something that eludes a generalizing conceptualization. Its essential indeterminacy is manifested in the fact that every piece of nature...is capable of becoming beautiful" (110/104). At the same time, the individuality or autonomy of each instance of natural beauty is shown by the fact that "every single object of nature that is experienced as beautiful presents itself as though it were the only beautiful thing in the whole world" (110/104).

What Adorno says about how natural beauty is perceived sheds light on another aspect of this autonomy. The individual instance of natural beauty has a strange quality of strength and power vis-á-vis the capacities of subjective perception. He speaks of "the weakness of thought—of the subject—in the face of natural beauty and its objective strength" (114/107–8). Natural beauty seems to stand apart from the subjective perceiver and to be independent from it: "Such objective expression could not exist without [subjective] receptivity, but it is not reducible to the subject; natural beauty testifies to the primacy of the object in subjective experience" (111/104). One indicator of this relative weakness of subjective perception is that natural beauty appears in perception as fleeting: "[T]he beautiful in nature flashes out, only to disappear immediately when one tries to pin it down" (113/107). This strength and its converse, fleetingness, mean that natural beauty is best perceived nonrationally: "Unconscious perception knows more about the beauty of nature than does the intense concentration with which we regard works of art. Natural beauty opens up, at times suddenly, in the continuity of unconscious perception.... The objectification brought about by attentive observation damages the eloquence in nature" (108/102). It is as though, Adorno says with a nod to Proust and Bergson, natural beauty could be perceived only in the *temps durée*. As a result of these qualities, natural beauty is perceived both as "compellingly valid and as something unintelligible that poses a question and awaits its solution" (111/104–5)—in other words, as enigmatic.

Art's mimetic relationship to natural beauty can be understood both as a response to these qualities and in the context of increasing rationality in the course of history. On the one hand, consciousness perceives this fleetingness of natural beauty as a problem, which inspires the desire to capture it in art, which is not fleeting but has duration. At the same time, natural beauty is increasingly seen as defective and archaic in its blindness (hence, Adorno says, its disappearance from aesthetic theory since Kant). As consciousness and rationality mature, blind perception is no longer felt to be acceptable or adequate, just as the unfreedom that is also inherent in nature and instinct is no longer acceptable or adequate. Increasingly "beauty lends itself to analysis," hence the demand that "the enigmaticness of natural beauty be reflected in art and thereby define itself in relation to concepts although, again, not as something inherently conceptual" (114/108). Art, in other words, will both fix and reflect natural beauty, though nondiscursively.

As he himself points out, much of what Adorno says about natural beauty is similar to what he says about works of art. Like fragments of nature, human artifacts—which become second nature—can become beautiful, and works of art, too, present themselves as though they were the only beautiful things in the world. Works of art may also need to be perceived in the *temps durée* and through a kind of blind apperception—the kind of mimetic behavior that the performer engages in. Works of art, too, are enigmatic. We are dealing here, in other words, with a continuity, in which art is a modification of natural beauty but still continuous with it. Aesthetic philosophy, too, as we will see later, is similarly both a modification of art and continuous with it. How consciousness, rationality, and conceptuality enter into this continuity and discontinuity is a central theme of *Aesthetic Theory*. One of the ways in which Adorno presents the theme is as a matter of language.

Let me approach the question of language by returning to the question of what it means to imitate natural beauty as such. First, it does not mean, as Adorno emphatically tells us, to *copy* nature, because natural beauty is something that appears, and appears as image, and to copy an image is to destroy its autonomous quality: "Nature as something beautiful cannot be depicted. For natural beauty, as something that manifests itself, is itself an image. There is something tautological about copying it" (105/99). The Old Testament taboo on graven images, Adorno tells us, has an aesthetic implication connected with this idea. It implies "that no such image is possible. In being duplicated in art, that in nature which manifests itself or appears is robbed of its inherent being, which is what the appreciation of nature feeds on" (106/100). But the appearing quality in nature, its being-in-itself, is also defined as a special kind of language, the language of nature, which, Adorno says, may be the closest thing we have to the language of creation, the language of things. This linguistic capacity of nature, its speaking quality, Adorno calls expression: "What qualitatively distinguishes the beautiful in nature is to be sought, if anywhere, in the degree to which something not made by human beings speaks, in its expression" (110–11/104). This language of nature as expression is what art imitates, trying to give voice in another, further sense to the language of nature: "Under the prevailing rationality, the subjective elaboration of art as a nonconceptual language is the only form in which something like the language of Creation appears.... If the language of nature is mute, art seeks to help this muteness speak" (121/115). Art, in other words, imitates the nonconceptual language of nature, "the model of a non-conceptual language, a language not pinned down in significations," as Adorno calls it elsewhere (105/99). When art copies not nature but natural beauty, it achieves something that converges with the language of nature. Adorno comments, for instance, that in Schubert's "Wanderers Nachtlied," "the subject falls silent within what it creates, as in every authentic work of art; but through its language the poem imitates the unsayable element of the language of nature" (114/108). And similarly, the pure sound in the most authentic works of Anton Webern, he says, turns into "the sound of nature; of an eloquent nature—nature's language—and not a copy of a piece of nature" (121/115).

Conversely, we could say that art takes over the enigmatic but authoritative nature of natural beauty, that this is what it imitates, and it can do so only insofar as it can create nonconceptual and enigmatic forms of language: "Art is imitation not of nature but of natural beauty. This aspect is entwined with the allegorical intention that it displays without decoding; with meanings that never become objectified as they do in discursive language" (111/105). Not attempting to decode nature's enigmas, this language of art retains an enigmatic quality. It is a language "without meaning, or, more precisely, a language whose meaning is severed or covered over" (122/116). Clearly this "language" of art is to be distinguished from discursive or communicative language. And of course it need not involve words or sentences at all. On the other hand, the artistic use of verbal language may transform it into the nonconceptual language of art, as when James Joyce and other modern writers, Adorno says, attempt "to transform communicative language into a mimetic language" (171/164).

What is this nonconceptual language that art uses to imitate natural beauty and that converges with the language of creation? It is none other than artistic form as such, which gives articulation to its material, its subject matter: "In form, all that is quasi-linguistic in works of art becomes concentrated" (217/208). The notion of articulation draws attention to the dual function of this languagelike quality of form. On the one hand, it allows the thing imitated to "speak," to become articulate. On the other hand, as articulation in the sense of organization—differentiation and integration—it is languagelike in providing structure and coherence, something analogous to a syntax, and thus a degree of rationality and universality, without becoming a formal discursive, conceptual language: "Works of art approximate the idea of a language of things only through their own language, through the organization of their disparate moments; the more they are immanently syntactically articulated, the more eloquent they become, together with their various moments" (211/203.)[16] In other words, the cognitive but nonconceptual nature of art—its logicity, to use another term of Adorno's—is its languagelike quality; the language of form is akin to reason in its organization and articulation. But at the same time, the language of art, or, more accurately, the languagelike quality of art, retains its continuity with mimesis, with the specific and the particular and thus also the opaque and enigmatic: "The quasi-linguistic moment in art is the mimetic moment.... The basis of the paradox that art both says something and does not say it is that the mimetic moment through which it makes its statement is opaque and particular and as such at the same time resists speech" (305/293).

The fact that the "language" of art retains its opaqueness, its mimetic character, is what gives it its affinity with silence and muteness and therefore with the enigmatic quality of natural beauty, or the language of nature. This is one of the crucial paradoxes of the aesthetic as Adorno conceives it. For to give expression to natural beauty, to let the thing itself speak, is at the same time to become mute and speechless, to fall silent. Expression is the achievement of the work of art and is languagelike in that it becomes the naturelike voice of things, but at the same time it is speechless and mute because it is not a discursive language: "The epitome of expression is the linguistic character of art, which is totally different from language as a medium of art.... In fact, the true language of art is speechless" (171/164). Adorno emphasizes this in referring to Samuel Beckett, in whose work the moment of muteness is so striking: "Aesthetic transcendence and disenchantment achieve unison in falling silent: in Beckett's oeuvre. It is the fact that a language removed from meaning is not a speaking language that creates its affinity with muteness. Perhaps all expression, which is the closest thing to transcendence, is this close to muteness, just as in great modern music nothing is so expressive as the sound that dies away, the tone that emerges naked from the density of form, the note in which art opens out into its natural aspect by virtue of its own movement" (123/117).

Here, with the element of speechlessness and muteness, we find ourselves again in the domain of the aura, for the muteness of natural beauty, or of the work of art, is at the same time a gaze, a mute enigmatic gaze. Indeed, expression, Adorno says, is "the gaze of works of art" (172/165). It is this speechless expressiveness, this mute enigmatic gaze that they turn on us in their imitation of natural beauty, that gives works of art their paradoxical autonomy. "The mimesis of works of art is their resemblance to themselves," Adorno says in one of the most enigmatic formulations in *Aesthetic Theory* (159/153). What this means is that what works of art express is their own beingness, their *haecceitas.* Commenting on the Etruscan vases in the Villa Giulia, Adorno says that "their similarity to language accords most closely with something like 'this is me' or 'here I come,' asserting a selfhood which is not carved out of the interdependent totality… by identifying thought but stands on its own. In the same way a speechless animal, say a rhinoceros, seems to be saying 'I am a rhino'" (171–72/164). (Here Adorno cites Rilke's line about there being "no place which does not see you.") With this evocation of an interdependent totality, a sphere of mute, gazing presences that resemble themselves by virtue of their resemblance to something enigmatic and indefinable, we have reached Adorno's equivalent of Benjamin's "world in a state of resemblance," just as with art's imitating not nature but natural beauty and in fact the language of nature, we have reached Adorno's elaboration of the aesthetic domain as one of "nonsensuous similarity." In both cases, this domain is one in which the subject/object paradigm as we know it does not hold— one in which subject and object, consciousness and matter, the human and nonhuman are on equal footing; one in which a language is "spoken" without subsuming the object to concepts through definition and conceptual identification.

There lingers, however, the question of philosophical language, the language of aesthetic theory, which is not the language of things and not, certainly, identical with the language of art. Earlier, I showed how enigma was the point of continuity and discontinuity between art and aesthetic reflection. With this investigation of natural beauty as what is imitated in art, we see something that looks more like a linear progression in which the enigmatic quality is transferred, in a series of shifts both continuous and discontinuous, from nature to art to philosophy or aesthetic theory. The language of nature is mute, and art tries to help it speak. But art speaks and does not speak; it, too, is speechless. The speechlessness of art in turn calls forth the speech of philosophy. "[A]rt needs philosophy, which interprets it in order to say what art cannot say, whereas in fact it is only art that can say it—by not saying it" (113/107). But just as it is the enigmatic quality of natural beauty that gives rise to art and is continued in the enigmatic quality of art, so, too, something of the enigmatic quality of art—or at least its paradoxical quality—is continued in aesthetic philosophy. To return to the context from which I just quoted: "Art [imitates] natural beauty as such. This [states] the aporia of aesthetics as a whole. Its subject matter is defined negatively, as undefinable. This is why art needs philosophy.... The paradoxes of aesthetics are imposed on it by its subject matter" (113/107).

Thus we have the semblance of a progression that is characterized both by a continuity of enigma or paradox and by an increase in rationality. At the same time, we seem to have an attempt to return to some of the qualities of natural beauty and its perception. Thus Adorno, on the "second reflection" of aesthetic analysis, says, "Second reflection takes up the work of art's mode of proceeding, its language in the broadest sense, but it aims at blindness" (47–48/40)—the blindness of that continuity of unconscious apperception in the *temps durée* that I referred to earlier. Equally, however, we may say that these appearances of linear progression and return are complementary and that the structure we are really dealing with in aesthetic mimesis is one of convergence. Like his comments on Webern's music cited earlier, Adorno's comments on the analysis of beauty, which resemble his comments on the mimetic nature of aesthetic experience, can be read to suggest this structure of convergence: "Analysis returns beauty to spontaneity and would be fruitless if there were not a moment of spontaneity hidden within analysis. When faced with beauty, analytic reflection restores the *temps durée* through its antithesis. Analysis terminates in something beautiful.... In doing so it retraces, subjectively, the trajectory described objectively by the work of art" (109/103).

This notion of a structure of convergence, or, in Benjamin's term, "convolution," is, I believe, linked with the experience of fleeting perception or flashes of perception that we saw in Adorno's description of natural beauty and that figures so strikingly in Benjamin's comments on language as a repository of nonsensuous similarity. Let me now return to Benjamin's work to pursue this connection more fully and attempt to link it with the question of philosophical form, the domain in which, if Jameson's suggestion is accurate, Adorno's mimesis of Benjamin ultimately takes place.

V   The Flashing of Constellational Form

To observe the interaction of aging and remembering means to penetrate to...the universe of convolution. It is the world in a state of resemblances, the domain of the correspondences.... When the past is reflected in the dewy fresh "instant," a painful shock of rejuvenation pulls it together once more.
—*Benjamin, "The Image of Proust"*

In "On the Mimetic Faculty," Benjamin presents the idea of language as a refuge for the mimetic faculty, hence an archive of nonsensuous similarity, in several versions, including the image of words in different languages arrayed in a configuration around a common center, and the image of similarity flashing up like a flame. Configuration and flashing flame would seem to have little in common, but they come together in the image of a constellation of sparkling stars. In this section, I explore what this conjunction suggests for a philosophical language and form consonant with the aesthetic dimension and its basis in mimesis, a philosophical language and form in which we would expect the mimetic dimension of language to play a role. I begin by drawing attention to some of the ideas linked with these two images in Benjamin's texts.

"If words meaning the same thing in different languages are arrayed about that thing as their center, we have to inquire how they

all—while often possessing not the slightest similarity to one another—are similar to what they signify at their center" (*Reflections,*
335). What is interesting about Benjamin's description of this mimetic, linguistic configuration is that the "thing" at the center, which
is not language, binds the dissimilar and in fact alien words together.
The nonverbal thing at the center plays the role of a crucial but enigmatic blank space, somewhat as the child-narrator of the *Berlin Childhood* can resemble things but not his own image. At the same time, it
is only in the configuration as a whole that the similarities become
evident. Described in this way, the configuration of words resembles
the Proustian world of mute, gazing, autonomous presences bound
together by opaque similarities. Benjamin's description of the way
nonsensuous similarity flashes up also links it to the image of the
configuration and the world of opaque similarities: "The coherence
of words or sentences is the bearer through which, like a flash, similarity appears. For its production by man—like its perception by
him—is in many cases, and particularly the most important, limited
to flashes" (*Reflections,* 335). The moment of entry into the world of
opaque similarities takes the form of a flash in which there is a conjunction of the present moment with a moment in the past. Benjamin speaks of the "concentration...in which things consume
themselves in a flash" and the "painful shock" that pulls time together (*Reflections,* 211).

Clearly, consciousness plays a role in this moment of "convoluted
time" that opens into and constitutes the "universe of convolution"
(*Reflections,* 211). In his texts on mimesis, Benjamin describes the
mind as "participating" in the moment, in the production of nonsensuous similarity, through the speed of reading and writing, which allows the semiotic and mimetic aspects of language to fuse and the
constellation to be illuminated, as it were, in a flash: "So speed, that
swiftness in reading or writing which can scarcely be separated from
this process then becomes, as it were, the effort or gift of letting the
mind participate in that measure of time in which similarities flash
up fleetingly out of the stream of things" (*New German Critique*
17:68). Similarly, with regard to the "reading" of the stars by the astrologer: "The perception of similarities...seems to be bound to a
time-moment. It is like the addition of a third element, namely the

astrologer, to the conjunction of two stars which must be grasped in an instant" (*New German Critique* 17:66).

Let me now turn to the implications of these ideas for textual form. I begin by returning to the miniatures of the *Berlin Childhood,* which Benjamin describes as "excursions into the depths of memory" and which we might thus expect to demonstrate some of what he elaborated with respect to Proust. The miniature entitled "Winter Evening" does in fact provide a very eloquent demonstration of how perceiving and remembering, image and language can be wrapped together in the convolutions of textual form:

> On winter evenings my mother often took me with her when she went shopping. It was a dark and unfamiliar Berlin that lay before me in the gaslight. We did not leave the old West End, whose streets were more pleasant and less pretentious than those that later became fashionable. The overhanging balconies and the columns were no longer visible, and the lights had come on in the housefronts. Whether it shone on gauze curtains or blinds or on a gas jet under a hanging lamp, this light revealed little about the rooms it illuminated. It was concerned only with itself. It attracted me and made me pensive. It does that even now when I recall it. Its favorite thing is to lead me to one of my postcards. The card depicted a square in Berlin. The buildings surrounding it were a pale blue, and the light sky with the moon was a darker blue. The moon and all the windows had been cut out of the layer of blue pasteboard. One was supposed to hold the card up against the light, and then a yellow glow shone from the clouds and the rows of windows. I was not familiar with the district portrayed. "The Halle Gate" was the caption. "Gate" and "Halle" merged in it to form the illuminated grotto in which I come upon the memory of Berlin in winter. (*Gesammelte Schriften* 7.1, 414)

We might initially try to understand this miniature as a picture puzzle in the sense of a rebus, presenting a series of pictures of objects that bear some relationship to one another and, taken together, make up some other thing that is the answer to their puzzle. In these terms, the miniature is made up of a sequence something like this: houses in the darkened streets of the old West End, gaslight, picture postcard, illuminated grotto. But this is not a satisfying construction. It seems to leave out too much, and the elements in this series are too disparate to fit the kind of series that would make up a conventional rebus. Looking again at the miniature, we might see that the similarity among these elements seems to consist in the fact that they are transformations of one another, with the precise transformational function, so to speak, remaining opaque. The picture postcard described has no one-to-one correspondence with the lighted houses; nor does the illuminated grotto in the mind have direct correspondences to the postcard or the original scene. Yet there is some kind of resemblance between them—a nonsensuous similarity. Further, there is light, an illumination, that pervades the whole text in different forms which again seem to be transformations of one another. In the initial scene, the light is described as "preoccupied with itself"; then it "leads" the narrator to the postcard and returns as the light the postcard is held up to, and it persists as the illumination in the interior grotto formed by the words of the caption. This light and its transformations, however, seem to be of a different order again from the houses, the postcard, the grotto, and their transformational relationships. Still, there does indeed seem to be some kind of sequence of transformations here, beginning with an actual cityscape, moving to an image of a cityscape (the postcard), and then to the words that title that image, and finally to the metaphor of the interior grotto.

But these attempts to identify linear sequences, even of different kinds of elements that are transformations of one another, are upset by the presence here of convoluted time. Past and present are joined enigmatically and indefinably as the light leads from the exterior scene to the postcard both then and now: "It made me pensive. It does that even now when I recall it. Its favorite thing is to lead me to one of my postcards. The card depicted..." Further, the last element in the text, the interior grotto, is the space in which the memory of Berlin in winter is encountered in the present—the same memory that has been recounted in its transformations leading up to the grotto in which it is contained. Finally, it is language in the form of the words of the postcard caption, "the Halle Gate," that forms the container for the memory. But this container of words is then redescribed as an illuminated grotto, only then to be reincorporated into the text as a whole as a linguistic structure—the text— which in turn incorporates external scene, artifactual image (the postcard), the words of the caption, and the image of the illuminated grotto.

We might say, then, that this is a text that both demonstrates its own genesis in childhood experience and recontextualizes the notion of such a genesis through its structure of convoluted time in which the genesis touches the present moment of its unfolding. The presence of the light in its different forms here might then be a muted equivalent of the flash that pulls time together, itself subjected to the distortions that govern the world in a state of resemblance. Further, we might say that the structure of convoluted time that governs this miniature is the structure that allows its language to form a constellation out of the disparate kinds of elements within it, a constellation in which they can be read as transformations of one another. Finally, we might say that language has this capacity to represent convoluted time and to name these disparate elements while suggesting that they are transformations of one another, because it is indeed an archive of nonsensuous similarities. These comments, which only crudely approach an articulation of the complex textual form of this miniature, nevertheless begin to convey the sense in which Benjamin's notion of language as the repository of the mimetic faculty can be actualized in textual form.

The miniatures of the *Berlin Childhood* are not, of course, works of philosophy or aesthetic theory. In such works, we are still more directly concerned with the cognitive moment, the moment of truth or knowledge, which is nevertheless present to some degree in works of art and indeed works of memory. Benjamin links enigmatic and convoluted time with truth and knowledge, just as he links them with the aesthetic dimension and the "world in a state of resemblance." There is a cognitive moment in the perception of nonsensuous similarity, as we saw in "The Stocking," with its message about truth in its discontinuous continuity with narrative. And the enterprise of understanding and awakening from historical experience that underlies not only the *Berlin Childhood* but also such works of original philosophical form as the *Arcades Project* or the "Theses on the Philosophy of History" also turns on convoluted time and the flash of constellational perception, which is a flash of understanding or knowledge.[17]

There is much to suggest, then, that Benjamin's conception of language as the repository of the mimetic faculty provides the basis of his original conception of philosophical form, the conception through which, as Jameson puts it, Adorno achieved liberation by mimesis. Accordingly, our final task here is to see whether the very philosophical form of Adorno's *Aesthetic Theory* can be illuminated by Benjamin's notions of language, and thereby of philosophical form as well, as the repository of the mimetic faculty. For one last time, however, I want to proceed by way of Benjamin, and to ask specifically what the philosophical form of the *Arcades Project*—surely his most daring example of a form based on this enterprise of historical awakening through the achievement of a convoluted time—might suggest for *Aesthetic Theory*, which as a culminating, enigmatic, and uncompleted work is certainly its analogue in Adorno's oeuvre.

Of course, it is with a degree of irony that I speak of the philosophical form of the *Arcades Project*, since it consists of an unwritten book in the form of a collection of materials.[18] Here I will simply speculate briefly on Benjamin's idea, which at least Adorno considered with interest,[19] that the *Arcades Project* might be a book consisting solely of quotations. Were that the case, the quotations would function something like the words in various languages arrayed around a "thing" at their center which they all mean, as in the image from "On the Mimetic Faculty." They would be linguistic, discursive in form in their original contexts but not discursive in function in the context of the *Arcades Project*. There, on the contrary, their mimetic function would come to the fore: language as artifact. Indeed, on another level, many of the quotations have to do with cultural artifacts and with the materials of material culture, such as iron and glass. Reading these groupings of quotations would presumably allow them to be constellated in a flash of perception that would illuminate them in their relation to one another and to that unspoken center that they all mean but cannot say directly; this constellation would be the convolution of the present with the historical moment, the convolution that permits awakening.[20]

How does this idea of a work consisting wholly of quotations illuminate the form of *Aesthetic Theory*, a work of some five hundred pages, which is, in contrast, almost strikingly devoid of quotations? There are a few quotations from Valéry and from Benjamin himself, to be sure, but essentially the book is one long series of sentences by

Adorno himself, in which even paragraph or section breaks are infrequent and inconspicuous. It is simply a matter, I believe, of the materials from which Adorno forms his constellations being different. Broadly speaking, his materials consist of contexts rather than quotations. Once we see this, Benjamin's notions about constellational form in its relation to nonsensuous similarity, as exemplified for instance in the *Berlin Childhood* or in the *Arcades Project* conceived as a book of quotations, suggest a number of perspectives on the form of *Aesthetic Theory*.

We see the idea of a constellation composed of contexts in one of Adorno's favorite analogies for constellational form as he expounds it in "The Essay as Form": the analogy of learning a foreign language without a dictionary, an analogy that bears a striking resemblance to Benjamin's notion in "On the Mimetic Faculty" of arraying words in various languages around the thing they all mean. "The way the essay appropriates concepts," Adorno writes, "can best be compared to the behavior of someone in a foreign country who is forced to speak its language instead of piecing it together out of its elements according to rules learned in school. Such a person will read without a dictionary. If he sees the same word thirty times in continually changing contexts, he will have ascertained its meaning better than if he had looked up all the meanings listed, which are usually too narrow in relation to the changes that occur with changing contexts and too vague in relation to the unmistakable nuances that the context gives rise to in every individual case."[21] *Aesthetic Theory* itself, as I suggested earlier, may be seen as composed of the disparate concepts from previous aesthetic theories, now taken out of their original contexts and set in relation to one another. In particular, we may think of mimesis as the undefined foundational concept, the blank center itself, surrounded by innumerable contexts of exposition, a number of which I listed earlier in my short display of contexts in which mimesis appears in *Aesthetic Theory*. In this sense, *Aesthetic Theory* might be described as a tracing around the various points in this constellation of contexts with mimesis at its center. Hence the feeling that there is no natural starting or ending point to it. Adorno shared this feeling, as he indicated in a letter about the "presentational difficulties" of the book, because of the fact that "the sequence of first and afterwards which is almost indispensable to a book proves to be so incompatible with the matter itself."[22] Mimesis is also like that blank "disfigured" center in that it remains alien despite its implication in these numerous contexts. Its presence is felt everywhere in *Aesthetic Theory*, but it is linked to the other which is not subject in such a way that the subject can never fully participate in it and still retain the sense of self; mimesis means assimilation to the other. In this sense, the enigmatic and indefinable quality of mimesis can be thought of as generating the seemingly infinite irresolvable set of contexts around it.

The contexts in *Aesthetic Theory*, however, are formed from individual sentences and the links between them. As I said earlier, *Aesthetic Theory*, more strikingly than other works, perhaps, consists of one long series of Adorno's sentences. Let us see if we can specify the role these sentences play in the form of *Aesthetic Theory*. Two critics have made suggestive, if not wholly satisfying, comments on the subject. In his essay "Subversive Mimesis," Michael Cahn notes that although Adorno considers the languagelike quality of artistic form to consist in its resemblance to syntax, sentences do not seem to be the basic syntactic units of Adorno's constellations, any more than individual words: "The syntactic order of a mimetic configuration, while following in some respects the Wittgensteinian turn from a word to sentence, nevertheless upsets this basic syntactic unit. Against the sentence it adopts the fragmentary as paradigm."[23] In fact, however, though technically unfinished, *Aesthetic Theory* does not have a fragmentary character. In contrast to Adorno's essays, which are often constructed of relatively self-contained "paragraphs," *Aesthetic Theory* seems to go on and on, each sentence linked with the next one, producing the concentric and paratactic quality Adorno speaks of in the letter on "presentational difficulties" quoted earlier.

Fredric Jameson, in contrast, who devotes some insightful comments to the mimetic or gestural quality of Adorno's sentences, points to the way the sentences create a kind of spatiality that expands outward: "Adorno's sentences try to recover the intricately bound spatial freedom of Latinate declension, objects that grandly precede subjects, and a play of gendered nouns that the mind scans by means of the appropriately modified relative. Chiasmus here becomes the structural echo by one part of the sentence of another, distant in time and space; and the result of these internal operations is the closure of the aphorism itself; definitive, yet a forthright act that passes on, not into silence, but into other acts and gestures."[24] Jameson is not talking specifically about *Aesthetic Theory* here, and indeed *Aesthetic Theory* is not constructed of aphorisms and has perhaps less of an aphoristic feel than many of Adorno's other works. Nevertheless, it is composed of aphorismlike sentences that pass quickly on to related or opposing ideas and from there to still others. Despite the limitations of their comments, Cahn is helpful, I believe, in pointing us beyond the sentence in looking at constellational form in *Aesthetic Theory,* and Jameson is helpful in pointing us to the way the interconnections between sentences in Adorno expand the space of the text outward into act and gestures that cross the boundaries of sentences.

Can these suggestions be linked back with what I have derived from Benjamin's work? Let me attempt to do so by proposing that we think of the sentences in *Aesthetic Theory* as the bearers of the flame in which we perceive the resemblance of one context to another, the flash in which the constellation around mimesis is created. The gestures and acts, to use Jameson's phrase, that make up *Aesthetic Theory*—the deconstruction and recontextualizing of one historical aesthetic theory and its concepts after another—are this flame. In them we perceive the connections and resemblances in which mimesis continues to operate in its enigmatic and undefinable way. The sentences are linked in this activity of recontextualizing, but without discursive adjudication. One assertion of position is transformed into another on the basis of resemblance, but the resemblance that permits the transformation is never definitively specified. "Logicity," that analogue in expository prose of the languagelike quality in art, is this state of resemblance at the conceptual, linguistic level. It retains the enigmatic quality that both constitutes and plagues beauty and the aesthetic, from natural beauty through art to aesthetic theory. And as if to put the seal on its enigmatic quality, *Aesthetic Theory* remains an unfinished torso, asserting, as if were, its incapacity to ever take on definitive form.

Let me say a little more about this notion of the flame of resemblance in contextualization that passes through the sentences of *Aesthetic Theory.* In *One-Way Street,* Benjamin has a suggestive passage on the tractatus form, a form characterized by its unobtrusive, undifferentiated exterior. Benjamin describes it in ways that invite comparison with *Aesthetic Theory*: "The surface of its deliberations is not pictorially enlivened but covered with broken, proliferating arabesques. In the ornamental density of this presentation the distinction between thematic and excursive expositions is abolished."[25] And although Benjamin does not make the connection explicit, the arabesque form, which consists of intertwining lines, also appears in the Proust essay as a spatial analogue of convoluted time: "When the past is reflected in the dewy fresh 'instant,' a painful shock of recognition pulls it together once more as irresistibly as the Guermantes way and Swann's way became intertwined for Proust" (*Illuminations*, 211). Although *Aesthetic Theory* is not labeled a tractatus, the notion of "unbroken, proliferating arabesques" seems peculiarly applicable to it. The series of sentences across which the flame of contextual resemblance passes has an internal structure that is reminiscent of such nonpictorial arabesques (*Aesthetic Theory* is curiously devoid not only of quotations but also of examples or "pictures"). Each sequence of sentences points in several directions, and the various themes contained in any sequence are interlaced, so that a certain theme can be traced through a sequence by omitting certain phrases or sentences, while a completely different theme can be followed in the same sequences by omitting other phrases or sentences. The full series will rarely be usable in support of any one idea or position.

This arabesque quality of interlacing themes has in fact been reflected in the way I have quoted from *Aesthetic Theory* in this essay. Take the passage, for instance, that I used in discussing Adorno's notion that art imitates natural beauty:

Natural beauty is defined by its indeterminateness, which is the undefinedness of the object as much as that of the concept. As indeterminate, and hostile to definition, natural beauty is undefinable, and in that it is akin to music.... As in music, the beautiful in nature flashes out, only to disappear immediately when one tries to pin it down. Art does not imitate nature, nor even individual natural beauty, but rather natural beauty as such. This goes beyond the aporia of natural beauty to state the aporia of aesthetics as a whole. Its subject matter is defined negatively, as undefinable. This is why art needs philosophy, which interprets it in order to say what art cannot say, whereas in fact it is only art that can say it—by not saying it. The paradoxes of aesthetics are imposed on it by its subject matter: "The beautiful may require the servile imitation of what is undefinable in things." (113/107)

This passage appears in parts throughout my discussion, the parts appearing in conjunction with parts of other passages, both preceding and following it. Embedded here, for instance, is the statement that art imitates natural beauty, a statement that seems to present a key idea. But this statement appears here in the context of natural beauty's undefinability, an idea which is better understood in relation to an earlier context in which it appears, on page 104. The notion of natural beauty flashing out is not explicitly connected here with either of those ideas, but it can be understood on the basis of comments in that earlier passage about the subject's relative lack of priority or strength in the face of natural beauty, a notion which then reappears in the paragraph following this one. The notion of language, too (what art can and cannot *say*), flashes out here but can be understood only in connection with comments that appear in a number of other contexts. Art's need for philosophy is stated here, first in a context that suggests that philosophy can speak when art cannot, because of the undefinability of art's subject matter, and then in a context that suggests that aesthetics retains the paradoxes of what it talks about, namely, both art and natural beauty.

On the one hand, the ideas here do not follow directly from one another from sentence to sentence but must be amplified through their connections with other passages, as though this text were foregrounding its nature as a complex weaving. On the other hand, there is some sense of coherence from one sentence to the next, a sort of opaque resemblance. (The same thing is true of Benjamin's writing, whose sentences also seem to be linked by opaque connections.) The coherence from one sentence to the next seems to be provided by the concept or image in a sentence showing first one face, which links it to the sentence preceding, and then another face, which links it to the sentence following. In this way, we may imagine each concept or image to be faceted like a jewel, with several faces that point in different directions.[26]

This comparison of the individual concepts and sentences in *Aesthetic Theory* to faceted jewels expands the idea of the constellational form of *Aesthetic Theory*. We may now imagine it as an interlacing of multitudinous constellations—a whole night sky, perhaps—whose nodes are those faceted jewels. This allows us in turn to imagine the difficulty of grasping this text; the various interlaced constellations and their nodes of connection flash up at one moment and are gone the next, for what reader has the speed to perceive and retain all of these interlaced constellations in the same act of concentration?[27]

Notes

A version of this essay will appear in my *Exact Imagination, Late Work: On Adorno's Aesthetics* (Cambridge, Mass.: MIT Press)

English translations from the German have sometimes been altered.

1. But see Josef Früchtl, *Mimesis: Konstellation eines Zentralbegriffs bei Adorno* (Würzburg: Königshausen & Neumann, 1986); and Karla Schultz, *Mimesis on the Move: Theodor W. Adorno's Concept of Imitation* (New York: Peter Lang, 1990), neither of which has figured prominently in English-language discussions of Adorno's aesthetics. For a detailed discussion of mimesis in Adorno in relation to the French discussion, see Martin Jay's "Mimesis and Mimetology: Adorno and Lacoue-Labarthe," in this volume. Regarding Auerbach, see Karlheinz Barck, "Walter Benjamin and Erich Auerbach: Fragments of a Correspondence," *Diacritics* 22, nos. 3–4 (fall–winter 1992): 81–83.

2. Fredric Jameson, *Late Marxism: Adorno, or, The Persistence of the Dialectic* (London and New York: Verso, 1990), p. 64.

3. Cf., for instance, the review of *Aesthetic Theory* by Henry L. Shapiro in the *Philosophical Review* 95 (April 1986): 288–89, which calls the book "shockingly difficult" and refers to its "enormous obscurity" and "long-winded manner."

4. Missac comments in his *Walter Benjamin's Passages* (Cambridge, Mass.: MIT Press, 1995) that Benjamin's "reciprocal interaction" with Adorno "ought to be studied in both directions, beginning with the seminar the young *Privatdozent* Adorno devoted to Benjamin's book on the German *Trauerspiel* in 1929 and extending to works Adorno published after the war, in which the authority of Benjamin is often invoked" (p. 26).

5. Cf. for instance, Michael Taussig, *Mimesis and Alterity* (New York: Routledge, 1993), with its repeated references to Benjamin and Adorno, or, specifically on Jakobson, Ann Jefferson, "Literariness, Dominance and Violence in Formalist Aesthetics," in *Literary Theory Today*, ed. Peter Collier and Helga Geyer-Ryan (Ithaca, NY: Cornell University Press, 1990), pp. 125–41.

6. Benjamin, "On the Mimetic Faculty," in Walter Benjamin, *Reflections* (New York: Harcourt Brace Jovanovich, 1978). Citations from "On the Mimetic Faculty" will afterward be noted in the text as *Reflections,* followed by the page number; this citation is from p. 333. "Doctrine of the Similar" is to be found in *New German Critique*, no. 17

(1979): 65–69. Citations to "Doctrine of the Similar" will afterward be noted in the next as *New German Critique* 17, followed by the page number.

7. *Reflections*, 335. By the "semiotic element" here, we must assume that Benjamin means language as characterized by signs with no inherent resemblance to what they signify. In "Doctrine of the Similar," however, he amplifies this by referring to the "semiotic or communicative element of language," making it clear that he means not only this technical linguistic idea but the ordinary discursive use of language: "The nexus of meaning implicit in the sounds of the sentence is the basis from which something similar can become apparent instantaneously, in a flash" (*New German Critique* 17, 68).

8. Quotations from Benjamin's *Berlin Childhood* follow the *Fassung letzter Hand* published in volume 7.1 of Benjamin's *Gesammelte Schriften* (Frankfurt am Main: Suhrkamp, 1989), pp. 385–432. The translations are from the unpublished manuscript of my translation of this work. Citations to the *Berlin Childhood* will afterward be noted in the text as *Gesammelte Schriften* 7.1, followed by the page number. This citation is from p. 418.

9. Jameson, *Late Marxism*, p. 256.

10. Quotations from *Aesthetic Theory* are given in my own translation. Here and afterward in the text, page numbers in parentheses following quotations from *Aesthetic Theory* refer to the corresponding pages first in the German original and then in the published English translation by Christian Lenhardt (London: Routledge & Kegan Paul, 1984).

11. See my essay "Subjective Aesthetic Experience in Adorno and Its Historical Trajectory," *Theory Culture & Society* 10, no. 2 (May 1993): 89–125.

12. One may approach this question of language from different directions. Albrecht Wellmer, in "Truth, Semblance, and Reconciliation: Adorno's Aesthetic Redemption of Modernity," in his *Persistence of Modernity*, trans. David Midgley (Cambridge, Mass.: MIT Press, 1991), pp. 1–35, argues that, although mimesis in art on the one hand and philosophical reflection with its rationality on the other may both be required for full aesthetic understanding, they nevertheless remain irreconcilable. Wellmer lays the blame for this aporia in Adorno's thought on the subject/object paradigm, the paradigm of consciousness and its objects, within which Adorno worked. He proposes to further our understanding of the aesthetic by substituting the paradigm of an intersubjective communicative rationality in language, along the lines laid out by Habermas, for the subject/object paradigm within which, he says, *Aesthetic Theory* is formulated. Language would then become the medium of reconciliation. I prefer, however, to explore the implications for language of the notion of mimesis implicit in Adorno and Benjamin's work, with particular reference to the suggestion of a continuity or affinity between subject and object in the mimetic or aesthetic dimension.

13. Walter Benjamin, "The Image of Proust," in his *Illuminations*, trans. Harry Zohn (New York: Schocken, 1969), pp. 201–15. Citations to this essay will afterward be noted in the text as *Illuminations*, followed by the page number.

14. Walter Benjamin, "On Some Motifs in Baudelaire," in his *Illuminations*, pp. 155–200. Citations to this essay will afterward be noted in the text as *Illuminations*, followed by the page number.

Shierry Weber Nicholsen

15. This passage from "The Mummerehlen" appears only in the earlier version, which can be found in Walter Benjamin, *Schriften*, vol. 1 (Frankfurt am Main: Suhrkamp, 1955), p. 607.

16. The importance of articulation as an aesthetic concept has not been sufficiently recognized. But see, for instance, Konrad Wolff, *The Teaching of Artur Schnabel* (London: Faber & Faber, 1972).

17. Benjamin's article "Theses on the Philosophy of History" is full of formulations of this kind. To cite just a few (all from *Illuminations*, 253–64): "The true image of the past flits by." "The past can be seized only as an image which flashes up at the instant when it can be recognized and it is never seen again." "History is the subject of a structure whose site is not homogeneous empty time, but time filled by the presence of the now [*Jetztzeit*]." "Where thinking suddenly stops in a configuration pregnant with tensions, it gives that configuration a shock, by which it crystallizes into a monad." "The present . . . as a model of Messianic time, comprises the entire history of mankind in enormous abridgement." The historian "grasps the constellation which his own era has formed with a definite earlier one."

18. For an imaginative improvisation on the status of these quotations, see Pierre Missac's *Walter Benjamin's Passages*, pp. 169–72.

19. Theodor W. Adorno, "A Portrait of Walter Benjamin," in his *Prisms*, trans. Samuel and Shierry Weber (Cambridge, Mass.: MIT Press, 1981), p. 329.

20. Here we are reminded of Benjamin's statement in *One-Way Street* to the effect that quotations in his works are like highway robbers who fall upon the reader and rob him of his convictions (*Schriften*, vol. 1, p. 591). This is the reverse or "shock" face of the speed of reading that allows the reader to snatch a glimpse of nonsensuous similarity, as a passage from "Doctrine of the Similar" makes clear: "Even profane reading, if it is not to forsake understanding altogether, shares this with magical reading: that it is subject to a necessary speed, or rather a critical moment, which the reader must not forget at any cost unless he wishes to go away empty-handed" (*New German Critique* 17, 68).

21. Theodor Adorno, "The Essay as Form," in his *Notes to Literature*, vol. 1, trans. Shierry Weber Nicholsen (New York: Columbia University Press, 1991), p. 13. Adorno himself of course, talks extensively about his own use of constellational form, and I have written about it elsewhere. See my "Toward a More Adequate Reception of Adorno's *Aesthetic Theory*: Configurational Form in Adorno's Aesthetic Writings," *Cultural Critique*, no. 18 (spring 1991): 33–64.

22. In a letter cited in the editors' epilogue to *Aesthetic Theory*, p. 496; my translation.

23. Michael Cahn, "Subversive Mimesis: Theodor W. Adorno and the Modern Impasse of Critique," in *Mimesis in Contemporary Theory*, vol. 1, ed. Mihai Spariosu (Philadelphia: John Benjamins, 1984), p. 41.

24. Jameson, *Late Marxism*, p. ix.

25. *Reflections*, p. 82.

26. Cf. the phrase from Mallarmé's *Le Mystère dans les lettres* that Pierre Missac uses to conceive the relationship between Benjamin and Mallarmé: "a distant sparkling reciprocity, or one presented obliquely, as a contingent event" leading back to its source (*Walter Benjamin's Passages,* p. 23).

27. I am reminded here of Christopher Alexander's book on the aesthetics of early Turkish carpets, *A Foreshadowing of 21st Century Art* (New York: Oxford University Press, 1993). Alexander argues that these carpets attain the wholeness and density of "beings" by virtue of being composed of a multitude of highly differentiated centers integrated across a number of levels. He talks at one point about asking his students to try to draw the design of a specific carpet and the difficulty they have doing so given their inability to "see" the various centers and their relations to one another. Similarly, he points out that the weavers who wove these carpets would have to attend to each knot with a concentration that would encompass the relationship of that particular knot to perhaps eight centers at once (see pp. 177–79). Some similar concentration must be required to properly read *Aesthetic Theory.*

4

Benjamin, Adorno, Surrealism

Richard Wolin

I

There is little doubt that one of the more enduring aspects of Critical Theory has been its contribution to the field of aesthetics. This is a fact that has seemed baffling and irksome to those for whom the inordinate concentration on the aesthetic dimension in the work of such thinkers as Adorno, Benjamin, Leo Löwenthal, and Herbert Marcuse cannot help but appear as the sublimated fulfillment of more deep-seated political urges—a form of ersatz praxis, as it were. Even the more intelligent and sensitive commentaries on Critical Theory that have appeared in recent years are not wholly free of the atavistic materialist suspicion that time spent away from the practical sphere is time ill spent. Yet such attitudes risk becoming a "defeatism of reason"[1] in an era in which not only has the applicability of the Marxian approach been thrown into serious doubt but that approach has become ideologically responsible for a historically new form of oppression.

At the same time, there can be little doubt that the aesthetic interest of Critical Theory retains an essential *radical quality* insofar as this interest is unfailingly wedded to questions of human emancipation. However, in this new frame of reference, such questions cease being reducible to the simplistic matter of changing the ownership of the means of production, the answer long associated with traditional socialist perspectives. Rather, they have become relevant to the *transformation of life in its totality,* that is, in its cultural, psychological, and everyday aspects, as well as its economic and political forms. Only a thoroughly reconstructed theoretical perspective would be capable of providing a framework adequate to such radical and wide-ranging needs; and it was precisely such a framework that Critical Theory sought to provide through its work in a variety of intellectual fields, not the least of which was the aesthetic.

The task of a systematic reconstruction of the aesthetics of Critical Theory would be an admirable and necessary subject of future research.[2] The present essay, focusing on the variegated links between two Critical Theorists—Benjamin and Adorno—and surrealism, represents only a very partial step in this direction. At the same time, it is important to note that in a historical era in which social theory had become "social science," philosophy was irredeemably scholastic, and objective prospects for social change were seemingly crushed beneath monolithic authoritarian and welfare-state formations, Critical Theory increasingly turned to the aesthetic sphere as a unique repository of qualitative difference, negation, and critique.

Benjamin once remarked, "My thought is related to theology like a blotter to ink. It is wholly soaked up by it. If it were left to the blotter, however, nothing would remain."[3] One could make an analogous claim concerning his innate attraction to surrealism. Indeed, the elective affinities between surrealist attitudes and Benjamin's characteristic mode of philosophizing account for one of the most fundamental motifs throughout his work.

Technically, one must date Benjamin's interest in surrealism from his 1925 reading of André Breton's "Manifesto of Surrealism." In a letter to Rainer Maria Rilke that year, Benjamin would write enthusiastically, "In particular what struck me about surrealism...was the captivating, authoritative, and definitive way in which language passes over into the world of dreams."[4] The following year, Louis Aragon's *Le Paysan de Paris* appeared, a work that would provide the ultimate stimulus for Benjamin's celebrated *Passagenwerk* (Arcades Project), the uncompleted masterpiece of his later years. At a later date, Benjamin described his initial reaction to Aragon's book as follows: "At night in bed I could never read more than two or three pages at a time, for my heartbeat became so strong that I was forced to lay the book down."[5]

Unquestionably, it was in the execution—as fragmentary as it remained—of the *Passagenwerk* that Benjamin's passionate encounter with surrealism was put to its most significant, if at times controversial, employment. To this crucial episode in Benjamin's development I will return shortly. However, in the present context, it is perhaps of equal importance to indicate that well before these momentous initial encounters, Benjamin's thought had already inclined in surrealistic directions.

Despite the fact that in his early years (1916–1925) Benjamin displayed a primarily *Germanistik* focus (with the important exception of his interest in Baudelaire and Proust), what one might call protosurrealist stirrings can be found in two significant works from this period: the 1918 essay "The Program of the Coming Philosophy" and the "Epistemo-Critical Prologue" to his 1925 *Trauerspiel* study (*The Origin of German Baroque Drama;* Benjamin's failed *Habilitationsschrift,* eventually published in 1928).

At first glance, it would seem inherently problematical to characterize "The Program of the Coming Philosophy" as "protosurrealistic." The focus of the essay is a Kant critique directed against the neo-Kantianism that had attained the status of a school philosophy during Benjamin's university years (the years 1912–1919). The brunt of Benjamin's criticisms are directed against the concept of experience that a Kantian theory of knowledge yields, one Benjamin correctly identifies as deriving unambiguously from a mechanistic, Newtonian worldview, and which he mercilessly castigates as being "of inferior rank."[6] "That Kant could commence his immense work under the sign of the Enlightenment means that it was undertaken on the basis of an experience reduced to a nadir, to a minimum of signification, so to speak," Benjamin observes, with reference to the physicalist biases of High Enlightenment thought.[7] Lest there remain any doubt concerning Benjamin's pronounced antipathy to a Newtonian conception of experience, in which all is calculable, predictable, and lawlike, Benjamin adds his conviction that this was "one of the most base experiences or views of the world."[8]

It is clear that what Benjamin found most objectionable about the remnants of a Newtonian, causalist perspective in Kant's theory of cognition was the resultant ontological separation between phenomenal and noumenal realms. Concerning the latter, according to Kant,

we could have no "knowledge," properly speaking: because the noumenal transcended the (Newtonian) bounds of experience, claims
directed toward this sphere of being remained hollow and empty, ultimately succumbing to the folly of "dialectical illusion." Yet this is
precisely what Benjamin desired from a "theory of experience" that
would be worthy of the name: access to noumenal truth, that is, contact with a form of knowledge/experience that would be transcendent vis-à-vis the predictable, lawlike regularities of the prosaic
phenomenal world. The latter worldview promoted a conception of
existence that was statistical and mechanistic, hence "inferior" in
Benjamin's eyes. Only what he dubbed a "superior concept of experience"[9] would be capable of doing justice to the true dignity and
worth of human existence and its higher capacities. As Benjamin remarks, "What the Enlightenment lacked was authorities, not in the
sense of something to which one would have to submit uncritically,
but rather as spiritual powers that would have been capable of providing experience with a superior content."[10]

    The conclusion Benjamin draws from this youthful Kant critique
prima facie could not be more removed from surrealist considerations: an authentically superior concept of experience must "render
possible not only mechanical but also *religious experience.*" However, if
one isolates the key positive conception found in the essay—that of a
"superior concept of experience"—the links with surrealism will
seem less parochial. Indeed, the surrealists, too, sought to surmount
the inherent narrowness of a Western rationalism that resulted in the
prevalence of a thoroughly mundane and routinized cosmos. This
rationalist spirit, or antispirit, had resulted in the unprecedented car-
nage of World War I, in which scientific knowledge had been applied
to methods of mass annihilation on a previously unimaginable scale.
Moreover, its killing sobriety was responsible for the banishment of
all mystery, romance, and transcendence from the center stage of
human existence, in favor of the bourgeois values of conformity, cal-
culation, and profit. As Fredric Jameson has remarked, "Surrealism
presents itself first and foremost as a reaction against the intellectual-
ized, against *logic* in the widest sense of the word, subsuming not only
philosophical rationality, but also the common-sense interest of the
middle-class business world, and ultimately reality itself."[11] The sur-

realist revulsion toward the spirit of bourgeois rationalism can be seen clearly from such "arational," privileged surrealist media as automatic writing, *l'hasard objectif*, and—of paramount importance for Benjamin—the realm of dream experience. As André Breton would remark in his 1925 "Manifesto," "I believe in the future resolution of these two states, dream and reality, which are so seemingly contradictory, into a kind of absolute reality, a *surreality*, if one may so speak. It is in quest of this surreality that I am going."[12] Indeed, it was a similar quest for an "absolute reality" that motivated so much of Benjamin's youthful literary activity.

The other moment of Benjamin's early development that may be described as incipiently surrealist was his theory of knowledge in the *Trauerspiel* book. Here, too, at first glance, cogent parallels would seem hard to come by. Nothing could be more foreign to the surrealist enterprise than the construction of a theory of knowledge, an all too traditional philosophical undertaking. To be sure, a thorough discussion of the hermetic prologue to Benjamin's *Trauerspiel* book would far transcend the scope of this essay and is a matter I have addressed at length elsewhere.[13] But there is little doubt that the methodological basis of Benjamin's theory of knowledge is the principle of *montage:* an immediate juxtaposition of intrinsically unrelated elements; a principle that Peter Bürger has referred to as "the fundamental principle of avant-gardiste art."[14]

The key to understanding Benjamin's early theory of knowledge (which he considered to be "dialectical," if not yet "materialist") is the concept of "constellation." By regrouping material elements of phenomena—the objects of knowledge—in a philosophically informed constellation, Benjamin sought the emergence of an "Idea" through which the "redemption" of the phenomena would be effectuated—insofar as contact with the Idea would facilitate their elevation to the homeland of unconditioned truth. In this admittedly recondite procedure, the function of conceptual (i.e., rational) knowledge is strictly delimited: its sole task is to facilitate the *arrangement* of the phenomena or material elements in the constellation. As Benjamin asserts, "Conceptual distinctions are above all suspicion of destructive sophistry only when their purpose is the salvation of phenomena in ideas."[15] But the ultimate goal of this process, the emergence of the ideas themselves, is to be a product of the montagelike juxtaposition of the material elements alone. It is not, strictly speaking, a result that is achieved by employing the traditional philosophical means of induction, deduction, or logical argumentation, if the latter nevertheless remain useful as auxiliary methods. To be sure, what Benjamin has in mind is something more akin to a momentary epiphany, a sudden burst of insight, that he would later explicitly associate with his materialist version of the constellations of the *Trauerspiel* book, the "dialectical image." As Benjamin would say of the latter, "The dialectical image is a flashing image. Thus, the past must be grasped as an image that flashes in the now of recognition. Redemption, which is accomplished in this way and only in this way, can be attained only as that which in the next instant is already irredeemably lost."[16] As a *Jetztzeit*, or "now time," the constellation or dialectical image approximates the Neoplatonic-theological notion of *nunc stans*. As defined by Franz Rosenzweig in *The Star of Redemption* (a work known to have influenced Benjamin), *nunc stans* signifies that "mankind is redeemed from the transience of the moment," and the latter is "refashioned as the ever-persisting and thus intransient, as eternity."[17] The theological distinction between "historical time," prone to decay and disintegration (*Verfall*), and "messianic time," a time of permanent fulfillment, was indeed one of the most enduring motifs throughout Benjamin's lifework; it dates originally from a crucial 1916 fragment "Trauerspiel und Tragödie"[18] and pervades the 1940 "Theses on the Philosophy of History," in which Benjamin speaks of the *Jetztzeit* as "shot through with chips of Messianic time," in contraposition to the empty and degraded "homogeneous" time of the historical era.

Benjaminian constellations (also described at times as "monads") bear affinities with the surrealist search for transcendence (a "surreality"). As we first saw with reference to his 1918 Kant critique, and again through his emphasis on a messianic time of permanence and fulfillment, the secular bent of Benjamin's philosophy is throughout interspersed with theological residues of no small moment. Yet if one observes carefully, it is apparent that Benjamin's search for transcendence transpires, like the surrealists', *within* the sphere of immanence. Hence, in his *Trauerspiel* book's theory of ideas, the latter, although of ontologically superior value, remain, unlike the Platonic doctrine, *this-worldly* in origin. That is, they emerge spontaneously from the conceptually mediated arrangement of the phenomena themselves. In Benjamin's theory, it is clear that ideas are denied an existence independent of phenomenal being. This claim is crucial, for it is the basis on which he hopes to surmount "dualism." As he observes at one point, "For ideas are not represented in themselves, but solely and exclusively in an arrangement of concrete elements in the concept: as the configuration [constellation] of these elements." He seeks to summarize the relationship between ideas and phenomena through use of the following bold, if characteristically elliptical metaphor: "Ideas are to objects as constellations are to stars."[19] That is, neither ideas nor constellations exist independently of the material elements that constitute them, but instead first emerge therefrom.

One can only date the explicit emergence of surrealist motifs in Benjamin's work from the aphoristic *Einbahnstrasse* (1928) and the seminal "Surrealism" essay of a year later. With reference to the former, Ernst Bloch was quick to see, in a 1928 review, that the basic intention was "to render philosophy surrealistic."[20] He recalls that Benjamin reacted favorably at a Berlin café when Bloch showed him a review that compared the book to a "store-opening, with the newest spring fashions in metaphysics in the display window."[21] Bloch noted further that Benjamin had consciously shunned a systematic, discursive means of presentation in favor of the surrealist-inspired principle of montage: "Surrealistic philosophy is exemplary as a montage of fragments that, however, remain pluralistic and unconnected."[22] In *Einbahnstrasse*, Benjamin first formulated the methodological precepts that would define the construction of the *Passagenwerk*, whose initial composition occurred during these years. As Benjamin remarks in his notes for the *Passagenwerk*, "Method of this work: literary montage. I have nothing to say. Only to show. I will pilfer nothing valuable and appropriate for myself no clever formulations. Only rubbish and refuse, of which I will make no inventory; rather, I will allow them to come into their own in the only way possible: by employing them."[23] This methodological plan was the object of an extensive critique by Adorno, who feared that the *Passagenwerk* in its entirety would ultimately be composed of a montage of citations, devoid of supporting commentary or interpretation. Support for this conviction is seemingly contained in the above-quoted dictum, "I have nothing to say. Only to show."[24]

What was it above all that Benjamin prized about surrealism? To begin with, the surrealist technique of montage seemed an ideal way of surmounting the staleness and convention of traditional, discursive philosophizing. It was a procedure more likely to yield sudden flashes of insight ("the dialectical image is a flashing image") than precalculated, deductive truths. In addition, the *imagistic* character of montage—for example, in the thought montages or collages that constitute *Einbahnstrasse*—lends it greater affinities with the sensuous, objective side of truth, that is, with the things themselves that truth seeks to grasp. Such a technique stands in opposition to the typical philosophical emphasis on "conceptual" primacy and against the modern philosophical preeminence of the epistemological subject. Benjamin was vehemently opposed to such conventional philosophical practices, which he felt could never truly reach the "in itself" of phenomena.

Moreover, surrealistic modes of apprehension—above all, surrealism's unhesitating immersion in the concrete particularity of everyday life—seemed to harmonize especially well with Benjamin's own partisanship for philosophical micrology: his conviction that the universal is not something that must be foisted on the particular from on high but must be gently coaxed from the latter of its own accord. To do otherwise would be merely to violate the delicate contours of particularity as such, to subject the latter insensitively to the abstract "will to power" of the conceptual sphere. Bloch has aptly commented on Benjamin's talents as a philosophical micrologist: "Benjamin had what Lukács so enormously lacked: he had a unique sense for the significant detail, for the near at hand, for the fresh elements which burst forth in thinking and the world, for singularities which are unsuitable for practical use and thus deserving of an entirely unique consideration. Benjamin possessed a peerless micrological-philosophical sense for such details, such significant signs of the off-the-beaten-track."[25]

Benjamin himself describes his methodological reliance on micrology and its relationship to montage in an important note to the *Passagenwerk*. There, Benjamin grapples with the problem of how to reconcile a "heightened sense of felicity to the subject matter [*Anschaulichkeit*]" with the "Marxist understanding of history." His conclusion: "The first step on this path will be to incorporate the principle of montage in the study of history. Thus, to construct the grandest edifices from the smallest, most precisely fabricated building-blocks. Thereby to discover the crystallization of the totality in the analysis of the small, individual elements."[26] Hence, the procedure of montage is designed both to surmount problems stemming from the abstract superimposition of "method" on "material" (method here being the "Marxist understanding of history") as well as to facilitate greater *Anschaulichkeit* or fidelity to the being-in-itself of the subject matter. It is a technique that inclines intrinsically toward respect for the material rather than promoting the abstract primacy of the concept.[27]

The enchanted, micrological transformation of fragments of everyday life was a quality of surrealism that Benjamin especially revered. In the letters referring to his 1929 "Surrealism" essay, Benjamin leaves no doubt concerning its theoretical centrality for the *Passagenwerk*. At one point, he refers to it as "an opaque paravent in front of the Arcades study"; at another he speaks of it as a type of "prolegomenon to the Arcades project."[28] The "Surrealism" essay, he says, represents an attempt "to determine the most concrete qualities of an epoch as they present themselves here and there in children's games, a building, or one of life's random situations."[29] Not only was the essay to be about surrealism; it was itself supposed to be surrealist in spirit.

Benjamin praises the surrealists for their attempt to narrow the gap between art and life. As such, one of the movement's most salutary features is its concerted assault on the bourgeois realm of belles lettres. It presents itself as a definitive challenge to the illusionistic, otherworldly complacency of "art for art's sake," which Benjamin describes as the "secular religion of art." He therefore praises Breton for "his intention of breaking with a praxis that presents the public with the literary precipitate of a certain form of existence while withholding that existence itself."[30] The *promesse de bonheur* of bourgeois art should no longer be confined to the supramundane sphere of aesthetic illusion but should instead be transferred to the plane of material life itself. As Breton declared, "'Transform the world,' Marx said; 'change life,' said Rimbaud. For us these two watchwords are one."[31] The writings of this circle had become bluff, demonstration, and pure provocation; they had thus ceased being works of art in the purist, affirmative sense. Yet for the surrealists, this transformed conception of the relationship between art and life praxis meant not only that was art to be brought closer to the domain of real life but also that shards of real life were to be absorbed within the artistic process. Once transformed within the surrealist collage, these shards, newly arranged, would produce inspired, "profane illuminations." In perhaps the most representative passage of the essay, Benjamin explains his veneration of the surrealist movement:

[The surrealists were] the first to perceive the revolutionary energies that appear in the "outmoded," in the first iron constructions, the first factory buildings, the earliest photos, the objects that have begun . . . to ebb from them. The relation of these things to revolution—no one can have a more exact concept of it than these authors. No one before these visionaries and augurs perceived how destitution—not only social, but architectonic, the poverty of interiors, enslaved and enslaving objects—can be suddenly transformed into revolutionary nihilism. Leaving aside Aragon's *Passage de l'Opéra*, Breton and Nadja are the lovers who convert everything that we have experienced on mournful railway journeys (railways are beginning to age), on Godforsaken Sunday afternoons in the proletarian quarters of the great cities, in the first glance through the rain-blurred window of a new apartment, into revolutionary experience, if not action. They bring the immense forces of "atmosphere" concealed in these things to the point of explosion.[32]

This "enchanted" relationship to the discrete phenomena of everyday life satisfied Benjamin's long-standing yearning for a "superior concept of experience." Moreover, it possessed the potential political advantage of existing in profane, exoteric form.

Undoubtedly, one of the most crucial links between surrealism and the arcades project stemmed from the former's emphasis on the superior experiential value of dream life. In his first manifesto, Breton affirms the value of dreams to such an extent that he ultimately calls into question the conventional priority of waking over dream life: "Freud very rightly brought his critical faculties to bear upon the dream. It is, in fact, inadmissible that this considerable portion of psychic activity...has still today been so grossly neglected. I have always been amazed at the way an ordinary observer lends credence and attaches much more importance to waking events than those in dreams."[33]

In Benjamin's work, too, dreams occupy a very special locus. For him, dreams become an autonomous source of knowledge and experience, a privileged key to the secrets and mysteries of waking life. In no uncertain terms, they become repositories of the utopian visions of humanity. Dreams provide a necessary sanctuary for the higher aspirations and desires of humanity, which are systematically denied on the plane of material life. Adorno touches on this point when he observes that, for Benjamin, "the dream becomes a medium of unregimented experience, a source of knowledge opposed to the stale superficiality of thinking." In dreams, "the absurd is presented as if it were self-evident, in order to strip the self-evident of its power."[34] Dreams thus represent the realm of the possible, the nonidentical; they serve to contest the pretension to "being-in-itself" of the dominant reality principle.

In an 1843 letter to A. Ruge, Marx makes his famous observation that "the world has long been dreaming of something of which it must only become conscious in order to possess it in reality"—a saying with which Benjamin was quite familiar and which he explicitly cites in the *Passagenwerk*.[35] Indeed, the Marx citation may be plausibly read as the theoretical germ cell of the *Passagenwerk* in its entirety. The work's central methodological concerns are unambiguously contained in the following remarks by Benjamin bearing on the relationships among dreams, awakening, and the nineteenth century:

The attempt to awaken from a dream as the best example of dialectical transformation.... The utilization of dream elements in awakening is the canon of dialectics.... Capitalism was a natural phenomenon with which a new dream-sleep, containing a reactivation of mythical powers, came over Europe.... The coming awakening stands like the Greek wooden horse in the Troy of the dream.... The collective expresses its conditions of life. In the dream it finds its expression and in awakening its interpretation.... The critique of the nineteenth century must in a word begin here. Not with its mechanism and machinism, rather with its narcotic historicism, its addiction to masks, in which however is hidden a sign of true historical existence that the surrealists were the first to grasp. The task of the present work is to decipher this sign. And the revolutionary, materialistic basis of surrealism is a sufficient guarantee of the fact that in the sign of true historical existence just mentioned, the economic base of the nineteenth century has attained its highest expression.[36]

Capitalism, as a "natural phenomenon," has unleashed a neomythological dream sleep over Europe, whose manifestations are the superstructural material elements of nineteenth-century life first investigated by the surrealists (who, moreover, through their salutary investigations of the latter, have provided a guarantee of "true historical existence") and soon to become the privileged phenomena of analysis in Benjamin's own *Passagenwerk:* phenomena such as the arcades, fashion, the world exhibitions, the bourgeois interior, the streets of Paris, and so on. The dream sleep signifies not merely false consciousness; that is, it is irreducible to the purely negative moment of objective delusion. Rather, it is simultaneously a repository of utopian potentials and wish images that point in the direction of a meaningful historical existence. The latter, of course, will accrue to humanity—the "collective"—only with the moment of historical awakening. The intention of the—inconsummate—*Passagenwerk* was nothing less than the redemption of the superstructural *Erscheinungsformen* from their indigent, natural state through their reassemblage in a surrealistically inspired montage; it was this procedure, and this procedure alone, that would release the utopian wish images from their reified imprisonment in the fetishistic world of bourgeois cultural consumption. In this respect, Rolf Tiedemann makes the pertinent observation in his introduction to the *Passagenwerk* that "Benjamin attempted to do for the superstructure of capitalism what Marx did for the economic base."

At several points in the study, Benjamin insists on the importance of the category "ambiguity." "Ambiguity is the metaphorical [*bildliche*] appearance of the dialectic, the law of dialectic-at-a-standstill. This standstill is utopia and the dialectical image thus a dream-image."[37] The ambiguity lies precisely in the fact that the phantasmagorical image sphere of the bourgeois cultural landscape can be conceived of neither strictly in terms of historical disintegration (*Verfall*) nor in terms of the modern theory of progress (on which Benjamin heaps such scorn in sheaf N of the *Passagenwerk*). Rather the regressive and utopian potentials are inextricably interlaced, and both moments are contained in the dialectical image. There is certainly little difficulty in making sense of this judgment from the standpoint of an orthodox Marxist lexicon. Marx always considered capitalism an "ambiguous" social formation, insofar as the development of objectively progressive forces of production was retarded by retrograde capitalist relations of production. Benjamin pays lip service to this insight when he comments that, in his chapter on commodity fetishism, Marx shows "how ambiguous the economic world of capitalism is—an ambiguity greatly enhanced by the intensification of the capitalist economy; this is very clear in the case of machines, which heighten exploitation instead of improving the lot of man."[38]

A detailed, lapidary summation of the methodological intentions of the project as a whole is provided in the following crucial remarks:

> There exists an entirely unique experience of dialectics. The compelling, drastic experience which refutes all "gradualism" and shows all apparent "development" as an eminently thoroughgoing dialectical transformation is the awakening from a dream.... The new dialectical method of historiography appears as the art of experiencing the present as a world of awakening in which that dream which we call the past is related to truth. To experience the past in dream-remembrance!—Thus: remembrance and awakening are intimately related. Awakening is namely the dialectical, Copernican turn of remembrance.... The state of a consciousness that oscillates between sleep and awakening need only be transposed from the individual to the collective. Much that is merely extrinsic to the individual is intrinsic to the collective: architecture, fashion, even weather are internal to the collective in the same way that organ sensations, the feeling of sickness or health are internal to the individual. As long as they persist in an unconscious, unshaped dream form, they remain mere natural processes such as the digestive process, breathing, etc. They stand in the cycle of the eternally same until the collective effects political mastery of them and sets them on the path of history.[39]

The foregoing observations indicate a seminal change in Benjamin's utilization of the surrealist-inspired notion of dream experience. Originally, like the surrealists, Benjamin valorized—indeed fetishized—the *manifest contents* of dream experience by viewing them as autonomous sources of value and meaning. In the more mature version of the *Passagenwerk,* however, the emphasis has switched from the manifest content of the dream images to the moment of interpretation or *awakening*. And here, in opposition to surrealism and in closer proximity to Freud, the category of awakening is emphatically associated with that of *remembrance*. The act of awakening is produced via a labor of interpretive remembrance. The *Passagenwerk* may thus be understood as an elaborate effort to remaster the historical past, which otherwise threatens to fall victim to the somnambulism of the dream state. It represents a quasi-Freudian attempt to make the unconscious conscious—albeit on the level of the *collective* rather than that of the *individual* past. It is Benjamin's own *Traumdeutung* in the service of human emancipation, that is, in the raising of historical life from the level of an unconscious "natural process" to something consciously produced and lived.

The *Passagenwerk*, then, represents the consummation of Benjamin's initial flirtations with surrealism in the 1920s, an attempt, as it were, to transpose surrealist "powers of intoxication" from the cafés of the right bank to the panoramic domain of nineteenth-century historiography.

That Benjamin never completed the project is a well-known fact and usually attributed to circumstantial considerations: his precarious situation as an impoverished German émigré in the 1930s, his untimely death on the Franco-Spanish border in September 1940. Gretel Adorno once suggested that Benjamin failed to consummate the work for deep-seated personal and psychological reasons. However plausible these explanations may be, I would like to suggest that the inconsummate nature of the *Passagenwerk* must be at least in part attributed to certain substantive difficulties inherent in the conceptual master plan of the work itself. I would like to bracket this claim and turn instead to discuss Adorno's critique of surrealism.[40]

II

When it comes to the question of Adorno's relationship to surrealism, the secondary literature displays a startling degree of unanimity. Indeed, the fine studies by Susan Buck-Morss, Eugene Lunn, and Martin Jay seemingly could not be more in agreement on this point.[41] All three commentators seize on what is assuredly the dominant thrust of Adorno's reservations toward the movement: the tendency of surrealism (at least in its *visual* manifestations) to succumb to a type of object fetishism. Surrealism absorbs the fragments and detritus of everyday life in its disjointed construction. Adorno's question, however, is whether the *unmediated absorption* of the fragments of immediacy in surrealist collages does not, in the last analysis, amount to a crass duplication of everyday life in its indigent given state. As Jay has pointed out, Adorno's critique of surrealism results in strange bedfellows: it dovetails surprisingly with Lukács's rejection of modernism tout court for fetishizing the immediacy of bourgeois fragmentation. Needless to say, Adorno and Lukács were, apart from their comparably damning judgments of surrealism, diametrical antipodes in aesthetic taste: Adorno was, as a rule, one of the staunchest defenders of aesthetic modernism, whereas Lukács championed the "critical realism" of such nineteenth-century authors as Stendhal, Balzac, and Tolstoy (and in the twentieth century, Thomas Mann, another figure on whom, curiously, Adorno and Lukács find themselves in agreement).[42]

Both Jay and Lunn, although resting their cases primarily on Adorno's 1956 essay "Looking Back on Surrealism," cite a revealing footnote from *Philosophy of Modern Music* to exemplify Adorno's reservations concerning surrealist art:

Surrealism is anti-organic and rooted in lifelessness. It destroys the boundary between the body and the world of objects, in order to convert society into a hypostatization of the body. Its form is that of montage. This is totally alien to Schönberg. In the case of surrealism, however, the more subjectivity renounces its rights over the world of objects, aggressively acknowledging the supremacy of that world, the more willing it is to accept at the same time the traditionally established form of the world of objects.[43]

To be sure, these remarks penetrate to the heart of Adorno's rejection of surrealist techniques. Here, the central thematic objection concerns the category of montage—precisely that aspect of surrealism that Benjamin found methodologically most serviceable. As a result of its renunciation of the category of mediation, surrealism accepts the material elements of bourgeois society as such and uncritically. For this reason it remains "inorganic and lifeless," since these elements remain untransformed in the surrealist constructions; that is, they are not reinserted in a new, conceptually integrated organic whole. Yet "inorganicity" and "lifelessness" were the chief traits of high capitalism under conditions of total reification, which fostered *social* relations between things—commodities—and *objective* relations between persons. Hence, Adorno's conclusion that surrealism, at its worst, celebrated a reified immediacy in its montages. He illustrates this contention in a frequently cited passage from the 1956 essay: "The montages of Surrealism are the true still-lifes.... In making compositions out of what is out of date, they create *nature morte*." This is true insofar as surrealism represents "abstract freedom's reversion to the supremacy of objects and thus to mere nature." He then goes on to make the following observations:

These [surrealist] images are not images of something inward; rather, they are fetishes—commodity fetishes—on which something subjective, libido, was once fixated. It is through these fetishes, not through immersion in the self, that the images bring back childhood.... Breasts that have been cut off, mannequins' legs in silk stockings in the collages—these are mementos of the objects of the partial drives that aroused the libido. Thinglike and dead, in them what has been forgotten reveals itself to be the true object of love, what love wants to make itself resemble, what we resemble. As a freezing of the moment of awakening, Surrealism is akin to photography. Surrealism's booty is images, to be sure, but not the invariant, ahistorical images of the unconscious subject... rather, they are historical images in which the subject's innermost core becomes aware that it is something external, an imitation of something social and historical.[44]

In this characteristically terse but essential passage, Adorno identifies the manifest weakness of surrealism's assimilation of psychoanalytic concepts. Early in the essay, he had already taken issue with the surrealist appropriation of dream life. The surrealists fetishized the manifest content of dreams, whereas in psychoanalysis, of course, it was always the latent dimension of *dream interpretation* that received pride of place. (Yet it must be pointed out that however much Breton et al. may have misunderstood the letter of Freud's doctrines themselves, they of course had no pretension to becoming *practicing analysts*. Hence, as *practicing artists*, if their creative misinterpretation of psychoanalytic principles yielded results that were aesthetically fruitful—so much the better!) Adorno also wished to point out that their claim to being in immediate contact with the unconscious or dreams, whose powers they claimed to be able to release at will for artistic purposes, was a sham. In the case of automatic writing, for example, such *écriture* could hardly be an unadulterated product of the unconscious, since the very act of sitting down at a desk, pen in hand—as well as the idea of a "program" of automatic writing itself—was the result of a prior conscious decision. He proceeded to cite the analytic truism that veritable contact with unconscious components of the psyche can only be the product of a concerted and laborious therapeutic reworking of the past. It is not something that can be summoned up at a moment's notice for artistic purposes, however worthy these might be.

Similarly, his criticism in the preceding citation warns of the dangers of a precipitate appropriation of psychoanalytic concepts. Above all, if the fragmentary imagoes of childhood are transposed *tel quel* into the surrealist collages without having first been conceptually (or therapeutically) deciphered, one runs the risk of promoting unilateral *regression*. This, in Adorno's opinion, is the upshot of surrealist "image fetishism." It recovers images of childhood libidinal attachment not as something first subjected to the healing powers of analytical self-insight ("self-immersion") but in unmediated, inchoate form, that is, qua "fixations." In focusing on the libidinally charged, dismembered torsos that figured so prominently in surrealism as a visual medium, Adorno seems to be operating with analytic concepts borrowed from the "object-relations" school rather than orthodox Freudianism.

At the same time, it is important to register Adorno's insistence that the "imagoes" of the surrealist collages are not reducible to the archaic, dehistoricized images of a Jungian stamp (the Benjaminian conception of archaic wish images would seem to fall victim to this characterization). Instead, their "truth content" seems to lie in a measure of fidelity to the "sociohistorical" present, albeit, a "reified" present, in which, as Adorno expresses it, the "innermost being of the subject appears as something external to it." A distinct sociohistorical component manifests itself in the surrealist montage, insofar as the latter is in large measure composed of veritable fragments of contemporary social life: familiar objects, such as railway tickets, newspaper headlines, and the like. It is precisely in their capacity to convey, however immediately, something of the historical present that surrealist collages avoid lapsing into ideology pure and simple (the case with Jung's archaic images) and establish a relation to truth.

To be sure, Adorno's hesitancies concerning surrealism and its favored technique of montage are already discernible in his criticism of certain of Benjamin's *Passagenwerk*-related studies from the 1930s. Two instances in particular are noteworthy. First, Adorno's epistolary response to Benjamin's 1935 arcades exposé, "Paris, Capital of the Nineteenth Century." Among the numerous elements Adorno found objectionable in this crucial, initial formulation of the designs of the *Passagenwerk* was Benjamin's uncritical employment of the surrealist belief in the sacrosanct character of dream experience. As a motto for what is perhaps the most seminal passage of the exposé, Benjamin cites Michelet's saying, "Chaque époque rêve la suivante" (Every era dreams the following one). He goes on to propound an undeniably fanciful theory whereby the prehistoric past, which Benjamin lauds as a "classless society," has deposited utopian wish images into the collective unconscious, which are reactivated as it were by the utopian potential of high capitalism. As Benjamin observes, "In the dream in which every epoch sees in images the epoch that is to succeed it, the latter appears coupled with elements of prehistory—that is to say, of a classless society. The experiences of this society, which have their storeplace in the collective unconscious, interact with the new to give birth to the utopias which leave their configurations in a thousand traces of life, from permanent buildings to ephemeral fashions."[45] It is precisely these utopian potentials that Benjamin wished to release in the dialectical images of the *Passagenwerk*.

Adorno literally pounces on the more tenuous aspects of Benjamin's construction. He objects stridently to the neoromantic characterization of prehistory as a "Golden Age"—a classless society; also to the uncritical reliance on the Jungian category of the "collective unconscious," which in Adorno's view is a mythological notion designed to mystify contemporary social antagonisms.

His fundamental objection, however, is to Benjamin's pseudosurrealistic attempt to recast the dialectical image as a dream. As he remarks, "If you transpose the dialectical image into consciousness as a dream . . . you also deprive it of the objective liberating power which could legitimate it in materialistic terms. The fetish character of the commodity is not a fact of consciousness; rather, it is dialectical in the eminent sense that it produces consciousness."[46] In other words, by equating the problem of commodity fetishism with the world of dreams, Benjamin risks occluding its true origins in the sphere of production. Hence, he risks reducing problems of material life to "facts of consciousness"—dreams; consequently, Adorno accuses him of an idealist deviation from the original materialist focus of the project. As a problem originating in the sphere of material life, commodity fetishism cannot be resolved—only mystified—by being transposed to the world of dreams, not to mention the specious role played by the Jungian "dreaming collective."

Three years later, Adorno and Benjamin would disagree over the first draft of the latter's Baudelaire study. Again the central point of contention concerned Benjamin's uncritical use of surrealist techniques; in this case, the technique of montage. Because this debate has received its due in the existing secondary literature,[47] I will merely confine myself here to its essentials. Adorno expressed his extreme reservations concerning the montage-inspired methodological orientation of the study, which resulted in an unmediated assemblage of data, wholly devoid of supporting commentary. Adorno could hardly disagree more with Benjamin's statement, "I have nothing to say. Only to show." What Benjamin's essay lacks, above all, according to Adorno, is "mediation." As he observes, "motifs are assembled but not elaborated. Panorama and 'traces,' flaneur and arcades, modernism and the unchanging, without a theoretical interpretation—is this a 'material' which can patiently await interpretation without being consumed by its own aura?"[48] In another passage from his detailed letter of criticism, he raises the following charges: "The theological motif of calling things by their names tends to turn into a wide-eyed presentation of mere facts. If one wished to put it very drastically, one could say that your study is located at the crossroads of magic and positivism. That spot is bewitched. Only theory could break the spell—your own resolute, salutarily speculative theory."[49]

The same principle is at issue in both Adorno's criticism of Benjamin's 1938 Baudelaire essay ("The Paris of the Second Empire in Baudelaire") and his 1956 discussion of surrealism: the unmediated absorption of material elements in montage constructions relapses into a positivist affirmation of the given, unless these elements are arranged according to a preconceived, theoretically informed plan. However, behind this disagreement lie contrasting estimations about the value signs proper to the "material elements." Benjamin wanted to view these as "ambiguous": they contained utopian potentials pointing toward immanent prospects for the realization of the realm of freedom once they were reconstituted in the dialectical image. For Adorno, in contrast, the moment of "negativity" was dominant: these elements were less the portents of an impending golden age than the signs of a Sisyphean, hellish, eternal recurrence: the presentation of the always-the-same as the eternally new that distinguished the logic of commodity fetishism.

In retrospect, Adorno seems to have been right about Benjamin yet wrong concerning surrealism. He was right in the former case insofar as Benjamin overestimated both the inherently redeeming powers of the dialectical image as well as the utopian aspects of a largely prosaic, disenchanted commodity-producing society. Benjamin's primary sin was trying to apply methods of literary analysis to sociological material of a very different order, expecting to produce "epiphanies" proper to the former realm of study in the case of the latter—which, it may be safely said in retrospect, has proven much more intractable than Benjamin imagined. His attempt to apply the aesthetic technique of the dialectical image to recalcitrant historical data thus invites the accusation of "misplaced concreteness": whereas Benjamin might have been able to effect the *aesthetic transfiguration* of social phenomena in the montage sequences of the *Passagenwerk*— following the artistic precedents established by Baudelaire and surrealism—the trajectory of sociohistorical life itself follows an independent developmental logic. In this respect, as a viable piece of social analysis, the *Passagenwerk* would have to supply the dimension of theoretical mediation Adorno found lacking or else succumb to the status of an aesthetically pleasing historical collage. Of course, it is impossible to say precisely what form the finished product might have taken. But on the basis of the evidence available, it seems doubtful that the *Passagenwerk* could have satisfactorily allayed Adorno's pertinent suspicions.

As far as his charge of "image reification" against the surrealists is concerned—the aspect of his critique that has received the most publicity—a more skeptical verdict is in order, though one must cede a measure of cogency to his standpoint. The surrealists were certainly wont to fetishize certain privileged representations, and these at times were distinctly tainted by regressive traits, as Adorno suggests. If Baudelaire could claim that genius was childhood recaptured, then much of modern art attempted to follow his lead in retrieving the element of naiveté that had been lost amid the refinements of civilization. Here, the paintings of Paul Klee, with their childlike insouciance, are models of success. Regression, however, is clearly the risk that any such attempt runs. Like any "ism," surrealism lays itself open to the dangers of formal codification and the attendant hazards of eternally repeating itself. Adorno identifies the historical etiology of this dilemma in his 1956 essay, when he observes that the "shocks" of surrealism lost their power following "the European catastrophe," which conferred an element of normalcy on shock by making it a category of everyday life.

Where Adorno errs, however, is in his attempt to measure surrealism qua artistic movement against standards appropriate to the theoretical sphere. The abdication of subjectivity, the refusal to mediate the component elements of the montage, results in the fetishization of a reified immediacy, argues Adorno. Yet he makes this point after already having exploded the myth of surrealist antisubjectivism: "The subject... is at work much more openly and uninhibitedly in surrealism than in dreams," Adorno readily confesses. In essence, surrealist symbols "prove [to be] much too rationalistic."[50] Contra Adorno, the lack of subjective input he finds in surrealism is probably no greater than in its nineteenth-century literary precursor, symbolism. After all, it was Adorno himself who incisively warned against the dangers of taking the programmatic pronouncements of surrealism at face value (e.g., the one concerning the primacy of the unconscious for automatic writing). He himself was forced to admit that montage, if "correctly done," is "by definition also interpreting."[51] Rigorous standards of theoretical construction, though certainly applicable to a project like Benjamin's, are out of place, however, when brought to bear mechanically on the aesthetic sphere, a fact Adorno readily admitted in other contexts. Finally, it would be a grave error to attempt to extend the charge of "image reification" from surrealism qua visual art form to the *poetic* and *literary* dimensions of the movement, aspects that are certainly less readily assimilable to Adorno's germane montage critique.

In point of fact, however, Adorno's sympathies for surrealism are much greater than may at first appear—a fact that suggests that the inordinate attention conferred on his critical remarks in the 1956 essay is misleading. I would like to develop this point in some detail.

To begin with, one must take cognizance of what was perhaps the pet methodological category of negative dialectics, "constellation," a term whose Benjaminian origins are self-evident. In my discussion of the *Trauerspiel* book, it was asserted that Benjamin's employment of the category reflected protosurrealist stirrings, especially with reference to the category of montage. Does not Adorno's philosophical modus operandi bear the same affinities? Given Adorno's critique of the montage idea of the *Passagenwerk,* this is certainly an analogy one would not want to push too far. Nevertheless, there exist unmistakable parallels between the paratactic, nondiscursive features of Adornian philosophical presentation—all of which hinge on the concept of constellation—and the surrealist technique of montage. This claim holds good as long as one recognizes that in Adorno's case, these thought montages remain *conceptually mediated* to an extreme, unlike those of the surrealists and, on occasion, those of Benjamin.

The procedural centrality of constellation is expressed by Adorno in the following passage from *Negative Dialectics:* "The unifying moment survives, without the negation of the negation, and without having to be responsible to abstraction as the highest principle, insofar as concepts do not progress step by step to the highest general concept, but instead enter into a constellation.... Constellations alone represent from without what the concept has excluded from within: the non-identical [*das Mehr*] that it wants to be so much but cannot."[52] In relying on constellations, Adorno incorporates an *aesthetic* dimension into philosophy in order to save the latter from categorical hierarchies in which the sensuous nature of things themselves is continuously sacrificed on the altar of ascending conceptual abstraction. In this way, he seeks to undo the metaphysical violence perpetrated by traditional techniques of philosophical conceptualization against things themselves, the nonidentical. This design can be achieved only via montage-derived philosophical procedure, for only the latter avoids the traditional philosophical hierarchical ordering of conceptual elements in favor of an equilateral and nondiscriminatory presentation of ideas.

The theoretical complement to Adorno's 1956 reflections on surrealism is provided by the related remarks in his posthumously published masterpiece, *Aesthetic Theory* (1970). These observations represent an elaboration of the conclusion of the earlier surrealism essay, which Adorno ends on an appreciative note, comparing surrealism favorably to the Neue Sachlichkeit, its historical contemporary. Adorno thus relativizes emphatically the negative comments concerning surrealism made earlier in the essay. The movement is lauded for its frank portrayal of the consequences of a repressive and reified social totality, facts denied by Neue Sachlichkeit's sobriety. Surrealist imagery represents

the quintessence of what the *Neue Sachlichkeit* makes taboo because it reminds it of its own object-like nature and its inability to cope with the fact that its rationality remains irrational. Surrealism gathers up the things the *Neue Sachlichkeit* denies to human beings; the distortions attest to the violence that prohibition has done to the objects of desire. Through the distortions, Surrealism salvages what is out of date, an album of idiosyncrasies in which the claim to the happiness that human beings find denied them in their own technified world goes up in smoke. But if Surrealism itself now seems obsolete, it is because human beings are now denying themselves the consciousness of denial that was captured in the photographic negative that was Surrealism.[53]

Surrealist "irrationalism" thus gives the lie to the dominant reality by revealing the bedrock of unreason on which it is based: the prohibition of desire, the perpetual postponement of the *promesse de bonheur.* Its "distortions" are merely the hidden truth of the pretension to objectivity, to being-in-itself, of the reigning social totality.

It is not as though in *Aesthetic Theory* Adorno's attitude toward surrealism has undergone a diametrical volte-face. Instead, his appraisal takes the form of a balanced constellation. The critique of surrealism for succumbing to a (Hegelian) dialectic of "absolute freedom"—in which the impotence of the subject vis-à-vis the external, empirical is revealed—is retained. As Adorno remarks, "Surrealism ... was done in by its illusory belief in an absolutely subjective being-for-itself, which is objectively mediated and cannot go beyond being-for-itself in the domain of art."[54]

Surrealism is also praised on many counts, however. It is, for example, lauded, along with impressionism, for having "put spontaneity on the agenda" of aesthetic modernism (AT 36). In a discussion that amplifies the conclusion of the 1956 essay, Adorno argues that "[c]urrents like expressionism and surrealism, the irrationality of which was highly disturbing to some, acted up against repression, authority and obscurantism" (AT 82). Rather than serving as a confirmation of a reified social order, as some would claim, irrationalism and the "chaotic features of authentic modern art ... are the ciphers of a critique of a spurious second nature; they seem to be saying: 'This is how chaotic your order actually is'" (AT 138). For Adorno, the use of irrational elements, for example, the "fantastic" dimension of surrealist painting, performs a crucial defetishizing function over against the dominant reality principle, whose rigidity and inflexibleness are thereby unmasked: the latter is indicted by what it refuses to tolerate. The social superego and its accompanying array of taboos and prohibitions is thus confronted with the absurdity of its own restrictions: "Look how easily things could be otherwise," might be taken as the secret motto of much surrealist art. For analogous reasons, Adorno endorses the "shock effects" of surrealist montage. In montage, "the paradox that the operation of a rationalized world is a result of historical becoming is perceived as shock: ... the sensory apparatus of the individual is traumatized by the discovery that the rational is actually irrational" (AT 440). The shock effect defetishizes by exploding the pretense of a rationalized capitalist life world to being natural and eternal. This realization is produced via the deconstruction and remounting of the everyday imagery of the life world itself, whose transient, historical character thus stands exposed.

Perhaps the most startling turnabout in *Aesthetic Theory* relating to surrealism is Adorno's concerted attempt to legitimate the category of montage. Certain dangers still inhere in montage as an artistic technique: "What makes montage feeble is its inability to expose individual elements...[its] adapting the ready-made material supplied from outside" (AT 83). Yet there are no artistic procedures immune from abuse—not even Schönberg's employment of the twelve-tone system.

Aside from this by-now-familiar criticism, Adorno goes out of his way to indicate the many positive contributions of montage. For one, montage effectuates a praiseworthy change in conventional habits of perception: as a technique that "reached its zenith with surrealism... montage shuffles and reshuffles elements of reality as seen by healthy common sense so as to wrest from them a change in direction" (AT 83). "Montage," Adorno observes, "arose in opposition to mood-laden art" (i.e., impressionism), which sought "to redeem aesthetically what was alienated and heterogeneous." For Adorno, this was a "flimsy conception, all the more so since the supremacy of prosaic thing-likeness over the living subject just kept increasing." Montage appeared on the scene in salutary contrast to all romanticizing, aesthetic tendencies, in order thereby to give the lie to premature ideological claims to universal harmony and well-being. Montage, which may be defined as the independence of individual elements vis-à-vis the whole, proves fatal to traditional conceptions of organic totality and thereby testifies to a permanent condition of non-identity. As Adorno comments,

It is against this romantic turn that montage reacted negatively. Montage goes back to the cubist practice of pasting newspaper clippings onto paintings, and so on. The illusion that art had of becoming reconciled with external reality through figuration was to be destroyed; the non-illusory debris of real life was to be let into the work; no bones were to be made about the break between the two; indeed, this break was to be used to good aesthetic effect.... Works of art that negate meaning must be able to articulate discontinuity; this is the role played by montage. Montage disavows unity by stressing the disparity of the parts while at the same time affirming unity as a principle of form. (AT 222)

Yet montage never remains wholly free of the danger of the "capitulation by art before what is different from it."

There are other features of surrealism that come in for special praise by Adorno as well. Surrealism represents the deathblow to the staid academicism of all neoclassical art. In it, the images of antiquity are toppled from their Platonic heaven: "In Max Ernst's work they roam about like phantoms among the late nineteenth-century middle class, for which art, neutralized to the form of a cultural heritage, had in fact become a ghost. Wherever those movements which temporarily touched base with Picasso and others focused on antiquity, it was in order to depict it as hell" (AT 415).

Adorno also acknowledges the surrealist dialectic of "art and anti-art," a tension that would define so much of artistic modernism. "The surrealist successors of Dadaism rejected art without being able to shake it off completely" (AT 44), he observes. "Surrealism once undertook to rebel against the fetishistic segregation of art as a sphere unto itself. But surrealism moved beyond pure protest and became art" (AT 325). Yet this ultimate rapprochement with what surrealism once scorned is in no way a compromise with its original intentions (with the notable exception of Dali, whom Adorno describes as a "jet-set painter"). Instead, this development signaled a process of maturation for surrealism, once it was recognized that the Dadaist procedures of bluff and provocation had themselves been recuperated by the insatiable bourgeois appetite for culture and elevated into a new aesthetic norm. Instead, surrealism now sought, unlike Dada, to undo bourgeois aestheticism from within, producing a new, deaestheticized version. As Adorno notes, "eminent surrealists like Max Ernst and André Masson who refused any collusion with commercial interests moved towards accepting formal principles... as the idea of shocking people wore off and needed to be replaced by a mode of painting. The step to non-representationality was taken at the moment when surrealists decided to expose the accustomed reality as illusion by illuminating it with the aid of a photographic flash, as it were" (AT 363).

In light of such remarks, the widespread belief that Adorno simply rejected surrealism in favor of a quasi-mandarin attachment to the music of the Vienna school or to "high" modernism in general would seem in need of substantial revision. Certainly, his critique of surrealism (both the 1956 and 1970 versions) was an indirect response to the methodological failings of Benjamin's *Passagenwerk;* that is, Benjamin's materialist conception of the dialectical image as an unmediated montage of *faits sociaux*. This concern accounts for the oftenascerbic character of his surrealism critique. As I have tried to show, his fundamental charge of "image reification" is certainly not without foundation. At the same time, his positive valuation of the movement's worth must also be recognized. It is a valuation that hinges on the surrealist dialectic of "art and anti-art": surrealism continues the Dadaist assault on bourgeois aestheticism—that is, on the bourgeois conception of art as highbrow divertissement; yet it astutely perceives that this assault "terminated in something trivial" (AT 44): infinite repetition or self-caricature. The question surrealism faces then is this: how does one continue to create art after the Dadaist unmasking of the extreme complacency of bourgeois aestheticism? The answer given by surrealism—and that aspect which Adorno singles out for praise—is that one incorporates the Dadaist antiaestheticist critique into the very heart of the work of art. In contrast to Dadaism, this means one still has "works of art." Yet these represent works of art of an entirely different nature from the *affirmative* works of the bourgeois tradition. Instead one is left with deaestheticized works of art: works of art that divest themselves voluntarily of the aura of affirmation, in which the moment of refusal or negativity is embodied in the work a priori.[55] For Adorno, this trait represents the hallmark of all authentic modern art.

Notes

1. Adorno's phrase in *Negative Dialectics* (New York: Seabury Press, 1973), p. 3.

2. An all too neglected step in this direction has been taken by Heinz Paetzold in *Neomarxistische Äesthetik* (Düsseldorf: Pädagogischer Verlag Schwann, 1974), 2 vols.

3. Walter Benjamin, *Passagenwerk*, vol. 1 (Frankfurt: Suhrkamp, 1983), p. 588.

4. Walter Benjamin, *Briefe*, vol. 1, ed. G. Scholem and T. W. Adorno (Frankfurt: Suhrkamp, 1966), p. 390. For a comprehensive discussion of Benjamin's relation to surrealism, see Margaret Cohen, *Profane Illuminations: Walter Benjamin and the Paris of the Surrealist Revolution* (Berkeley: University of California Press, 1993).

5. Benjamin, *Briefe*, vol. 1, p. 663.

6. Walter Benjamin, "Das Programm der kommenden Philosophie," *Gesammelte Schriften* 2:1 (Frankfurt: Suhrkamp, 1974), p. 158.

7. Ibid., p. 159.

8. Ibid.

9. Ibid., p. 160.

10. Ibid., p. 159; emphasis added.

11. Fredric Jameson, *Marxism and Form: Twentieth-Century Dialectical Theories of Literature* (Princeton: Princeton University Press, 1971), p. 96.

12. André Breton, *Manifestoes of Surrealism* (Ann Arbor: University of Michigan Press, 1969), p. 14.

13. Richard Wolin, *Walter Benjamin: An Aesthetic of Redemption* (Berkeley: University of California Press, 1994); see especially pp. 79–106. See also Susan Buck-Morss, *The Origin of Negative Dialectics: Theodor W. Adorno, Walter Benjamin and the Frankfurt Institute* (New York: Free Press, 1977).

14. Cf. Peter Bürger, *Theory of the Avant Garde* (Minneapolis: University of Minnesota Press, 1984), p. 72. For Bürger, surrealism becomes the paradigm of the "historical avant-garde." I have criticized Bürger's interpretation of surrealism, in my essay "Communism and the Avant-Garde," *Thesis eleven* no. 12 (August 1985): 81–93.

15. Walter Benjamin, *The Origin of German Tragic Drama* (London: NLB, 1977), p. 33.

16. Benjamin, *Passagenwerk*, vol. 1, pp. 491–92.

17. Franz Rosenzweig, *Der Stern der Erlösung* (Frankfurt: J. Kauffmann, 1921, The Hague: Nijhoff, 1976), p. 323. For a conceptual history of *nunc stans*, see *Historisches Wörterbuch der Philosophie*, vol. 6 (Darmstadt: Wissenschaftliche Buchgesellschaft, 1986), pp. 990–91.

18. Benjamin, *Origin of German Tragic Drama*, p. 34.

19. Ibid.

20. Ernst Bloch, "Revueform in der Philosophie," in *Erbschaft dieser Zeit* (Frankfurt: Suhrkamp, 1962), pp. 367–71.

21. Ernst Bloch, "Erinnerungen," in Adorno et al., *Über Walter Benjamin* (Frankfurt: Suhrkamp, 1970), pp. 22–23.

22. Bloch, *Erbschaft dieser Zeit*, p. 371.

23. Benjamin, *Passagenwerk*, vol. 1, p. 574.

24. It should be pointed out that Rolf Tiedemann, editor of the magisterial six-volume edition of Benjamin's work, has recently challenged Adorno's idea that the *Passagenwerk* was to consist of a "montage of citations." Cf. "Einleitung des Herausgebers," *Passagenwerk*, vol. 1, p. 13.

25. Bloch, "Erinnerungen," p. 22.

26. Benjamin, *Passagenwerk*, vol. 1, p. 574.

27. For Adorno's systematic epistemological reflections on the problem, see the section of *Negative Dialectics* entitled "Vorrang des Objekts," mistranslated in English as "Preponderance of the Object."

28. Benjamin, *Briefe,* vol. 2, pp. 489, 496.

29. Ibid., p. 491.

30. Benjamin, "Surrealism," in *Reflections: Essays, Aphorisms, Autobiographical Writings* (New York: Harcourt Brace Jovanovich, 1978), p. 179.

31. Breton, *Manifestoes of Surrealism,* p. 241.

32. Benjamin, *Reflections,* pp. 181–82.

33. Breton, *Manifestoes of Surrealism,* p. 241.

34. T. W. Adorno, *Über Walter Benjamin* (Frankfurt, 1970), pp. 53–54.

35. The Marx citation can be found in *The Marx-Engels Reader,* ed. Robert C. Tucker (New York: Norton, 1978), p. 15. It is cited by Benjamin on p. 583 of the *Passagenwerk.*

36. The first two quotations are from pp. 1002 and 580 of the *Passagenwerk.* The ensuing citations are culled from the section entitled "City of Dreams, Future-Dreams, Anthropological Nihilism," pp. 493–96.

37. Benjamin, "Paris, die Hauptstadt des XIX. Jahrhunderts," *Passagenwerk,* p. 55.

38. Benjamin, *Passagenwerk,* p. 499.

39. Ibid., p. 491–92.

40. In terms of the general aesthetics of Critical Theory, it would be extremely germane to examine Herbert Marcuse's attempt to integrate surrealist principles. Marcuse's major discussion of surrealism can be found in *An Essay on Liberation* (Boston: Beacon Press, 1969).

41. Cf. Buck-Morss, *The Origin of Negative Dialectics;* Eugene Lunn, *Marxism and Modernism: An Historical Study of Lukács, Brecht, Benjamin, and Adorno* (Berkeley: University of California Press, 1982); and Martin Jay, *Marxism and Totality: The Adventures of a Concept from Lukács to Habermas* (Berkeley: University of California Press, 1984) and *Adorno* (Cambridge, Mass.: Harvard University Press, 1984), p. 129.

42. For a representative sampling of Lukács's aesthetic judgments, one might consult the following of his works: *Realism in Our Time: Literature and the Class Struggle* (New York: Harper & Row, 1964), *Studies in European Realism* (New York: Grosset & Dunlap, 1964), and *Essays on Thomas Mann* (New York: Grosset & Dunlap 1965). See also the discussion by Lunn, *Marxism and Modernism,* pp. 75–145.

43. T. W. Adorno, *Philosophy of Modern Music* (New York: Seabury Press, 1973), p. 51.

Richard Wolin

44. T. W. Adorno, "Looking Back on Surrealism," in *Notes to Literature*, vol. 1, pp. 86–90. The German original can be found in *Noten zur Literatur*, vol. 1 (Frankfurt: Suhrkamp, 1958), pp. 155–62.

45. Walter Benjamin, *Charles Baudelaire: A Lyric Poet in the Era of High Capitalism* (London: NLB, 1973), p. 159.

46. T. W. Adorno, in Ernst Bloch et al., *Aesthetics and Politics* (London: Verso, 1977), p. 111.

47. Cf. Buck-Morss, *The Origin of Negative Dialectics; Lunn, Marxism and Modernism*, pp. 162–72; Wolin, *Walter Benjamin: An Aesthetic of Redemption*, pp. 198–207.

48. Adorno, in *Aesthetics and Politics*, p. 167.

49. Ibid., pp. 129–30.

50. Adorno, "Looking Back on Surrealism," p. 87.

51. Cited in Buck-Morss, *The Origin of Negative Dialectics*, p. 269n.

52. Adorno, *Negative Dialektik* (Frankfurt: Suhrkamp, 1966), p. 162.

53. Adorno, "Looking Back on Surrealism," p. 90.

54. T. W. Adorno, *Aesthetic Theory*, trans. C. Lenhardt (London: Routledge & Kegan Paul, 1984), p. 44. All subsequent references will appear in parenthesis.

55. Cf. R. Wolin, "The De-aestheticization of Art: On Adorno's *Aesthetische Theorie*," *Telos* 41 (fall 1979): 105–27.

5

Concept, Image, Name: On Adorno's Utopia of Knowledge

Rolf Tiedemann

In memory of Leo Löwenthal

The true might be neither whole nor a part: this insight, implicitly a critique of knowledge, can be reached through an immanent analysis of these concepts themselves. Indeed, Adorno does reach it this way in *Against Epistemology: A Metacritique.* The insight leads Adorno to the aphorism that the whole is, in any case, false,[1] a maxim evident from experience itself—if not provided by insight alone—and which meanwhile has proliferated incomparably since Adorno put it down in a notebook in August of 1942.[2] Certainly, the "whole" may mean something different in each of the following two cases. For Hegel, in *The Phenomenology of Spirit,* the true is precisely the whole, absolute knowledge existing in and for itself; in *Minima Moralia,* which in 1951 finally carried Adorno's maxim into print, the whole is real society. Yet this difference does not amount to much; as Adorno observed repeatedly, conceptual equivocations reveal, in any state of affairs, an objective commonality. Negative dialectics discerns—even in the most abstract epistemological categories—the compulsive nexus of real domination. For this, of course, the price must be paid. Persisting even in the face of the negation of the negation (an equation no longer certain, mechanically, to yield the positive), the truth of negative dialectics has become aporetic; in Adorno's words, it has become a fragile, vulnerable thing. If the societal whole is false, and its untruth pervades the whole of thought, then it is only with utopian intention that one can speak of "true society" (with the emphasis Adorno's thinking so provocatively employs). Because knowledge has been misconstructed as the unity of perception and concept, a true construction of knowledge would instead *fulfill* the concept, which can be construed solely from the perspective of the messianic. To the perpetual annoyance of those who underwrite the belief that what cannot be will not be, Adorno unswervingly defends this perspective. Though Adorno would ultimately turn against it, his thought nonetheless further developed Ernst Bloch's version of the "*single* idea of utopia and breakthrough,"[3] which Bloch introduced into philosophy. Without utopian thinking, negative dialectics could hardly have traced the ontology of the false state of things: that what is, is not everything, nor really yet anything at all. This is what one would like to call (following Schopenhauer's pronouncement on death) the "inspirational genius or the Mousagetas"[4] of Adorno's philosophy—if one only could be certain not thereby to add fuel to the fire of those who think they can incinerate this philosophy with a triumphant "Everything is mere aesthetics." Once, someone even blurted it out: after attesting to "how splendorously conceived" the *Minima Moralia* was, Botho Strauss did not recoil from the unspeakable sentence: "Without the dialectic, from the get go we think more stupidly; but it has to be: without it!"[5] *Why* stupidity must be is to be read on the preceding page: "Writing also means going against the individual gaze, fending off the specifying detail. We have lived too long from the richness of difference. Coarseness and sameness are the interesting thing; reality is inconsequential."[6] Thought must forbid itself individuation and differentiation, because they bring to mind that reality still does without them. Such writing as Adorno's, which insistently troubles itself over every detail and, where it has found the appropriate detail, at least in thought anticipates something of fullness and richness—even fulfillment and happiness—again and again provokes rancor. Such writing transgresses the primordial bourgeois taboos on incest and exogamy. For Adorno, and perhaps this is always the case, the dominant work ethic remains bound to the pregenital phases and thus repressed; utopia is the erotic counterpart to this ethic. Although during its glory years psychoanalysis provided the model of the repression of the nether regions (reminiscent of privies and cloacae) and all that remained regressive in the face of civilization, in its wake, one would rather repress that which transcends civilization even by the most minuscule amount: the thought that is merely well formulated but termed "splendorous." Better to comport oneself according to the coarseness and sameness that is, treacherously enough, called "interesting." "Mere aesthetics" is not the thinking of Adorno but rather the decisionism of stupidity that orients itself masochistically to the "inconsequential." Meanwhile, such stupidity continues—abundance lying before its eyes—if only in the reflection of what it nonetheless denounces as the "splendor" of Adorno's thought. "Inconsequential reality" means in the end to let the world play out as it is, against "splendor" and its promise of abundance. This amounts to the sabotage of possibility.[7] To this, Adorno, like Bloch, never lent himself.

Already in 1960, when Bloch's *Principle of Hope* appeared in West Germany, Jürgen Habermas noted the minimal exchange value of utopia. Today, in light of the ghosts of renewed or reunified nationalisms, utopia is not handled at all, traded on the stock markets of neither science nor society. Arnold Gehlen's well-known thesis that history has reached its plateau, that qualitative changes can no longer be expected in either the base or the superstructure, and that we have arrived, finally, at posthistory, was to a large extent implicitly accepted, even in the politically left camp. Theoreticians like Foucault or Derrida—not to mention their German acolytes—in this respect hardly distinguish themselves from the first structuralists or belated Schmittians like Jacob Taubes. To the theories of postmodernity, so fashionable in the 1980s, Adorno's philosophy might at least have offered an occasion for irritation. Insofar as the former did not simply derive their central motifs from the latter, they inevitably found themselves anticipated by it. Whether it is the infirmity of ratio or history coming to a halt or the supposed borrowing of knowledge from art, all are arrows from *Dialectic of Enlightenment, Negative Dialectics,* or *Aesthetic Theory,* drawn from the quiver to be used, though in a terribly dulled condition, for deconstruction. In every Adornian category, the tips of critique are turned toward society and against the thinking that is one with society—such tips had to be broken off before they could serve as playing pieces in the happy, fully nonirritating game that postmodernism claimed itself to represent, the game it intended as the prelude for the ascent of posthistory. Just as the eclecticism of postmodern architecture merely appears different from the Alexandrian, some of these playing pieces may appear to distinguish themselves from their Adornian originals only by a nuance. The interpretive immersion in inherited texts, which Adorno supported and practiced, is nuance nonetheless aiming at the whole; naturally, postmodernism wants to know nothing of this, and so knows nothing. Still other concepts essential to Adorno's philosophy are also missing in postmodernism. The whole merely one of them, history yet another, utopia together with its theological archetype of reconciliation a third. Not inappropriately, postmodernism has been defined as a modernism that has taken its leave of history and emerged without utopia. As the placeholders of utopian thought, Bloch and Adorno are also, as always, heretical Marxists, completely unsusceptible to any departure from history. Though utopia may have portrayed itself to them as, in a certain sense, the end of history—as Adorno formulates it, "it could be said that progress occurs where it ends"[8]—by the same token, they did not imagine "true society" could be produced in any way other than through historical labor. They are thus in agreement with Marx, who knew that the "true realm of freedom" can only "blossom with the realm of necessity as its basis," and who, regarding freedom's construction, added lapidarily, "The shortening of the work-day is the basic condition."[9] In light of the final solution, be it ecological or nuclear—the preparation for which always appears to be the most effective means of ensuring employment—it is unlikely, indeed improbable, that utopia will ever be realized. As always, the thought of utopia is possible only when it finds fragmentary points of reference in the here and now. Thus Bloch derives utopia from the "traces" he finds in the unassuming, irrelevant, and apocryphal, and Adorno follows his lead: it is expressly from the details that Adorno's thinking hopes for something other than the dominant madness.[10] Still, the philosopher of *Negative Dialectics* could not concede that hope is a *principle*. He criticizes Bloch for undertaking to construe the "form of the unconstruable question," for hammering together the edifice of a system—as great as it is violent—in which things ultimately happen not so very differently from other systems. Systems and principles are sublimated forms of the domination of nature, forms that fall prey to the "Dialectic of Enlightenment." Therein, the concrete can appear only in a truncated form—cut short, robbed of its best, robbed indeed of that quality whereby everyone already can be and is witness to utopia. The "appearance" (*Vor-Schein*) in intentionless things that Bloch made fruitful for philosophical theory in *Traces* (*Spuren*) is "levelled off to intention" in *The Principle of Hope*, in which "the color Bloch is after becomes gray when it becomes total."[11] Adorno defends the imagelessness of utopia against the positivistic collecting and cataloging of image worlds in Bloch's work; Adorno's defense is the biblical "thou shalt make no graven images," secularized and translated into the profane. The prohibition against what Adorno calls the "painting in" of utopia returns almost topically: against utopias identified as such or designed with specific content. Utopia is not determinable as that which *should* be; "should be" is much more consistently amalgamated with determination, with domineering subjectivity—just that totalitarianism which utopia wants to reconcile. According to Adorno, thinking knows nothing of reconciliation except through determinate negation, whereby thinking can show in what exists only why it is *not* the "true whole." What the true whole would be, thinking cannot anticipate.[12] Yet each of Adorno's thoughts, even without the hope of being able to suffice, unmistakably lays claim to the whole truth. Their assertiveness is founded in what *Negative Dialectics* calls "the conduct of language": where language in philosophy "appears essentially as language, becomes a form of representation,"[13] here is where Adorno's thinking ascertains its methexis in the utopian.

In 1969, in an essay written directly after Adorno's death, indeed as a sort of necrology, "The Primal History of Subjectivity—Self-Affirmation Gone Wild," Habermas employs a sentence from *Negative Dialectics* that comes the closest of any of Adorno's to what one could call a definition of his concept of utopia: "The reconciled condition would not be the philosophical imperialism of annexing the alien. Instead, its happiness would lie in the fact that the alien, in the proximity it is granted, remains what is distant and different, beyond the heterogeneous and beyond that which is one's own."[14] Thus, Adorno; but Habermas continues:

He who reflects on this sentence will realize that the circumscribed condition, although never real, is our closest and best known one. It has the structure of cohabitation in noncoercive communication. And we necessarily anticipate the latter according to its form each time we want to speak the truth. The idea of truth, which was implied in the very first spoken sentence, allows itself, namely, to be built solely on the ideal of the idealized consensus reached in communication free of domination. In this respect the truth of assertions is bound to the intention of a true life.[15]

Clearly, this is no interpretation of Adorno's sentence on the "reconciled condition," nor does it wish to be. It is the beginning of the "theory of communicative action": an attempt at founding critical theory anew as language philosophy or, one could say, at overcoming critical theory and negative dialectics. According to Habermas, the transformation of negative dialectics into the theory of communicative action follows a systematic obligation to which Adorno did not want to bow, even if he supposedly stood under its objective subjugation. In what follows, instead of discussing the necessity and conclusiveness of the Habermasian project, it will merely be asked whether Adorno's theory actually proceeds inconsistently when it does not bow to this pressure, or whether it does not have, in the end, other grounds to show for its utopian thought, its idea of universal reconciliation. This is a philological formulation of the question, which can be handled quite readily by means of immanent interpretation, or which might just as easily be served by a systematic interpretation with specific interests. Adorno would have admitted that the truth of assertions is bound to the intention of a "true life" as surely as he would have refused to recognize this intention in the structures of colloquial speech, however idealized. But Adorno's philosophy knows that it guarantees its idea of reconciliation through language. Ultimately, reconciliation is due less to any systematic obligation than to a historical-philosophical necessity, though Adorno's philosophy also claims that it is grounded in precisely that moment in language when the communication of people with one another is at odds with itself: *in language as an autonomous moment.*

As an expression of the thing itself, language is not fully reducible to communication with others. Nor, however...is it simply independent of communication.... Language as expression of the thing itself and language as communication are interwoven. The ability to name the matter at hand is developed under the compulsion to communicate it, and that element of coercion is preserved in it; conversely, it could not communicate anything that it did not have as its own intention, undistracted by other considerations. This dialectic plays itself out within the medium of language itself; it is not merely a fall from grace on the part of an inhumane social zeal that watches to make sure that no one thinks anything that cannot be communicated.[16]

Language "as something autonomous"[17] is the opposite of language as communication. Autonomous, it does not exhaust itself striving for the "expression of the thing itself" but "incorporates the expression of nature into language"; it is "the act in which the human being becomes language, the flesh becomes word."[18] What stands here before his eyes Adorno first saw truly realized in art, in the works of Eichendorff and Rudolf Borchardt. Here, too, lies one of the roots of his affinity to Beckettian solipsism, whose untenability as a philosophical doctrine he no doubt realized. In a certain sense, the expression of the incommunicable is philosophical language's only object, the only object of the labor and exertion of the theoretical mind. Yet, in a treatise written at the beginning of the 1960s, Adorno observes the opposite: "communication dictated by the market...weighs upon language to such an extent that language forcibly puts a stop to communication in order to resist the conformity of what positivism calls 'ordinary language'."[19] With this pronouncement, Adorno both foreshadows the manner in which his radical critique will later be turned against him and substitutes his dialectical presentation of things for the implicit, conventional discourse on them.[20] The topography of traditional philosophy can be discerned in Adorno's thought without much violence. His work includes epistemology as well as social theory; the philosophy of history, moral philosophy, and aesthetics are also represented. One discipline of the inherited canon is largely missing: one finds language-philosophical theorems only scattered and piecemeal, and often in enigmatic abbreviation. Yet in the objects of Adorno's philosophizing, language possesses a special dignity, one reminiscent of Humboldt. The paramount significance that Adorno always accorded questions of representation culminates at last in the work on his unfinished *Aesthetic Theory*, in which he describes a model, fashioned after Hölderlin, of a paratactic representational form. The model tries to draw the consequences for linguistic form from the content of thought—the annihilation of a privileged first, the πεῶτον of the philosophical tradition—and searches for a form that might transcend hierarchically ordered argumentation, beyond hypotactic subordination to language. Under given social conditions in which not all are equal nor is everything equidistant, it is more than questionable whether philosophy can speak such a language. That Adorno is so broodingly devoted to language proves that, for him, at least, the function of language, especially as he sees it used poetically in Hölderlin, qualitatively outweighs the standard function of philosophy.[21] Language is not one of the objects of Adorno's thought but the medium and driver of his thinking. Just as, on the one hand, Adorno's critical enterprise, construed on Kantian grounds as the critique of foundational philosophy and positivism, was always the critique of both language and of the restrictions logic places on language, on the other hand, he developed the utopian from the idea of a language in which word and thing might unite without truncation or violence.

The language of philosophical knowledge is the language of concepts and logical forms; in it, conceptuality terminates in judgments and conclusions. Knowledge employs language as a means or a tool, without encountering it as purposive in itself. If the full demand of language is thereby resigned, such resignation is necessary; it is the presupposition of enlightenment that it aims at "liberating men from fear and establishing their sovereignty,"[22] as rulers over nature, since nature inspires fear only so long as it remains unknown. What Horkheimer and Adorno register in *Dialectic of Enlightenment* is that enlightenment has not completed its program. Nature perfectly subjugated has not thereby brought about the freedom of human beings but multiplied their fear. The historical failure of enlightenment is grounded in an instrumental reason that rules history and amounts to nothing but dominance over nature. The resignation that lies at the very origin of discursive knowledge, irrevocable as it is, nonetheless demands—according to *Dialectic of Enlightenment*—renewed reflection to reliquify knowledge. In *Against Epistemology: A Metacritique* and in *Negative Dialectics,* Adorno attempts to carry through in detail such "second reflection" for the conceptuality of philosophical language. In the face of a thing as itself, every concept resigns. A concept meets a thing only particularly by reducing its specificity to that wherein it agrees with other specificities: its generality. Concepts are characteristic units of whatever is grouped under them. Striving for the formal sameness of things, they seek "something objective... [that] is subjectively captured by means of a fixed concept."[23] Words betray what conceptualization demands: grasping, touching, and catching are the forms according to which concepts seize on objects. They confiscate them, turn them into property, and therewith make them arbitrarily available. In *Against Epistemology*, the mechanism of concept building is ascertained as deriving from the character of numbers: mathematicization's "accountability of the stock"[24] is the prerequisite for its collecting and administrating. In data banks, each individual is entered as an abstract number, to be called up at will for purposes of manipulation or supervision. Such data banks stand at the end of a development that began when the Socrates of the *Phaedo* refused to view things for himself and instead took refuge in concepts.[25] Conceptualization is one with abstraction. The reduction of concrete things to what is identical in concepts is, in Adorno's formulation, nothing other than the reflexive form of a society whose "standard structure" is reflected in the form of exchange.[26] The form of rationality most available to this society is that of abstraction, since only abstraction permits equating real differences by disregarding them, thereby enabling the exchange of commodities. Abstraction is the calculating rationality of the capitalist, who is interested not in use value but profit. Just as profit is the balance after the entire cost of production is subtracted,[27] so the objectivity of instrumental knowledge is residual: it is what remains after the abstraction from all that is nonconceptual in the elements. Abstraction is untruth that is nevertheless true. Untrue, it deceives about the very thing it depends on: full concretion. True, it is the precise expression of the fact that the concrete humans of commodity society are being swindled. From here it appears but a small step to the insight that the people cheat themselves and that they need not, yet this step is also the longest, since it must reach beyond society as it is. Even negative dialectics cannot want to eliminate abstraction only to substitute another type of knowledge that would recoil, impotent, from reality. Negative dialectics is not the unmediated reflection of the thing but the reflection of what hinders perceiving the thing as it is. It is a reflection of the social limitation of knowledge, a reflection possible only through abstraction and conceptual language. Such reflection does not want to leap beyond discursivity but "wants to use concepts to pry open... [what] cannot be accommodated by concepts."[28] Although Adorno never shied away from speaking definitively of the knowledge that hovered before him, he always bound it to the conceptual: "The utopia of knowledge would be to disclose the nonconceptual with concepts while not imitating them."[29] And yet the nonconceptual—the thing itself, the fully concrete, the true object, the nonidentical and unintentional—are concepts by which Adorno attempted to describe something that might be other than a category's own example. This something has not already been given, nor is it waiting to be found in some place knowledge has not yet penetrated. It would first "come to fulfillment only in the development of [its] social, historical, and human significance"[30] but retains its potential in abstract concepts, and this necessitates going beyond their rigid fixation on closure. Negative dialectics seeks to satisfy this constraint and to do so—after the categories have once and for all classified what is and brought it to stasis—in such a manner as to again open the categories to the new. In this sense, negative dialectics is not the attempt simply to continue translating language into logic but, finally, "to bring logic to speak."[31]

Whatever remains necessarily inaccessible to language as a mere semiotic system Adorno's thinking tries to approach by another path: that of the *interpretation of images*. As early as his 1931 introductory academic lecture, "The Actuality of Philosophy," Adorno set up a program from which he has never strayed, that of philosophy as interpretation: philosophy should not break open reality by intentionality but should read the unintentional itself. From texts philosophy should transform and decipher the puzzling figures of being; it should, as *Dialectic of Enlightenment* phrases it, "interpret... as writing" the images into which the world has shriveled before physiognomic sight.[32] Adorno inherits this program from Benjamin; it is that of the *Passagenwerk*, which sought to "put to the test the extent to which it is possible to be 'concrete' in the context of the philosophy of history."[33] Such a concretion Benjamin expected to gain from the presentation of the most recent past—in the case of the *Passagenwerk*, the Paris of the nineteenth century—as an ensemble of dialectical images. The development of the theory of dialectical or historical images has not been passed down fully in written form. Benjamin himself never found his way to a more exhaustive explication of the category of the dialectical image; the term never once appears in the texts published during his lifetime. It reached the public only via Adorno's *Habilitation* thesis, published in 1933, in reference to its Benjaminian origin. There Adorno writes that, in such images (just as in the Kierkegaardian *intérieur*), the dialectic comes to a standstill; he cites "the mythical in the historically most recent as the distant past: nature as proto-history."[34] Apparently, the theory of dialectical images was developed mainly in conversations between Benjamin and Adorno, and, on at least one of these occasions, which Benjamin later called "historical,"[35] Horkheimer also took part. These conversations traced the entwining of myth and the new, of the ever-same (*Immergleichem*) and history, back to the commodity fetishism analyzed by Marx. This is confirmed in a 1935 letter in which Adorno informs Horkheimer about the first draft of the *Passagenwerk*. He characterizes Benjamin's project as "an attempt to disclose the nineteenth century as 'style' through the category of the commodity as a dialectical image," and he continues:

This conception has you to thank, as much as it is dear to me (and as indebted to it as I have been for many years). In that memorable conversation ... that you, Benjamin and I ... carried on years ago about dialectical images, you were the one who claimed that this characteristic of the historical image was central to the commodity, and from that talk dates a definite reconfiguration of the corresponding thought of Benjamin and myself. The Kierkegaard book contains it rudimentarily, the *Passagenwerk* draft fully and explicitly.[36]

Without attempting to detail the transformations the theory of dialectical images has undergone, let alone trying to explicate the variance between Adorno's version and Benjamin's, let a 1962 passage of Adorno's exemplify what he, at any rate, understood by "dialectical images." From the essay "Progress," in the collection *Interventions and Catchwords,*

The interlocking of the ever-same and the new in the exchange relation manifests itself in the *imagines* of progress under bourgeois industrialism. What seems paradoxical about these *imagines* is that something different ever appears at all, that the *imagines* grow old, since the ever-sameness of the exchange principle intensifies by virtue of technology into the domination by repetition within the sphere of production. The life process itself ossifies in the expression of the ever-same: hence the shock of photographs from the nineteenth century and even the early twentieth century. The absurdity explodes: that something happens where the phenomenon says that nothing more could happen: its disposition becomes terrifying. In this experience of terror, the terror of the system forcibly coalesces into appearance; the more the system expands, the more it hardens into what it has always been. What Benjamin called "dialectic at a standstill" is surely less a Platonizing residue than the attempt to raise such paradoxes to philosophical consciousness. Dialectical images: these are the historically objective archetypes of that antagonistic unity of standstill and movement which defines the most universal bourgeois concept of progress.[37]

In a philosophy that holds definitions as suspect as Adorno's, it is extraordinary to see the definition form applied to one of its most central, certainly most expounded-on theorems. This much may be clear from the citation: dialectical images are in no way something for which concepts could or should be substituted. As Adorno occasionally prodded Benjamin about,[38] such images are not facts of consciousness but produce a most specific consciousness: alienation under the conditions of market society. Dialectical images are a means of looking at historical material and helping to bring it to expression; this helping into expression, this interpretation, however, is quite unimaginable except through concepts. So concepts also constitute the material of philosophy, for Adorno—each one "prejudiced in favor of idealism."[39] The theory of dialectical images seeks to correct such leanings, just as later *Negative Dialectics* seeks to correct, to a certain degree, the encroaching prioritizing of the object. Indeed, no philosophy can "glue" material "into its texts," like the method of many montage techniques. Nonetheless, philosophy can try to absorb material by sinking itself interpretively into the material's blindness and opacity and deciphering its figures. Further, the theory of images does not aim to be ahistorical or universal. It is the theory of historically exact, particularized images: those from the superstructure of commodity-producing society. Adorno, like Benjamin, tests the theory exclusively on images belonging to the nineteenth century. The interpretation the images undergo is a negative one; it follows the model of determinate negation. But if the dialectic "interprets every image as writing," the following should also be valid: "It [the dialectic] shows how the admission of its [the image's] falsity is to be read in the lines of its features—a confession that deprives it of its power and appropriates it for truth. [Thereby, language becomes more than a mere semiotic system.]"[40]

How can interpretive language that turns to historical images be more than mere semiotics; how is it able to burst the bounds of abstract-discursive language? The question leads at first to the distinct contradictoriness according to which Adorno treated the problem of the givenness of images. In the quotation from the "Progress" essay, images are defined as historically objective archetypes, which would mean that thought always finds images already finished and complete and need not itself first produce them. Yet precisely the opposite is said of them in countless other places in Adorno's oeuvre, and actually seems to describe his position more accurately. For example, as early as his introductory lecture in 1931, he says that images are "not simply self-given. They do not lie organically ready in history.... Rather, they must be produced by human beings.... They are ... instruments of human reason.... They are models, by means of which the *ratio*, examining and testing, approaches a reality which refuses to submit to laws, yet can imitate the pattern of the model every time, provided that pattern is imprinted correctly."[41] Dialectical images are not reproductive; as models, they are constellations in which thought groups the *membra disiecta*. The images Adorno intends are not pictures stretched on stable frames but thoroughly temporary figures that, like those in a kaleidoscope, fall apart to be grouped anew by thought—if indeed thought hopes to achieve new meanings from new groupings. In 1955, while he was working on the edition of Benjamin's writings, Adorno penned a draft on dialectical images as constellations of concepts. The draft remains unpublished:

Why dialectical images and not concepts: because Benjamin's thought takes up the paradoxical attempt, through thinking, at setting off course from what thought, through abstraction, preparation, and classification, inflicts on its object. If Benjamin's philosophy does not recognize boundaries...then this means that it concerns itself in a certain sense for the thing itself, and the images in which his philosophy should result (according to its intent) serve this end. Yet these images are not unmediated intuitions, but rather emerge from constellations of concepts, and presuppose thinking labor—namely, expanded theory—: these are constructions out of concepts. The utopian effort of this method, which amounts to the utopian goal of Benjamin's philosophy, simultaneously fixes the impossibility of its completion: the fragmentary character is the irrevocable price that Benjamin's philosophy must pay for its refusal to leave off from the absolute.[42]

It is conceivable that Adorno did not take this note into account in his introduction to Benjamin's *Schriften* because he could not ultimately convince himself that what was presented here was the theory of his friend, rather than the theory to which he had changed it. At any rate, in 1966, there is still to be found in *Negative Dialectics* excurses on constellative thought that clearly touch on the ones cited above on Benjamin's philosophy. It is language, particularly in Adorno's later work, that gives to concepts

objectivity by the relation into which it puts the concepts, centered about a thing. Language thus serves the intention of the concept to express completely what it means. By themselves, constellations represent from without what the concept has cut away within: the 'more' which the concept is equally desirous and incapable of being. By gathering around the object of cognition, the concepts potentially determine the object's interior. They attain, in thinking, what was necessarily excised from thinking.[43]

Adorno's thinking would like, nonetheless, to grasp and hold fast in constellations whatever falls through the net of abstracting conceptuality as well as whatever cannot be comprehended by it at all.

In his claims, Adorno neither overlooks nor denies the "daring, anticipatory, and not fully redeemed"—or what is kept irredeemable by thought alone—but takes these up, as it were, in his theory. "Irresponsibility," for him, is an "aspect of all truth,"[44] and "abandoned by play truth would be nothing but tautology."[45] By means of play, fantasy, and spontaneity, he attempts to find what otherwise would be lost irretrievably to thought. Philosophy as interpretation appears related to that "construction of fantasy" which Adorno grasps as the idea of Schoenberg's twelve-tone composition. If Adorno grants validity only to those musical works that tend immanently toward knowledge, then his entire theoretical work undertakes to mobilize the potential for knowledge contained in reality but speechlessly closed off—and to which artworks nonconceptually lend witness. Adorno's thinking had no aversion to contact (*Berührungsangst*), nor was he above learning from art. Thus has he been exposed to the mockery of the thought police from all schools of thinking. Heinz-Klaus Metzger has defended the staggering thesis that the concepts of knowledge and composition are basically synonymous in Adorno.[46] Metzger relies on a passage from *Negative Dialectics* that discusses a methodology of Max Weber's, according to whom "sociological concepts [should] be 'gradually composed' from 'individual parts to be taken from historic reality.'" Essential, according to Adorno, is

that to which Weber gives the name of "composing," a name which orthodox scientivists would find unacceptable. He is indeed looking only at the subjective side, at cognitive procedure; but the "compositions" in question are apt to follow similar rules as their analogue, the musical compositions. These are subjectively produced, but they work only where the subjective production is submerged in them. The subjectively created context—the "constellation"—becomes readable as a sign of an objectivity: of the spiritual substance. What resembles writing in such constellations is the conversion into objectivity, by way of language, of what has been subjectively thought and assembled.[47]

The indecisiveness governing the referential syntax of the last three sentences is extremely confusing but not unintentional. "*These* are subjectively produced, but they work only where the subjective production is submerged in them:" "these" clearly refers to musical compositions. "The ... context [*it*] created ... becomes readable as a sign of an objectivity:" "it" is subjective production—thus musical composition—but so, too, the compositions of Weberian sociology, which are treated only in the final sentence, for "the conversion into objectivity, *by way of language,* of what has been subjectively thought and assembled" does not occur in music. In no way did Adorno formulate this loosely. It is precisely the fluctuating nature of his formulation that gives entry to that most fragile context in which Adorno's language speculations form theological and ultimately mystical motifs.

Philosophy as interpretation, the reading of images, presupposes that an encoded text lies hidden in the materials from which the images are made—and that things possess their own language, that things themselves take part in language. In the essay "On Language as Such and on the Language of Man,"[48] the young Benjamin asserts exactly this: the methexis of language with every thing in animate and inanimate nature. Adorno cited Benjamin's theorem in the most diverse contexts; it would not leave him alone. A note, for example, from 1948 reads, "If one were to impute to Benjamin's theory that things, even soulless ones, in the strictest sense have language, painting then would have to be defined as an attempt on the part of humans to answer the language of things; at the same time, this would be painting's threshold before photography."[49] Not just painting and music[50] but so, too, Adorno's philosophy itself might well be understood as just such an attempt at answering the language of things. In images, whose characters are expressive of commodity fetishes, language appears exhausted. Interpretation wants to conjure a unity from these alienated features, to prepare the way for an "agreement between people and things."[51] This would be the only theory of communication Adorno would not have hesitated to endorse. The utopia of knowledge, which he courted with such intensity, aims for "the absolute unity of thing and sign, which in its immediacy is lost to human knowledge."[52] Such a knowledge would not make itself like a thing. Nor would it identify the object as some subjective thing. This knowledge would endeavor, rather, to resemble the thing on its own, in some sense, to copy it. Such a knowledge, in contrast to merely interpretive, signifying language, would have to appropriate to itself mimetic powers. It would not be a mythic divisionlessness of subject and object but the as yet unrealized "state of distinctness without domination, with the distinct participating in each other."[53] Far from being exhausted by the "structure of cohabitation in noncoercive communication," the condition Adorno has in mind aims for nothing less than reconciling human beings with nature, of which reconciling human beings with one another would be a part. The condition's linguistic idea is that of the *name*, a concept that does not merely denote the thing θέσει, but rather meets it φύσει itself, retaining—in the midst of irreversible nominalism—the fragile rights to the realism of linguistic expressions. The name denotes the final consequence of nominalism: it is a concept valid only for particulars. Simultaneously, since the construction of the name does not require abstraction from these particulars, it "adumbrates a Platonic idea of truth."[54] Thus, in *Negative Dialectics,* Adorno attempts, in a Proustian-Platonic fashion, to realize "in the happiness...promised by village names" "what metaphysical experience is."[55] The name alone, if one could have it, "would fulfill the concept of the concept;"[56] it would bring home what philosophy has been seeking fruitlessly under the rubric of intellectual intuition: the nonidentically determined, the indelible color of the concrete. In *The Origin of the German Play of Lamentation*, Benjamin unconditionally reclaims Adamic name giving for philosophy, "the word, reclaiming [anew] its name-giving rights."[57] Adorno did not follow him in this. Rather, Adorno doubted whether any nonidentical thing (which the name would reveal) "is there at all" and suspected that the nonidentical was "[more likely] what Kant outlined in his concept of the idea."[58] In Adorno's works, the name occurs nowhere as a key; for him, the name is a seal that at once guards what is promised and yet holds it closed off. Just as *Dialectic of Enlightenment* finds this in the Jewish religion, where "the bond between name and being is still recognized" and continues precisely "in the ban on pronouncing the name of God,"[59] so Adorno forbids himself to name the name, instead turning all his energies toward determinate negation, the unmasking of false names that propagate themselves as real ones.

For Adorno, music reaches closest to the name. He once wrote of music that "[i]ts Idea is the divine Name which has been given shape. It is demythologized prayer, rid of efficacious magic. It is the human attempt, doomed as ever, to name the Name, not to communicate meanings."[60] And elsewhere Adorno states,

The relation of music to philosophy lies in the utopian and likewise hopeless efforts to reach the name, due to which efforts music in its idea stands incomparably closer to philosophy than any other art. But in its name music appears solely as pure sound, set free from its carrier, and therefore the opposite of any meaning, any intention for the senses. Yet since music does not directly know the name—absoluteness as sound—but rather, if one can phrase it so, attempts to conjure up its construction through a whole, a process—thus is itself simultaneously woven into the process by which categories such as rationality, sense, meaning, language are validated. It is the paradox of all music that it unfolds itself—as the effort to reach the unintentional, for which the insufficient word 'name' was chosen—precisely only thanks to its participation in rationality in the broadest sense.[61]

Philosophy, on the other hand, remains committed to words as carriers of a meaning in which the name is not incorporated. Because

meaningless or nonsensical thinking would not really count as thinking at all, thinking cannot shake off the intention of meaning—precisely that which the name escapes. Nor does philosophy know the
name directly; even philosophy can attempt the name's construction
only by means of reason; it can, at most, reach beyond the concept
only by means of the concept.[62] Through discursivity alone, philosophy may hope to be absorbed in the intentionless and nonidentical
and thereby, nevertheless, approach the name. Adorno, for whom
examples were deeply dubious, nevertheless once gave an example
of the way the name can flicker up in music:

> If, shortly before the end of the first measure of the sonata *Les Adieux* by
> Beethoven, the clattering of horses can be heard as the "meaning" of the
> three beats—with a fleetingly receding association—so this passage (which is
> superior to words) says that this most mortal thing, the ungraspable sound
> of vanishing, enfolds more of the hope of return in itself than would ever be-
> come visible through reflection on the nature of the form-seeking tone.[63]

What follows from this for philosophy, however, is that "only a philosophy that truly succeeded at affirming to the innermost such micrological figures from the construction of the whole would achieve
contact with the nature of the puzzle, without however daring to flat-
ter itself of the solution."[64] In the vanishing, the hope still contained
is that the absolute might yet remain bound to the most mortal. This
denominates the innermost impulse of Adorno's thinking. It is solidarity with the lost, an objection to mortality, a refusal to reconcile
with death. With the name as salvation for the particularized, the
wholly ephemeral, and the contingent, Adorno appeals to a mystical
theologumenon. Yet his treatment of the concept of progress is evidence that he does not have a restoration of theology in mind. The
failure of enlightenment and civilization, let alone the near-to-hand
possibility of apocalypse, is more than enough to resign progress to a
transcendental intervention or a historical hiatus; even Benjamin
tended toward this. Recognizing that such messianism "evaporates
into ahistorical theology,"[65] Adorno finds it precisely the thing to resist. He insists that such emphatic concepts, to which hope once
bound itself, are intertwined in the historical process; the process itself, however, due to its continuing blindness and growing irrational-

ity, needs to reflect the transcendental telos of those concepts that realize theological names. Only for the sake of immanence did Adorno allow himself the thought of transcendence—for the sake of the mortal, he would not leave the eternal alone. A sketch from the final year of his life reads,

Yesterday I wrote in *Aesthetic Theory:* no transcendence without that which would be transcended. Yet doesn't that reach far beyond art? Doesn't the answer to the question of contingency's endless relevance for the unconditioned—the kernel of mystical experience—lie enclosed in thought? For if the absolute is so only in relation to the contingent—any talk of the absolute would be wholly senseless otherwise—then it would be very bad and abstract to characterize the relationship according solely to this dichotomy. If the absolute cannot be without the contingent, the contingent itself thereby falls into the absolute, which is then still contingent. This corresponds exactly with the life-feeling that everything here in life is at once quite irrelevant and so too of endless relevance (the feeling that one has nothing but just this nothingness and that it is therefore endlessly important, is parodied by metaphysical experience and leaves open whether, in the end, the most banal experience doesn't coincide with the sublime—). Therein lies nothing less than the communication between all that is, the objectivity of mimesis. Of utmost importance, demonstrate (*Höchst wichtig, ausführen*).[66]

The name, as form (*Gestalt*) of the absolute, suggests possibility, which still has been betrayed by every reality and yet is indeed glimpsed only from reality.[67] The name is nonbeing (*Nichtseiende*), which only being (*Daseiendes*) knows and toward which it therefore reaches;[68] the absolute, which would not be were it not for the contingent: that "god" whom the mystics knew "cannot live a moment without me." In his mystical remembrance of the divine name, Adorno's thinking appears most spiritual. But it is, in truth, perfectly materialistic.

Translated by Ellen Anderson and Tom Huhn

Notes

1. Cf. Theodor Adorno, *Gesammelte Schriften* (Frankfurt: Suhrkamp, 1970–1986), vol. 4, p. 55. Hereafter, *Gesammelte Schriften* will be abbreviated GS and followed by a numeral before the slash referring to the volume of the collected edition; the number following the slash will be the page of the corresponding volume. (If the reference is

142

Rolf Tiedemann

to a writing by Adorno that has been translated into English, the published version will be cited and its reference will follow the citation to the German original. In this case: *Minima Moralia: Reflections from Damaged Life*, trans. E. F. N. Jephcott [London: NLB, 1974], p. 50.)

2. Cf. Theodor W. Adorno, from a "Scribble-In Book," in *Perspektiven Kritischer Theorie. Eine Sammlung zu Hermann Schweppenhäusers 60. Geburtstag*, ed. Christoph Türcke (Lüneburg: Klampen, 1988), p. 9.

3. GS 11/247; *Notes to Literature*, trans. Shierry Weber Nicholsen (New York: Columbia University Press, 1991), vol. 1, p. 213.

4. Arthur Schopenhauer, *Sämtliche Werke*, ed. Wolfgang von Löhneysen, vol. 2: *Die Welt als Wille und Vorstellung II*, (Darmstadt, 1980), 590. ("Mousagetas," or "leader of the muses," is one of Apollo's epithets.)

5. Botho Strauss, *Paare, Passanten* (Munich: Hanser, 1981), p. 115.

6. Ibid., p. 114.

7. In the era following Hoyerswerda and Rostock, Strauss speaks unabashedly of "the criminal dialectic of leftist terror": if the older renunciation of the dialectic was already unspeakable, how should one characterize this newest verdict? How about "terroristic"? Out of Strauss's weakness for the "raw and the same" grew a plea for "what's ours" and against the foreign: with this, at any rate, this lawyer of the *ius sanguinis* has "finally turned out to be that famous...characterization." (Cf. Botho Strauss, "Anschwellender Bockgesang," *Der Spiegel* 6 [1993]: 203.)

8. GS 10.2/625; "Progress," in *Interventions and Catchwords*, trans. Henry Pickford (New York: Columbia University Press, forthcoming).

9. Karl Marx and Friedrich Engels, *Werke*, vol. 25: *Das Kapital* (Berlin, 1968), p. 828.

10. Cf. GS 6/43; *Negative Dialectics*, trans. E. B. Ashton (New York: Seabury Press, 1973), pp. 32–33.

11. GS 11/248; *Notes to Literature*, vol. 1, p. 213.

12. In May or June of 1968 Adorno noted, "On the controversy with Bloch. My position is to show that all dreams today of a better life are pale and powerless, or kitschy. Wedekind showed this for erotic utopia (hence his dialectic), Proust for the experienced life. Utopia lies strictly, exclusively *only* in determinate negation. The rest is Schinderhannes-Ché Guevara. (Very important.)" (Unpublished manuscript; Theodor W. Adorno Archive, notebook a, pp. 29ff.)

13. GS 6/164; *Negative Dialectics*, p. 162.

14. GS 6/192; *Negative Dialectics*, p. 191.

15. Jürgen Habermas, *Philosophisch-politische Profile*, 3d, expanded edition (Frankfurt: Suhrkamp, 1981), p. 176; the essay in which this passage appears was not included in the English edition, *Philosophical-Political Profiles* (Cambridge, Mass.: MIT Press, 1983).

16. GS 5/339; *Hegel: Three Studies,* trans. Shierry Weber Nicholsen (Cambridge, Mass.: MIT Press, 1993), p. 105.

17. GS 11/83; *Notes to Literature,* vol. 1, p. 68.

18. GS 11/83; *Notes to Literature,* vol. 1, p. 69.

19. GS 5/340; *Hegel: Three Studies,* p. 106.

20. The most resounding critique of the concept of communication is to be found in "Zu Subjekt und Objekt," one of Adorno's last works: "If speculation on the state of reconciliation were permitted, neither the undistinguished unity of subject and object nor their antithetical hostility would be conceivable in it; rather, the communication of what was distinguished. Not until then would the concept of communication, as an objective concept, come into its own. The present one is so infamous because the best there is, the potential of an agreement between people and things, is betrayed to an interchange between subjects according to the requirements of subjective reason." GS 10.2/743; "Subject and Object," in *The Essential Frankfurt School Reader,* ed. Andrew Arato and Eike Gebhardt (New York: Urizen Books, 1978), pp. 499–500.

21. Cf. GS 11/473; *Notes to Literature,* vol. 2, pp. 132–33.

22. GS 3/19; Theodor W. Adorno and Max Horkheimer, *Dialectic of Enlightenment,* trans. John Cumming (New York: Seabury Press, 1972), p. 3.

23. GS 10.2/741; "Subject and Object," p. 498.

24. GS 5/17; *Against Epistemology: A Metacritique; Studies in Husserl and the Phenomenological Antinomies,* trans. Willis Domingo (Cambridge, Mass.: MIT Press, 1983), p. 9. Oxford: Basil Blackwell, 1982.

25. Cf. GS 5/17; *Against Epistemology,* p. 9.

26. GS 10.2/745; "Subject and Object," p. 501.

27. Cf. GS 10.2/751; "Subject and Object," pp. 505–6.

28. GS 11/32; *Notes to Literature,* vol. 1, p. 23.

29. GS 6/21; *Negative Dialectics,* p. 10 (translation altered).

30. GS 3/43; *Dialectic of Enlightenment,* pp. 26–27.

31. GS 5/47; *Against Epistemology,* p. 40.

32. GS 3/41; *Dialectic of Enlightenment,* p. 24.

33. Walter Benjamin, *Gesammelte Schriften,* ed. Rolf Tiedemann and Hermann Schweppenhauser, vol. 5, 3d ed. (Frankfurt: Suhrkamp, 1992), p. 1086; *The Correspondence of Walter Benjamin 1910–1940,* ed. Gershom Scholem and Theodor W. Adorno, trans. Manfred R. Jacobson and Evelyn M. Jacobson (Chicago: University of Chicago Press, 1994), p. 333.

34. GS 2/80; *Kierkegaard: Construction of the Aesthetic*, trans. and ed. Robert Hullot-Kentor (Minneapolis: University of Minnesota Press, 1989), p. 54.

35. Cf. Benjamin, *Gesammelte Schriften*, vol. 5, p. 1117; *Correspondence of Walter Benjamin*, p. 489.

36. Benjamin, *Gesammelte Schriften*, vol. 7, 2d ed. (Frankfurt: Suhrkamp, 1992), pp. 860–61.

37. GS 10.2/637; "Progress."

38. Cf. Benjamin, *Gesammelte Schriften*, vol. 5, p. 1128; *Correspondence of Walter Benjamin*, pp. 494–503. An alternate translation of this same letter appears in *Aesthetics and Politics*, ed. Ronald Taylor (London: NLB, 1977), pp. 110–20.

39. GS 6/531. Although this text has been translated into English as *The Jargon of Authenticity*, trans. Knut Tarnowski and Frederic Will (London: Routledge & Kegan Paul, 1973), the phrase quoted here appears in a note appended to the German volume with an explanation that it was written shortly before Adorno's death, apparently with the intention of forming part of an expanded introduction to the next edition of *Negative Dialectics*.

40. GS 3/41; *Dialectic of Enlightenment*, p. 24; the published English translation inexplicably omits the second sentence of the passage.

41. GS 1/341; "The Actuality of Philosophy," in *Telos*, no. 31 (spring 1977): p. 131.

42. Adorno, "Zum Begriff des dialektischen Bildes," unpublished manuscript, Theodor W. Adorno Archive, Ts 30481.

43. GS 6/164–65; *Negative Dialectics*, p. 162.

44. GS 11/13; *Notes to Literature*, vol. 1, p. 6.

45. GS 11/29; *Notes to Literature*, vol. 1, p. 20.

46. Cf. Heinz-Klaus Metzger, "Mit den Ohren Denken. Zu einigen musikphilosophischen Motiven von Adorno," in *Adorno-Noten*, ed. Rolf Tiedemann (Berlin, 1984), pp. 21–22.

47. GS 6/167–68; *Negative Dialectics*, p. 165.

48. Walter Benjamin, *Reflections: Essays, Aphorisms, Autobiographical Writings*, trans. Edmund Jephcott (New York: Harcourt Brace Jovanovich, 1978), pp. 314–32.

49. Theodor Adorno, "Sketch without Title," unpublished manuscript, Theodor W. Adorno Archive, notebook 13 (Scribble-In Book 2), p. 160.

50. Cf. GS 4/252; *Minima Moralia*, pp. 222–23.

51. GS 10.2/743; "Subject and Object," pp. 499–500.

52. GS 18/154.

53. GS 10.2/743; "Subject and Object," p. 500.

54. GS 5/284; *Hegel: Three Studies,* p. 39.

55. GS 6/366; *Negative Dialectics,* p. 373.

56. GS 6/366; *Negative Dialectics,* p. 374.

57. Benjamin, *Gesammelte Schriften,* vol. 1, 3d ed. (Frankfurt: Suhrkamp, 1990), p. 217; *The Origin of German Tragic Drama,* trans. John Osborne (London: NLB, 1977), p. 37.

58. GS 10.2/752; "Subject and Object," p. 507.

59. GS 3/40; *Dialectic of Enlightenment,* p. 23.

60. GS 16/252; *Quasi una fantasia; Essays on Modern Music,* trans. Rodney Livingstone (London: Verso, 1992), p. 2.

61. GS 18/154.

62. Cf. GS 6/27; *Negative Dialectics,* p. 15.

63. GS 18/156.

64. GS 18/156.

65. GS 10.2/621; "Progress."

66. Adorno, "Zur Metaphysik," unpublished manuscript, Theodor W. Adorno Archive, notebook Z, pp. 138ff.

67. Cf. GS 6/62; *Negative Dialectics,* p. 52.

68. Cf. GS 6/66; *Negative Dialectics,* p. 57.

6

Concerning the Central Idea
of Adorno's Philosophy

Rüdiger Bubner

"I do not want to decide whether my theory is grounded in a particular understanding of humanity and human existence. I deny, however, that it is necessary to have recourse to such an understanding." This lapidary statement occurs at the end of the *Aktualität der Philosophie,* the inaugural lecture with which Theodor W. Adorno began his academic career in 1931.[1] The lecture is important because it foreshadows many of the main ideas of his later philosophy. The statement itself reflects an orientation toward philosophy Adorno would maintain throughout his life.

Adorno's philosophical theses arise from certain fundamental assumptions, as do all meaningful propositions and especially those expressing pure theoretical insights. His intentional and emphatic refusal, however, to give an account of his premises is responsible for the form these assumptions take in the course of their theoretical development. Most assumptions that inform our everyday thinking and discussions about the world are so self-evident we pay no attention to them whatsoever. It is, however, theory's unique task to provide the most exhaustive and airtight account possible of just such tacit assumptions. Since its inception, philosophical theory has embraced an ethos urging the establishment of rational grounds. Adorno's startling statement, of which there are many others like it, does not deny that theories are constructed in this way. Instead, it calls into question our received ideas about theory in order to challenge their claims. For Adorno, the point is not to discover a different type of theory or to jettison theory tout court and replace it with a new, irrational mode of expression. Adorno remains firmly oriented toward an understanding of theory that "refuses to abandon philosophy."[2] Only against the backdrop of this explicitly philosophical orientation does Adorno's refusal to account for first principles, in the traditional sense, have any meaning at all. Nothing else, however, pervades Adorno's philosophy so thoroughly as his unremitting refusal to meet theory's traditional demands.

In the inaugural lecture, Adorno goes on to appeal to the essay as the appropriate form for philosophical discourse.[3] Later on, this approach, from which Adorno's mature theory will emerge, is formulated in various ways. For example, "critical theory" characterizes his entire undertaking. "Negative dialectic" describes the leading intention behind the polemics he wages against Hegel. An important catchphrase is the "dialectic of enlightenment." Adorno's thought, however, finds its definitive expression in the title *Aesthetic Theory*. This posthumously published work has proven to be his true philosophical testament. As is well known, the title is equivocal. "Aesthetic theory" does not only mean that theoretical aesthetics is one subdivision of an extensive, theoretical edifice. More important, it means that the text's main concern is the process by which theory itself becomes aesthetic—the convergence of knowledge and art. "Aesthetics is not a form of applied philosophy, rather it is in itself philosophical."[4] What does this mean?

Historical Diagnosis

The question I pursue here aims at discovering the reasons that, for Adorno, theory must give way to aesthetics. Even to raise this question is tantamount to dismissing out of hand both Adorno's refusal to reveal what his premises are and the verdict that the question itself is petty and lacks refinement. Such a purely stylistic concern, which makes it taboo to tamper with an argument's finely wrought unity, is usually a manifestation of sophistry and of little philosophical value. Adorno would have certainly fended off questions like the one I just raised by saying that there is no place within the structure of his work where they can gain a foothold. This objection is to be rejected. To maintain a stony silence when confronted with a call for the reasons that ground the type of theory Adorno advocates does not make the theory in any way more plausible.

Adorno, however, does give a thorough explanation of his motivation for encouraging silence. He argues *historically*. The demand to specify the foundations presupposed by theory is a relic of idealism's overestimation of philosophy's importance and continues to foster the illusion that thought contains an absolute beginning.

"Philosophy, however, that no longer presumes to be autonomous, that no longer believes reality to be grounded in the *ratio,* but time and again assumes the transgression of an autonomous, rational legislation by a Being that is not adequate to such legislation and cannot be rationally construed as a totality, will not pursue to the end the path leading back to rational premises but will come to a standstill wherever irreducible reality intrudes. . . . The intrusion of irreducible reality occurs concretely and historically, and this is why history keeps the movement of thought from returning to presuppositions."[5]

To begin with, it is not at all convincing to denounce every theory's search for grounds as being tainted with idealistic presumption. Ever since the Socratic challenge of the *logon didonai,* it has been one of philosophy's most basic tenets to give an account of why we say what we say. In addition, rationalism's various systems have claimed to provide proof that their respective principles were absolute and could not be surpassed by any other. That was true for Spinoza and especially for Fichte and Schelling, who both, not by chance, returned to Spinoza. In contrast, Hegel, whom Adorno quotes with particular relish when it comes to idealistic hubris, showed much more caution than his contemporaries, who were always too quick to assert that they had surpassed each other in building unsurpassable systems. The absoluteness Hegel's philosophy in fact lays claim to did not arise out of historical myopia or the arbitrary positing of abstract principles. Rather, it was acquired on the basis of consistently confronting the one immutable idea of philosophy with the experience of the historically contingent forms the idea must assume if there is to be philosophy at all. All of this, however, does not directly concern us.[6] What is at issue here is Adorno's reluctance to give an account of his own underlying philosophical premises.

Adorno's reference to an *irreducible Being*, which intrudes on philosophy through the backdoor of history, is either a surreptitious way of establishing grounds or nothing more than an empty incantation. The first alternative gives rise to difficulties that I will consider below. Understood as an example of the polemics Adorno continually wages against Heidegger, the second alternative is pointless to pursue. The surprising parallels between Adorno's early works and Heidegger's *Seinsphilosophie*, do, however, bear closer examination.[7] From early on, Adorno never tired of pillorying the "new ontology" as the form par excellence of ahistorical hypostasis.[8] With the publication of *Being and Time* (1927), which immediately received wide recognition, Adorno must have clearly sensed his unsettling philosophical proximity to Heidegger. The way Heidegger sometimes expresses his hope for a Being that will directly reveal itself at the end of traditional metaphysics' long history of decline, a Being that only makes itself known within the dimension of concrete existence, beyond the reach of philosophical insight, comes very close indeed to mirroring many of Adorno's theses. In order to undermine the outward impression that he might have shared similar insights with Heidegger, Adorno emphasized, in the strongest possible terms, the substantial differences between their two philosophical standpoints.

Adorno thus pursues throughout his *Habilitationsschrift* on Kierkegaard the ulterior motive of contesting existentialism's appropriation of this church father of the protest against Hegel's brand of idealism.[9] Adorno also takes Heidegger to task for his dubious and, in terms of style, not exactly surefooted attempts to take refuge in poetic metaphor in order to avoid the atrophy that, according to Heidegger, had overtaken the expressive power of the language traditionally used by philosophers.[10] Only later, however, did Adorno succeed in delivering the decisive blow that contributed to removing Heidegger from the center of public influence. As Heidegger's star began to fade during the period of Germany's restoration after the Second World War, Adorno's essay called "The Jargon of Authenticity," intended as a pamphlet, certainly came at precisely the right moment. Since then, the laconic expression *Sein* has been taken out of circulation and replaced by the more complicated sounding *das Nichtidentische*. What is meant in both cases is that reality eludes or, in Adorno's words, is not absorbed by the philosophical concept. Only insofar as the concept recognizes reality can the dimension of truth really be disclosed to it. As Adorno writes, "[C]oncepts for their part are moments of the reality that requires their formation."[11]

Those who are not satisfied with bare, emphatic assertions can interpret the reference to historical experience, which forbids recourse to rational premises, as itself an unacknowledged premise for the type of theory Adorno has in mind. The grounding of theory must be carried out in a way which shows that precisely today, under the prevailing conditions of the here and now, and after society has reached its present level of historical development, it has become impossible to return to the old naive way of pursuing philosophy. Adorno's work resonates from many sides with similar formulations. But why should an account of the historical hour be sufficient to bid "traditional theory" a final farewell and to put in its place a form of theory whose sole function is "critique," a theory "which holds that the core of truth is historical, rather than an unchanging constant to be set against the movement of history"?[12] The blanket answer to this question is *mystification* [*Verblendungszusammenhang*], that is, the profound and all-pervasive blindness to sociohistorical truth that sets in once society has fallen under the sway of ideology.

According to this thesis, in all societies in the grip of late capitalism, ideology has become so total and totalizing that there is no way to escape its influence. Even the simple act of stating what is falls prey to mystification, for it necessarily fails to add that everything that is should not have been in the first place. Thus, every statement made in the interests of serving truth must simultaneously recant the insight it was meant to express. Such a paradoxical use of language immediately exhausts theory's already-limited possibilities. All hope must now be directed toward another type of language, toward art. "The true is revealed to discursive knowledge, but for all that, not attained; the knowledge that is art has the true, but as something incommensurable."[13]

Drive toward Totality

Before it is possible to understand how art can function as a substitute for theory in the context of the above considerations, we must discuss the difficulties implicit in Adorno's historical diagnosis that underlies the transition from theory to art. The controversy surrounding historical diagnosis has nothing at all to do with actual assessments of the current political situation or with occasional ad hoc attempts to improve it. Nor does it have anything to do with a strategy of moral intimidation that all too easily silences naive doubt, by holding up examples of cataclysmic historical events. Rather, what is problematic is the paralysis the diagnosis brings on itself by assuming that everything is exactly as it makes it out to be. The belief in the totalizing power of ideology to mystify all aspects of modern life, including our own individual powers of judgment, thoroughly deprives theory of the freedom to move within its own sphere of operation. Under the distorting lens of historical diagnosis, everything, without exception, appears reified. As a result, theory completely succumbs to the very same coercive ideology it was, in fact, enlisted to describe.

Trading in hypotheses, tedious to-and-fro argumentation, ponderous deliberations, proofs, objections, questions raised about other theories and about itself—all this drops away as soon as the diagnosis calls the universal spell by its proper name. Thereafter, it would be an example of systematic self-delusion if theory carried on as if nothing at all had happened. The moment at which historical truth is revealed simultaneously ushers in the moment at which historical truth slips forever beyond theory's grasp, a negative *kairos*. Because it now senses that all of its knowledge is unavoidably false, theory also realizes that truth by means of theory is no longer possible. With this insight, its concepts are subjected to an entirely heteronomous determination.

The paralysis that has overtaken theory now sets in on its object and affects the process by which theory determines what its appropriate field of inquiry should be. This, however, fundamentally contradicts the avowed intentions of *critique* and *dialectic*. The very same totality, with which theory has invested the *bruta facta* of ideology, consistently ties the hands of critique. Confronted with the opponent's superior strength, theory has only one viable recourse—to strike back with the most stringent, thoroughgoing form of negativity. Because, as theory itself has shown, there can no longer be any exceptions to the global rule of ideology, it is forced to denounce everything under the sun as being a product of ideology. The bogus ideal of totality, which theory in its newly won role of critique attributes to traditional systems, insidiously turns back on theory with the same intensity with which it afflicts everything else.

In order to preserve its critical edge over against a world dominated by the totalizing effects of ideology, theory must target the objects of its inquiries before it has direct knowledge of them. It must maintain a critical attitude toward these objects to ensure that it deals with them impartially and remains immune to whatever charms they may hold for it. Theory must keep itself at a safe distance from the flux of phenomena and reestablish this distance whenever they threaten to lead it astray. To sustain its opposition toward what is immediately given, theory is forced endlessly to redefine itself by successive acts of reflection. This means, however, that theory winds up being driven by an inner necessity to validate itself and thus replicates the dogmatic self-certainty displayed by the philosophical concept—the object of Adorno's unmitigated contempt.[14]

As much as Adorno would like to claim that the emergence of Critical Theory is historical and concrete, the truth of the matter lies elsewhere. In fact, it is based on sweeping, a priori assumptions. These assumptions, guiding the course of Adorno's earlier thinking, remain just as much in force later on. Adorno himself confirms this in a chance observation: "Actually, there is one ontology maintained throughout history, the ontology of despair. If, however, ontology is what is perennial, then thought experiences every historical period as the worst and, most of all, its own which it knows directly."[15] To be secure in the belief that from its very beginning the world has always been thoroughly degenerate makes every present historical moment appear in the most dismal light. Because historical diagnosis is guided by such foreknowledge, it necessarily cuts off all discussion.

As we have just seen, Critical Theory does, in fact, rest on a *full-fledged theory of history that claims ontological status.* If such a theoretical foundation did not exist, Adorno would not have proposed so vehemently that we renounce traditional theories in favor of one whose sole function is to unmask the workings of ideology. Of course, to avoid the penalty of transgressing all that Critical Theory stands for, the actual underlying ontology must remain out of the discussion.

The validity of such a foundation, however, can be tested only when it is openly defended in discussion. This would allow for an undogmatic assessment of Critical Theory's soundness. Adorno, however, deliberately formulates all his arguments to preclude such a possibility. We thus have no other choice but to follow the clues implicit in his silence. This will lead us into the terrain of aesthetics.

Adorno bans discussion not out of a desire to surround his argument in an aura of mystery. On the contrary, the strategy of keeping silent acquires an overt and novel function within the architectonic that underpins a highly intricate thought progression. Adorno's position, that theory is no longer viable in a world dominated by ideology, must be construed as his attempt to demonstrate the necessity of the transition from philosophy to aesthetics. Yet in order to continue to give expression to theory's departure from its traditional function of establishing grounds, Adorno offers a special form of discourse. Instead of following Wittgenstein's famous maxim to keep silent on that about which there is nothing to say, Adorno transforms aesthetics into the one legitimate way to speak about the ban on speaking about theory per se.

Dialectic of Enlightenment

It has been often observed that the *Dialectic of Enlightenment* holds the keys to understanding Adorno's *Aesthetic Theory*.[16] The studies or "philosophical fragments" that constitute the *Dialectic of Enlightenment* were written while Horkheimer and Adorno lived in exile in the United States. The text is characterized by the authors' own political and existential concerns, translated into general philosophical terms. It occupies a central place in their thought because it does not, as is usually the case with their other work, subject external issues to critique but turns critique back on itself so that it becomes its own object: "the point is... that the Enlightenment *must consider itself*."[17] Against the backdrop of their historical experience of fascism, as well as Stalin's perversion of Marxist theory, they felt it had become imperative to embark on a critique of ideology, which, since Marx, had remained nothing more than a desideratum.

If the critique of ideology is not based on a "socially detached intelligentsia," as Karl Mannheim's sociology of knowledge would have us believe, what then is the special form of objectivity the critics are so deeply rooted in that they are not blinded by the universal mystification caused by ideology?[18] Or is the critique of ideology secretly just as prone to ideological appropriation as all those theories it relentlessly takes to task? Lukács was one of the first to be struck by the problem of how enlightenment becomes stymied once orthodoxy sets in. His remedy is to introduce Hegel's concept of reflection into Marx's concept of class consciousness. One should not underestimate the role Lukács's important book *History and Class Consciousness* played in inspiring the Frankfurt School. Nevertheless, Lukács's attempt to identify the one revolutionary class, the proletariat, as the sole bearer of historically correct consciousness could not, in the final analysis, prevent the decline in political relevance of a theory that had once been the source of so much hope.

The idea of a "dialectic of enlightenment" deals with the paradox that a dialectic plays with enlightenment instead of explicitly working in its interests. In contrast to Marx, whose dialectical method coincided with the possibility of real historical progress, Horkheimer and Adorno conceive the process of enlightenment itself as succumbing to a dialectical reversal into its opposite, a reversal that takes place behind the back of enlightened reflection.[19] This, however, should not be confused with Hegel's critique of enlightenment, which was meant to overcome the biased nature of enlightened reflection in order to open the way for a truly speculative movement of ideas. Adorno and Horkheimer specifically intend that their dialectic of enlightenment should not culminate in absolute knowing. Indeed, for them, idealism's final configuration continually serves as an ominous reminder of how philosophy is brought to a standstill. How is it possible to make use of Hegel's dialectic and, at the same time, be dead set against its logical and historical consequences?

To prevent theory from being absorbed by idealist speculation, it is necessary to check the automatic, dialectical progression from reason's critique of enlightenment, as carried out in the realm of the understanding, to the autonomy that theory achieves in Hegel's system. This requires, in defiance of enlightened thinking, that a natural prerogative be granted to all those deep-seated prejudices and superstitions from which enlightenment promises to emancipate humankind. The privileged position these irrational beliefs have in our thinking, however, is obvious from the fact that, despite all its efforts, enlightenment always fails to dislodge them. All the exertion expended in good faith to raise this intractably irrational substance to the level of the concept comes to absolutely nothing. The more enlightenment is convinced of itself and the correctness of what it does, the more it risks being dominated by the same irrational principle it struggles to supplant. Thus, in the end, reason's omnipotence turns out to be just as irrational as nature's despotism, against which all the first cultural revolutions were fought. In this way, the dialectic of enlightenment is made to atone for the Fall that, before all recorded time, drove humankind out of paradise and into history.

In order to describe this hard-to-grasp dialectical reversal of enlightenment into its opposite, Adorno and Horkheimer introduce a concept of myth that, however much it may have been inspired by Judeo-Christian tradition, is at odds with all usual meanings of the word. We might consider Rousseau's ambivalence toward modernity in general and the Enlightenment in particular to help see how a projection back through history to an original state of nature is solely a consequence of the Enlightenment's having reached the zenith of its historical development and yet, at the same time, is the standard by which the Enlightenment measures reason's historical progress. Understood in this way, Rousseau's fictional reconstruction of the state of nature serves as a mirror in which the hopes of the Enlightenment are reflected from afar, and the sins, inherent in cultural progress, seem to be completely wiped away. Myth is not a word for a primordial state out of which human reason slowly and successfully evolved. On the contrary, reason is already present in the earliest myths; conversely, the mythical maintains its presence throughout the Enlightenment's entire historical development. The culmination of the Enlightenment in scientific knowledge is, in fact, a reversion to earliest times, which shows, contrary to the expectations of philosophers and other enlightened thinkers, that nothing at all has changed.

Precisely understood, the word "myth" maps out a dimension that is not affected by the dialectic of history, because it forms the basis of this dialectic.[20] This reveals the limits and futility of believing in open-ended historical progress; in whatever direction history may happen to push forward, it cannot escape this pregiven situation.[21]

Of course, corresponding to this understanding of history is a vaguely defined ideal of an *eschatological reconciliation* in which all differences are eliminated, all errors are avoided, and historical change is brought to an absolute standstill. Knowledge of this reconciliation lies beyond the finite capacity of our rational faculties and, therefore, also avoids being compromised by our ideological thinking. As mere mortals, however, we can experience such a reconciliation only in the limited way afforded to us by the pseudoreality created by art.[22]

Philosophy has a concept available that, as a product of reason, marks out, in the most subtle way, reason's own limits—the concept of *illusion*. Although, in the first place, illusion is something other than the philosophical concept, nevertheless, it is illusion only because the concept recognizes it as such. Philosophy has always seen the true nature of art mirrored in the concept of illusion.[23] It is one of the terms in which the problem of the *Dialectic of Enlightenment* is articulated. To designate illusion as the locus where this problem can be adequately addressed means to obscure the line of division that separates art from philosophy.[24]

The Dogma of Contradiction

Schelling's philosophy of art is the appropriate court of appeal for a type of philosophy whose most deep-seated intentions are to be transposed into the medium of art.[25] Schelling thought that the absolute indifference of subject and object could be brought to the level of intuition by means of art. Philosophy cannot achieve this identity without transcending itself and ceasing to be philosophy. The last point reached by reflection, where it abandons its own claims for the sake of absolute, seamless unity, simultaneously reveals the limits of discursive philosophy. In contrast to philosophy, art realizes this unity on its own accord and without distortion. In order, however, for art to succeed in this undertaking of speaking for philosophy, both sides of the relation between art and philosophy must be adequately determined.

The younger Schelling drew on the idea of an *organon*[26] to conceptualize the relationship in which philosophy establishes a close proximity to art. This allowed Schelling to use art as an antidote to philosophy's shortcomings without art's merely substituting for philosophy. On the one hand, this lets art remain autonomous and prevents the intentional and unintentional transformation of art into a philosophical hybrid that solely serves the interests of philosophical proof. Art must not be defined as an *ancilla philosophiae;* it is precisely art's autonomy that enables it to serve the function philosophy requires of it. On the other hand, the function art assumes on behalf of philosophy must lend itself to characterization so that art remains accessible to philosophy. Nothing is to be gained either by an intoxicated feeling of identity that blurs all distinctions between art and philosophy or by a neutral coexistence in which philosophy and art have nothing to say to each other. Considering the extreme nature of the opposing demands philosophy makes on art, the Aristotelian model of an organon is only, at best, a makeshift solution. Art is not, at any price, to be instrumentalized by philosophy, the way, for example, tools are subordinated to the ends they serve. Art is able to express philosophy's most difficult paradoxes only when it has parity with philosophy and, therefore, like philosophy, is not a means to an end but is an end in itself. This is the reason Schelling later abandoned the organon model and relied less heavily on the problematic relationship between philosophy and art.[27]

Critical Theory's general program is informed by a tension whose extremes are characterized by Kant's doctrine of the *Ding an sich* and Hegel's absolute concept, whereas the arena in which these two extremes are battled out was prepared by Marx and the Young Hegelians. Adorno's aesthetics, which emerged from these conditions, is best understood, however, in connection with Schelling, a connection almost all interpreters of Adorno and modern aesthetics have failed to take into consideration. If, for once, this suggestion is taken to heart, then the question of defining the relation between philosophy and art can be posed more clearly than Adorno would have been willing to admit. Adorno himself always stressed that philosophy and art converge in knowledge. It will be more difficult, however, to understand what the terms of this convergence are.

To begin with, not all forms of art entail knowledge per se. As opposed to idealist naiveté, the critic of ideology makes a strict distinction between liberal or "enlightened" art and art that, as part of the "culture industry," is complicit in furthering the general deception produced by ideology. This distinction does not automatically coincide with qualitative distinctions based on pure aesthetic categories. Rather, it presupposes a highly attuned awareness of prevailing historical conditions. The art critic's aesthetic sense becomes more finely honed through knowledge that is extraneous to aesthetic considerations, that is, philosophical and sociological insights into the factors determining the present state of society and possible prospects for the future. By emphasizing that artworks of true aesthetic import are also ones that boast a *progressive* outlook, Adorno forces aesthetic and political judgments to overlap. This echoes Walter Benjamin's tenuous attempt to understand the "artist as producer" in such a radical way that the mastery of the technical side of art production and "the correct political tendency" are predicated on each other.[28] Increase in technical skill and keeping in step with the course of history amount to the same thing—progressive art.[29]

In referring, on the one hand, to the expertise involved in discerning art's purely formal aspects and, on the other, to the knowledge involved in evaluating its content according to the degree it furthers the cause of humanity, the term "progressive art" brings aesthetic and political concerns under one roof. Sometimes the language Adorno uses to reconcile the universal with the particular is reminiscent of *classical poetics*, for example, Goethe's concept of symbol.[30] At the same time, however, the critic must rein in the writer of poetic theory in order to prevent the deception from insinuating itself should it be forgotten that the reconciliation achieved by art is fictive, that it is not present in reality but lies forever in a distant, utopian future. Art must simultaneously present things in two different ways. On the one hand, it must present the concrete particular as something that is not eclipsed by abstract universality but exercises its own right in harmonizing with the universal; on the other hand, art must make manifest the irreality of such a reconciliation.[31] The status of important artworks is established by the contradiction that takes shape between harmony and its disillusionment. What constitutes the historical meaning of works of art must find expression in their artifical construction.

Adorno's theory thus presupposes that the extra-aesthetic categories that form the basis of the critic's interpretations are directly embodied in the artworks themselves. Strictly speaking, then, art expresses only what someone who already has knowledge of historical processes can possibly understand. In fact, this remarkable type of art, with just such an interiorized awareness of its own historical position, is modern art. Complete rejection of the traditional canon, which we have come to expect of modern art, seems to provide the paradigm for Adorno's theory. Obviously, here, the contradiction has become real between art's immanent, self-contained harmony and the sudden shattering of this longed-for harmony. The critic's task is to bring out what is already embedded in the structure of art, and consequently the critic is reduced to a mere recipient to whom art provides whatever he or she might require. The critic's role would be completely redundant, were it not for the complication that not all of the art produced in the last hundred years can be counted as progressive, even when some works seem to look or sound "modern." In the updated *musée imaginaire,* it is once again a question of separating the sheep from the goats. The critic's function, which seemed to have entirely merged with the structure of artworks, is given a new and apparently independent lease on life. The critic's task, however, is no longer to distinguish between good and bad art. Rather, the critic must now distinguish between progressive and reactionary art, a distinction that obviously is no longer based solely on aesthetic criteria.

In relation to modern art, the rehabilitation of the critic's function shows that in truth the formal laws supposedly governing modern art production are merely invoked to divert attention away from criteria introduced by critical aesthetics. Untutored perception alone can never disclose the meaning of art. In order to penetrate art's structure, it is necessary to have command over the history of philosophy and its categories. "To be sure, an immanent method of this type always presupposes, as its opposite pole, philosophical knowledge that transcends the object. The method cannot, as Hegel believed, rely on 'simply looking-on.'"[32] This is the difference between progressive art and all other forms of art production, which only seem to be comparable to it. Without such philosophical and historical categories, the controversy Adorno stages, for example, between Schönberg, the standard bearer of "true" modernity, and Stravinsky, the incarnation of "false" modernity, would be nothing more than an academic debate between two opposing schools of musical composition.[33] Philosophy thus adds what is not already contained in innocent artworks, indeed what can never be contained in them: the interpretation of their meaning as *the negation of existing reality*.

With this, the cornerstone of Adorno's aesthetic theory is in place. It will be obvious now why it is necessary to compare art and social reality from an *external* vantage point in order to discover the moment of contradiction in certain works—by no means art in general. If all art were to stand opposed to reality, then the distinction between art shot through with ideology and progressive art would be totally meaningless. By the same token, if the pseudoreality created by art represented the complete negation of existing reality, then art would lose its oppositional stance toward the external world and would forfeit its function as critique. In the guise of uncompromising protest, art would then be guilty of passing off its illusion of harmony for the real thing. Thus Adorno is perfectly consistent in rejecting all forms of "engaged" art;[34] only art that is entirely itself, and does not attempt to have an effect outside of itself, is able to confront reality's most dominant features with sufficient autonomy to allow the contradictions to force themselves on the spectator. The universal mystification of social reality and art's complete autonomy stand radically opposed to each other. But only from a *third position*, totally removed from ideology, which affects all aspects of everyday life and art production, can mystification be exposed in all its ramifications. This position can be assumed only by the critic.

I needed to pursue the analysis to this point in order to arrive at an approximate answer to the question raised above. In connection with the discussion concerning transformation of philosophy into aesthetics, the question was posed as to the possibility of *determining both sides of the relationship between art and philosophy*. A confused mirroring of philosophical concepts in artworks and vice versa will not yield the knowledge of social reality for whose sake art was introduced into the consideration in the first place. It turns out, however, that two corresponding, fundamental assumptions are presupposed that work in tandem to support the thesis that art and philosophy converge in knowledge. By insisting, on the one hand, on reality's completely ideological character and, on the other, on the complete autonomy of art production, philosophy and art are forced to act on each other in such a way as to make the truth of social reality totally transparent. Adorno's conclusions can be made to appear persuasive only if a strict separation is dogmatically presupposed between art and reality, both of which, with equal right, follow their own internal laws and remain directly opposed to each other.

The unique relationship art and philosophy share with regard to knowledge can only be established once it has already been accepted on good faith that art stands diametrically opposed to reality. According to this ungrounded dogma, art is the adversary of fetishized reality that, by carrying out its own form of negation, is capable of breaking ideology's spell. Thus, as if by an act of providence, art comes to the aid of philosophy as it struggles to break free from the dialectic of enlightenment. Only the critic's powers of interpretation, however, can make us aware of this feat of negation, accomplished in and by art.

Mimesis and Works of Art

Things become more complicated when we turn to aesthetic experience. According to Adorno, to view paintings or to listen to symphonies does not automatically give us access to their truth content. If we want art to perform the additional service of ideology critique, then we must relinquish the classical idea that beauty imparts its truth unaided. All aesthetic experiences require theory in advance. "The demand of artworks to be understood by taking hold of their content [*Gehalt*] is tied to a specific experience of them. This, however, can only be completely fulfilled by a theory that reflects upon experience."[35] If only theory is able to complete what is laid out in experience, then art's critical *function of enlightenment* depends, once again, on its undiminished *autonomy*. As we have seen, autonomy means in this case that art remains independent of philosophy and is not used for the purposes of supporting or validating philosophical insights. What art has to say will come to the fore against the backdrop of philosophy, so long as philosophy does not impose its interests on art.

By means of the oldest concept known to the philosophy of art, Adorno's aesthetic theory attempts to find a way out of this self-imposed impasse. *Mimesis,* which has certainly undergone a remarkable change in meaning and importance, was understood by the tradition as an imitative mode of representation, parasitic on an independently given and higher-order reality. Plato thought that mimesis was inimical to truth, because it produced likenesses "three removes" from reality,[36] and Aristotle classed mimesis among those most fundamental attributes that make humans "the most mimetic of all animals."[37] For Adorno, mimesis is a virtue, because it resists being defined by reason, and because it is so firmly rooted in human behavior. He also places a high value on the necessarily derivative nature of all mimetic forms of representation, something that was anathema to the tradition. Philosophy's recourse to mimetic behavior is intended to repair the damage mimesis suffered at the hands of the philosophical concept. "There is no way for the concept to plead the case of mimesis, without losing itself in mimesis, which it itself supplanted, other than by incorporating something of mimesis in its own conduct. In this respect, the aesthetic moment is not accidental to philosophy, though for reasons quite different from the ones Schelling proposed."[38]

By way of mimesis, Spirit is restored to a quasi-prehistorical attitude toward the phenomenal world. Spirit adapts itself to experience as its other without offering any resistance and abandons its need to dominate the concrete. Blind imitation, which philosophy has held in contempt since the advances made in perfecting conceptual representation, is now seen as a corrective to what has become philosophy's idling machinery of empty categories. Philosophy comes into closer proximity to art, for which it had so little respect, the more theory's sovereignty is called into question. Mimesis in art acquires an altogether new meaning once theory's monopoly on appropriating reality has been challenged.

Adorno's new assessment of mimesis, as a corrective to theory, was fated to run against the grain of the *traditional copy theory of art.* Above all, Adorno objected to reviving axioms of traditional mimetic art theory in a neo-Marxist principle requiring that art produce mirror images of reality. Starting out from Marxist premises, Lukács, in his later writings, adhered to a thoroughly orthodox theory of art that called for faithful reproductions of a pregiven reality. Considering Adorno's understanding of the relation of art to reality, it is not surprising that he vehemently opposed such a misuse of mimesis, which substitutes images for knowledge and prefers concealment to disclosure. "The most fundamental weakness of Lukács's position may be that he...applies categories that refer to the relationship between consciousness and reality to art as though they simply meant the same thing here. Art exists within reality, has its function in it.... But nevertheless, as art, by its very concept it stands in an antithetical relationship to the status quo."[39]

Adorno's newly accentuated concept of mimesis can be defended against entrenched traditional views only by dint of ingenious argumentation. Understood as a basic form of assimilation, capable of overcoming the concept's rigidity, mimesis is not a remnant of another age that has come down to us intact so that the worn-out concept can revert to it at any time. It would be an illusion for philosophy to believe that mimesis can, with the touch of a magic wand, restore a more direct relation to reality. Without the help of well-reasoned explanations, the concept of mimesis has no meaning whatsoever. This becomes all too obvious in the dispute between Adorno and Lukács, in which bare assertions are traded back and forth and the continually cited crown witnesses, Adorno's Samuel Beckett and Lukács's Thomas Mann, are given permission to speak only when they can give testimony on behalf of the respective positions.[40] Seen in this way, Adorno's recourse to mimesis, as a form of "mimicry" of spirit, fails to persuade.

One last consequence remains to be considered. For the sake of the coherence of his own insights into modern art, Adorno cannot get around reinstating an *unqualified work category* in his aesthetic theory, even if the theory itself constantly maintains the opposite. Where else can the concrete and the universal be reconciled in a way that is far removed from all conceptual schematizations, if not within the autonomous sphere created by artworks? What else is to serve as a mirror for exposing "bad" reality, if not an objective example? What else can reflection cling to as it founders in the vortex created by the dialectic of enlightenment, if not a tangible product of mimetic behavior? In spite of whatever statements Adorno may have made to the contrary, it is beyond all doubt that the work category plays a central role in his undertaking. The theory as well as the actual writings on art criticism bear witness on every page that Adorno systematically presupposes the given fact of artworks.

Just as little can it be doubted, however, that modern art, the basis of Adorno's aesthetic theory, represents one continuous process, *the demise of the work category*.[41] If the diverse forms of art production crudely classified as "modern" permit being reduced to one common dominator, then the main trend embodied by modern art is the steady subversion of the traditional work category. In the absence of the work category, modern art has resorted to a number of strategies, ranging from playful skepticism to ironic distortion and surrealistic shock, from the systematic destruction of unity and the radical reduction of planned construction to the increased, constitutive function assigned to chance; readymades, found objects, happenings, and performance pieces are the most obvious examples. Modern art denies the ontological status of a second reality that, although derivative, would be equal to the first. *Ergon*, as an independent bearer of meaning, has disappeared from art altogether. Where modern art does not aim to disappoint the traditionally passive spectator, who usually expects to find a full-fledged work, it often serves to inspire the spectator's imagination and active participation, at least to some degree. What used to be attributed to the creative process of actual art production has been transformed by modern art into a process that is automatically set in motion after the work has been completed.[42] In this way, the entire notion of the autonomous artwork has been overtaken by aesthetic experience, which, according to Adorno, is always a "reciprocal" experience between the work of art and the spectator.

This understanding is not new. Nor, to be reminded of it, do we need to turn to Adorno, who, with considerable insight, describes how modern art eroded the central role the traditional work category formerly played in art production and aesthetic theory. All the same, it is worth mentioning two arguments that are often raised and profess to jeopardize this thesis. It is often said that the demise of the traditional work category, in fact, only makes room for *new kinds of artworks*. If this is true, then the entire modern art movement is by no means as revolutionary as it is made out to be. Modern art would represent only a further phase in a long series of style changes and historical shifts to be indifferently classified by the art historian. Above all, those analyses that are of vital importance to Adorno's aesthetic theory would prove to be invalid. For Adorno, what is truly innovative about modern art and specifically distinguishes it from art of all other periods is precisely its protest character; therefore, it should be interpreted in this way. If we subscribe to critical aesthetics, then we can hardly take seriously the argument just mentioned.[43]

The second argument is based on the conviction that modern art simply makes explicit what is implicit to art in general. Fragility is art's true abiding essence, whereas substantiality is make-believe. This argument takes two forms. First, current ideas about art are simply projected back on the entire past, so that modern art is not seen as modern but merely as a new expression of what we understand art to have always been. To draw conclusions about the past on the basis of the present and to level all historical differences results in a distorted foreshortening of historical perspectives. Second, similiar to Marx's famous dictum that the anatomy of man is the key to the anatomy of the ape, this argument often reverts to a teleological model that presupposes the most recent stage of art's historical development to be the culmination of art's entire history, and thus allows all the preliminary stages leading up to a completed process of historical development to be taken in at a glance. Apart from the dubious nature of the method involved in historical teleology—which even in Marx's case, despite his materialist examples, had strong roots in idealism—such a belief in progress, together with the claim of rendering ever more transparent the origins of the current historical moment, once again robs aesthetics of its potential as critique. As Adorno saw, rational capacity does not develop according to the dictates of an inner telos. Art that opposes the advance of rationality and, like Faust's return to the mothers,[44] reverts to fundamental, mimetic levels of human existence is the last place of refuge from where it is possible to expose the new and ever-deeper inroads deception continues to make into history.

To conclude, we cannot avoid *synthesizing the following two irreconcilable sides of modern art.* On the one hand, modern art undermines the traditional work category, and it is thanks to this that it acquires its protest character. On the other hand, modern art has no means of expression other than individual concrete works; aside from their autonomous structure, no place remains where they can carry out their mission of critique. Adorno resolutely engages both sides of this paradox. Theory cannot provide us with any solution. The paradox can be defused only by means of casuistry. On the basis of case-by-case analyses of literary texts and musical scores, the two sides of the paradox can be set off against each other, that is, modern art's need to destroy unity for the sake of preserving its critical function and its need to maintain unity for the sake of giving expression to its critical function.

Merely providing examples, however, can in no way substitute for establishing the grounds for a theory. As plausibly as Adorno may have sometimes demonstrated his general insights with regard to particular literary and musical works, he provides little in the way of evidence to ground the application of these insights. Every one of his interpretations hinges far too much on his hermeneutical starting point and rhetorical skill to serve as evidence for the conclusions he draws. If the same works are considered from a different perspective and with different intentions, then, to a certain extent, the resulting interpretations would also make sense. The ultimate ploy, which Adorno all too gladly uses to give his interpretations an authoritative tone, is to insinuate that all possible alternative interpretations are to be suspected of being ideologically biased or, worse still, philistine. This, however, only camouflages the shaky foundations on which his own interpretations are built. To shift the burden of fundamental aesthetic issues intentionally onto the shoulders of interpretation underhandedly obscures the difference between aesthetic theory and aesthetic experience.

Aesthetic Experience

The role aesthetic experience plays in Adorno's aesthetic theory is particularly puzzling. In fact, the tautological character of his analysis of how art affects us renders his theory incapable of shedding light on the structure of aesthetic experience; it presupposes a definite effect, which it then uses to account for its findings. The possibility of analysis slips away when theory is fashioned after an aesthetic paradigm, which should, in fact, form the object of analysis. Since art is at theory's beck and call to produce exactly the kind of knowledge theory wants, the outcome of actual encounters with concrete artworks is always determined in advance. Theory knows art has a critical effect, because it knows art's autonomy is the last bastion of resistance in a world blinded by ideology. Theory, therefore, also knows how to distinguish between truly avant-garde art that looks ahead and art that, despite its modern trappings, is reactionary.

Because art always reconfirms the structural insights theory brings to bear on the wealth of aesthetic phenomena, there is no longer, to put it bluntly, a need for individual aesthetic experience. The undeniable attraction of the concrete interpretations Adorno offers us in his numerous essays lies in his versatility and in the keenness for detail with which he makes aesthetic experience meet the conditions laid down by aesthetic theory, rather than in the freedom and range of understanding with which he is prepared to confront the unexpected in aesthetic experience.

Because it makes all actual experience superfluous, the absolute certainty that art is the source of a type of knowledge is the weakest aspect of Adorno's theory. This is why Adorno's aesthetic theory tends toward dogmatic self-validation,[45] shutting itself off in narcissistic reflection from doubt and from anything else that might disturb its conception of itself. If we use Adorno's theory as a guide to aesthetic experience, nothing out of the ordinary will ever happen to us; we will see, hear, feel nothing new, because the theory has already accounted for every possible reaction we might have. True aesthetic experience is predicated on the willingness to remain open to what is unexpected. An ironclad theory can never be a substitute for this openness, which allows art to provoke us into seeing the world in new, unchanneled ways.

The true antidote to traditional theory's dogmatic self-certainty, which Adorno's aesthetics was meant to provide, consists in giving precedence to the possibility of engaging art in a way not already thoroughly determined by theory. *Aesthetic experience must be made the basis for aesthetic theory* and not the other way around. The entrenched illusions generated by ideology can be dispelled only when there is freedom to confront the official face of reality with alternatives. This freedom is first and foremost acquired by an *unfettered play of reflection,* which can be set in motion only by genuine aesthetic experience. Let us consider this a bit more closely.

In contrast to our everyday experiences of the world as we find it, encounters with aesthetic phenomena are unique in that they do not require organization by the understanding; nor, strictly speaking, do artworks prescribe how these encounters will turn out. Aesthetic experience encourages consciousness to engage in a form of reflection that does not restrict it in any way. This highly unusual experience opens up for consciousness new and previously unrealized possibilities. The age-old solution to the problem of how to reawaken deadened forms of perception lies entirely in the possibility of being moved by art. The extreme nature of modern art production, however, makes openness and breadth of vision especially necessary to have such experiences.

I have deliberately introduced this description of aesthetic experience in order to bring Kant to mind. It is time to rediscover his analysis of how aesthetic phenomena affect consciousness, an analysis that Schelling and Hegel thought they had consigned to history.[46] Kant's insights into the structure of reflective judgment, applied to modern art, not only dispense with a fixed, traditional work canon but also make it imperative that we reconsider aesthetic experience, not in terms of confirming what we already think or know about the world but as the way art enhances our powers of perception and understanding. To account for the basis of aesthetic experience in terms of what Kant called our disinterested pleasure in objects allows us to define art without directly identifying it with knowledge. The true nature of art thus consists in its capacity to stimulate thought without restricting it and to bring reflection to a level of independence where it is no longer bound to concepts. Because it loosens reflection's ties to specifically determined cognitive functions, only the type of art that is capable of initiating the free play of reflection can do without the services of thought.

In contrast, art whose entire function is critique is in fact not conducive to critique, as Adorno would have it. Rather, just the opposite is true. Instead of freeing knowledge, it succeeds only in trammeling knowledge. Art that takes on meaning only in opposition to reality is the reverse side of art that merely copies reality. In both cases, consciousness is condemned to fixed, predetermined, almost mechanical reactions in its apprehension of art. Neither of these concepts of art is capable of bringing about the freedom of reflection necessary for true aesthetic experience.

Dialectic of Limits or Philosophy and Art

Hegel's dialectical method, which Adorno unabashedly employs at strategically crucial moments, may help us understand why the latter places so little value on true aesthetic experience. Hegel's objection to Kant's concept of the *Ding an sich,* resurrected in Adorno's concept of the *Nichtidentische,* involves the *dialectic of limits.* Hegel's argument maintains that in order to define the limit of something, a position must already be assumed outside of that limit. Limits can never be drawn from only one side. To recognize a limit thus implies the possibility of overcoming it. Within the context of his debate with Hegel there is no way, other than blind obstinancy, that Adorno can circumvent the consequences this insight has on his own "negative dialectic." Adorno must first explicitly complete the dialectic of limits in order then to sublate it again.[47] *Theory's transformation into aesthetics* rests squarely on this step.

Insight into theoretical knowledge's limitations cannot lead to theory's consummation by transcending its limits. According to what I have identified as Adorno's a priori principle, which accounts for the convergence of art and philosophy in terms of their shared orientation toward knowledge, this insight into theory's limits would seem to fall within the purview of art. By locating the point of convergence in art, however, the mediation is cut short, which prevents the dialectic from culminating in an absolute system. If this mediation were to be completed, then theory would be able to draw its own limits, which would make art's limiting role superfluous. That theory's limits are determined by art, however, is by no means a self-evident truth. In fact, theory imposes its limits on itself and thus determines what its proper domain should be. Aesthetics, as the limit of theory, can be determined only by theory. This, however, sets the dialectic of limits in motion again.

This relationship can be understood as the *inversion of the relationship* in which Hegel ranks art with respect to philosophy. According to Hegel, art is historically prior to philosophy, but because art represents absolute Spirit only in its immediacy, art is subordinate to philosophy. Spirit's unmediated presence in art gives rise to a mediation by which Spirit comes into its own as philosophy. Philosophy, in spelling out what is spiritual in art, necessarily destroys art's autonomous sphere. To raise art to the level of the concept means to put an end to how aesthetic illusion creates its unrestricted effect, which depends on immediacy. Illusion recognized as illusion is robbed of its power and magic. The advent of the philosophy of art thus rings out the age of art.

Neither with respect to its content nor its form is art the highest and most absolute way for Spirit to bring its true interests to consciousness. The type of creation and works peculiar to art no longer fulfill our highest needs.... For this reason, in our age, the *science* of art is much more of a prerequisite than for those times in which art pure and simple really did offer complete satisfaction. Art invites us to consider things in a thinking way; not for the purpose of creating new works of art, but rather to know, in a scientific way, what art is.[48]

In a certain sense, it can be said that Adorno's aesthetics reverses the process by which Hegel's philosophy destroys art's independent sphere. Although Adorno discovers in art philosophy's most fundamental interests, he does not subject art to a philosophical concept of truth, as Hegel does. To do so would deprive art of its power to impose limits on philosophy. In order to save art from sinking back to the level of one of Spirit's irrelevant, preliminary stages, Adorno would rather dispense with reflection. This would reveal, of course, that it was philosophy, in the first place, that had conferred the status of knowledge on art. Adorno thus conceals from himself that it is only by way of philosophical interpretation that art can be put on an equal footing with philosophy. The fact that he does not admit philosophy's constitutive role gives art the aura of independence. The truth of the matter, however, is that Adorno uses art as a deus ex machina, which he hauls in to save the day for philosophy. Perhaps,

Rüdiger Bubner

in spite of all its self-effacing gestures, it is Adorno's aesthetic theory that treats art with the most extreme condescension, the condescension of an anonymous sovereign power.

All these complications could have been avoided if Adorno had once and for all given up the dream that it is possible for philosophy to remain itself and at the same time be different from itself. *The aestheticizing of theory impoverishes a theory of the aesthetic.* Although Adorno professes to promote art's autonomy, he always has theory's interests at heart. In this way, aesthetics is rendered thoroughly heteronomous. The line of argumentation that begins with the insight into universal mystification and extends through the dogma that art and reality are diametrically opposed to each other, in the end, transforms art into an agent of critical theory's interests. Because these interests cannot be openly articulated, they are imputed to the artworks themselves, thus determining in advance how we will experience them. In this way, theory prevails in the very act of denying that it plays a constitutive role in aesthetics.

Translated by Cara Gendel Ryan, from "Kann Theorie ästhetisch werden? Zum Hauptmotiv der Philosophie Adornos," in Rüdiger Bubner, Ästhetische Erfahrung (Frankfurt: Suhrkamp, 1989).

Notes

1. Theodor W. Adorno, *Gesammelte Schriften (GS)*, vol. 1 ("Die Aktualität der Philosophie"), pp. 325–44, 343. See also the preface to Theodor W. Adorno, *Negative Dialektik* (ND) (1966), GS 6:9; trans. E. B. Ashton (New York: Continuum, 1973), p. xix.

2. Max Horkheimer and Theodor W. Adorno, *Dialektik der Aufklärung. Philosophische Fragmente* (DA) (1944/1947 and 1969), GS 3:10; trans. J. Cumming (New York: Seabury Press, 1972), p. x.

3. See also Theodor W. Adorno, "Der Essay als Form" (1958), in *Noten zur Literatur*, vol. 1, GS 11:9–33; trans. as "The Essay as Form," *Notes to Literature*, vol. 1, trans. Shierry Weber Nichelsen (New York: Columbia University Press, 1991), pp. 3–23.

4. Theodor W. Adorno, *Ästhetische Theorie* (AT) (1970), GS 7:140, trans. C. Lenhardt (London: Routledge & Kegan Paul, 1984), p. 134 (translation modified).

5. GS 1 ("Die Aktualität der Philosophie"), p. 343.

6. For a detailed account, see my essay "Problemgeschichte und systematischer Sinn der 'Phänomenologie' Hegels," in *Dialektik und Wissenschaft* (Frankfurt: Suhrkamp,

1973). This essay has been translated as "Hegel's Concept of Phenomenology" for a book on Hegel's *Phenomenology of Spirit*, ed. Gary K. Browning (Netherlands: Kluwer Academic Publishers, 1997).

7. For an extensive treatment of the philosophical similarities, see Hermann Mörchen, *Adorno und Heidegger. Untersuchung einer philosophischen Kommunikationsverweigerung* (Stuttgart: Klett-Cotta, 1981).

8. See GS 1 ("Die Idee der Naturgeschichte" [1932]), pp. 345–65.

9. *Kierkegaard, Konstruktion des Ästhetischen* (1933); GS 2; *Kierkegaard: Construction of the Aesthetic,* trans. R. Hullot-Kentor (Minneapolis: University of Minnesota Press, 1989).

10. Theodor W. Adorno, "Parataxis. Zur späten Lyrik Hölderlins" (1963/1964), in *Noten zur Literatur,* vol. 3, GS 11:447–91.

11. ND, GS 6:23; trans., p. 11.

12. DA, GS 3:9; trans., p. ix.

13. AT, GS 7:191; trans., p. 183 (translation modified).

14. These are sketches of analyses I have dealt with in more detail in my essay "What Is Critical Theory?" in R. Bubner, *Essays in Hermeneutics and Critical Theory,* trans. E. Matthews (New York: Columbia University Press, 1988), pp. 1–35.

15. Theodor W. Adorno, "Offener Brief an Rolf Hochhuth" (1967), in *Noten zur Literatur,* vol. 4, GS 11:591–98, 598.

16. For example, see T. Baumeister and J. Kulenkampff, "Geschichtsphilosophie und philosophische Ästhetik," in *Neue Hefte für Philosophie,* no. 5 (1973):pp. 74–104.

17. DA, GS 3:15; trans., p. xv.

18. Karl Mannheim, *Ideology and Utopia: Introduction to the Sociology of Knowledge,* trans. L. Wirth and E. Shils (London: Routledge & Kegan Paul, 1948). See M. Horkheimer, "Ein neuer Ideologiebegriff?" (1930), in *Gesammelte Schriften,* vol. 2 (Frankfurt: Fischer, 1987), pp. 271ff.; "A New Concept of Ideology?" in *Between Philosophy and Social Science: Selected Early Writings,* trans. G. F. Hunter, M. S. Kramer, and J. Torpey (Cambridge, Mass.: MIT Press, 1993), pp. 129–49. This essay is similar to Adorno's "Das Bewußtsein der Wissenssoziologie" (1937, first published 1953), in *Prismen. Kulturkritik und Gesellschaft* (1955), GS 10/1:31–46; "The Sociology of Knowledge and Its Consciousness," in *Prisms,* trans. Samuel and Shierry Weber (Cambridge, Mass.: MIT Press, 1981), pp. 35–49.

19. In his essay on Samuel Beckett's *Endgame,* Adorno refers to this reversal as follows: "The irrationality of bourgeois society in its late phase rebels at letting itself be understood; those were the good old days, when a critique of the political economy of this society could be written that judged it in terms of its own *ratio.*" ("Versuch, das Endspiel zu verstehen" (1961), in *Noten zur Literatur,* vol. 2, GS 11:281–321, 284); "Trying to Understand *Endgame,*" *Notes to Literature,* vol. 1, p. 244.

20. See Adorno's essay "Zum Klassizismus von Goethes Iphigenie" (1967), in *Noten zur Literatur,* vol. 4 GS 11:495–514, 512ff.

21. "As far back as we can trace it, the history of thought has been a dialectic of enlightenment." ND, GS 6:124; trans., p. 118.

22. Compare AT, GS 7:16, 67, 114; trans., pp. 78, 60, 108.

23. For example, consider Plato's *Republic X*.

24. DA, GS 3:36–37; trans., pp. 18–19. Cf. also T. Adorno, *Philosophie der neuen Musik* (1949) (Berlin, 1972), pp. 20ff., 189.

25. DA, GS 3:36–37; trans., pp. 18–19; AT, GS 7:120, 197, 511; trans., pp. 113–14, 189, 457; ND, GS 6:26–27; trans., p. 15.

26. Friedrich Schelling, *System des transzendentalen Idealismus* (1800).

27. Friedrich Schelling, *Philosophie der Kunst* (1802/1804) (Darmstadt, 1959), pp. 8ff.; *Vorlesungen über die Methode des akademischen Studiums* (1803), lecture 14.

28. W. Benjamin, "Der Autor als Produzent," in *Versuche über Brecht* (Frankfurt: Suhrkamp, 1968), pp. 96ff.; "The Author as Producer," in *Reflections*, trans. E. Jephcott (New York: Harcourt Brace Jovanovich, 1978), pp. 220–38.

29. For example, T. W. Adorno, *Ohne Leitbild. Parva Aesthetica* (1967/1968), GS 10/ 1:289–453, 299ff.

30. Theodor W. Adorno, "Zum Klassizismus von Goethes Iphigenie," in *Noten zur Literatur*, vol. 4, GS 11:502ff. (Cf. Goethe, *Maximen und Reflexionen*, no. 751.) For a pertinent observation about Adorno's essay, see Gerhard Kaiser, "Adornos Ästhetische Theorie," in *Antithesen* (Frankfurt: Athenäum, 1973), pp. 309ff.

31. Citing "historico-philosophical reasons" and referring to his favorite example, Samuel Beckett, Adorno demonstrates the following "change in the a priori of drama: the fact that there is no longer any substantive, affirmative metaphysical meaning that could provide dramatic form with its law and its epiphany. That, however, disrupts the dramatic form down to its linguistic infrastructure. Drama cannot simply take negative meaning, or the absence of meaning, as its content without everything peculiar to it being affected to the point of turning into its opposite." "Versuch, das Endspiel zu verstehen," *Noten zur Literatur*, vol. 2, GS 11:282; "Trying to Understand *Endgame*," in *Notes to Literature*, vol. 1, p. 242.

32. Theodor W. Adorno, *Philosophie der neuen Musik*, p. 31. Adorno's reference to Hegel is completely misleading. What Hegel describes as "simply looking on" [*das reine Zusehen*] refers specifically to the method appropriate to a "phenomenology of Spirit." It does not apply to his philosophy in general, nor does phenomenological *Zusehen* mean that systematic premises are lacking. See *Phänomenologie des Geistes*, in *Werke*, vol. 3 (Frankfurt: Suhrkamp, 1986), p. 77; *Phenomenology of Spirit*, trans. A. V. Miller (Oxford: Oxford University Press, 1977), p. 54. In this connection, see my essay "Hegel's Concept of Phenomenology."

33. Such an innocuous observation, as F. Busoni made in his *Entwurf einer neuen Ästhetik der Tonkunst* (1916; new ed., Frankfurt: Suhrkamp, 1974), does not at all come to grips with the problem: "Ephemeral qualities constitute what is 'modern' about a work of art; the immutable qualities save it from becoming 'old-fashioned.' For 'mod-

ern times,' just as much for 'former times,' there is good and bad, authentic and inauthentic. The absolutely modern does not exist. There is only what comes into existence earlier or later, what flourishes longer or fades away more rapidly. There have always been things which are modern and things which are old" (p. 8).

34. AT, GS 7:134; trans., p. 128. In his essay "Engagement" (1962), Adorno chooses to make Sartre and Brecht into opponents (*Noten zur Literatur,* vol. 3, GS 11:409–30).

35. AT, GS 7:185; also 189, 193ff., 391; trans., p. 179; also pp. 181–82, 186ff., 370–71 (translation modified).

36. Plato, *Republic* 595c ff.

37. Aristotle, *Poetics* 1448b.

38. ND, GS 6:26; trans., pp. 14–15 (translation modified). See also AT, GS 7:86ff., 180ff.; trans., pp. 79ff., 174ff.

39. Theodor W. Adorno, "Erpreßte Versöhnung" (1958), in *Noten zur Literatur,* vol. 2, GS 11:251–80, 260; "Extorted Reconciliation," *Notes to Literature,* vol. 1, pp. 216–40, 224.

40. On the background and orientation of this debate about materialistic aesthetics, see my essay, "Über einige Bedingungen gegenwärtiger Ästhetik," in R. Bubner, *Ästhetische Erfahrung* (Frankfurt: Suhrkamp, 1989), pp. 23ff.

41. Ibid., esp. pp. 30ff.

42. For a good standard work on *Rezeptionsästhetik,* see Wolfgang Iser, *Der implizite Leser. Kommunikationsformen des Romans von Bunyan bis Beckett* (Munich: Fink, 1972); *The Implied Reader: Patterns of Communication in Prose Fiction from Bunyan to Beckett* (Baltimore: Johns Hopkins University Press, 1974).

43. That holds for Peter Bürger, *Theorie der Avantgarde* (Frankfurt: Suhrkamp, 1974). See my essay, "Moderne Ersatzfunktion des Ästhetischen," in *Ästhetische Erfahrung,* pp. 76ff.

44. Johann W. v. Goethe, *Faust. Der Tragödie zweiter Teil,* 6216ff.

45. From an external standpoint, this consequence is particularly striking, as Marc Jimenez has shown in his insightful analysis in *Theodor W. Adorno: Art, idéologie et théorie de l'art* (Paris: Union générale d'éditions, 1973), pp. 270ff.

46. See, R. Bubner, *Ästhetische Erfahrung,* pp. 34ff.

47. Compare, ND, GS 6:9, 397ff; trans., pp. xix, 405ff; *Philosophie der neuen Musik,* pp. 20ff., 189.

48. G. W. F. Hegel, *Vorlesungen über die Ästhetik,* ed. H.G. Hotho (1842), *Werke* 10.1:13ff., 16.

7

Why Rescue Semblance? Metaphysical Experience and the Possibility of Ethics

J. M. Bernstein

Disenchantment

"Nature, in ceasing to be divine, ceases to be human.... We must bridge the gap of poetry from science. We must heal the unnatural wound. We must, in the cold, reflective way of critical system, justify and organize the truth which poetry, with its quick, naive contacts, has already felt and reported."[1] The author of these sentences was not T. W. Adorno but the young John Dewey, writing in 1891. Yet there is hardly any distance at all between Dewey's words and, for example, Adorno's "But although art and science became separate in the course of history, the opposition between them should not be hypostatized."[2] What the instrumental rationality exemplified by natural science begets—and what is socially borne into everyday life by industrialization and technology, for Dewey, and by the ever-expanding domination of exchange value over use value, for Adorno—is the disenchantment of the world, the creation of an unnatural wound between human nature and nature. This wound is unnatural, or contrary to nature, because the human is a part of the natural world. In raising ourselves above it, in making the world an object of representational knowing in which, ideally, even the perspective of the knower would disappear (or, what amounts to the same, become just another item within the object world), all subjective response to the world, and thus the world as it *appears* to human subjects, disappears.[3] By this route, which is the path of enlightenment, the knife of a proclaimed self-sufficient methodological rationality slices into the flesh of the one who wields it. The blood that is let is the subjectivity of the modern subject and the meaning (*Sinn*) of the object world. The cultural crisis generated by science (by technology, by capital) is a crisis of subjectivity and meaning; the disenchantment of the world is the proximate and ground cause of this crisis.

In listing the support of Dewey, whose views in this respect converge with other first-generation pragmatists,[4] my intention is only to provide corroborative evidence for Adorno's contentious thesis that there is a crisis of modernity; that this crisis is best understood in terms of a diremption, a "wound," whose manifest image is the gap between art and science; and that the cause of this gap is progressive disenchantment. These views, variously formulated, were until recently what self-consciously modernist thinkers and artists considered constitutive of the problematic of modernity. Ironically, in part because of the quiet success of pragmatism in installing itself as the "rational" postmetaphysical outlook, they have been "forgotten." When they are mentioned, they appear anachronistic, as if the attempt to engage with them raises the stakes too high, beyond, say, what is pragmatically intelligible. Nonetheless, without an adequate focus on the phenomena of disenchantment and diremption, Adorno's philosophical practice will be misunderstood.

Adorno's philosophy is "speculative" in Hegel's sense of that term; its primary aim is to provide a conceptual articulation of the experience of diremption. Hegel's *Phenomenology of Spirit* sought to articulate the diremption of "subject" and "substance," as expressed, for example, in the Enlightenment separation of pure insight from faith.[5] For Adorno, other than the diremption between science and art, the diremption is said to be between universal and particular, concept and object, concept and intuition, sign and image, communication and expression, autonomous subject and subjectivity. In quite broad terms, Adorno's two major philosophical works engage this diremption from competing perspectives: *Negative Dialectics* attempts to demonstrate that the disenchanted conception of the concept involves an illegitimate diremption of concept from object. Concepts cannot be self-sufficient and independent from what they are about, any more than linguistic meaning can be made fully deter-

minate (and thus a transparent medium of representation) independently of social and historical usage (practice).[6] *Aesthetic Theory*, in
contrast, works at the dislocation of universal from particular from
the perspective of the disenchanted particular. Works of art form the
object of Adorno's concern here since, prima facie, they are particulars that claim attention, that is, insinuate meaning (*Sinn*) and substance (import: *Gehalt*) while not being subsumable under any one
concept or theory. If rationalized concepts can be shown to require
the nondiscursive resources of object and image, and if aesthetic particulars thrown up by artistic modernism can be shown to suggest
(invoke, imply) meaning and cognitive significance, then concept
and object belong together in a manner not recognized by the re-
gimes of enlightened reason and rationality at work in contemporary
discursive practices (social, economic, political, etc.).

This tidy picture of Adorno's speculative philosophy is, in two respects, a bit too tidy. First, and most evidently, that the speculative
comprehension of disenchanted particulars should focus on works of
art is problematic, because, trivially, such works are not "real" particulars at all; rather, they are shot through with "nonbeing," with being
"fictions," "illusions," unrealities. How and why should the claim of
particulars in opposition to the reigning universal (call it, again, enlightened reason, capital) be lodged from the perspective of these indigent items? Should not the claim for particulars be made from the
vantage point of fully worldly particulars—ecological habitats or the
poor, women, ethnic minorities—at present not adequately recognized as being of substance and worth by science and rationalized society? Second, and even more emphatically, Adorno's writings do not
read as straightforwardly speculative discourses, even if it is conceded
that his major works do appear to intrigue a speculative pairing together of concept and object, philosophy (the discourse of the pure
concept) and art (the practice of the particular for its own sake). How
are we to account for the discrepancy between Hegel's and Adorno's
speculative philosophies? How can Adorno's philosophy be speculative and a negative dialectic opposed to a positive, identifying closed
dialectic? We can only make sense of the project of *Aesthetic Theory*—
of Adorno's attempt to sanction the claim of the particular against
the universal by considering the illusory particulars evidenced by

modernist artworks—by charting the divergence between his and Hegel's conceptions of a speculative dialectic.

The Withering of Experience

Hegel's speculative philosophy ponders the *experience* (*Erfahrung*) of diremption, the experience of the dislocation of particular from universal, of certainty from truth; for example, the experience of the unhappy consciousness who regards God as the universal and as thus representing his true essence.[7] Hegel's phenomenology here traces the unfolding experience of the unhappy consciousness as it attempts to make sense of, give expressive articulation to, its separation from and its unity with its timeless, unchangeable Other, which it takes to be the truth about itself. The changing relationship between consciousness and object, the way in which consciousness redefines who it is and what its object is as a consequence of attempting to articulate its identity and difference with its Other is roughly what Hegel means by the notion of experience (*Erfahrung*). There can be this experience because there is an inner, intentional relation between consciousness and object, because "the" object, whatever it is, is construed as, or comes to be experienced as, essential to self-consciousness, and because consciousness's recognition of its other is always simultaneously a misrecognition. So, in the case of the unhappy consciousness, "what it does *not* know is that this its object, the Unchangeable, which it knows essentially in the form of individuality [i.e., as Jesus], is *its own self*, is itself the individuality of consciousness."[8] As a consequence, the attempt by the unhappy consciousness to affirm the universal and unchangeable by sacrificing its particular material life to it is necessarily self-defeating. The ascetic and masochistic pleasure consciousness has through the pain of bodily self-mortification not only keeps bodily existence as the focus of attention, but such renunciation eventually reveals the ineliminability of sensuous fulfillment as integral to the search for spiritual transcendence. The coming to be of this revelation of the entwinement of (unchanging) universal and (changeable) particular is Hegelian experience.

Experience is hence the fundamental *medium* of Hegel's speculative discourse, which attains its fullest objectivity when experiences are given an appropriate narrative order in memory. This is equally, according to Adorno, Proust's "method": "The measure of such objectivity is not the verification of assertions through repeated testing but rather individual human experience, maintained through hope and disillusionment. Such experience throws its observations into relief through confirmation or refutation in the process of recollection."[9] Experiences of hope (e.g., of spiritual transcendence) and disillusionment (e.g., of bodily pain and pleasure in the very activities that seek to remove it as essential) are individual occurrences of general claims; hence the path of experience, the way of despair, is always of a failed relation between universal and particular from within the perspective of the particular. Because the claims of universality only ever arise as claims about the ideal significance of particular lives, the perspective of the individual cannot be departed from. The question as to whether a *path* of experience is exemplary and objective is answerable only as a work of recollection and narration that interrogates the orderliness of the path traversed. Narrative recollection, with its prospective openness to contingency and retrospective closure, is or was the dominant form in which the discourse of human experience could achieve a level of objectivity that surmounted the singular path from which it arose without departing from that path.

The thought that recollective narratives no longer possess authority is a familiar one. For Adorno, however, the collapse of the authority of developmental narratives is itself an effect of a more fundamental collapse—of experience. It is precisely the medium of experience, Adorno believes, following the lead of Walter Benjamin, that progressive disenchantment has made all but unavailable: we no longer directly experience the diremption of subject from object, universal from particular. There has been a "withering of experience."[10]

The disproportion between the all-powerful reality and the powerless subject creates a situation where reality becomes unreal because the experience of reality is beyond the grasp of the subject. The surplus of reality is reality's undoing. By slaying the subject, reality itself becomes lifeless.... The marrow of experience has been sucked out of the concrete. All experience, including experience that is removed from economic life, has been emaciated. (AT 53–54/45–46)

On Adorno's view, the fundamental determinants of everyday life no longer go through the experience of individual subjects; what practices and things now might mean is determined by macrostructures that work behind the backs of the individuals who are their functionaries.

Only our self-preserving narcissism prevents us from experiencing this absence of experience. So entrenched is this ego-protecting narcissism that Adorno can quip that "the very people who burst with proofs of exuberant vitality could easily be taken for prepared corpses, from whom the news of their not-quite-successful decease has been withheld for reasons of population policy."[11] Adorno's sarcasm here needs to be well timed, like a good joke, since he is speaking about us. Somewhat more austerely, in an essay on Proust, Adorno appears to be supporting Benjamin's interpretation of Proust's project as the "synthetic" production of experience under conditions in which "there is less and less hope that it can come into being naturally,"[12] when he avers that "undamaged experience is produced only in memory, far beyond immediacy.... Total remembrance is the response to total transience, and hope lies only in the strength to become aware of transience [the collapse of *Erfahrung* into *Erlebnis*] and preserve it in writing."[13]

A withering of experience thus involves two basic features. First, that the universals that are potentially constitutive for singular lives are no longer found to be immanently formative for those lives; as a consequence, no exemplary process of hope and disillusionment is manifest in individual lives. The highest values have devalued themselves—for us. Second, where a claim to truth or universality is encountered, its objectivity is regarded as in principle independent of individual experience. The claims of experience are reduced to the impersonal and repeatable protocols of experiment and evidence.

The withering, the destruction, the collapse of experience haunts and burdens Adorno's philosophy: how is speculation possible if the diremption of subject and substance is unexperienced and unknown? How can there be a dialectic of recognition and misrecognition when there is no experience of the Other to recognize or misrecognize? What if, like those beings bursting with exuberant vitality, we can manage perfectly well without experience, without meaning, without the Other? Might not a fully functional life, one wholly adapted to the demands of existing society, be sufficient unto itself? What if, then, the diremption or wound that eviscerates life to the level of mere appearance has become so routine that it has become our second nature, and the drive of self-preservation sufficient for the reproduction of social life?

From Auschwitz to Metaphysics

Implicitly, these are the questions Adorno himself poses in the concluding study of *Negative Dialectics*, "Meditations on Metaphysics." Two overlapping sets of reflections are pursued in the "Meditations." In sections 1–5 (ND 354–74/361–81) Adorno attempts to demonstrate how the questions and ideas of metaphysics in its most traditional sense, namely, ideas concerning what transcends the context of human life as immanently understood, necessarily emerge as relevant again to thought in virtue of the extreme of their denial as exemplified by "Auschwitz." Sections 6–11 (ND 374–97/381–405) repeat the previous dialectic of radical immanence as generating the necessity for some form of transcendence, only here the focus of Adorno's reflections are Kant's ideas of pure reason, above all the ideas of freedom, God, and the immortality of the soul that are postulated as necessary supplements to practical reason.

The *event* of Auschwitz is a historical hyperbole; it projects the figure of a world reduced to self-identity without remainder, a world without an outside and without possibility. However, as a worldly event, it forces us to place our reflective self-understanding in relation to it and thereby in relation to the image projected by it. In this way, it conditions our reflective relation to culture and philosophy. The event of Auschwitz

demonstrated irrefutably the failure of culture. That this could happen in the midst of the traditions of philosophy, of art, and of the enlightening sciences says more than that these, and their spirit, lacked the power to take hold of men and to change them. In those fields themselves, in the autarky that is emphatically claimed for them, there is untruth. (ND 359/366)

This thought involves a double inscription. On the one hand, it demands a radical self-critique of culture, one that acknowledges culture's impotence while nonetheless recognizing that only via such an

autocritique is change possible—culture is all we possess to overcome the depredations it purveys. On the other hand, this demand
equally affects metaphysics, since its transcendent ideas are at one
with culture's traditional self-conception of being concerned wholly
with "higher things," with "spiritual life": "After Auschwitz there is no
word tinged from on high, not even a theological one, that has a
right to remain unchanged" (ND 360/367).

Auschwitz irrevocably, and from a variety of directions, questions
whether a life conceived of in purely immanent terms, a life as
bounded by the terms, say, of a "postmetaphysical" naturalism or
pragmatism, can be self-sufficient. If life were the highest good, then
death would be the worst that could be feared; but Auschwitz has
taught us that there is worse than death (ND 364/371). To acknowledge that there is something that is worse than death, that death is
an extreme and a figure of the deprivations of life, entails that the
"impossibility" that the event of death once securely marked off can
no longer be considered external to what transpires within life.
Hence, life does not of itself carry the promise of possible experience, of possible meaningfulness. Just carrying on is not the same as
human possibility. Life without experience is equally life without possibility. Auschwitz thus questions the meaning of possibility and impossibility by projecting a context of pure immanence in which they
cannot be separated. But our capacity to reflexively capture this indifference implies there is something more to be said, something
more that can be said. If immanence were self-sufficient and complete, then despair would be rational and final because unknown
and unknowable. If Auschwitz could happen in the midst of our enlightened, rational moralities, then those moralities must lack the resources to ensure that it does not happen again. There must be
"more" than this (AT 122/116), something that transcends the context of radical immanence.

Conversely, this "more" cannot be what metaphysics always
claimed it to be, not only because "high" culture has failed but
equally because our sense of the injustice of Auschwitz involves an ineliminable "bodily sensation" of moral abhorrence at the "unbear-
able physical agony to which individuals" were there exposed. No
rationalized morality can provide full acknowledgment of human

suffering; that the acknowledgment we do offer has a mimetic, somatic source speaks in favor of "materialism" in opposition to such moralities and the culture they are a part of: "The course of history forces materialism upon metaphysics" (ND 358/365).

In accordance with his practice of providing paratactically arranged "constellations" of thought rather than deductive argument, nearly every section of the "Meditations," and often even single paragraphs of sections, works a double movement whereby Adorno confronts a version of the claim for radical immanence that reveals itself to be incomplete or self-stultifying, and as thus requiring a metaphysical supplement, with an argument showing that the metaphysical supplement itself cannot be the absolute "beyond" it was taken to be by the philosophical and theological tradition. The contrapuntal critique of absolutist metaphysics, the critique that is to bring about a union of materialism and metaphysics, begins with the very first sentence of the "Meditations": "We cannot say any more that the unchangeable (*Unveränderliche*) is truth, and that the mobile, transitory is appearance (*Schein*). The indifference of temporality and eternal ideas is no longer tenable." The statement is meant to recall the experience of Hegel's unhappy consciousness. But whereas Hegel ascribed the self-defeating logic of sacrificing the changeable to the unchangeable to individuals in their actual lives, our sacrifice is collective and cultural: the "indifference" of temporality and the eternal is the moral indifference of the lives of some to others—morality failing to be immanent to conduct when it mattered most. The cancellation of this indifference is our bodily sensation of moral abhorrence. This, Adorno intends to claim, must be relevant to what is conceived of as transcendent.

As this thought is reconfigured throughout the opening sections, as recent history is brought to bear on how we regard what is metaphysical, Adorno begins explicitly to urge the claim that, in fact, we find the kind of exteriority traditionally ascribed to the metaphysical ideas in concrete, worldly occurrences: "And yet it is tempting to look for meaning (*Sinn*) not in life in general, but in the fulfilled moments—in the moments of present existence that make up for its refusal to tolerate anything outside it" (ND 371/378). Almost nothing is said here about what such "moments" (*Augenblicken*) might be.

It is, then, the unfolding historical entwining of materialism and metaphysics that generates the central question orienting the "Meditations": is metaphysical experience in general still possible? This question, in its turn, leads to the dominant theme of section 4 of the "Meditations": what is a metaphysical experience (ND 366/373)? One might have thought that Adorno had already answered this question many times over in the course of *Negative Dialectics*, that everything he had to say about the nonidentical, about what does not fall under the disenchanted concept, about what rationalist idealism leaves out of its systems, about the somatic moment repressed by the Kantian idea of autonomy—that all these were, in some way, just what might be denoted by the idea of metaphysical experience. But this would be to misread the austerity of a negative dialectics that pursues the critique of the abstract concept, which in broad terms should be considered extensionally equivalent to Kant's notion of the understanding (*Verstand*), from the perspective of that concept by using it against itself. As a consequence, Adorno's procedure locates the logical or rational insufficiency of identity thinking without stating what sort of evidence might be relevant to vindicating that claim or providing evidence of something other. The practice of negative dialectics is austerely philosophical: it never explicitly steps outside what is immanent to the logic of the concept.

However, it is just this fact that is the ultimate fault with the rational concept and hence with traditional philosophy: they presume their own self-sufficiency. And, we are now to understand, it is this same "postmetaphysical" self-sufficiency that is fulfilled and refuted by the event of Auschwitz. As a consequence, three distinct concepts begin to converge: the nonidentical, metaphysics, and experience. The first is Adorno's technical term for what the disenchanted concept excludes and vanquishes. Metaphysics comes to overlap with the nonidentical once rational cognition proclaims itself to be a "postmetaphysical" affair of pure immanence. And these both come to overlap with experience once the autarky of the mind and culture is dissolved, forcing metaphysics to reconcile itself with materialism. Metaphysical experience, were it possible, would be of what, *in esse*, transcends the rationalized context of immanence.

The Broken Good: Despair and the Intelligible World

If the deity did not exist, only the wicked would reason rationally. The just man would be merely mad.

—*Kant*

Although Adorno provides, in section 4, a brief Proustian exemplar of metaphysical experience as the promise of happiness accorded to certain childhood experiences, rather than following through on this, he suddenly switches to an extended discussion of Kant two sections later. The reason for this new tack is that, having elicited metaphysical experience as the only possible repository of a counter to the despair and nihilism of a context of pure immanence, he must somehow locate the possibility and characterization of such an experience as it might appear from within a *philosophy* that is itself fully committed to enlightened rationality. Nor is Adorno's choice of Kant's philosophy arbitrary, since it both legislates radical immanence as the condition for possible knowledge and acknowledges the inevitability and necessity of thinking that transcends the bounds of experience.

In turning to Kant after his discussion of Auschwitz and the fate of metaphysics in contemporary culture, Adorno is implicitly contending that, from the perspective of the philosophy of history, Kant's aporetic accounting of immanence and transcendence is more applicable to the present than Hegel's more sanguine speculative dialectic, which presupposed metaphysical experience: self-recognition in absolute otherness. Hegel's fundamental philosophical problem was to demonstrate that what Kant took to be transcendent, as a thing-in-itself beyond appearances, as noumenal or belonging to an intelligible world, was in truth already ideal (an intentional correlate of consciousness) in virtue of its being posited by us. For Adorno, the Enlightenment drive toward immanence, the drive to realize idealism, has been all too successful. Our post-Auschwitz problem is thus the opposite of Hegel's: we have lost sight of the moment of transcendence, of absolute otherness, of the "something" without which our mediations would be mere mirrors of our eviscerated subjectivities. The thing-in-itself thus *becomes* what is to be rescued:

What survives in Kant, in the alleged mistake of his apology for the thing-in-itself—which the logic of consistency (*Konsequenzlogik*) from Maimon on could so triumphantly demonstrate—is the memory of the refractory moment opposing the logic of consistency: nonidentity. This is why Kant, who surely did not misconceive of the consistency of his critics, protested against them and would rather convict himself of dogmatism, than absolutize identity, from whose meaning, as Hegel was quick to recognize, the reference to something nonidentical is inalienable. The construction of thing-in-itself and intelligible character is that of a nonidentity as the condition of possible identifications; but it is also that which categorially eludes identification. (ND 286/290)

Nonidentity—variously, object, image, somatic moment, or indigent particular—is the condition of possible identifications, because without it there would be nothing to identify. Concepts *depend* on the objects they are about while disavowing that dependency. From the point of view of the rationalized concept, all meaning, all sense, all import comes from it. Hence particular "intuitions" are subsumed by concepts; events provide evidence for the truth of theories; use values are evaluated by the market in terms of exchange values; maxims of actions become valid only through a universalistic procedural formalism. In each case, cognition and rationality are wholly on the side of the universal; the particular plays a functional role but lacks a speaking part: it eludes identification. If dependence is real, then the claim to constitute meaning on the part of identifying thought is illusory. Hence, identifying thought lives off what it cannot not acknowledge and what it must disavow. In the "exchange" between particular and universal, there is a complex logic of dependence and independence that belongs to both sides of the relation. This complex logic is both causal (factual) and conceptual. It is this logic of dependence and independence, with its dual character, that Adorno perceives in the Kantian thought of the thing-in-itself; it thus becomes the model for his concept of the nonidentical: it is what grounds and makes identifying thought possible while making its claim to totality impossible. For us, as for Kant, there is a "block" preventing access to the nonidentical, the metaphysical, but this "block" is historical not a priori.

What is most difficult and rebarbative about Adorno's argument at this juncture is that he is binding his defense of metaphysical experience to a materialist rereading of Kant's moral theology, the very element of Kant's moral theory that his contemporary followers find most otiose. Resistance to the centrality Adorno offers to philosophical aesthetics is coextensive with past resistance to Kantian theology. Yet the *problem* to which Kant's moral theology is an intended response is an urgent one for contemporary moral and political thought.

The contemporary versions of Kant's problem concerns the diremption between impartial, universalistic moralities (Kantian, utilitarian, Habermasian) that subsume individual ends under the requirements of what is followable by, or acceptable to, all or what would provide the great happiness for all, on the one hand, and moralities that take their bearing from individual projects or attachments (leading to *eudaimonia* or authenticity), on the other.[14] Habermas, for example, has been brought to distinguish the logic of ethical reason, which concerns what is good, or even absolutely good for me (a good life), and moral reason which relates to the validity of a maxim as it might be acceptable to everyone (a right life).[15] Unavoidably, the distinction between the moral and the ethical points to the diremption that Adorno contends is the source of the Kantian block: the divorce of the intellectual and the sensual, itself a legacy of the split between intellectual and manual labor: "The separation of sensuality and the Understanding, the nerve of the argument in favor of the block, is a social product; by the *chorismos,* sensuality is designated a victim of the understanding because, all arrangements to the contrary notwithstanding, the state of the world fails to content sensuality" (ND 382/ 389). The contingent character of this separation is what Habermas denies when he argues that morality and ethics have incommensurable logical forms or, for example, when he asserts that duties "point the will in a certain direction and give it orientation but do not compel it as impulses do; they motivate through reasons and lack the impulsive force of purely empirical motives."[16] Here we are being confronted with a claimed logical, indeed quasi-transcendental separation between the sensual and the intellectual: "orientation" belongs to reason alone, whereas the impulses causally "compel." What is it, Adorno could ask (ND 226–230/226–230), to "motivate" without empirical motives? To make something move without touching?

Of course, Adorno's confidence that this diremption between the particular and the universal is historical and contingent derives from his belief that the universality of existing society, its appearance as a system of cooperation, hides the fact that it perpetuates itself through individual, class, and national antagonism. The peaceable whole is one of conflict and antagonism, and it thereby uses individuals, sacrifices them, to its universality. In this respect, it may be said that the whole is contradictory or false. But this falsity is precisely what constitutes the context of immanence, making any conception of reconciliation a matter of what does not fit into this context.

What draws Adorno to Kant's account of the diremption of universal and particular is that Kant perceives the question of the separation of the mental from the sensual, of moral goods from nonmoral goods, *as* a diremption, which therefore has a direct bearing on the intelligibility of moral action itself. As Adorno reiterates, what motivates Kant's construction of an intelligible world is "the unthinkability of despair" (ND 378/385). What would cause unrelieved and unconditional despair is if moral struggle and moral achievement in their narrow, universalist construal were *wholly disconnected* from the achievement of human happiness; if, then, there were overriding reasons to believe that the natural course of things was such that evil flourished in this life and one wide grave, swallowing good and evil indifferently, was the ultimate end. It is because the existing world is like this that Kant postulates the existence of God and the immortality of the soul as rational "instruments" that make the idea of the highest good itself possible. What is central here is the disconnection, the diremption of moral worth and human happiness. It is their actual, empirical separation from one another and their "rational" belonging together that is the speculative core of Kant's moral theology, even in the first *Critique.*

Happiness, taken by itself is, for our reason, far from being the complete good. Reason does not approve happiness (however inclination may desire it) except in so far as it is united with worthiness to be happy, that is, with moral conduct. Morality, taken by itself, and with it, the mere *worthiness* to be happy, is also far from being the complete good. To make the good complete, he who behaves in such a manner as not to be unworthy of happiness must be able to hope that he will participate in happiness.... Happiness, therefore, in exact proportion with the morality of the rational beings who are thereby rendered worthy of it, alone constitutes the supreme good of that world wherein, in accordance with the commands of a pure practical reason, we are under obligation to place ourselves. This world is indeed an intelligible world only, since the sensible world holds out no promise that any such systematic unity of ends can arise through the nature of things.[17]

What is at stake in this passage is the intelligibility *überhaupt* of moral conduct, and hence the reality of the moral perspective: "If we could not even conceive of another order than the one implied by our rational calculations, we would have to conclude that the moral perspective is *illusory*."[18] This potential illusoriness relates primarily to the rational status of moral conduct itself. If virtue is not its own reward—a skeptical, stoical thesis that a priori discounts worldly experience as mattering to morality—then it must be connected in some way to the "natural" ends of human conduct. To urge that virtue is utterly independent of empirical eventuality gives license to instrumental rationality as the sole logic of empirical practice. If the virtuous person can point to nothing empirical that is morally salient, then the claim of virtue must be empty for finite beings. If there is no inner coordination (synthetic, a priori connection) between worthiness to be happy (say, whatever the rational demands are for coordinating action among many individuals) and happiness, then either one sacrifices oneself to the demands of the whole or one seeks one's own ends in complete disregard to the ends of others. Only speculation—the demonstration that the world projected by instrumental reasoning is not *the* world, and hence not self-sufficient, a closed totality—can save the just person from being irrational and fantastical, that is, mad. Hence, speculatively, the happiness of the Nazi and the suffering of his or her virtuous victim will bespeak a moral deformity in the world order, of what counts *as* a world, a deformity intelligible as a deformity only if happiness and virtue are essentially incomplete, non–self-sufficient goods; thus, the thought of their unity, happiness proportionate to virtue, forms the ineliminable place from which judgment on the world is made and conduct originates.

The speculative articulation of virtue and happiness, the rational and the sensible, would provide *the moral image of the world*. Such an image is ontological, because it concerns making room for the (highest) good *within* worldly experience. Speculation continues the project of transcendental philosophy critically, hence nontranscendentally, in the precise sense that it concerns the conditions of possible experience. Because one of the characteristics of how the world appears now is as a context of radical immanence in which experience in its robust sense is absent, the task of speculation is to demonstrate the possibility of experience in this sense.

Necessary Semblance

What, again, is supposed to distinguish speculative from abstract identities is the return to the experience of diremption. But it is precisely this experience that is lacking in the Kantian construction: empirically, the evil do flourish and the virtuous do suffer; when the two do harmonize, their harmony appears as wholly contingent, a matter of moral luck. Hence, empirical experience vindicates the logical hiatus separating the logic of moral reasoning from the logic of ethical self-realization. It is thus no accident that Kant finds it necessary to postulate the existence of another, intelligible world as the moral counterpart to this world in order to avoid the conclusiveness of despair. Yet, as stated, the idea of the highest good cannot be accepted, because its instruments (God and the immortality of the soul) and its setting outside all sensibility themselves offend against reason. If human striving must presuppose an intelligible world that lacks all connection with the sensible, then we lose any grasp of what human, sensible striving is for. The conditions of rational striving hence come to make such striving appear irrational and thereby confirm the very despair the idea of the highest good was meant to dissolve.

As Adorno remarks, however, metaphysical experience "was never located so far beyond the temporal as in the schoolbook use of the word metaphysics" (ND 365/372). If the intelligible world refers us to "objects," including for Kant freedom, then there is something contradictory in assuming their *existence* beyond what can be given in a possible perception: "What Kant alludes to with respect to freedom would apply to God and immortality as well, only more so. For these do not refer to any pure possibility of conduct [as freedom does]; their own concepts make them postulates of things in being, no matter of what kind. These entities need "matter," and in Kant's case they would depend entirely upon that intuition whose possibility he

excludes from the transcendent ideas" (ND 383/391). It is this fact
that makes Kant's conception of an intelligible world hopelessly
aporetic, poised in an apparently impossible space between the real
and the merely imaginary.

If even the thought of despair requires nondespair in order to be
thought—"Grayness could not fill us with despair if our minds did not
harbor the concept of different colors, scattered traces of which are
not absent from the negative whole" (ND 370/377–78)—that is, if the
conclusiveness of despair could be only posited, and therefore not absolute, then Kant must be thinking "something" through the ideas of
reason. Yet if the notion of an intelligible world, the traditional home
of metaphysical ideas, is incoherent, and indeed on Kantian grounds,
then the space between the real and the imaginary that it projects
must be materialistically reconfigured. And that reconfigurement
must be twofold. First, it must be reflectively constructed as relation-
ally bound to the logic of the understanding that initially rejects it,
namely, as the negation of that logic: "Paradoxically, the intelligible
sphere which Kant envisioned would once again be an 'appearance': it
would be what that which is hidden from the finite mind shows to that
mind, what the mind is forced to think and, due to its own finiteness,
to disfigure. The concept of the intelligible world is the self-negation
of the finite mind" (ND 384/392). Adorno takes this self-negation to
be what is thought in Kantian idealism—we know appearances only
and not things in themselves—once it is drawn out of the armor of its
method. The necessity of postulating an intelligible world cancels the
claim to completeness concerning empirical existence of the mind
that asserts it; empirical existence itself must include more than what
the understanding projects it as including.

Second, Kant's austerity is itself well taken: we cannot presume
that what *must* be thought through the self-negation of the understanding exists simply because we (rationally) must reflectively enact
that negation. The necessity of postulation can be convicted of mere
wishful thinking, of blind hope: because moral conduct is not intelligible without positing transcendence does not entail the validity of
what is thereby posited. But Adorno has already undermined the purity of Kantian postulation, a purity that assumes an a priori disjunction between the sensible and the intelligible, by showing that it is

the logic of the understanding itself, identity thinking, that forces the harmonization of the sensible and the intelligible into a transcendent beyond. The issue, then, is not, as Kant supposed, a matter of providing a theological supplement to the understanding but of dissolving the understanding's claim to hegemony over what belongs within the domain of possible experience. Of course, to the degree to which the understanding can rationally and empirically claim dominion over possibility, what appears as other must appear as illusory, as semblance. To the degree to which what is illusory is necessary for the understanding itself (identity thinking lives off of nonidentity), the unequivocal distinction between empirical possibility and logical possibility is brought into question.

Hence, the corrective of the understanding must truly inhabit a space between the real (empirical possibility) and the imaginary (logical possibility). This is the space of necessary semblance: "What finite beings say about transcendence is the semblance of transcendence; but as Kant well knew, it is a necessary semblance. Hence the incomparable metaphysical relevance of the rescue of semblance, the object of aesthetics" (ND 386/393). Everything we have observed Adorno argue turns on the space between the real and the imaginary not being exhaustive, either cognitively or "metaphysically," that is, with respect to what bears on what can be known and therefore be true, and with respect to the meaning of the being of the world. Artistic semblance is the successor and the materialist transformation of metaphysical illusion: if religion and traditional metaphysics demand the immortality of the soul, art, which is inevitably bound to its material medium, must reject the separation of body and soul; its hope, the hope projected in its practice, would be for the transfigured body.

The Rescue of Semblance

Adorno calls the drive behind the unthinkability of despair the "rescuing urge" (*Begierde des Rettens*); the task of rescue, of redemption, can be thought only through the rescue of semblance. Thus, aesthetic semblance must take on all the ambiguity and tension that once was lodged in the hope and despair of the idea of an intelligible world. The difficulty of aesthetic semblance is that its claims cannot be unequivocally charted in accordance with the understanding's own concepts of possibility and potentiality, because those concepts reflect the duality between the imaginary (what is only logically possible or conceivable) and the real (what is stored up and thus a potentiality in the existing configuration of what is). The question of aesthetic semblance is the question of the possibility of possibility, of a conception of possible experience that transcends what is now taken to be the parameters of possible experience. And this question makes sense only if occurrent conceptions of what is understood by both "possibility" and "experience" can be revealed to be contestable, despite their being the terms that form the horizon of empirical intelligibility. Hence, Adorno's contention is that aesthetic semblance rides adrift of, and calls into question, our most sophisticated elaborations of the logical, epistemic, and causal modalities. Nor should this be surprising if, as Adorno avers, in the materialist reinscription of metaphysics the dignity once accorded to the universal and the atemporal is now to be transferred to the contingent, the indigent particular: "There is no origin save in ephemeral life" (ND 158/156).

In section 5 of chapter 5 of *Aesthetic Theory* (AT 128–29/122–24), Adorno provides some indication of the fineness of balance required in order to heed the claims of artistic semblance without either reifying or dismissing them. The work of heeding is the effort of philosophical aesthetics as rescue. For our immediate purposes, what is most relevant about this section is that it presents a classification of the different senses adhering to, or better, the different claims being made by a semblant particular, that is, a nonexistent being (*Nichtseiende*), that comes on the scene as if it were real. Throughout *Aesthetic Theory*, Adorno argues that, paradigmatically, only autonomous, modernist works of art fully satisfy the criteria for being semblant particulars in an emphatic sense. In each such nonexistent item, at least four claims are to be registered: (1) particular things can be unsubsumable, nonfungible, and yet sources of meaning; (2) the promise and possibility of happiness as an immanent human possibility are different from the mere satisfaction of desire; (3) as an inference from (1) and (2), claims about the categorial status of "possibility" and "experience" can arise outside the self-conceived sphere of philosophical reflection and hence become essential for it (i.e., philosophy must be in a relation of dependence to nonphilosophy, art, as a condition for philosophical reflection on "possible experience"); and (4) what aesthetic items claim, however "objective" those claims must be regarded as being, nonetheless may be sheer lie and illusion.[19] The vindication of these four claims would be the philosophical core of a rescue of semblance. Although the task of vindication is beyond the scope of this essay, a slightly elaborated sketch of these claims themselves is a necessary preliminary to understanding Adorno's speculative reconstruction of the moral image of the world.

1

The familiar Kantian construal of aesthetic judgment contends that the specificity of such judgments resides in their being singular judgments that lay claim to intersubjective validity, made only when the judger is exposed to an individual object, without constitutive recourse to descriptive predicates. Although a good deal of Adorno's general philosophical strategy involves the attempt to provide aesthetic reflective judgment with a scope beyond the domain of the aesthetic that would contest existing views of epistemic judgment, he also deploys the elements of Kantian aesthetic judgment to model the constitutive features of modernist works. It is such works themselves that are singularities that do not derive from existing concepts (i.e., aesthetic forms, genres, etc.) that raise claims to intersubjective validity beyond what we had heretofore believed to be constitutive of such validity. Traditional autonomous works accepted existing genre and form specifications and standard criteria for unity, harmony, and integration. In contrast, modernist art operates through the negation of existing forms, normative criteria, and extra-artistic assumptions about meaning while continuing to produce items that are recognizably works. Such works are "new" in their incommensurability with everything thought constitutive of what art is or could be.

Thus, where the aesthetic semblance of modern autonomous works of art radically parts company with Kantian metaphysical illusion is in what appears through such works—their intentional objects—necessarily adhering to specific and concrete individuals. These individuals are apparitions, appearances *of* intentional objects whose existence does not formally exceed, and therefore cannot be separated from, particular works. Aesthetic semblance, the mode of appearance or apparition specific to the aesthetic, is not gathered from, for example, taking up an "aesthetic attitude" nor from an item belonging to the "artworld" nor from there being a transcendental category that inscribes the "artistic" in general. Rather, it is a concrete particular—"this" poem, symphony, painting—that presents itself while being nonetheless a semblance, a nonexistent: "The appearance [the artwork itself] is not exchangeable because it is neither a torpid particular being, replaceable by other particular beings, nor an empty universal, subsuming and leveling specific beings in terms of some common characteristic." The thesis that there is no origin save in ephemeral life is raised by each authentic work of art to the degree to which each is an "origin," making a claim that exceeds and defies every preestablished source of authority, every universal, while remaining a particular that cannot be replaced by any other particular.[20] This challenges our extant understanding of the sensible particular by portending the thesis that sensibility is not categorially distinct from the intelligible, because what appears as belonging solely to the domain of the sensible, for example, "this" abstract painting, is also intelligible.

2

It is central to Adorno's critique of idealist aesthetics that it conceives of the sensual moment of art, through its formation, as providing a distinct pleasure (say, the harmony of understanding and imagination) and thus as satisfying a desire, a longing. This sins against artistic form by not taking aesthetic form, and thus the spectator's knowledge that what appears is a semblance, seriously. To consider art in terms of pleasure and satisfaction would reduce it to the gustatory—a matter of "taste" in the most reductive sense of that term. Modernist works, like Kafka's stories, underline this removal of art from desire by calling forth "responses like real anxiety, a violent drawing back, an almost physical revulsion" (AT 26/18). Yet these reactions of psychic defense are more closely related to desire than to the Kantian stance of disinterestedness, which is supposed to underwrite the objectivity of aesthetic pleasure. Art works do not give satisfaction to existing desires but, passing through a stage of disinterestedness, incite longing, provoke desire: "The unquenchable longing excited by the beautiful... is the longing for the fulfillment of a promise," the *promesse du bonheur*. This promise arises from the belief that if something can materially appear, even in the mode of semblance, it must be possible to imbue what it figures with being; this thought is almost definitive of the ontological proof of God's existence, which Hegel, who regarded the logic of semblance as also a logic of truth, saw as not so flatly false as Kant's refutation portrayed it to be. The ontological proof could be flatly false only if the distinction between the intelligible and sensible worlds was absolute; but that thesis, we have seen, cannot be sustained.

Adorno's deployment of the concept of "promise" is thus significant, because it is in part what distinguishes the claiming of works from the claiming of fantasies, which place the syntheses of disparate elements before us as if they really existed, and idealities that construe syntheses as being self-sufficient but belonging to an order independent of the world's material order. Art works do not claim existence pure and simple or self-sufficient ideality for their syntheses; rather, by being forms of resistance to what is commensurable with immediate desire satisfaction, which is the moment of painful "sublimity" in modernist works, while yet holding, sustaining, and heightening perceptual attention, they open a possibility of responding and relating to objects (including other subjects) that is not presently available. Art thus enacts a categorial promise, and it is the modality of promising itself that most accurately captures the form of "possible experience" projected by works. In part, then, artworks' being "semblances" is to be understood by construing promising as a modal function; promising is for Adorno a categorial specification of (transcendental) possibility. It is along these lines that we should interpret Adorno's claim that in modernist art "disinterestedness [as the correlate of the moment of resistance] reproduces interest immanently, in a different form. In a false world, all *hedone* is false. This goes for artistic pleasure, too. Art renounces happiness for the sake of happiness. In this way desire survives in art" (AT 26/18).

3

Artworks lodge a promise of happiness as intricated with the idea of a world in which the universal fungibility of particulars is dissolved; this is how the idea of the immortality of the soul becomes the hope for a "transfigured body (*verklärten Leib*)" (ND 393/400), the hope for a different regime of embodiment in which the sensual and the spiritual would be indissolubly entwined. Yet it is no more in art's power to declare that such happiness and such nonfungibility of particulars are really possible than it was in philosophy's power, once upon a time, to underwrite the immortality of the soul a priori. A rift has occurred in the mode of these two promises, however: the authority of traditional philosophy's claim was bound to a self-sufficient reason that operated in defiance of its own material conditions of existence. Art's promise is bound to irreducible particulars that claim attention for themselves only through their own immanent resources. By itself, this challenges the claim of reigning universality and, thereby, the very idea that philosophy, as the self-articulation of unrestricted conceptuality, can self-sufficiently draw the categorial map of existence. To concede the first two claims about the nonexistent is already to deny philosophy's self-sufficiency.

Once that concession is made, its converse directly follows: artworks raise categorial modal claims. As such, artworks directly call forth philosophical reflection; reflection on existence and nonexistence, reality and possibility; and reflection on the fact that it is art that raises claims on these matters in opposition to all that already exists. Works of art draw their *authority* (a category thought refuted by enlightened rationality?) from this capacity to call forth philosophical reflection, the capacity to reveal to philosophy that its claiming about modality must relate to a practice that it cannot legislate for in advance. This is the reflective implication of art's promising: if philosophy cannot legislate in advance the transcendental parameters of art, if artistic practice can exceed the very idea of art, then the possibilities of experience cannot be bound by philosophical reflection. Further, the conditions of possible experience (perhaps) do not derive from what is atemporal and universal but can advance through particulars. If the thesis that the universal lives off of the particular is true, it would follow that the conditions of possible experience can advance only through particulars.

4

Insofar as there are authentic works of art, the previous claims must be taken as objective: they are intrinsic to the authenticity of the works themselves. Yet it is beyond works themselves, and beyond what philosophy can say about the claims of such works, to categorially separate the objectivity of art's promise from the lapse of such promising into mere illusion, its telling lies. This gives to these claims a different aporetic character than that which applied to the intelligible world. We must, if we take works seriously, regard their claims as objective, hence as projecting a possibility or potentiality that outruns present existence. Nonetheless, we are powerless to vindicate the truth of this objectivity; that it is all illusion must remain an open possibility. Thus, philosophy cannot unconditionally support art's objectivity: "Works of art take an advance on a praxis which has not yet begun. Put the other way around, nobody knows whether a future praxis will redeem art's draft." The fragility of art's promising and the indeterminacy of its "advance on future praxis" should not be interpreted as a concession to the idea that artworks, inscriptions of the imagination, explore human possibilities by the elision or suppression of empirical or categorial constraints on reflection. Such an interpretation would make artworks idealities, in the pejorative sense, once more. Because art does abstract from the material processes of social reproduction, artworks are without instrumental purpose; the charge of ideality can never be fully answered. Nonetheless, the objectivity (or intersubjective validity) of works itself urges a bracketing of the bad infinity of the conditional ends presupposed by instrumental rationality. As a consequence, the fragility and indeterminacy of art's promising should be construed as direct corollaries of Adorno's particularistic materialism: if works of art could really promise more, they would be universal and not particular, their claim of transcendence flatly transcendental and not critical or reflective.

Experience (Again): Aura and Subjectivity

Benjamin states at the end of "On Some Motifs in Baudelaire" that Baudelaire "battled the crowd—with the impotent rage of someone fighting the rain or the wind. This is the nature of something lived through (*Erlebnis*) to which Baudelaire has given the weight of an experience (*Erfahrung*)."[21] Baudelaire's modernist poetry provides us with experience *of a world constituted by the absence of experience*. Such, for Benjamin and Adorno, is the remarkable constitutive character of modernist works of art in relation to the world they inhabit. Because works of art are sensuous particulars that provide experiences, they appear as objective realities; because they depart from the productive ends of empirical life, they are powerless to redeem their promise of experience—they are semblances; because the promises that artworks make transcend the context of immanence, they are metaphysical; because works of art provide an experience of the absence of experience that has metaphysical import, they provide an experience of diremption of particularity from rationality (particular from universal); by providing an experience of categorial diremption, works of art call forth philosophical reflection; this philosophical reflection is speculative in Hegel's sense. This chain of claims makes good our initial difficulty with the thesis that Adorno's philosophy is speculative. The fundamental diremption that Adorno surveys is not drawn from everyday life but from its reflective forms: art and philosophy. Art's capacity to render the absence of experience into an experience underwrites its categorial claiming on behalf of sensuous particularity against the reigning universal as expressed by philosophical rationality. *Aesthetic Theory* is philosophy living off of art's nonidentity with it and avowing that relation of dependency. *Aesthetic Theory*, one might say, rehearses philosophy's (self-consciousness's) self-recognition in the absolute otherness of modernist art. This speculative relation between philosophy and art expresses the diremption between universal and particular in empirical life.

Nonetheless, that somewhat formal-sounding account of the meaning of Adorno's thought as speculative requires that the idea of speculation itself be interpreted more fully. Adorno's handling of

Kant's conception of the intelligible world, I suggested, evidences the thesis that what is at stake in eliciting the speculative identity and difference of universal and particular is the provision of the moral image of the world, which itself provides the necessary conditions for the rationality of ethical conduct. Thus, another way of articulating the above chain of claims would be to say that aesthetic experience itself projects a categorial articulation of subject and object that would provide the moral image of the world fulfilling, in materialist terms, the requirements of Kant's moral theology.

In order to help this more exorbitant claim along, let me begin by saying something general about the concept of experience. To experience something is, in accordance with colloquial usage, to have had an "experience." To have an experience is to undergo something, to suffer something, and to do so in such a manner that one is changed thereby. What is experienced is something one had not anticipated or predicted, something that occurs counter to expectations. Because unexpected exposure to something unprecedented entails that experiences are "undergone," "experience" invokes ideas of passivity and even loss of control. Experience is the arena in which we learn through "suffering."

From these uncontentious characterizations of experience, three inferences may be drawn. First, novelty is intrinsic to the structure of experience; it is this characteristic that makes experience contrary to the goals of scientific knowing. In science, the unexpected is what falsifies a theory; the ideal of science would be never to be surprised and hence for theory to be complete and determinate, independently of the objects and events it explains (which, broadly, is the most basic definition of what Adorno means by identity thinking). To imagine experience coming to an end, conversely, is to project a world in which nothing would or could "matter" to an individual, in which the course of events was neutral with respect to subjectivity. Second, if the transformation undergone in an experience occurs at the behest of a specific object or event, then the state of the subject that eventuates from the experience is determined by, and depends on, that object or event. From this it follows that experience always depends on individuals' being present to what they experience, and that the ensuing transformation remains a relation between individual and object or event. Experiences of love, war, childbirth, friendship, freedom, desire, beauty, courage, sympathy, and so on, expose individuals to a domain of meaning that remains bound to the events that precipitate the exposure. It is because experience is bound to the concrete events precipitating it that the articulation of experience must be rendered through narrative recollection. Finally, having an experience involves both a transformation of the individual and the emergence of a new object domain for consciousness. Although this conception of transformation or conversion may model what occurs in paradigm changes in natural science, the goal of science is to be done with such changes. The image of life without experience is finally the image of life without history, as if the meaning of life were in its eternal cessation: death. There cannot be historical life without experience; only lives articulated through experience can be fully and self-consciously historical.

Adorno's and Benjamin's belief that there has been a pervasive destruction of experience is itself drawn from art (and philosophy), since only reflectively is it possible to evaluate the types, sources, and availability of meaning current in a particular society. Reflective practices operate a closure on the basic terms supportive of meaning in a culture and submit them to "tests" for coherency and consistency that are supplied by the principles of the practice itself. So, for example, that philosophy cannot integrate the moral and ethical—what is good for everyone and what is good for me—or ground moral norms except procedurally, says something about the possibilities of moral conduct and the idea of a "good life" in our society. Analogously, that the most stringent attempts to narrate empirical existence show everyday life no longer to possess narrative coherence through time, or that painterly representations of the natural world appear kitschy or sentimental when representational and attain to artistic authenticity only when they are abstract, says something about the possibilities of the meaning of a life or the meaning of the natural world that is hidden from everyday life. This is the sense in which art and philosophy are their own time apprehended in thought.[22]

Although the notion of experience is not prominent in *Aesthetic Theory*, its cognates, surrogates, and analogues are: for example, expression, suffering, shudder, aura, mimesis, affinity, the plus or more of appearance. One of the less conspicuous terms, "aura," will do for the purposes to hand. In Benjamin's later thought, the destruction of experience and the disintegration or decay of aura are versions of the same thing. A useful place to begin is with a passage of Valéry's quoted by Benjamin that is pivotal for his account of aura in section 11 of the Baudelaire essay. Valéry's depiction of the work of art corresponds almost point by point to what was said above about experience:

> We recognize a work of art by the fact that no idea it inspires in us, no mode of behavior that it suggests we adopt could exhaust it or dispose of it. We may inhale the smell of a flower whose fragrance is agreeable to us for as long as we like; it is impossible for us to rid ourselves of the fragrance by which our senses have been aroused, and no recollection, no thought, no mode of behavior can obliterate its effect or release us from the hold it has on us. He who has set himself the task of creating a work of art aims at the same effect.[23]

Keying his account to this passage, Benjamin defines aura as a phenomenon of "distance" in the sense that no voluntary activity (thought or action) can get on level terms with the auratic object—it cannot be absorbed. But our inability to absorb auratic objects, to reduce them to transparently communicable truth claims, suggests an independence from subjectivity whose only model is the ineliminable separateness of subjects from one another. Our gaze does not exhaust the other precisely because it can gaze back, placing us within its perceptual horizon. But this return of the gaze by the other should not be comprehended in terms of Sartrean objectification of the other; on the contrary, it is the depth of subjective response, the odor of the madeleine, that is indefinitely dependent on its object that is being evoked here. The gaze is that of a lover not an impersonal, god-like other. Hence, the Benjaminian thesis that objects possessing aura return our gaze: "To perceive the aura of an object we look at means to invest it with the ability to look at us in return."[24] Benjamin thus considers the experience of aura a matter of transfering a response typical of, or at least appropriate to, human interaction to the relation between humans and inanimate objects or nature. Indeed, it is difficult not to consider Benjamin's conception of the return of the gaze as equivalent to Hegelian recognition, which is itself the model for Hegelian speculative identities, that is, the unity of identity (the unity of spectator and object) and nonidentity (the object remains independent of the spectator, who thus remains dependent on it).

Whatever Adorno's earlier strictures about aura, all his references to it in *Aesthetic Theory* are affirmative. In his longest discussion of aura (AT 407–10/384–87; this passage is summarized at AT 122–23/ 117), he begins by suggesting that aura is like the mood of a work of art, only to suggest at the end of his account that the analogy falsely converts a valid aspect of works, something objective, into a subjective mode of response. What is at issue in this conclusion is whether or not Benjamin was correct in thinking of aura as the mere transfer of a mode of human interaction to the interaction between humans and what is not human. If a transfer is what occurs in auratic experiences, then aura would be an instance of anthropomorphic projection, the basic and most primitive form of the enchantment of the natural world. But, at least with respect to works of art, the idea that our response to them involves an illegitimate projection onto them of qualities they otherwise lack appears deeply implausible.

In responding to, say, Robert Motherwell's "Elegy to the Spanish Republic 34" by noting its black, biomorphic shapes, the bluish-white background, the small, blocked red on the far left, are we *projecting* onto the canvas a *merely subjective* set of appearances? Adorno contends, rather, that aesthetic perception, breathing the aura of an artwork, moves in precisely the opposite direction, essentially involving "the Hegelian notion of 'freedom towards the object.' Instead of projecting on to the work what goes on in his head, so as to see himself confirmed and satisfied on a higher plane, the viewer must externalize himself, recreating the work and assimilating himself to it" (AT 409/387). The experience of aura, which is the experience of experience ("aura" names "experience"), is attained in modernist works of art themselves through a process of negation. What is negated in this process are all those elements of works that might with some justification be regarded as projections of the human on to the inanimate. That radically negative, abstract works (Beckett, Berg, Rothko) still possess auratic qualities, possess them in opposition to our ability to project onto them and through their deliberate work of negativity, is some confirmation that it is not projection in any obvious sense that is occurring.[25] Adorno goes so far as to claim here that the auratic element that survives or occurs through deliberate negation is the element that is modeled on nature and is responsible for works' likeness to nature rather than any representational likeness they might possess (AT 409/386). Hence, Adorno's emphatic claim, "As apparition, as appearance and not as copies (*Abbild*) are artworks images (*Bilder*)" (AT 130/124).

According to Adorno, the project of the Enlightenment, its work of disenchanting the world, is essentially a project of demythologization. The legitimate ground for the project of demythologization is the discovery that features of the world previously believed to be intrinsic to it turn out to be anthropomorphic projections. Demythologization is anti-anthropomorphism. Adorno's whole project turns on his contention that the critical project of demythologization, however progressive originally, is inherently skeptical, since it is structured by a wholly negative *skepsis*: neither "myth" nor "projection" nor "independent of subjectivity" are defined, and no natural terminus or determinate end to the negative process is offered. Whatever appears is subject to the skeptical doubt of natural science that it is only an appearance, a projection. Hence, what began with the critique of myth and religion continues with the elimination of values and secondary qualities until only the mind's own forms (method, logic, and mathematics) remain.[26] These identitarian forms are Enlightenment's own mythic spell on nature.

The question raised by modernist works as to whether the ascription of "spiritual" qualities to the sensible features of the world is a projection is the question about the limits of intellectual abstraction, the limits of the pure concept, and hence the limits of identity thinking. To interrogate those limits through the *same* procedures of abstraction and negation that provide for Enlightenment disenchantment is hence determined by the attempt to determine or reveal the limits of disenchantment itself. The limits of abstraction and the limits of disenchantment are, for Adorno, the same. In eliminating, for example, secondary qualities as objective features of the natural world, what is eliminated simultaneously are those features through which humans respond to the world. But without the somatic features of perception (images, sounds, smells, tastes, feelings), all that remains of the subject

are its mental powers for abstraction, analysis, and synthesis: the rational, autonomous subject, in eliminating its own natural capacities for
response, simultaneously eliminates subjectivity, which, a fortiori, can
be seen to reside in its somatic stratum. Autonomous works contest
this result by processually negating the grounds on which the authority of works can be denied as projective. In his "Ocean Park" series, Richard Diebenkorn eliminates everything that might be thought
essential to landscape, leaving only light, color, and line to let the
world (natural and artificial) outside his studio window appear. The
integration of elements Diebenkorn self-consciously produces is something more than their "production"; his intentional act is there and yet
not what provokes our gaze, gazes back at us. The work fixes our look,
holds it beyond merely subjective desire or interest. This disenchanted
landscape, a landscape without explicit likeness to sky, sea, beach, window frame or telephone pole, is the appearance of its object beyond
how that object appears. This appearance, Adorno claims, is the
work's immanent transcendence (AT 122–23/116–17), aesthetic appearances being, in the true sense, appearances of an other, of what is
other to the context of immanence. In this way, desire survives in art.

Thus, in aesthetic experience, we have a "metaphysical experience," an experience of transcendence and otherness. But this experience is one of diremption, of our separation from the intentional
object of the work itself, since what appears is semblance. The intentional object of the work itself appears through its not appearing;
only what is not like the intentional object appears. At the limit, the
intentional object of modernist works is the bare otherness of a
meaning beyond identitarian meaning, the recognition that this is
not all, that "the phantasm of eternity is only its curse."[27] Above, I
noted that a central characteristic of semblance is its promise of happiness. In aesthetic experience is thus syncopated a difficult objectivity, a sense of the meaning of the object as beyond will, want, and
interest yet connected to the realization of what is most untransfer-
ably personal and subjective—happiness. Hence, Adorno's all but
opaque claim that "[h]appiness, the only part of metaphysical experience that is more than impotent longing, gives us the inside of objects
as something at once removed from them" (ND 367/374). In this
sentence, we should now be able to hear a materialist, aesthetically

driven rewriting of Kant's speculative reconciliation of virtue and happiness.

The element of "virtue" in Adorno's account is the works' independence from us, their uniqueness and integrity, their ability to gaze back. Yet that independence is not a threat to subjectivity but engages and intensifies it. Only through respect for the other, the distance that passes through the stage of disinterestedness, does what is most subjective in the subject become operative and is the promise of happiness invoked. To experience the aura of an artwork is thus to experience the possibility of experience in its robust sense. To experience this possibility is to be in possession of the moral image of the world—in semblance. This experience is metaphysical not only because it relates to what transcends the context of immanence but because it provides an account of the world in relation to the fundamental rational powers (of response, synthesis, judgment) of the subject; in this respect, too, Adorno's critical procedure tracks the program of German idealism. Like Kant's own attempt to circumscribe the understanding by reason and supplement pure practical reason (the categorical imperative) with an immanently necessitated moral theology, so the rescue of semblance circumscribes identity thinking by revealing a possibility of a form of meaning, and a form of interaction between subject and object that is not identitarian. Because this formation of meaning and interaction is riveted to the conditions of possible perception, the exposure of the subject to a singular object, it is materialist. Because it is materialist, it recognizes that transcendence is, finally, not vertical but horizontal, a promise—toward a future habitation of this world.

Transcendence, Adorno states, "feeds on nothing but the experience of immanence" (ND 390/398). But this immanence is that of the aesthetic object; access to what was once the concern of metaphysics and theology lives on in artistic semblance and its rescue in aesthetic theory. Art's promise of happiness is of a transfigured world in which happiness and virtue would be reconciled; only through the rescue of semblance is this speculative thought utterable. Yet without it, without its guidance, ethical conduct would lapse into either cynicism, despair, or evil, this latter being, of course, also a work of despair.

In the risk of taking his metaphysical bearings from the domain of art, Adorno knew his project would appear as "folly." But folly, he said, "is truth in the form which men are struck by as amid untruth they will not let truth go." He continues:

Art is semblance even at its highest peaks; but its semblance, the irresistible part of it, is given to it by what is not semblance. What art, notably the art decried as nihilistic, says in refraining from [determinate] judgments is that everything is not just nothing. If it were, what is would be pale, colorless, indifferent. No light falls on men and things without reflecting transcendence. Indelible from the resistance to the fungible world of exchange is the resistance of the eye that does not want the colors of the world to fade. Semblance is the promise of nonsemblance. (ND 396–97/404–5)

Notes

* The English translations of Adorno's writings have been modified where accuracy demanded it.

1. John Dewey, "Wandering between Two Worlds," quoted in John Patrick Diggins, *The Promise of Pragmatism* (Chicago: The University of Chicago Press, 1994), p. 4.

2. T. W. Adorno, *Notes to Literature*, vol. 1, trans. Shierry Weber Nicholsen (New York: Columbia University Press, 1991), p. 7.

3. I am referring to a variety of epistemological positions, from Descartes's "absolute" conception of knowledge to more recent versions of naturalized epistemology. For a lucid statement of the sort of view at issue, see Thomas Nagel, *The View from Nowhere* (New York: Oxford University Press, 1986), chap. 5.

4. See Diggins, *The Promise of Pragmatism*, chaps. 1–6.

5. G. W. F. Hegel, *Phenomenology of Spirit*, trans. A. V. Miller (Oxford: Oxford University Press, 1977), pp. 10–14, 329–55.

6. Because rationalist philosophies often use concept determinacy as a criterion for the self-sufficiency reason, it should be unsurprising that meaning determinacy involves precisely the same structure of identity thinking in the philosophy of language that the autonomy of reason did earlier on, especially in Kant. For a Wittgensteinian-type critique of the ideal of determinate meaning, see Mark Sacks, "Through a Glass Darkly: Vagueness in the Metaphysics of the Analytic Tradition," in *The Analytic Tradition: Meaning. Thought and Knowledge*, ed. David Bell and Neil Cooper (Oxford: Basil Blackwell, 1990), pp. 173–96.

7. For Hegel's methodological claims for "experience," see *Phenomenology of Spirit*, pp. 54–56.

8. Ibid., p. 131. Within the *Phenomenology*, the location of the moment of what is essential or universal shifts, being locatable either inside or outside the subject. What makes the unhappy consciousness prefigurative for the forms of consciousness Adorno analyzes is that it is a structure of universality that deracinates transient, sensual particularity. What makes Adorno's object different is that overcoming sensual particularity is no longer a goal but has always already occurred and for that very

reason is unknown to us. For an interesting take on the Hegel–Adorno relation to which I am indebted, see Simon Jarvis, "The 'Unhappy Consciousness' and Conscious Unhappiness," forthcoming.

9. *Notes to Literature*, vol. 2, trans. Shierry Weber Nicholsen (New York: Columbia University Press, 1992), p. 8.

10. T. W. Adorno, *Minima Moralia: Reflections from Damaged Life*, trans. E. F. N. Jephcott (London: NLB, 1974), p. 55.

11. Ibid., p. 59.

12. Walter Benjamin, *Illuminations*, trans. Harry Zohn (London: Collins/Fontana Books, 1973), p. 159.

13. *Notes to Literature*, vol. 2, p. 317.

14. For a contemporary contestation of the Kantian project that sides with individual self-realization, see Bernard Williams, *Moral Luck* (Cambridge: Cambridge University Press, 1981), pp. 1–39.

15. *Justification and Application: Remarks on Discourse Ethics*, trans. Ciaran P. Cronin (Cambridge, Mass.: MIT Press, 1993), chaps. 1–2.

16. Ibid., p. 41. For an immanent critique of the ethics/morality dualism in Habermas, see my *Recovering Ethical Life: Jürgen Habermas and the Future of Critical Theory* (London: Routledge, 1995), chaps. 4–6.

17. Immanuel Kant, *Critique of Pure Reason*, trans. Norman Kemp Smith (New York: St. Martin's Press, 1965), pp. B841–42. For a discussion of this problem in the context of the problem of reflective judgment, see Immanuel Kant, *The Critique of Judgement*, trans. James Creed Meredith (Oxford: Clarendon Press, 1952), sec. 87.

18. Dieter Henrich, *Aesthetic Judgment and the Moral Image of the World* (Stanford, Calif.: Stanford University Press, 1992), pp. 12–13. The central, implied thought that connects the two parts of the title of Henrich's book, and which thereby reads Kant's construction as adumbrating Adorno's speculative account, concerns the imagination's (reflective judgments) role in providing the subjective conditions for concept acquisition and application: "Yet a symptom of the possession of a concept is always the possibility of its being *exhibited* in intuition. One cannot even search for concepts unless one conceives them already in the light of the way in which they can be *exhibited*" (p. 49; emphasis added). The hard work in this area involves separating the conditions for "exhibition" (the aesthetic *in* the cognitive) from truth and verification conditions; Kantian conditions for "exhibition" are to be considered along the lines of Adornoesque "mimesis" and "affinity" and, therefore, as being somehow antecedent to these more familiar notions.

   In what follows, I presume that if virtue amounts to no more than the conditions for coordinating action among a plurality of agents, however that is cashed out, then the moral and the instrumental become equivalent, as Hobbes claimed they were. In ways I cannot hope to demonstrate here, Adorno believes that this reduction of the moral to the instrumental is a consequence of the separation of virtue from happiness. From an Adornoesque perspective, that there is a question of action coordination is a symptom of the lapse of ethical life. Conversely, therefore, Adorno presumes that the conditions for action coordination will always already be satisfied if we possess a structurally undeformed ethical life. I take up these issues in a forthcoming book on Adorno's ethical thought: *Adorno: Of Ethics and Disenchantment* (Cambridge: Cambridge University Press), forthcoming.

19. For this breakdown of Adorno's argument, I am indebted to a seminar paper by Ståle Finke, Unversity of Essex, spring 1994. Unattributed quotes in the rest of this section are from AT 128–29/122–24.

20. For this way of construing artworks as "origins," see Jacques Derrida's discussion of Heidegger's "The Origin of the Work of Art," in Derrida's *Truth in Painting*, trans. Geoff Bennington and Ian McLeod (Chicago: University of Chicago Press, 1987), pp. 255–382; and my *Fate of Art: Aesthetic Alienation from Kant to Derrida and Adorno* (Cambridge, England: Polity Press, 1992), pp. 140–59. Throughout my discussion, I have sought to underline the structural homology between identity thinking living off of (nonappearing) nonidentity and the thought of *différance*. Although underlining the nontranscendental character of Adorno's critical program, I hope to take up this issue at some later date with respect to the status of the "promise" in Adorno and Derrida.

21. Benjamin, *Illuminations*, p. 196.

22. See Lambert Zuidervaart, *Adorno's Aesthetic Theory: The Redemption of Illusion* (Cambridge, Mass.: MIT Press, 1991), pp. 152–54.

23. Quoted in Benjamin, *Illuminations*, pp. 188–89.

24. Ibid., p. 190.

25. For reflections on Adorno's treatment of Beckett in line with the argument being presented here, see Zuidervaart, *Adorno's Aesthetic Theory*, chap. 7. I have taken it here that it is worthwhile focusing on the question of secondary properties, above all the significance of configurations of secondary qualities, since it is now not uncommon to believe that the objectivity of color predicates and of value predicates (and by extension, use values) succeed or fail in the same way. If we were to treat value predicates analogously with Adorno's treatment of configurations of secondary qualities, then his ethical thought would naturally fall out as a form of particularistic realism.

26. T. W. Adorno and Max Horkheimer, *Dialectic of Enlightenment*, trans. John Cumming (New York: Seabury Press, 1972), pp. 3–13.

27. Adorno, *Notes to Literature*, vol. 1, p. 273. In a sense, the Diebenkorn example is slightly unhappy. The *explicit* intentional object of a Diebenkorn is the unperceived natural landscape. However, the *explicit* intentional object of, for example, a classical Pollock is the work itself, whereas its *implicit* intentional object would be the promise of another relation to the perceptual world in general. The explicit and implicit intentional objects of high modernist works are, of course, only analytically separate; their intrication is what Adorno conceives of as the "truth content" of a work, which, precisely because of the distinction and overlap between implicit and explicit intentional objects, requires philosophical elucidation. The image/likeness distinction, which preserves the direct (perceptual) unavailability of the natural world (the world of sensuous particularity is unseen and unknown by us), is what permits the

treatment of less-radical works (Diebenkorn, Giacometti, Proust) on analogy with the more-radical ones (Pollock, Beckett). To perceive an image within a likeness, where the very idea of image is derived from the moment of high modernism, is what permits traditional artworks to become modern, and so relevant again to us. For a treatment of some of these problems, see my "Death of Sensuous Particulars: Adorno and Abstract Expressionism," *Radical Philosophy* 76 (1996): 7–18.

8

Adorno's Notion of Natural Beauty: A Reconsideration

Heinz Paetzold

There are several ways to characterize postmodernity from a theoretical perspective informed by, and related to, topics of Adorno's critical theory. According to Andreas Huyssen, Adorno is, like Clement Greenberg, a spokesman of emphatic modernism. Huyssen questions Adorno's distinction between high and low culture, however, and argues that postmoderns are beyond and after the "great divide" between the culture industry and authentic art.[1] Jean-François Lyotard, on the other hand, often refers to Adorno's conviction that philosophy today, even if postmetaphysical, should not forget its solidarity with metaphysics at its decisive breakdown (*Sturz*) under the catastrophes of the twentieth century.[2]

Contrary to these lines, I focus in this essay on Adorno's notion of natural beauty. Of course, in this case, too, we find a postmodern tuning. In postmodernity, aesthetics has split into aesthetics in the sense of a philosophy of art and aesthetics in the sense of an (ecological) aesthetics of nature. The first two sections of my essay lay bare central motifs that Adorno had in mind when he introduced the notion of natural beauty. Then I turn to two recently developed aesthetics of nature, one by Gernot Böhme and the other by Martin Seel. I argue for a position that maintains the systematic link between philosophy of art and the aesthetics of nature. This link is a heritage of Adorno's aesthetic theory.

I

I start by exploring Adorno's introduction of natural beauty into his aesthetic theory. One can distinguish here between a more methodological argument concerning the internal structure of aesthetics and a more materialistic argument.

The methodological argument has to do above all with the very structure of aesthetic theory. It is Adorno's conviction that aesthetic theory (and philosophy in general) should not invent new notions and topics; rather, it should reevaluate and reflect on topics already known to philosophical aesthetics. It is not the task of aesthetics to give descriptive or normative narratives of modern art history, nor is aesthetics to be restricted to art criticism.

Adorno claims that aesthetics must be related to the internal dynamics of philosophy itself. The idea and the state of philosophy are changing to such a degree that philosophy must incorporate aesthetics. Accordingly, aesthetics must be structured by three theoretical moves that cannot be separated from each other.

The first move of Adorno's aesthetic theory consists in a rereading of classical aesthetics, that is, the philosophical aesthetics of German idealism, which started with Alexander Gottlieb Baumgarten and reached its peak in Kant and Hegel. Kant was a decisive modern philosopher who broke with the Platonic triad of beauty, truth, and moral good. Kant destroyed the metaphysical state of these three ideas, which had been developed in Western history from Plato through Plotinus, the Renaissance Platonism of Marsilio Ficino and Giordano Bruno, and the modern versions of Leibniz and Shaftesbury. Kant's *Critique of Judgment* marked a turning point in history insofar as he rejected metaphysics as the foundation of philosophy and aesthetics.

Hegel, for his part, ratified the shift of aesthetics toward the philosophy of art that was introduced by Schiller and Schelling. Hegel set art in a philosophical perspective by revealing its realm as the "Ideal." But the realm of art had to be considered a historical one. Art as an autonomous cultural form has a history of its own; the symbolic, the classical, and the romantic stages are the marks in this history. The history of art, however, can be grasped only if it is conceived with reference to the development of different sorts of art, such as architecture, sculpture, painting, music, and poetry.

In other words, Hegel was, besides Schelling, Schiller, and the Schlegel brothers, the philosopher to relate the realm of art to the question of cultural and social modernity. Famous theorems like the "end of art" make sense only if they are understood as questions concerning the status of modern culture. Modern people understand works of art not as embedded in religious rituals and cults, Hegel says in a famous passage of his *Lectures on Aesthetics,* but as aesthetic objects.

This passage also reveals that, if we deal with art philosophically, then questions of religion and of philosophy itself arise immediately. Hegel does not separate out art as a realm exclusively centered in itself but rather treats art as something interwoven with all aspects of modern culture, yet having its own internal contradictions and internal rules.

The first move of Adorno's aesthetic theory, then, entails an awareness or a recollection of notions, topics, theorizations, and strategies related to classical aesthetics. The reason for this move is that, within the frame of philosophical idealism, beauty and truth and moral goodness are not separated from each other. They are brought into a discursive continuity or mutual interrelationship.

But Adorno was by no means a historicist. His aim is not a hermeneutic reappropriation of classical aesthetics, nor does he want merely to contribute to their correct understanding. His second move consists in confronting classical notions and topics with explicitly modern experiences of contemporary art. We can no longer continue to speak about style in the same manner as did Goethe and Hegel. After the vanguard movements, with their mocking of all styles, this notion must be redetermined. To a certain extent, one might understand Adorno's second move as a kind of deconstruction. But only from its methodological result is such a reference valid. Adorno's paratactic way of writing and his dethroning of metaphysical dichotomies (essence versus surface, idea versus semblance, form versus material) could be mentioned in this context.

Adorno works through the notions of the philosophical heritage by redetermining or deconstructing them. Experiences with contemporary art must be shaped and structured with reference to "inherited" notions. The stress lies on the articulation of contemporary aesthetic experiences. These experiences achieve the state of reflected experiences only if they are shaped and modeled according to "inherited" notions. But one has to keep in mind that Adorno's deconstruction affects both: the philosophical status of the notions or categories of aesthetics is undermined, and the experiences receive a notional or discursive structure.

This is the appropriate point to introduce the third move, which involves historical materialism. In order to avoid a petitio principii— aesthetic experiences must be articulated within a philosophical frame; the philosophical frame is changed by the means of confrontation with contemporary experiences—Adorno is obliged to introduce a third point of reference. Historical materialism relates philosophical notions to the potential for political emancipation, including individual emancipation. Emancipation means not only liberation from theoretical dogmatism but also the liberation of the body. All the restraints that a society based on the production of commodities lays on its members should be overcome. A reconciliation of the spirit with the body, of culture with nature, of society with nature, should be taken into account, even if only in utopian perspective. This historical-materialist perspective marks a difference from Derrida's idea of deconstruction. In Adorno's case, the deconstruction of the metaphysical heritage is linked to universal emancipation and sensual happiness for all.

II

Having outlined the philosophical framework of Adorno's aesthetic theory, I now turn to some details of his approach to the notion of natural beauty. According to Adorno, the steps toward a theory of natural beauty must be taken in such a way that (1) beauty in nature cannot be pitted against beauty in art and (2) the historical and theoretical process of dethroning natural beauty is deciphered as an increasing idealization of the spirit itself. The human spirit has lost its roots in the bodily senses.

Adorno starts by positing that the rehabilitation of natural beauty must take into account the theoretical improvements brought about by the shift of philosophy toward works of art. This shift, initiated by Schelling's move toward a philosophy of art, was accompanied by a break with (or a reconsideration of) the Platonic metaphysical heritage. Nevertheless, the notion of natural beauty remains a *Wunde*, a "wound." Something has been "repressed" (*verdrängt*).[3] For that reason the notion of natural beauty must be reconsidered. But such a reconsideration makes sense only if it can be linked with art theory itself.

In explicitly modern art, something comes to the fore that reaches "beyond the aesthetic immanence" but belongs nevertheless to art's internal conditions as well. The advantage of aesthetic reflection under modernism brought with it a high price, such as the "symbolically" presumed "reconciliation" in works of art. The price that had to be paid for the shift of aesthetics toward philosophy of art consisted, according to Adorno, in the "Selbsterhöhung des Tiers Mensch über die Tierheit," in the "prideful elevation of the animal 'man' above the animal realm" (ÄT 99; AT 92). The bourgeois presumes an internal dignity that entails a total separation from the environmental surrounding and empties nature of all its inherent qualities and promises. Because of modern capitalist ways of production, nature is degraded to a pure "material" useful for all formative powers laid on it (ÄT 99; AT 92).

Even if we concede that since the nineteenth century all subject matter whatsoever can be treated by art, and even if we concede that this process heightens the internal capacities of art, there still remains a substratum that was overridden by the cultivation of artistic expression. This substratum can be identified as natural beauty, to which authentic works of art silently refer in order to distance themselves from their own rigid identity. With reference to Kant, Adorno speaks of the "Gestus des Heraustretens," the "posture of stepping-outside-into-the-open" (ÄT 100–101; AT 94), in order to underline such a "trace" of reference to something outside the aesthetic immanence. As people of modern times, we cannot capture nature immediately. All our images of nature and of the natural are predetermined and prestructured by history. In the last instance, nature itself is a product of historical processes. History, on the other hand, is not totally independent of nature.

Adorno discusses, as an exemplification of natural history, the case of "cultural landscape" (*Kulturlandschaft*) (ÄT 101–2; AT 94–96). What qualifies a cultural landscape as an aesthetic experience of natural beauty? Cultural landscapes are close to aesthetic experiences of nature, because they stimulate images that reconcile natural conditions and cultural activities. From the viewpoint of cultural history, the idea of cultural landscape can be traced back to romanticism's cult of the ruin. Cultural landscapes provide us with an image of history that we understand immediately but that also makes us realize that "the expression of history" is in the same moment tinged by "past real sufferings" (ÄT 102; AT 95–96). These sufferings are indicated in that we realize the restrictions and restraints of history, but the restrictions do not trouble our aesthetic pleasure.

Here a remarkable point is touched on. It was Georg Simmel who first stated, in his essay "Philosophie der Landschaft" (1913), that perceiving environmental nature as landscape is an eminently modern phenomenon. It presupposes that the "*Allnatur*" of the Middle Ages is left behind. To experience nature as landscape is preconditioned by the modern divisions of the social body. We animate surrounding nature by perceiving it at a distance; that is, as a landscape. Nature loses its former threats. Joachim Ritter has theorized landscape as a specific secularized phenomenon of modern society.[4] The metaphysical *theoria tou kosmou* returns under the conditions of modern society, which is characterized by a domination of human beings over nature. The prior metaphysical understanding of *theoria tou kosmou* shifts to an aesthetic reconciliation. What formerly belonged to the privilege of priests and then was secularized to a metaphysical activity becomes, under the conditions of modernity, a means of reconciling modern human beings with their natural environment. The peasant struggling with nature does not experience it as landscape. The phenomenon of landscape is a result of a process of societal modernization that includes the division of labor and the social division in labor and leisure time. It is only in leisure that we experience the landscape aesthetically, but this experience presupposes human mastery of nature.

Adorno adds two decisive arguments to Ritter's rehabilitation of the experience of landscape as an eminent example of the modern aesthetic experience. First, landscape is to be conceived as natural history. We esteem in cultural landscape the utopian figuration of a reconciliation of nature and culture. It is a utopian figuration because we project our longings for reconciliation into landscape. Cultural landscape is not a pure given but a utopian semblance.

Second, images of cultural landscape are images of "a memento" (ÄT 102; AT 96). Historical memory and historical mourning must be invested in order to save the utopian figure of reconciliation between culture and nature. Adorno stresses the link between the aesthetic experience of nature and the aesthetic experience of works of art. They have in common the fact that they are images. Nature appearing as the beautiful is not conceived as an object of action. The purposes of self-preservation are transcended in both the work of art and the aesthetic experience of nature (ÄT 103; AT 96–97).

Art does not want to be nature, as philosophical idealism from Kant up to Hegel suggests but rather art intends to redeem what nature promises. "Art accomplishes what nature strives for in vain: it opens its eyes. Nature in its appearance—that is, nature in so far as it is not an object to be worked upon—in turn provides the expression of melancholia, peace or what have you" (AT 97).[5] Aesthetic experience of nature on the level of modernity allows us to perceive expressiveness in nature, and, by perceiving nature's expressiveness, we reach something beyond myth. Myth, as *Dialectic of Enlightenment* (1947) teaches, is a human attempt to escape the threats of nature, but myths articulate experiences of nature as spell. Nature is "always the same," and for that reason nature is seen as destiny (ÄT 105; AT 98–99). Art tames the powers of myth by transforming them into images (ÄT 180, 202, 211, 277; AT 173, 194, 203, 266). The same is true for natural beauty. Because aesthetic experiences of nature reveal images and not reproductions of nature, it is the quality of images that overcomes the immediacy of nature and allows a distance from its menaces (ÄT 105; AT 98–99).

Adorno's theorizing of natural beauty has its core in trying to show that natural beauty parallels aesthetic experiences of explicitly modern art. Both reveal the "expressiveness" of things (ÄT 111; AT 104). Furthermore, both artworks and natural beauty represent models of experience that transcend the totality of the principle of exchange and commodity production (ÄT 107; AT 101). But Adorno does not ignore the fact that such a position outside the world of exchange and commodities is increasingly nullified and made impossible. Nature has become an object of preservation (*Naturschutzpark*) or an alibi for immediacy. The experience of silence has become a social privilege. Nevertheless, natural beauty is an allegory of a sphere beyond the mediations of societal immanence. "In spite of its social mediatedness, the beautiful in nature remains an allegory of that beyond" (AT 102).[6]

Adorno stresses the allegorical character of such a being beyond societal immanence. Otherwise, if taken as an example of realized reconciliation, natural beauty would become ideology and reaffirm the existing society. Today we cannot picture our experiences of natural beauty according to principles of symmetry or harmony (ÄT 110, 117; AT 104, 111), nor is nature a substantial residue that could be explained in terms of Schelling's philosophy of nature (ÄT 120; AT 114).

Rather, the aesthetic experience of nature can be sensed in a contemporary work of art. Both frustrate identifying rationality and discourse. Rationality in its modern version presumes to capture all things through the process of identification in order to rule over them. But works of art, like natural beauty, claim the promise of being rational, even though both have the ability to escape rational discourse:

The beautiful in nature is the residue of non-identity in things, in an age when they are otherwise spellbound by universal identity. As long as this spell lasts, non-identity has no positive being. Therefore natural beauty remains sporadic and uncertain. But what it promises is all the more significant, going as it does beyond subjective sensation. Pain in the presence of the beautiful—which pain is especially vivid in one's experience of nature—is both the yearning for what is promised but never unveiled by beauty and the suffering in face of the insufficiency of the phenomenal appearance which wants to be like the beautiful but does not succeed. The same holds true of art. (AT 108)[7]

Natural beauty and modernist works of art have in common that they provide us with "traces" of the nonidentical. Such "traces" are comprehensible in the promises of a language that is beyond signifying meaning (ÄT 115; AT 109). Artworks and natural beauty alike ask us to realize the primacy of the object as opposed to subjective meaning (ÄT 111; AT 104–5).

Adorno offers a metacritique of Hegel's aesthetics, in which the beauty of art, art's "Ideal," is supposed to be a result of the insufficiency of natural beauty. Adorno follows Hegel in thinking that natural beauty cannot be treated as separate from beauty in art. Hegel is right when he states that natural beauty is not to be thought of as something immediately conceived: philosophical reflection must be added in order to save natural beauty. But Hegel hypostatizes "subjective spirit." He is unable to grasp nature as something that is not spiritual (ÄT 117–18; AT 111–12). Hegel states correctly the prosaic character of natural beauty, but he does not realize that modern art explicitly tries to escape the practical that is a reflex of ongoing disenchantment, "Entzauberung" (ÄT 119; AT 113).

The ongoing spiritualization of modern art, art's reflexivity and rationality, does not lead it away from natural beauty but rather propels art's spiritualization in line with nature and with natural beauty. Spiritualization cannot be conceived as identification with scientific rationality. Art tries to articulate something beyond human meaning and beyond human intentionality:

In actual fact, the spiritualization that art underwent in the past two hundred years and which has allowed art to achieve maturity did not signify an estrangement of art from nature. To say that it did is an interpretation dished up by reified consciousness. In truth, as art grew up, it moved closer to the beautiful in nature. A theory of art that simplistically equates art's tendency to subjectivization and the development of science in accordance with subjective reason may have some plausibility, but it misses the essence of the drift in artistic development.... Pure expression in art works... converges with nature, just as in the most authentic works of Anton Webern the pure sound... turns into its opposite: the sound of nature.... While nature's language is mute, art tries to make this muteness speak. (AT 115)[8]

To summarize, let me stress that for Adorno a theory of natural beauty must be developed in line with a theory of artistic beauty. The theory of art and the theory of natural beauty are to be linked. The images that natural beauty stimulates are fueled with the images that explicitly modern works of art provide.

In the remainder of this essay, I pursue this line of reasoning vis-à-vis recently developed aesthetic theories of nature. I do not neglect the new motifs introduced by Gernot Böhme and Martin Seel—times have changed since Adorno—but, as we will see, Adorno's voice should not be forgotten.

III

I begin by describing some systematic aspects of Böhme's theory. It is important to bear in mind that his ideas for an aesthetics of nature are linked both to a revised philosophy of nature and to modern aesthetics, in the narrow sense of the term. He presents his ecological aesthetics of nature as a revision of the philosophy of nature.

After environmental crises, such as Chernobyl, Sellafield, and Bopal, we have sufficient grounds for believing that the natural sciences should no longer be the prime source of our knowledge and understanding of nature. The philosophy of nature can no longer be thought of as an extension of the natural sciences, as has been the case in recent history.[9] We cannot place it within the tradition of speculative philosophy or in relation to Schelling's romanticist or Hegel's antiromanticist philosophies of nature. Hegel, for example, did not take the evolution of nature into account; furthermore, he perceived philosophy as a whole as a reconciliation of spirit and nature.

The need for a contemporary philosophy of nature is generated by the crisis in humanity's relationship with the environment.[10] Today we experience the consequences of humanity's interaction with nature as disastrous, and we increasingly feel the necessity for a thorough revaluation of the idea of scientific/technological progress.

What should a philosophy of nature constitute now, and how should we begin to develop a new aesthetics of nature? According to Böhme, both the aesthetics and the philosophy of nature should be grounded in the idea of an anthropology having pragmatic intent. This is also Kant's line in *Anthropologie in pragmatischer Absicht*.[11] Human beings must learn that we ourselves are, and always will be, of nature. Unless we cease to negate the nature we are part of, we will never achieve a shift in our attitude toward what is around us. Nature is not merely the totality of what is given to the senses, as Kant suggested, referring to the two central elements of Cartesian metaphysics. On the contrary, nature and the human world are fundamentally interconnected, and it is for this reason that philosophy must dispense with the notion that the primacy of pure reason marks the essence of what is human.[12]

According to Böhme, the philosophy of nature should focus on those characteristics that underlie, determine, and get revealed by all natural processes. Physiognomic knowledge should also be taken into account; this is a mode of understanding what is different from ourselves, such as another person. Understanding rests not on rational deduction but on intuitive insight into nature's characteristics or "traits." These characteristics are not models; they are articulated in sentences, and they signify complex experiences. As Böhme says, the characteristics of nature "articulate an intuitively conceived total impression of nature and formulate it in a physiognomic mode."[13] They are connected on both sides: to the experience of the life world, and also to scientific knowledge.

Within the natural sciences, characteristics might function as a kind of "heuristic device" but not as hypothesis.[14] Nature's characteristics were touched on by Aristotle, according to whom nature implements nothing in vain, strives for the best, and avoids the infinite.[15] In this context, we should also remember the ancient philosopher Heraclitus, who proposed that nature prefers to hide or conceal itself, or Galileo, who compared nature to a book written in mathematical formulas.

The characteristics of nature can be determined today by deconstructing classical writings on the philosophy of nature, on the one hand, and by reflecting on the results produced by the natural sciences, on the other. For example, in the light of the natural sciences, the classical tenet *lex continui* (nature does not make jumps) should be applied today as a law that holds true only in the macroscopic sphere of the body. It does not apply to the world of molecules and elementary particles.[16] Insofar as the law of continuity states divisibility of further divisibles, the legitimacy of this principle is in question even in the area of macrophysics.

Today, the natural sciences perceive absolute orders of magnitude and absolute scales of temperature; natural bodies are inscribed into special categories of size and the temporal order of cosmic eras into scales of temperature.[17] Characteristics of nature are revealed in the realm of living beings, in other words, in the organic.[18] The conditions of life are discerned through the development of such notions as self-regulation, circular causality, and autopoiesis. Despite the strong connection often made in modern philosophy between the notions of subjectivity and self-awareness, this link has now become obsolete. Böhme's notion of *Lebendigkeit*—the status of being alive—is conceptualized in the natural sciences today as a process of communication, that is, a process of the recognition and transferral of form. In this context, the notion of information, in the sense of understood structure, plays a crucial role.[19]

IV

How are we to develop an aesthetics of nature? How can we find a link between a new philosophy of nature and aesthetics in the narrower sense of the term? According to Böhme, such an aesthetics of nature should be grounded primarily in our bodily and sensuous perceptions of nature. In Baumgarten's definition of aesthetics, the construction of a theory of sensuous cognition plays a crucial role. Today such a theory should be developed with reference to a phenomenology of the body. Working from Aristotle's theory of perception in *De Anima*, Böhme proposes that all perceptions contain three poles.[20] The perceived manifests itself, in its actuality, only in the act of perceiving. However, this act is dependent on a medium in which is registered the actuality of that which is perceived: the bodily organ is the sphere of the presence of the perceivable.

This Aristotelian theory of perception can become a fruitful starting point for an aesthetics of nature by way of the following reformulation.[21] The sense that, according to Aristotle, is active during the process of perceiving is *Befindlichkeit,* or bodily awareness. *Befindlichkeit* is the bodily presence of the perceiving "subjectivity." In most cases, however, this subjectivity is not autonomous; bodily awareness is subject to, and influenced by, "atmospheres" within which the body inevitably exists. Atmosphere is a kind of tuning, *Stimmung,* that colors perception. It exists in space, although its parameters cannot be defined.

Bodily awareness of natural things is an awareness, above all, of their physiognomy—their "coming to the fore" (*Heraustreten*), their coming into being, or, as Böhme says, their ecstasy. At issue here are the modes by which things present themselves.[22] Aristotle once called this the process of catching the "image" or "form" of things, their *eidos,* without "matter."[23] It is in such modes of coming to the fore, the processes whereby things present themselves, that the characteristics of things are revealed. Here the aesthetics and the philosophy of nature come together. Böhme says, that *Aussichheraustreten* (coming to the fore) is the main characteristic trait of the natural object: "By 'characteristics of nature' I mean the superior principles of our understanding of nature, which define nature, more or less, in all their singular appearances, but above all in the play which occurs between them as a whole. The aesthetic theory of nature is that theory of nature which elaborates nature's main trait of the stepping forth (*Hervortreten*) or the coming to the fore (*Aussichheraustreten*) of natural things and which makes this trait a leading principle for the disclosure of nature."[24]

There are two remarkable consequences of opening up philosophy of nature to aesthetics and of the problem of nature for aesthetics. One is the intuition of an aesthetics of the ephemeral and the need for reevaluating the aesthetic notion of "semblance."[25] This is a preeminent trait of natural characteristics,[26] implicit in Heraclitus's statement that nature likes to conceal itself; in human sexual relations, for example, the erotic experience veils the purpose of reproduction.

Since its development, after Kant, into a theory of aesthetic judgement and subsequently into a theory of the work of art, modern aesthetics has been unable to develop an adequate notion of semblance. As Hegel says, the philosophical idea must be immanent within the notion of semblance. In response to the fear of being absorbed into the ephemeral or into the passing moment, dissipated in the trivial (*Verschwendung*), the notion of semblance has been devalued to a transitory medium. An aesthetics that derives from the awareness of the senses ("Sinnenbewußtsein"—R. zur Lippe), however, emphasizes perception as the sensuous gaze that is stimulated and fascinated by things rather than merely serving a process of identification and registration.

The second consequence of opening up the problem of nature for aesthetics is a reevaluation of the art of gardening. According to Böhme, the theory of the English garden as developed by Hirschfeld is historically and systematically important for an aesthetics of nature.[27] The English garden or park was intended to present nature in the form of picturesque, scenic arrangements whose objective characteristics of expression and atmosphere are revealed, little by little, only through the bodily experience of moving around. These were romantic, melancholic "gardenscapes" in which not only plants, trees, and shrubbery but also the elements played their parts.

To avoid a Eurocentric view, we should also consider non-European gardens, such as the Japanese, in which we can distinguish three models. One is the garden as a miniature world, which we find at the Katsura, in Kyoto, or in Kamakura, at the Engaku-ji. Here stones, trees, and waterfalls stimulate the full range of our senses, especially sight, hearing, and smell. The second model presents the garden as a landscape in which as in Shūgaku-in, in Kyoto, artificial lakes are perceived from various viewpoints. Finally, there is the Zen Buddhist stone garden, in which small stones are arranged around rocks and greenery, and the morning ritual of raking this gravel (the alignment of the stones represents the path of the soul) constitutes an act of meditation, as in the fifteenth-century Ryoan-ji, or the Ginkaku-ji, both in Kyoto.

We have, then, an important point for the aesthetics of nature. We should not hope to go back to an "original," untouched state of nature. This no longer exists. As Böhme emphasizes again and again, nature has already been both appropriated and cultivated. The need for an aesthetics of nature is generated by the fact, which we have learned through experience, that the idea of nature as a core of essences no longer holds true. The traditional oppositions between nature and technology, nature and art, nature and culture—between the natural and the artificial—have lost their validity.[28]

V

Perhaps this is an appropriate place to introduce my critique of Böhme's aesthetics of nature, making reference to Adorno. Against Benjamin, who hoped that the new media of photography and film would be a useful tool for emancipating the masses, Adorno argues that technology functions as an instrument for maintaining social control. It is dependent on a social framework that, even today, is controlled by the powers of capital. Adorno claims that only in the sphere of art is there any real shift in the role or agenda of technology, because here it is not mediated by processes of social control. As art incorporates technological procedures into its purpose, that technology undergoes a transformation and acquires new meaning. Thus, within art, technology is geared toward purposes outside or beyond the domination of nature. For Adorno, such domination is no more than an extension of the domination of the social world, which results from the power of capital. By making use of technology, artworks can surmount such social restraints.

We find a similar conclusion in Lyotard. For him, avant-garde art articulates a *différend* by refusing the techno-sciences and their performative power. Whereas the techno-sciences dominate our modes of interpreting nature, art undermines the socially established modes of symbolic representation. The artwork refers to something that cannot be represented, and thus performs the *différend* by which the societal link between technoscience and social domination is broken.

I would argue, then, that a decisive shift in humanity's social condition is conceivable only through an affirmed aesthetic awareness of nature. Such awareness, in turn, is achieved through the experiences we have with the work of art. We should realize that technology may have a totally different meaning from the socially established, one-dimensional role of control or domination.

VI

Böhme approaches the problem of an aesthetics of nature through the perspective of the philosophy of nature. Because the natural sciences are integrated within a technological framework, it is no longer valid for them to put forward their visions of nature as a whole. We can face today's ecological catastrophe only if we recognize, through our bodily experiences, that we ourselves are part of nature.

Whereas Böhme enters the aesthetics of nature through the philosophy of nature, Martin Seel introduces the aesthetics of nature in order to go beyond the limited role of aesthetics as a philosophy of art. Moral/philosophical questions concerning the aesthetic experience of nature provide his focus.

Seel distinguishes among three marked aesthetic attitudes toward nature. First, there is the contemplative attitude, which involves the sensuous awareness of things and the importance of this awareness. Here, perspectives of meaning are surmounted by the experience of synaesthetic sensations. The predominance of the gaze throughout history no longer holds. Acts of contemplation presuppose an articulation of the world, but this articulation and its meaning are transcended at the moment of contemplation. Aesthetic contemplation is purely sensuous, and for this reason it is distinguished from the theoretical contemplation in the tradition of metaphysics until Schopenhauer.

Alongside this contemplative attitude toward nature lies a second paradigm: the experience of nature in the sense of a corresponding place. Here nature is perceived as an inspiring background to an unburdened existence. The physiognomy of a region plays an important role in this, with climate and history contributing to the tangible sense of "being in the world" (Heidegger). In tandem with this model, which could be linked to a notion of beauty, there is also "ugly nature." Ugly nature could be called a negative experience of correspondence, in which the world works against any possibility of feeling at ease within it; the world around us, and the human life it contains, are inadequate.[29] A related possibility might occur when nature is experienced as "sublime," when magnitude and power elicit in us the sense of our possibilities for a "supernatural destiny" (as both Kant and Edmund Burke have suggested).

The third paradigm of aesthetic attitudes is that wherein nature is regarded as the essential realm of our ongoing imagination and we experience nature as a prototype or a model in art. In experiencing a landscape, we make an analogy to the paintings of Caspar David Friedrich or William Turner. Nature alone is able to inspire our fantasy. But when we make analogies with the models we find in art, our imaginative capacity is intensified.[30] We might apply the notion of beauty to those cases in which the world of our imagination is intensified, whereas when our imagination suffers disturbance, we might think more of the notion of the sublime. In these cases, nature is experienced as having more dignity and more power than an artwork could ever hope to achieve.

The objectives of Seel's aesthetics of nature are directed above all to the questions of practical life. Whereas contemplation helps to put the many outlooks on life into perspective, the experience of correspondence intensifies our existential feelings and ideas. The imagination, when fueled by the great power of nature, can offer us new visions of the world.[31]

All three attitudes imply different modes of experiencing temporality: contemplation is related to our experience of the present and to a heightened awareness of its passing moments; the experience of correspondence is directed more toward the past; and the experience of the imagination is oriented toward the future. In all three attitudes, however, we experience nature as free, unfettered by human domination.

Not unlike Adorno, Seel argues that we realize the unity of all three aesthetic attitudes in the experience of landscape. Our images of landscapes are powerfully stimulated by works of art. If we experience landscape, then we attempt to attain a contemplative attitude. But for Seel this aesthetic experience of nature is contingent. For that reason, he criticizes Adorno for suggesting that works of art reduce the contingency of the aesthetic semblance.[32]

VII

For the purposes of my own discussion, it is important to mention that Seel himself relates the aesthetics of nature to the philosophy of art. In experiencing art, all three attitudes are brought to bear, subtly tempered according to the type of art in question. In architecture, for instance, correspondence plays the dominant role.[33]

Of course, great differences remain between the experience of art and the aesthetic experience of nature. The unity of all three aspects inheres in the structure of art, whereas in nature the unity fluctuates. The work of art is constructed with intention, whereas in nature the "work" is subjective and unauthorized.[34] Here, I touch on a problematic aspect of Seel's theory. He stresses the eternal character of artworks and speaks of "bleibenden Werken" as an ever-present background to the lifeworld.[35] Such reflections overlook the many changes that have taken place during the development of modern art: Beuys's idea of art as a "social sculpture," "land-art," and many other concepts of site-specific work do not fit into Seel's vision of the artwork as something permanent.

VIII

Although Seel fails to develop an adequate idea of contemporary artistic practices, his ideas on the ethical impact of the aesthetic experience of nature are more convincing, and this topic is important for a complete notion of natural beauty. Adorno, for his part, does not connect natural beauty explicitly with ethical issues. But how should we, today, relate the aesthetics of nature to ethics?

Recently, a sharp distinction has been made between ethics in the sense of individual conduct, in which we speak of advice and recommendations, and ethics in relation to the social world, where we discuss morally relevant social norms, precepts, or even imperatives.[36] The ethical implications of the aesthetic experience of nature revolve around an ethics of the "good life" of the individual. Social obligations, on the other hand, play a decisive role within communication processes and raise questions of intersubjectively valid responsibility.

Technological actions, in the sense of instrumental action (Habermas), may dominate nature, but liberating nature through technological means is also possible.[37] In neither case, however, is there space for that distance from nature that is one prerequisite for any aesthetic attitude, for even liberation occurs during processes of interaction with nature.

According to Seel, the ethical relevance of aesthetic experiences of nature must be viewed against the background of the social life of a smaller community, that is, in relation to the political practices of a geographically determined region.[38] Our experiences of nature through modes of aesthetic awareness may or may not influence our attitudes toward these practices. Whereas contemplation allows us to create a space of distance and imagination inspires us to new perspectives on the forms that life may take, the experience of nature as a corresponding place enables us to maintain a participation in communal or regional practices.[39] The product of Seel's theorizing is a critique of philosophies that place these attitudes in a hierarchy. Nietzsche, for example, stresses the power of the artwork to encourage contemplation and an intensified imagination.

The ethical dimension of aesthetic attitudes toward nature occupies much of Seel's theory. Complementary reflection concerning the intersubjective moral dimension is very slight. From a moral point of view, Seel argues, we have to take care of nature, especially the great variety of animal species. If we do not, enriched human life is endangered. Our experiences with the beauty of nature enable us to distance ourselves from the established outlooks on life. The destruction of nature is morally unacceptable, because the "destruction of an eminent and an irreparable sphere of the human world" would result.[40] In other words, it is our responsibility, as human beings, not to destroy nature or the natural environment of our existence.

IX

I agree with Böhme's proposition that the natural sciences can no longer hold the monopoly over our knowledge of nature. Furthermore, to discuss an aesthetics of nature in terms of an "anthropology with pragmatic intent" is highly convincing. Only when we recognize and affirm that our bodies are rooted in natural processes might a politics of the body emerge that can confront the environmental crises of our days. We need visions of nature. We need a politics of the body. However, neither version of the aesthetics of nature that we have discussed here, neither Böhme's nor Seel's, takes into account contemporary modes of artistic production. These modes might be seen as means for a social habituation of sensuous awareness and for changes in the social imagination. Artworks might be conceived as positions or sources of resistance to the manipulations of those atmospheres used, for example, in advertising. By stimulating reflective, sensuous awareness, artworks can challenge the power of manipulation.

In a time when global alternatives for social uses of technology are not being found, integrating technology into the work of art may still be seen as a means to a new kind of experience of technology. This is the lesson we can learn from Lyotard and Adorno.

It should be clear that I am arguing for continuing an aesthetics of nature in the line of Adorno. Böhme's criticism that Adorno stressed, rather one-sidedly, the alliance between the philosophy of art and the aesthetics of nature[41] could easily be levied against Böhme himself. Because Böhme does not have a full awareness of contemporary artistic productions, he misses the interrelationship between the aesthetics of nature and the philosophy of art.

With respect to another point, however, I would like to follow Böhme's suggestions. Böhme argues that philosophical aesthetics after Baumgarten was threatened by the aesthetic semblance. The ephemeral was feared and, accordingly, semblance was regarded as something provisional that should be overcome by the idea. Even Adorno does not succeed in getting rid of this philosophical heritage.[42] I do not want to enter the discussion here of whether Böhme is completely correct on this score. I only want to stress that we keep in touch with contemporary art productions when we introduce notions like "the ephemeral," "the transitory," "the event."

To my mind, a perspective informed by Adorno finds access to contemporary discussions only if we stress the above-mentioned characteristics. Then it should not be difficult to find entries to postmodern discourses as stimulated by Lyotard, Gianni Vattimo, Luce Irigaray, Julia Kristeva, and others.[43]

Vattimo's notion of art as oscillation, Lyotard's distinction between a "slackened" postmodernism and a radical postmodern position that maintains the experimental heritage of modernity, Kristeva's link between the symbolic power of avant-garde art and the semiotic of the body, Irigaray's vision of art as a means to create symbols of the hitherto-suppressed feminine—all could be read from a perspective informed by Adorno. In doing so, we regain the practical relevance of Adorno's thought today. The link between aesthetics as it relates to art and aesthetics as it relates to nature should not be forgotten.

Notes

1. See Andreas Huyssen, *After the Great Divide: Modernism, Mass Culture and Postmodernism* (London: Macmillan, 1993).

2. See Wolfgang Welsch, "Adornos Ästhetik: Eine implizite Ästhetik des Erhabenen," in *Das Erhabene. Zwischen Grenzerfahrung und Grsößenwahn*, ed. Christine Pries, (Weinheim: VCH Acta Humaniora, 1989), pp. 185–213.

3. Theodor W. Adorno, *Ästhetische Theorie*, ed. Gretel Adorno and Rolf Tiedemann (Frankfurt: Suhrkamp, 1973), p. 98; hereafter, cited in the text as ÄT. *Aesthetic Theory*, trans. C. Lenhardt (London: Routledge & Kegan Paul, 1984), p. 91; hereafter, cited in the text as AT.

4. Joachim Ritter, *Landschaft. Zur Funktion des Ästhetischen in der modernen Gesellschaft* (Münster: Aschendorff, 1963).

5. "Was Natur vergebens möchte, vollbringen die Kunstwerke: sie schlagen die Augen auf. Die erscheinende Natur selbst gewährt, sobald sie nicht als Aktionsobjekt dient, den Ausdruck von Schwermut oder Frieden oder von was immer." (ÄT 104)

6. "Das Naturschöne bleibt Allegorie dieses Jenseitigen trotz seiner Vermittlung durch die gesellschaftliche Immanenz." (ÄT 108)

7. "Das Naturschöne ist die Spur des Nichtidentischen an den Dingen im Bann universaler Identität. Solange er waltet, ist kein Nichtidentisches positiv da. Daher bleibt das Naturschöne so versprengt und ungewiß wie das, was von ihm versprochen wird, alles Innermenschliche überflügelt. Der Schmerz im Angesicht des Schönen, nirgends leibhafter als in der Erfahrung von Natur, ist ebenso die Sehnsucht nach dem, was es verheißt, ohne daß es darin sich entschleierte, wie das Leiden an der Unzulänglichkeit der Erscheinung, die es versagt, indem sie ihm gleichen möchte. Das setzt im Verhältnis zu den Kunstwerken sich fort." (ÄT 114)

8. "Tatsächlich hat Kunst durch die Spiritualisierung, die ihr während der letzten zweihundert Jahre widerfuhr und durch die sie mündig ward, nicht, wie das verdinglichte Bewußtsein es möchte, der Natur sich entfremdet, sondern der eigenen Gestalt nach dem Naturschönen sich angenähert. Eine Theorie der Kunst, welche deren Tendenz zur Subjektivierung in einfache Identität setzt mit der Entwicklung der Wissenschaft gemäß subjektiver Vernunft, versäumte zugunsten von Plausibilität den Gehalt der künstlerischen Bewegung.... Der reine Ausdruck der Kunstwerke...konvergiert mit Natur, so wie in den authentischesten Gebilden Anton Weberns der reine Ton...umschlägt in den Naturlaut.... Ist die Sprache der Natur stumm, so trachtet Kunst, das Stumme zum Sprechen zu bringen." (ÄT 121)

9. Gernot Böhme, *Natürlich Natur. Über Natur im Zeitalter ihrer technischen Reproduzierbarkeit* (Frankfurt: Suhrkamp, 1992), p. 36.

10. Ibid., pp. 34, 58.

11. Ibid., pp. 91, 120.

12. Such a deconstruction of the modern tradition of philosophy was put forward by Gernot and Hartmut Böhme in their book *Das Andere der Vernunft* (Frankfurt: Suhrkamp, 1985). See also Böhme, *Natürlich Natur*, pp. 38, 50–54.

13. Böhme, *Natürlich Natur*, p. 67.

14. Ibid., p. 67.

15. Ibid., pp. 63ff.

16. Ibid., pp. 68ff.

17. Ibid., pp. 70–72.

18. Ibid., pp. 72–75.

19. See Gernot Böhme, *Für eine ökologische Natur-Ästhetik* (Frankfurt: Suhrkamp, 1989), pp. 53, 122–23.

20. Böhme, *Natürlich Natur,* pp. 126–31.

21. Ibid., pp. 136–40.

22. Böhme, *Für eine ökologische Natur-Ästhetik,* pp. 52ff.

23. Böhme, *Natürlich Natur,* p. 130.

24. Ibid., p. 132.

25. Böhme, *Für eine ökologische Natur-Ästhetik,* pp. 166–89.

26. Böhme, *Natürlich Natur,* pp. 86ff.

27. Böhme, *Für eine ökologische Natur-Ästhetik,* pp. 79–95.

28. Böhme, *Natürlich Natur,* pp. 9–25, 107–24.

29. Martin Seel, *Eine Ästhetik der Natur* (Frankfurt: Suhrkamp, 1991), p. 95.

30. Ibid., p. 144.

31. Ibid., p. 191.

32. Ibid., p. 181, with reference to ÄT 122; AT 116.

33. Ibid., pp. 220–32. It goes without saying that artworks stimulate our imagination.

34. Ibid., pp. 270–72.

35. Ibid., p. 239.

36. Ibid., pp. 298ff.

37. Ibid., pp. 178–84.

38. Ibid., p. 323.

39. Ibid., pp. 330–36.

40. Ibid., p. 343.

41. Böhme, *Für eine ökologische Natur-Ästhetik*, pp. 19–23.

42. Ibid., pp. 176–78.

43. See my book *The Discourse of the Postmodern and the Discourse of the Avant-Garde* (Maastricht, The Netherlands: Jan Van Eyck Akademie, 1994).

9

Kant, Adorno, and the Social Opacity of the Aesthetic

Tom Huhn

The light dove, cleaving the air in her free flight, and feeling its resistance, might imagine that its flight would be still easier in empty space.
—*Immanuel Kant*

How do you know but ev'ry Bird that cuts the airy way, Is an immense world of delight, clos'd by your senses five?
—*William Blake*

I want to consider the relation between the aesthetic theories of Kant and Adorno. I want to suggest that Adorno closely follows Kant not only in the elaboration of the subject of aesthetics but also in the subjectivity elaborated in the aesthetic. What I would like to demonstrate is that the only substantive difference between Kant and Adorno lies in the history of the last two hundred years; that history consists of a transplantation of whatever it is that was once embodied by aesthetic judgment into what now occurs as the history and process of art. My hunch is that Adorno reads the *Critique of Judgment* as, simultaneously, the richest, most nuanced treatise on aesthetics, and as a site of immense repression. Rather than fault Kant's text for the latter, Adorno instead reads that repression as integral to the aesthetic and thereby attempts to set back in motion the frozen Kantian dialectic between beauty and the sublime. Adorno's insight into the aesthetic is both akin to and modeled on Kant's: Kant finds *aesthetic judgment* the reverse and hence visible image of subjective constitution, whereas

Adorno theorizes the work of art as both that same reverse image as well as the attempt to see not only by means of it but also through it. It is as if Kant and Adorno are peering at the same phenomenon from opposite points of view. Kant glimpses a view of the constitution of subjectivity and intersubjectivity by suppressing the view of the object that, ironically, is the occasion for the judgment of beauty. Kant's aesthetic theory is thus a mimetic recapitulation of the very dynamic by which judgment functions. Adorno's aesthetic theory, on the other hand, rather than attempting to look past the object in order to discern the subject, focuses on the object as a way of illuminating both object and subject. The object of aesthetic judgment thereby reveals itself as subjectivity in its otherness. It is now the artwork, and no longer Kant's aesthetic judgment, that has become for Adorno the most privileged site of alienation.

My hope for the present essay is twofold: I want to prompt a reconsideration of Kant's aesthetics by showing the extent to which Adorno is indebted to it; and I want to suggest that a profound intimacy continues to exist between Kant's and Adorno's texts, precisely in the inextinguishability of the aesthetic hope for reconciliation within human life. Though this hope for reconciliation registers itself in Kant as a refusal to forsake nature as the realm in which human freedom comes to fruition, Adorno proceeds instead to recount the historical migration of this hope from the site of natural beauty to that of the sublime and finally (or at least up until the present) to art beauty. Adorno's critique of the third *Critique* is that it attempts to hold the dialectic within the aesthetic at a standstill, to keep natural beauty separate from art beauty, and to keep both these instances of taste separate from the judgment of the sublime that occurs within— but seemingly above—the all too civilized heads of people.

I begin by considering some of Adorno's remarks on Kant's account of the sublime. The Kantian sublime, as is well known, resides not in art but only in the presence of nature: "This sublimity, Kant argues, is something we ought to feel in the face of nature, but measured by the subjective theory of constitution, this means that nature itself must be sublime. Self-reflection in the face of nature's sublimity anticipates something of a reconciliation with it" (AT 293/281).[1] The sublime is a promise, indeed a much more substantive and emphatic promise than the one made by beauty—Adorno's fondness for Stendhal's dictum that beauty is the *promesse de bonheur* is revealed by how often he repeats it—for the sublime also promises reconciliation and thereby redemption. But for Kant, such promise and such redemption might occur only with nature. Indeed, we might well say that for Kant this promise and redemption have meaning and content only insofar as they are made with and in nature. For a sublime art—nearly an oxymoron for Kant—the promise of life and redemption would instead amount to the resignation of subjectivity to its already-fallen state.

Perhaps the most important element in Kant's account of the sublime is an incessant dynamism, or better said, a negative dialectic. (For Adorno, the Hegelian dialectic inevitably collapses the distinction and distance between subject and object in favor of the subject and at the expense of the object; Adorno's negative dialectic instead favors the object at the expense of the subject. The dynamism of the Kantian sublime, like negative dialectics, registers the too-ready and too-complete erasure of the object.) The sublime is not itself redemption but the persistent performance of the expectation that redemption ought to be at hand. It is the refusal to relinquish not just hope but the immediacy and presence of real life. The sublime, however, is not Christian—it does not require a fallen subjectivity. Neither, then, is it nostalgic—it does not seek to recover what it imagines once existed. Neither is the sublime allegorical, premising its present on an overly dead something else. The sublime is instead a mimetic, proleptic production of nature—human (social) nature, which is to say, second nature.

If this second nature is reduced to a merely phenomenal scale, the art that heralds it is likewise often reduced to one version or another of morality. Although beauty might indeed at times function as a *symbol* of morality, the sublime resists such functioning in order to continue to suggest that which exceeds the grasp of the phenomenal: "No longer under the sway of spirit, nature would free itself from the cursed embrace of naturalness and imperious subjectivity. This liberation would amount to a return of nature, more specifically a return of the sublime, the counterimage of mere life" (AT 293/281).

A persistent theme of Adorno's aesthetics is that nature might indeed "free itself from...imperious subjectivity" by an art aligned in opposition to us. Adorno suggests this opposition might also be taken as the revenge of nature on us. Not revenge for what we have technologically inflicted on nature but for our having left off holding regard for nature in any of its guises. Art's contrariness, then, is a product of the sublime's having migrated, after Kant, from nature into art. The historical era of the sublime in nature, let us say the second half of the eighteenth century, Adorno describes as coincident with a development in which "[t]he unleashing of elemental forces was one with the emancipation of the subject and hence with the self-consciousness of spirit" (AT 292/280). The subject comes into its own and (mis)recognizes itself as sublime nature. But this misrecognition, this hope and reflection, cannot persist, because of the subjective failure to realize itself as indeed something more than mere life.

We might well describe Kant's account of taste—the experience of beauty in contrast to that of the sublime—as the diagnosis of its subjective attempt to universalize itself. For Kant, subjectivity succeeds as a universal product in the moment of aesthetic (tasteful) pleasure, but so, too, must we judge that same moment—by Kant's own account—as a failure insofar as it is precisely the universality of that moment which remains unrecognized by subjectivity. Indeed, it is precisely this opacity, the failure of aesthetic subjectivity to recognize itself as an agent, that calls forth the need for a critique of aesthetic judgment.

Subjectivity *realizes* itself in taste but fails to *recognize* itself therein, and thereby likewise fails to reproduce itself as social. Though the singular success of taste lies, according to Kant, in the achievement of positing intersubjectivity, its failure nonetheless is twofold: taste fails either to transform its achieved universal intersubjectivity into something objective or, what seems the very least, to apprehend its achievement—hence, its continuing opacity. This particular failure of taste—again, in the very moment of its success—sets in motion the project of the sublime. The first task of the sublime is to remove from taste the presentation that allows it to misrecognize itself as objective. For Adorno, the migration of the sublime from nature to art is not the product of nature's revenge alone: it is also a symptom of the reciprocally increasing reification of the social and the subjective. If the sublime begins as the withdrawal of the purportedly objective, it continues more purely as the force of the negative. As reification increases, so, too, does the urgency for a dynamism that cuts across it.

The migration of the sublime into art might then well be construed not merely as the disregard of nature but also as the signal of an increased reification within the confines of art itself. If art was ever a realm of free play, the arrival of the sublime indicates that art exists no longer as such. Because art, for Adorno, now requires the sublime, it is no longer the realm of mere appearance but, beyond that, the realm of false appearance, which is to say, of appearances that demand to be disavowed. If aesthetic appearance once served as a goad to reflection and life, pace Nietzsche, it must have since hardened into an impediment, indeed especially to itself.

We also find in Adorno the suggestion that it is just the success of art that allows the sublime to migrate toward it. Adorno borrows Nietzsche's aesthetic schematism regarding the principle of individuation in art in order to describe the particular problematic that art both creates and seemingly resolves: "It is the fact that art must at all costs individuate itself that makes universality problematic" (AT 300/289). Perhaps in homage to Nietzsche's critique of Euripidean drama, Adorno notes that a deus ex machina is the visible intervention of a technological machinery to assist, or rather force, the transition from particular to universal. Ideally, the particular artwork would dialectically make the transition on its own. Adorno's explanation of individuation and universalization centers again on Kant: "The more specific a work is, the more faithfully it actualizes its type: the dialectical precept that the particular is the universal has its model in art. Kant was the first to have sighted this, but he immediately defused it. From the standpoint of Kant's teleology, reason in aesthetics has the task of positing totality and identity" (AT 300/288). Presumably, what Adorno has in mind here is Kant's notion of the exemplar, which Kant formulates—in distinction to the example, which would be merely an instantiation of a general rule or model— as an instance that is simultaneously a particular and a rule or principle. The exemplar is by definition particular insofar as it is singular, but also it is more than a model, since it exists as ideal for any possible further instances.

Adorno faults Kant for positing too smooth and seamless a relation between particularity and universality in the object of beauty— because, despite his aesthetic theory, Kant helps keep invisible the technological machinery of transition. The object of beauty, whether artistic or natural, is for Kant less a site of promise or reconciliation, because it consists wholly of a harmonious identity between particular and universal. In short, there is no tension, dialectic, or slippage in Kantian beauty. It is as if beauty too readily achieves what Adorno considers art's inescapable goal: "Since time immemorial, art has sought to rescue the particular; advancing particularity was immanent to it" (AT 299/287). Yet for Adorno, the Kantian redemption and promotion of the particular object (but so, too, surreptitiously of the subject) come at too high a cost: the complete obliteration of the persistent tension between particular and universal as well as the eventual total effacement of the object of beauty itself. In Kant, beauty severs forever—in order to gain the universality of subjectivity—whatever ties remained that bound it to the particularity of the object. With this effacement of the object for the sake of beauty, or with what Adorno calls the evisceration of art, art's immemorial project of redeeming and promoting the particular now becomes the problem of the sublime. More simply put, Kant's formulation of beauty resolves, but all too quickly and completely, the immemorial tension between particular and universal. It is this tension that migrates to the sublime.

Kant's favoring of natural over artistic beauty is the implicit recognition of the importance of some resistance to an all-pervasive and seamless identity of particular and universal. For Adorno, natural beauty is precisely a cipher of that which resists identity: "The beauty of nature is the residue of nonidentity in things spellbound by universal identity. As long as this spell rules, nothing nonidentical is positively there" (AT 114/108). Natural beauty is not itself the nonidentical but the cipher or promise that nonidentity might be possible. "Natural beauty partakes of the weakness of all promisings: they are inextinguishable" (AT 114/108). And this inextinguishable promise is also fragile: "The reason one shies away from natural beauty is that one might wound the not yet existing by grasping it in what exists" (AT 115/109). The sublime, as we will see, bears no regard for this fragility in its attempt to extinguish the promise once borne by natural beauty, while attempting to make the not yet existing come into being.

If we turn to a passage in which Adorno comments on Hegel's aesthetics, we will come to understand that it is not only the sublime that migrates into art but the beauty of nature into art beauty:

> Contrary to Hegel's philosophy of identity, the beautiful in nature is close to the truth, except that at the moment of greatest proximity it conceals itself anew. This, too, art has learned from the beautiful in nature. What draws the line against fetishism and pantheistic make-believe as pleasant-looking disguises of an endless evil fate is the fact that nature, as it tenderly, mortally stirs in its beauty, does not yet in the slightest exist. (AT 115/109)

In other words, the beauty of art now carries the burden of what nature once promised in the guise of natural beauty. Natural beauty might then be understood as a dynamic, indeed a dialectical one: it begins as the hope of identity and comes near to achieving identity, but in the proximity of this near identity it "conceals itself anew," which is to say it retreats from positing identity. It would not be amiss here to suggest that what Adorno means by the autonomy of art may well be a reference to the historical piling up of functions onto art and art beauty such that art, merely by the accumulation and variety of tasks and expectations that fall to it, comes to be autonomous. Art thus functions as the default sphere into which migrate the historic frustrations of failed dreams and projects of human emancipation. Yet insofar as this sphere serves not only as a reservoir of these frustrations but also maintains them, the aesthetic sphere of art thereby—for Adorno—becomes an active, independent agency. This of course is not to suggest that all art is autonomous or that all or any art making occurs in autonomy but that what some art or aesthetic judgment *achieves* is autonomy. Put differently, the autonomy of art signals the transfer of human autonomy (which is to say, freedom) from the human subject to the aesthetic artifact. When we speak of the spirit of art, we do not just infer our own alienation but so, too, posit *the* privileged site of alienation.

The sublime, like natural beauty, is hope. It is also a good deal more, and less. It is more than hope insofar as it attempts to make actual the hoped-for identity between particular and universal. The sublime, in this regard, is the refusal of the solace of hope evoked by natural beauty. We might well recall here Adorno's statement explaining how,

in the late eighteenth century, the sublime and taste came into conflict as a result of the "unleashing of elemental forces" that was "one
with the emancipation of the subject" (AT 292/280). The subject,
however, was not emancipated—and, to paraphrase a well-known passage from *Negative Dialectics*, we might say that the moment when the
subject was to realize itself has passed. The residue of this passed moment, of a subject born still, is not the hope for some future birth but
the refusal of nature as the locus of generation and regeneration. The
sublime, after Kant, thus migrates to art, to the realm of artifice par excellence. And the fact of this migration means that hope has not been
extinguished but transferred. The question is how this migration affects the hope and whether there is more to hope for from art and art
beauty than once was allowed by nature and natural beauty.

In order to consider the transformation of hope, and art, by the
migration of the sublime, we need first to know how Adorno interprets Kant's account of the sublime. The reason Kant has an account
of the sublime is, I have suggested, the result of taste's having
achieved a too successful harmony of particular and universal, of
subject and object. I have also suggested that this harmony occurs at
the cost of obliterating the object as well as subjectivity's failure to
recognize its achieved universality. I want now to suggest that implicit
in Adorno's account of Kant's sublime is the thought that this sublime already registers the faults within the success of taste. It is thus
in the account of the sublime that we find the symptomatic expression of what ails the success of taste.

The sublime arrives in the eighteenth century as the most advanced dialectical technique for producing human freedom. Adorno
describes the traditional concept of the sublime as an "infinite
presence...animated by the belief that negation could bring about
positivity" (AT 294/282). However, since this positivity fails to occur
(or occurs all too negatively in taste), the negativity of the sublime
comes to the fore:

Sublimity was supposed to be the greatness of man as a spiritual being and as
nature's tamer. However, once the experience of the sublime turns out to be
man's self-conscious realization that he is not natural, it becomes necessary
to reconceptualize the sublime. Even in the context of the Kantian formulation, sublimity was tinged by the nullity and transience of man as an empiri-

cal being that was to have thrown in relief the eternity of his universal characteristic, i.e., spirit. (AT 295/283)

The sublime fails to achieve the *Aufhebung* of spirit, in part because it misconceives what is not spirit. In sacrificing empirical existence so readily, the sublime thereby also discards nature, just that realm until then requisite for prolonging the hope provided by natural beauty. With the sublation of human existence in the hoped-for transcendence of the sublime, the place and means by which reconciliation might occur is disregarded. And if this sweeping, purposive disavowal is, as I have tried to suggest, already a feature of natural beauty, then the negation of empirical existence effected by the sublime is but a more-thorough version of the effacement of nature achieved according to Kant's account of taste. The salient difference, then, between Kant's accounts of taste and the sublime is that natural beauty still required nature (whatever that might have been or comes to be) as an *occasion* for an aesthetic experience, for the harmony of particular and universal, even though Kant's account explains the functional importance of that occasion as merely an opportunity for subjectivity to misrecognize itself.

Power figures in most accounts of the sublime, from Longinus to Burke. Kant's account of the sublime, however, begins by exponentially increasing the power of the sublime into something capable, literally, of overpowering power; Kant's term for this superpower is dominance (*Gewalt*). It is as if the weakened power of subjectivity to reproduce itself in an experience of natural beauty demands a supercharged power. And because power has no overt opportunity to recognize itself in beauty, the sublime becomes the locus for the return of what was beautifully repressed. In this fashion, the power that expresses itself only implicitly in the experience of beauty becomes explicit and overpowering in the sublime. The sublime is the promise not just of identity but of overt recognition of subjective dominance, of self-conscious dominance, and so, too, of pleasure therein. The sublime might then be construed as the dialectical continuation of beauty, registering its sins and propelled by what remains unfinished in it. This continuation makes explicit, then, the complicity of domination in the aesthetic, in this case the sublime:

"By situating the sublime in an overwhelming magnitude, in an antithesis of power with impotence, Kant betrayed an unmitigated complicity with domination" (AT 296/284). This complicity, I want to suggest, is already foreshadowed in the judgment of beauty, especially the judgment of natural beauty, where the object is swept away by the tide of subjective universality even though the illusion of its presence remains. The sublime, then, is the dialectical removal of the veil of illusion that sustains judgments of beauty. The *reflective* judgment of beauty depends on the not quite seeing through that this veil provides. The critical mission of the sublime is to remove this veil. That mission fails, however, with the failure of subjectivity to complete it. The sublime continues historically as a downward spiral into sheer negativity: "Radical negativity, as bare and nonillusory as the illusion once promised by the sublime, has become its legacy" (AT 296/284).

The sublime, however, was never just sheer power and complicity with domination. It was, according to Adorno's interpretation of Kant, the primary means of subjective resistance to nature—in short, the means by which freedom is won. Because that freedom has not been won, or rather continues to be won only piecemeal and momentarily, the dynamic of the sublime not only turns inward to feed on itself but also returns, dialectically, to art. Art seeks to "reverse what the sublime wanted to sustain" (AT 296/284). The attempt by art to bring to fruition what remains unfulfilled in the sublime is likewise an attempt by art to complete the impetus underlying natural beauty. Beauty, as we have come to realize through an analysis of the sublime, is about domination:

As a transition in domination, the transition from natural to artistic beauty is dialectical. Art beauty is that which is objectively dominated in an image and at the same time transcends domination by virtue of its objectivity. Works of art free themselves from domination by taking the aesthetic behavior we display toward nature and transforming it into a productive labor, which is modeled on material labor. Like the dominated as well as reconciled language of humans, art seeks to revivify what has become opaque to humans in the language of nature. (AT 120/113–14)

If we read this passage as a commentary on the third *Critique*, we might well conclude that Kant was attempting to forestall the historical dynamism propelling natural beauty into art beauty. His account of the sublime might then be read as a displacement of a historical dynamism into what he hoped would be an entirely separate aesthetic experience. The continuing value of the third *Critique* lies, then, in its attempt to keep separate the three most crucial elements of the aesthetic: individuation, power, and freedom. Despite the letter of Kant's text, the programmatic analysis of these elements is testament to the lack of reconciliation among them. Kant's text itself resembles the aesthetic insofar as it embodies the desire and hope for reconciliation while nonetheless displaying aesthetic judgment, whether of beauty or the sublime, as an already compromised and coerced reconciliation.

In the quoted passage, we not only witness the dialectical transition in domination from natural to art beauty but also come to understand the dialectic between subjectivity and objectivity as it plays itself out in the recent history of beauty. Adorno implies that art beauty achieves an objectivity not allowed natural beauty. Contra Hegel's notorious elimination of natural beauty for the sake of a fully subjectivized art beauty, Adorno insists on an achievement of objectivity by precisely what has been relegated to the wholly subjective. The Kantian critique that invokes a universal subjectivity at the cost of any objectivity whatsoever is fulfilled then, for Adorno, in the constitution of a universal, albeit momentary, objectivity. It is in this light that we can best understand Adorno's frequent calls in the *Aesthetic Theory* to return to the object, the artwork. What was once construed, under Kant, as the dynamic of a universalizing judgment is turned via Hegel into a momentarily universalized object, and finally *returned* by Adorno into its autonomous particularity.

What kind of achievement, or fall, is this? The first caution that needs to be exercised is in response to the too-hasty surmise that the objectivity of the artwork is to be understood as reification. The artwork becomes—after the historical migration of the sublime to it—like the evanescing moment of Kant's aesthetic judgment. Its objectivity lies not in something that can be grasped or sustained, just as absolutely central to Kant's account of taste—and to Hume's—is our utter inability to supply the principle of aesthetic judgment. The inexorable nonappearance of the standard of taste has its complement in the, curiously enough, nonappearance of the object of art. And this nonappearance is the historical achievement premised on the historic failure of the sublime. Nonappearance is formulated in Adorno's aesthetics as afterimage. The artwork is not itself image; image implies, despite itself, presence and realization. (And image, for Adorno, is itself the revelation of what fails to appear.) Afterimage instead implies residue and trace, that the moment has passed. In this regard, the artwork as afterimage is a trace not just of the nonidentity between thing and image, or even thing and thing, but of the nonidentity within temporality itself. The afterimage is a site of mourning, but of hope as well. The closest approximation we find in Adorno to what the objective appearance of the artwork might look like is in his characterization of fireworks:

Fireworks are apparitions *par excellence*. They are an empirical appearance free of the burden of empirical being in general, which is that it has duration; they are a sign of heaven and yet artifactual; they are both a writing on the wall [*Menetekel*], rising and fading away in short order, and yet not a writing that has any meaning we can make sense of. (AT 125/120)[2]

Let us return to the question of whether the transition of the aesthetic from subject to object might best be read as achievement or fall. It is of course both. As an achievement, it means subjectivity's return to a state of affairs in which the object demands recognition— just that recognition that subjectivity failed to provide itself in the experience of the sublime. The transition to art beauty is thus premised on the failure of subjectivity. And it is just this failure that paves the way for a return of the thwarted force for universality. If subjectivity cannot recognize itself as universal, dialectically the only place to turn is toward the object, just that object already sacrificed surreptitiously in the judgment of natural beauty and overtly in the sublime. The impetus toward unity and universality thus appears in art beauty as the return of the repressed. The artwork, historically then, becomes objective just as, historically, the subject comes to fruition, albeit momentarily, in aesthetic judgment.

The objectivity of the modern artwork, because of its dialectical history, is best understood as the reverse image of universal subjectivity. Modern artworks, in short, have become the most profound instances of subjective alienation; most profound because they are at once both at the farthest remove from subjectivity and its most fulfilled *expression*. Adorno's repeated call to focus on the art object and likewise his insistence on the objectivity of the artwork might then be interpreted as the resistance to taking the achievement of the artwork as the achievement of subjectivity. That is, Adorno wants to forestall the collapsing together and coerced reconciliation of objectivity and subjectivity. If humanism defines itself by measuring the status and progress of humankind according to the achievements of its products, what might be called Adorno's antihumanism ought to be in turn taken to mean that any such achievements always occur only in default of subjective progress. The critical mistake of humanism, the mistaking of objectivity for subjectivity—just the reverse of Kant's description of the judgment of natural beauty—is, for Adorno, prohibited rather than encouraged by the artwork. The artwork witnesses not the achievement of subjective freedom but the continuation of its failure to ever fully arrive. Hence, the objectivity of the artwork is the literal embodiment of the distance between where we are and freedom. The artwork stands not just as testament but also as reminder of our unfreedom.

From this conclusion, it is but a short step to the view, posited variously by Schiller, Nietzsche, and Marcuse, that the artwork not only testifies to the absence of freedom but also impedes our progress toward it. In their hands, the objectivity of the artwork becomes an obstacle on the path of human emancipation. Culture turns into not just the symptom of human lack but something more like the persistent commitment to it. For Adorno, however, the artwork has become the surrogate for an emancipating subjectivity. (This explains his statement to the effect that all artworks fail—they fail not only to liberate subjectivity but also to produce a subject. This is what remains literally inhuman in art.) As a surrogate the artwork remains incomplete, hence the need for an aesthetic theory as a reminder that, no matter how complete any art object might be taken to be, insofar as it is an art object its completion is possible only as a return to subjectivity. The historical orbit of the artwork around subjectivity has reached its heretofore most distant point from the subject, repulsed to this furthest distance by the nearly successful program of the sublime—

counterprogram of capital—to unite the subject with her own alienated projects. After the failure of the sublime, the artwork becomes the objective counterimage of subjectivity; the achievements of modern art are to be read in direct proportion to the failure of the sublime. The modern artwork might thus be taken as whatever bears the closest resemblance and serves as the nearest analogy to the subject. And what do we see in this object?

Perhaps the first thing to take notice of is its hermetically sealed nature. The modern artwork, as many have noted, seems destined to reside in templelike museums. Philip Fisher has eloquently and persuasively described how modern artworks are produced exclusively with that end in view.[3] More relevant to my focus on aesthetic judgment is to note the contrast between the artifacts of modern art and those occasions for finding nature beautiful. For Kant, objects of natural beauty are an invitation to reconcile the subjective with the natural and thereby propose an opportunity to realize human freedom by creating a space between nature and artifice. Modern artworks, on the other hand, seem to offer no occasion for reconciliation with nature. They do still invite reconciliation, but the site has changed. The site now seems to be wholly within culture itself—as if artworks can only imagine and prescribe a reconciliation between subjectivity and itself. Still, though other than the reconciliation prompted by natural beauty and the sublime, this would nonetheless amount to no small achievement; the question posed objectively by modern art is whether subjectivity can recover possibilities it jettisoned before they were ever realized.

Let us consider what Adorno proposes under the term "technique" as the means of producing some of these possibilities. And let us recall that the goal in the dialectic between nature and artifice is neither the imitation nor the avoidance of nature:

Being-in-itself, which artworks follow after, is not an imitation of something that already exists but an anticipation of a being-in-itself that does not yet exist, something unknown but that determines itself by way of the subject. Works of art state that there is something that exists in itself, but they do not spell out what it is (AT 121/114).

In regard to the question of technique, Kant and Adorno again share a crucial insight concerning the status of the artwork, for both define what constitutes the entire sphere of art as the means-end rationality of technology. It is just this rationality that decides Kant in favor of natural beauty and, in the case of art beauty, even allows him not only to distinguish pure from dependent beauty but to favor the former over the latter by dint of its liberation from intention. For Adorno, beginning in the late eighteenth century, "technologization [of art] set up control as a general principle" (AT 94/87). It seems, too, that Adorno distinguishes *technique* from *technology,* on what amount to Kantian grounds: if technology is both the application and increasing centrality of instrumental rationality to human praxis, then the concept of technique appears in Adorno's text as the dialectical overcoming of technology. It is means-end rationality pushed up against itself. Dialectically then, successful appearances of technique feel like the magic of not being subject to means-end rationality: "The technologization of art is triggered both by the subject's disillusioned consciousness and distrust of the obscuring quality of magic, and by the objective situation of art, which is that artworks are becoming more and more difficult to bring off" (AT 94/87).

We find a striking confirmation in Kant of this dialectic between nature and artifice. For Kant, the successful work of art—a beautiful work—conveys its beauty precisely by seeming to be a work of nature. That is, art beauty is possible only as the successful concealment, or we might say transformation, of the means-end rationality inherent in intentionality. Thus, for Kant, beauty is the dynamical transformation of technology, just what Adorno describes as technique. The proof that Kant's aesthetics is fully dialectical is likewise afforded by his contention that natural beauty's success depends in turn on its appearing as if it were artifactual. Indeed, it might even be recalled that Kant has a technical term for the dialectical nature of beauty: exemplary beauty. In addition to exemplarity, there is in fact a good deal in Kant's aesthetics that attests to a dialectic of technology and technique: think, for example, of the crucial character of "purposeless purposiveness" in aesthetic judgment, or of the definition of genius as the overcoming of all subjective particularity. Indeed, why not describe the whole of the third *Critique* as the attempt to formulate the aesthetic as the *means* by which subjectivity, unintentionally and without malice toward nature, overcomes its own particularity and *means*-spiritedness to thereby realize itself as unity? Further, this unity is to have its model and precursor—again unintentionally—in nature. Technique, on this model and like beauty, is second nature.

"The autonomous work of art, which is functional only in reference to itself, aims at attaining through its immanent teleology what was once called beauty" (AT 96/89). Technique is the means by which the autonomous work of art achieves its telos. But rather than this means-end relation's confirming the artwork's thralldom to technology, Adorno instead posits technique as the dialectical overcoming of instrumentality. Technique, then, is the transformation of technology into pure expression: "What is called reification approaches, when it is radicalized, the language of things. Reification brings itself near the very idea of nature, which extirpates the primacy of human meaning" (AT 96/89). Artistic technique here allows us to understand the dialectical trajectory of reification. Technological reification, what might be considered the instrumentality par excellence of subjectivity, can also, by a "radical use of reification," become an expression of nature, insofar as the latter has been defined—technologically, we might add—as what stands in opposition to us. The radicalization of reification is thus a radicalization of the alienated relation between subjectivity and nature. Technology, in this light, is thus a mimetic approximation and acceleration of the nonidentity between things and us. So, too, is it potentially, especially if pushed far enough, a self-alienation that opens a space for something else to speak. In short, what makes technology akin to what nature might be is that both are the refusal of content, substance, and meaning. Technology is a means only, a method whose premise is the disavowal of significance. Nature appears dialectically to us as a dynamic that not only invites but, more important, resists any significance we might want to extract from it.

Technique is the acceleration of the meaninglessness of technology and reification that may well prompt an evisceration of whatever meaning we might once have imagined having. Technique achieves what Kant describes as natural beauty: an occasion whose lack of intentionality allows the appearance of what an intentionality might nonetheless have produced. Technique, then, occurs with the same opacity as natural beauty. But what is opaque in both cases is not simply intentionality—for this is precisely what has been overcome.

Rather, what is opaque in both beauty and technique is the universality of subjectivity. In judgments of beauty, what we fail to discern—though it is just this failure that allows beauty to occur—is intersubjectivity, the version of universal subjectivity unearthed by Kant's critique. Likewise, in our encounter with technique, what we fail to discern is precisely the thoroughly social nature of this most advanced form of production.

We are blind to technique insofar as we particularize it by ascribing it to an individual. Rather than fetishize the object produced, which is what we do in naming masterpieces, we fetishize the activity of making by describing it as technique. The recognition of technique *as* technique is thus inextricably bound up with both blindness and insight. To discern technique is already to reify an agency that has just itself overcome the reification of technology; thus, it is an insight premised on blindness. But to fail to discern technique is likewise to fail to find production a subjective (which is to say, thoroughly human) act; thus, it is a blindness premised on an insight. This dialectical web of technique maintains the opacity of the social.

In this regard, technique is but the historically most advanced participant in *das Immergleiche*. Thus, there is no reason to posit a historical development within the history of aesthetic judgment or aesthetic theory: Adorno's explication of technique is merely the twentieth-century equivalent of Kant's theory of natural beauty. But if instead we assume there is a history—indeed, a dialectical one—within the aesthetic whereas there is history nowhere else (consider in this light Hegel's history of the aesthetic), then the telos of the aesthetic is one and the same with human emancipation. (Art, pace Hegel, is not only the expression of temporality but the embrace of it—hence, perhaps, its commitment to deathliness.) And this thought concurs with the trajectory of Hegel's aesthetics into an exclusively subjective realm. But the thought likewise confirms Hegel's aesthetics as a dialectical continuation of Kant's insofar as it continues the effacement of any and all too-particularistic expressions of subjectivity, indeed expressions of subjectivity at all. What makes Hegel's aesthetics such an integral part of the history of the aesthetic is not the removal of nature as a realm in which human freedom is to be won but rather the explicit recognition that the bulk of the work to emancipate subjectivity will have to be done within and against subjectivity. The task, in other words, is first and foremost an internal one. This is already implicit in Kant's analysis of beauty but especially in his account of the sublime. Adorno locates this potential more generally in the political implication of Kant's version of subjective interiority: "Interiority, for Kant as well, is also a protest against the order, heteronomously imposed on subjectivity" (AT 177/169).

To consider for a moment this constellation of terms in light of *Dialectic of Enlightenment* would be to understand the order Odysseus places on (and within) himself as the technical, mimetic approximation of the heterogeneity he nonetheless feels imposed from outside. In this regard, technology originates as the disavowal of mimesis. The technology of self-production arises within the dynamic of mimesis that denies its own origin. So, too, the self that arises fails, in turn, to recognize its own origin. Dialectically then, it should come as no surprise that Adorno names Kant as one who takes interiority as a protest against order even though it is Kant who formulates the categorical imperative as the means by which that same interior most properly orders itself. But there is something amiss for Adorno in the dialectic between mimesis and technology—something extra and undigested. He uses the term "expression" (*Ausdruck*) for what occurs between the cracks of the dialectic: "Expression is an interference phenomenon, a function of technical procedure no less than one of mimesis. Mimesis, for its part, is called forth by the density of technical process, whose immanent rationality nonetheless appears to labor in opposition to expression" (AT 174/167). In a perfect world, technology and mimesis would seamlessly and unendingly transform themselves into one another. Subjectivity would project itself as other and then accommodate itself thereto. But expression is instead a kind of Ludditelike moment within this generation and regeneration. It is the protest spoken against itself; in this way, it is akin to critique, since it, too, depends on no external factors. Expression, therefore, speaks on behalf of no one but rather of those not yet allowed; subjective expression is an oxymoron: "This leads to a subjective paradox of art: to produce what is blind—expression—from reflection, through form; not to make the blind rational but instead to aesthetically first make it up" (AT 174/167). The blind needs to be produced in order for us to have something nonmimetic and technologically defective to follow. Blindness, in short, is a mimetic approximation of expression. And it is precisely at this juncture that we come to understand best the Kantian legacy in Adorno as well as the advance the latter attempts to make on him. The genius of Kant's aesthetics of beauty lies in its recognition of the absolute necessity of the opacity of the object—and the experience—we call beautiful. The incipient transition in Kant's aesthetics from beauty to the sublime is the recognition that the opacity of the object is unfortunately complemented by the opacity of subjective agency.

For Adorno, a modern artist might make this subjective opacity productive as technique; the term *Formgefühl* (intuitive feeling of form) describes the artistic subject's own cognizance of an opacity that is nonetheless productive. Not only does this term have an affinity with Kant's account of artistic genius but Adorno also finds that it solves the dilemma of Kantian aesthetics:

It resolves the Kantian problem through a category of mediation. Though for Kant art is utterly nonconceptual and subjective, it nonetheless contains a moment of universality and necessity, just that aspect which, according to the critique of reason, is the preserve of discursive knowledge. *Formgefühl* is at once the blind and binding reflection of things, on which it must in turn rely. *Formgefühl* is hermetic objectivity that falls on subjective mimetic ability. This ability strengthens itself in turn on its opposite, rational construction. The blindness of *Formgefühl* corresponds to the necessity in things. (AT 175/167–68)

Oddly then, what we become in following *Formgefühl* (whether by making or experiencing) is an instance of both technology and technique. We follow a method, however opaque, in the hope of further reflecting—though now as a dynamic—what has already hardened into a thing. Aesthetic judgment, then, becomes a mimetic approximation of the artwork, which is already a technical, mimetic approximation of us. The reflexivity inherent to the aesthetic doubles itself, and this doubling reflection occurs only if there is already some moment of blindness. It is on that opacity that reflection ignites itself. Hence, Adorno's description of *Formgefühl* as blind *and* binding. Because it is opacity that sets reflection in motion, there must, dialectically, be a return of opacity, just as in Kant's aesthetics we witnessed the absence of the standard of taste as corresponding to achieving the blindness of subjectivity.

The category of mediation fulfilled by the *Formgefühl* might likewise be construed as a model for subjectivity. The importance of this model is that it recapitulates the important lesson of the sublime in which all models and modeling are dispensed with for the sake of a vision of subjectivity as itself process and change. "Technologically discernible is that artworks are not being but becoming" (AT 262–63/ 252). Adorno continues in the same passage by asserting that artworks consist of an "immanent dynamic," again, I would want to say, like the immanent dynamism of Kant's account of the sublime. Artworks, then, are *models* of movement and becoming, though they nonetheless come into existence only if they are congealed as reified things—this is the price they must pay. Adorno insists that the movement that artworks are can be discerned only technologically—movement can be grasped only as a process that itself imitates the being of a static thing. Yet artworks embody the jolting reminder that all artifacts are but the forestalled, hence blind, mimesis of human fulfillment. The advantage of technology—perhaps akin to self-blinding subjectivity—lies in its incomplete reification. And incomplete reification, like opacity, holds the promise of a vision of something more.

Notes

I want to thank Leo Damrosch, Gregg Horowitz, Bob Hullot-Kentor, Jan Heller-Levi, and Lambert Zuidervaart for careful, generous and insightful readings of earlier versions of the essay.

1. Nearly all of the passages from the *Aesthetic Theory* that appear in the essay are either modifications of, or substitutions for, Lenhardt's translations.

2. Leo Damrosch reminds me that fireworks are, in French, *feu d'artifice*. Fireworks appear as a figure for aesthetic experience in accounts other than Adorno's. Burke, for example, in discussing magnificence as a source of the sublime, writes, "There are, however, a sort of fireworks, and some other things, that in this way succeed well, and are truly grand." Edmund Burke, *A Philosophical Enquiry into the Origin of our Ideas of the Sublime and Beautiful*, ed. James T. Boulton, University of Notre Dame Press, 1958 [1757], p. 78. Genet describes his own work with the same figure: "This book is only literature, but let it enable me to glorify my grief so that it emerges by itself and ceases to be—as fireworks cease to be when they have exploded." Jean Genet, *Pompes funèbres (Funeral Rites)*, *Oeuvres Complètes*, III, Éditions Gallimard, 1953. Cited in Edmund White, *Genet; A Biography*, New York: Knopf, 1993. p. 281. And from *Ulysses*: "And Jack Caffrey shouted to look, there was another and she leaned

Kant, Adorno, and the Social Opacity of the Aesthetic

back and the garters were blue to match on account of the transparent and they all saw it and shouted to look, look there it was and she leaned back ever so far to see the fireworks and something queer was flying about through the air, a soft thing to and fro, dark. And she saw a long Roman candle going up over the trees up, up, and, in the tense hush, they were all breathless with excitement as it went higher and higher and she had to lean back more and more to look up after it, high, high, almost out of sight, and her face was suffused with a divine, an entrancing blush from straining back and he could see her other things too." James Joyce, *Ulysses*, New York: Penguin Books, 1977 [1922], pp. 363–64.

3. Philip Fisher, *Making and Effacing Art; Modern American Art in a Culture of Museums* (New York: Oxford University Press, 1991).

10

Art History and Autonomy

Gregg M. Horowitz

Art and society converge in substance, not in something that is extraneous
to art. That also applies to art history.... This explains why art is a recollection of transience. Art preserves the transient, bringing it before our eyes by
changing it. This is the sociological explanation of art's temporal core. Seeking to steer clear of social praxis, art becomes a schema of social praxis just
the same: every authentic work revolutionizes art.

—*Aesthetic Theory*

Authentic works must wipe out every memory trace of reconciliation—in
the interest of reconciliation.

—*Aesthetic Theory*

I

The problem of how art is related to history emerges, not coinciden-
tally, at the moment it becomes clear that art has a historical
dimension. Hegel has been called the father of art history for his
monumental treatment of art as the spirit of its various ages in sensuous form, indeed, as spirit's very relation to sensuousness in those various ages. His analysis of art in terms of the culture that is expressed
through it is an attempt to locate the proper place of art within the totality of social life and thus to open art to understanding in light of
the relation between it and other moments of the totality. Joined to
his view that any particular social totality is itself but a part of the unfolding in time of the totality of spirit, such that the structure of any

particular moment is itself a function of the place it occupies in history, Hegel's treatment of art becomes a full-blown historicism. If Hegel's view is correct, art is properly grasped as the appearance of broader historical processes that can be witnessed, crystallizing, through it.

Although it might be argued that Hegel's dialectical analysis ought not to license it, nonetheless his historicism has provided the framework, if not the foundation, for reductionist analyses of art with history as the reducing base. Put differently, a key consequence of Hegel's arguments has been a commitment to explaining both art's internal dynamic and its development in terms of determinately nonaesthetic factors.[1] In this essay, I argue against any such reductionism, by attempting to recover a better understanding of the concept of the autonomy of art against which historicist reductionism shapes its project.

To start, it is important to recognize that Hegel's analysis of art is a kind of *retrieval* of art for the historical totality, a retrieval in the face of, specifically, the Kantian claim for the autonomy of art. A trace of this Kantian idea remains active in Hegel insofar as, despite his pronounced goal of providing an account of art and its development in terms of historical contexts, Hegel preserves the distinctness of the sphere of art by generating a reductive, analytic technique especially for it rather than letting that analysis merge into a generalized cultural anthropology. In this sense, Hegel's treatment takes the separation of art from the rest of social life as a presupposition to be overcome, sublated, in his historicism. Despite all of Hegel's arguments, this Kantian element continues to function as a source of tension in his philosophy of art; that art must be *retrieved* for a totalizing historicism is already a recognition that there is something about art, something about the structure of its mediatedness that is expressed in the claims about its autonomy, that at least *apparently* resists reduction to historical context. If this is so, of course, then any successful rehistoricization of art will also be an overcoming of art's capacity to be of distinct value and interest.[2] Hegel famously recognizes as much by announcing simultaneously with his philosophy that art is now a thing of the past, that his penetration of art's veil is the philosophical expression of the end of art's ability to resist being made, so to speak, transparent to history. Hegel argues not only that art is dead but that its grave digger was named "art history."[3]

From our historical vantage, it is obvious that the dialectical relation between art and history, between art's autonomy and historicist retrieval, did not end with Hegel. Even a quick canvass of the ongoing methodological strife among Hegel's progeny shows this particular fatherly self-understanding to be one of the more spectacular instances of philosophical self-misrecognition. The epochal figures of post-Hegelian art history and theory—Jacob Burckhardt, Heinrich Wölfflin, Alois Riegl and Erwin Panofsky, E. H. Gombrich and Clement Greenberg—all structure their positions by trying to forge a compromise between, on the one hand, the internal dynamics of works of art whose internality, that is, whose autonomy from external determination, constitutes their inner artistic identity and, on the other hand, the contexts within which that internality takes form. If Hegel is indeed the father of art history, it is, it would seem, not in virtue of having offered his children any solutions but in virtue of having initiated a problem against which they, too, must break their heads. This repetition bespeaks an original trauma of some sort—if Hegel is right, it will be a version of the inability to bury the dead— such that we must entertain the possibility that Hegel committed a perhaps unique philosophical error; rather than the familiar mistake of confusing the symptom with the disease, in claiming a historicist overcoming of the autonomy of art, Hegel, instead, mistook the symptom for the cure.

I argue in this essay that the appearance of contradiction between history and art that Hegel declares to be sublated is an objective structural feature of the post-Kantian aesthetic era. Specifically, I claim that the idea of a history for art arises only along with the idea of its autonomy, only as a consequence of that autonomy; hence, art and history come to stand in objective contradiction to one another. My arguments are not idealist, however; because I treat art and its autonomy as themselves historical phenomena, the contradiction between art and history also turns out to be a contradiction of the historical totality with itself. Art's self-presentation as autonomous is thus seen to generate a need for a nonreductive history of "apparent underdetermination" by, precisely, history itself. This is the basis for the tension within art history.

Although any effort to recover the neglected historical dimensions of art's autonomy must proceed by rereading Kant, such a project also helps in understanding Adorno's defense of the autonomy of art against the tendency in the sociology of art and knowledge to "assign art its proper place in society" (AT 355). Adorno's philosophy of the work of art is also a philosophy of social explanation that resists historicism and sociologism for the sake of grasping dialectically the contradictions of the social totality that express themselves as contradictions within critical social practices and theories.

> History is constitutive of works of art. Authentic ones give themselves over completely to the material substance of their historical period, rejecting the pretence of timelessness. Unbeknown to themselves, they represent the historiography of their times, which is why they are related to knowledge. Historicism grossly falsifies this historical substance of art by seeking to reduce art to history conceived as an extraneous datum. (AT 261)

Historicist analysis of art, like functionalist sociological explanation, posits a point of view from which the play of subjectivity can be seen as one more atomic factor in a field of pure external determination. Historicism thus simultaneously obscures the tension between art's having a proper place and its being in pursuit of its own ground *and* imagines for itself a social site immune from just the kinds of "subjective illusions" it attributes to putatively autonomous art. In obscuring the internal contradictions of autonomous art, historicists and functionalists

> [h]ewing to an ideal of value-neutrality...flatter themselves that their knowledge is superior to what they discredit as a collection of subjective standpoints in art and aesthetics. Efforts like these must be combated. They quietly seek to enforce the primacy of the administered world over art, whereas art wishes to be left alone and acts up against total socialization. (AT 355)

For Adorno, the ideological aim of the proper historicist placement of art (and knowledge) is to reconcile the impulse of reason to grasp the nature of social determination and the administered social world that blunts that impulse at every step. The conceptual precondition for doing so is the typical historicist inability to account for its own ability to remain (ostensibly) immune from the very processes of external determination it analyzes. Put differently, the cost of the historicist demolition of autonomy claims, wherever it finds them, is its inability to grasp dialectically its own rational capacities; in the process, it reduces those capacities, too, to mere atomized externalities having no claim, despite their self-proclaimed rationality, to any epistemic privilege. Nondialectical historicism thus becomes the agent of reason's self-abolition. Discussing Mannheim, in "The Sociology of Knowledge and Its Consciousness," Adorno writes,

> The answer to Mannheim's reverence for the intelligentsia as "free-floating" is to be found not in the reactionary postulate of its "rootedness in Being" but rather in the reminder that the very intelligentsia that pretends to float freely is fundamentally rooted in the very being that must be changed and which it merely pretends to criticize (P 48).

Despite Adorno's hostility to historicism and sociologism, he does not defend art's autonomy against them by idealizing it. On the contrary, his opposition to historicism is that it flattens the historical nature of the autonomy it claims to historicize by opposing, nondialectically, the demands of social explanation to the nature of social contradiction. In defending a dialectical interpretation of the autonomy of art, Adorno develops a philosophy of sociohistorical explanation that does not presume that explanation requires a point of view detached from the history it explains. One simple way to put this is that historical explanation is itself a historical action, such that critical history, in order to be truly historical, requires dialectical self-consciousness about its own conditions of possibility. Dialectical self-consciousness, or self-criticism, is but another name for the refusal of any externally *determined* proper place in the historical totality; it is, in other words, a form of opposition to a given state of society, or, dialectically understood in a way I will demonstrate, it is autonomy.[4] Dialectically self-conscious history, in striving to take the external determinations it represents into itself and so deprive them of their mere externality, thus enacts theoretically what the work of art enacts sensuously. "Art," Adorno writes, "is an unconscious form of historiography" (AT 366). Autonomous art, hence, is social and historical not because it is externally determined by society, although it is that, but also because, like self-conscious historiography, it strives to stage the conflict between itself and its determinations.

> Art … is not social only because it is brought about in such a way that it embodies the dialectic of forces and relations of production. Nor is art social only because it derives its material content from society. Rather, it is social primarily because it stands opposed to society. Now this opposition art can mount only when it has become autonomous. By congealing into an entity unto itself—rather than obeying existing social norms and thus proving itself to be "socially useful"—art criticizes society just by being there. (AT 321)

Autonomous art criticizes society just by being there because the "there" where it is is no "proper" place. This formulation makes legible the contradiction within art between art and history that gives rise to the tensions within art history that are my subject. It goes without saying that I will not be offering a way beyond this tension. I will be offering neither a theory of art as nonhistorical nor a renovated theory of historical explanation. Rather, following Adorno, I will proceed as if one of the central tasks of philosophical aesthetics is to preserve this contradiction in as much of its richness as the spirit of our age permits.

II

A proper way to begin is by considering what is at stake in the thesis to which Hegel was responding that art is autonomous. Kant's theory of the fine or beautiful arts is derived from his theory of the judgment of taste as disinterested, that is, as a judgment that abjures consideration of purpose.[5] Because the judgment of taste ranges over both natural objects and human artifacts, for works of art to be proper objects of aesthetic judgment, they, too, must be judged without regard to purpose. This, however, generates a puzzle: if an artifact is distinguished from a natural object in having a determinate purpose (CJ 170), and a work of art is an artifact made to be the object of a judgment of taste (CJ 173), then a work of art is an artifact made with the purpose of not seeming to have a purpose, of not seeming to be an artifact.

This paradox creates both a dilemma and an opportunity for Kant. The dilemma develops as follows: an object is an artifact if it has been made as the object of a human purpose. If an object exists with no such purpose in its history, then it is instead a natural object. Thus, for an artifact to not look like an artifact, it must seem to be, without really being, nature (CJ 173–74). The object must be made through a rational choice but that choice, must be, so to speak, made invisible. But this is a recipe for trickery not art, and a trickery all the more deviously purposive the more successfully achieved. Kant provides the following example to illustrate the aesthetic failure of trickery:

> What do poets praise more highly than the nightingale's enchantingly beautiful song in a secluded thicket on a quiet summer evening by the soft light of the moon? And yet we have cases where some jovial innkeeper, unable to find such a songster, played a trick—received with greatest satisfaction initially— on the guests staying at his inn to enjoy the country air, by hiding in a bush some roguish youngster who (with a rush or reed in his mouth) knew how to copy that song in a way very similar to nature's. But as soon as one realizes it was all deception, no one will long endure listening to this song that before he had considered so charming. (CJ 169)

For achieving the look of nature to be an achievement of art, the charge of trickery must be repelled by a blindness, a nonpurposiveness on the part of the artist that corresponds to the abjuring of judgment in terms of determinate purposes on the part of the judge of art. The invisibility of purpose must be the product of a real absence of determinate intention; it must be the appearance of that absence, in the making of what is, after all, an artifact, a purposive object. That is the dilemma: Kant's theory of art demands the production of artifacts that exhibit an absence of purpose in their production. But how is this possible?

It cannot be said that Kant fully answers this question. His description of the hidden artifactuality of art is sufficiently like the common eighteenth-century academic imperative that art not smell of the workshop that it is possible he did not quite see how strange a conclusion he had drawn. That the artwork not appear to be produced with academic rules foremost in the artist's mind, that "the academic form must not show" (CJ 174), is in keeping with the more traditional artistic goal of illusion. But that it not appear rule-governed, that it appear natural, because not really rule-governed, despite, of course, still being an artifact, is an altogether different demand. Indeed, insofar as the rule for this class of artifacts—to have no determinate rule—is a contradiction, the demand is perhaps unsatisfiable. But it is just here that Kant transforms a dilemma into an opportunity, albeit an opportunity he does not fully seize, by filling in the conceptual hole with a mutation in nature itself, nature in the form of genius.

The Kantian genius often seems to be the romantic genius, unconstrained by rules, magisterially creating without precedent but thereby establishing precedent for the generations that will be beholden to his original acts of creation. Because the work of the genius is performed in the absence of conscious rules of production, the genius is a force of nature, but one that thus manifests the freedom of the genius from social convention. The genius in this sense symbolizes a reconciliation of nature and freedom, what Nietzsche would later call the reconciliation of nature and her lost son, man.[6] The conceptual space for this idea of genius is held open by the contradictory artifactuality of the artwork, and it is just here that the world-founding idealisms of romanticism in philosophy and art would frolic.

It is crucial to remember, however, that despite Kant's providing a positive characterization of the features of the mind that he calls genius and out of which the romantic reading would grow, his motivation to propose the concept at all within his aesthetics is the underlying concern not with what genius is but rather with how it may *appear*. Kant's paradox, again, is how an artifact can look like nature, so the deep problem of genius for him is how an artifact can look like a work of genius, which is to say, how it can look free of determinate purpose. To understand what he is really after, despite his own imperfect clarity about it, we must hew closely to Kant's concern with appearance.

If we read Kant in the way he was read by idealists like Schiller, then the concept of genius would indeed mark a moment of reconciliation between freedom and nature. However, Kant at times explicitly recognizes that the nonpurposiveness of the work of art, that is, the work of genius, can appear only as a *lack* of reconciliation, at least between the artist and purposive structures. The idea that genius appears when the standard relation between purpose and artifactuality is swept away, when the artist ignores issues of technique, is rejected by Kant as a mistake that produces misguided protocols, or a misguided lack of protocols, in artistic education. Where "genius" appears *instead of* purposive activity, out of indifference to it, there we have not art appearing like nature but nonsense (CJ 188–89); this version of genius reeks of the adolescent conviction that authentic selfhood depends on the liquification of the grounds of selfhood. For Kant, the work of art is an artifact, and so genius appears not instead of purposive activity but by means of it. That is, genius appears when the technique that guides the production of the artifact *visibly* fails to produce its appearance. An artifact is thus a work of art when the mechanical relation between purpose and artifact is seen to be broken, when something shows itself as the underdetermination of the artifact by any specific purpose.

Kant's acknowledgment that the appearance of genius is a moment of nonreconciliation, a lack of fit between determinate purpose and the object whose concept it is, is notable in several similar passages, which are all puzzling on idealist readings:

It is advisable . . . to remind ourselves that in all the free arts there is yet a need for something in the order of a constraint, or, as it is called, a mechanism. (In poetry, for example, it is correctness and richness of language, as well as prosody and meter.) Without this the spirit, which in art must be free, would have no body at all and would evaporate completely. This reminder is needed because some of the more recent educators believe that they promote a free art best if they remove all constraint from it and convert it from labor into mere play. (CJ 171)

The spirit, Kant says, must be free in art, which is to say it must be undetermined by any purposive structure. At the same time, though, it must be constrained by a mechanism, because without constraint it evaporates, turns to mere spirit, mere vapor. It appears Kant is saying that for spirit to be free, it must be bound to a body, bound by a mechanism. This sounds like a contradiction plain and simple, despite the fact that it does correspond to standard practices in the training of artists. However, it is a contradiction only if we take "constraint" to mean that which imprisons; in that case, Kant would be saying something like "the free person is the one who lives in a jail cell," which, although neither an unheard of nor an unreasonable proposition from a certain otherworldly point of view, is entirely non-Kantian. That Kant does not mean it this way is highlighted by his qualification of what is needed as "something in the order of a constraint," which suggests something like a constraint yet not, something like a constraint that does not constrain.

To get closer to the moment of nonreconciliation Kant is imagining, let us reflect on the synonym he provides for the constraint that makes free spirit possible, that is, "mechanism." The other synonym used in this argument is "body," which, in its invocation of nature, seems the obvious alternative to freedom in Kant's metaphysics. However, given arguments Kant develops elsewhere regarding heteronomous and autonomous determination of the human will, nature does not as such have the power to function as a constraint on freedom;[7] indeed—and this is the issue that highlights one of Kant's central purposes in writing the *Critique of Judgment*—the freedom of the will, that is, moral agency, is constituted by an indifference to nature, a turning away from the realm of heteronomous determination as such. Kant, in other words, typically treats nature not as a constraint on freedom but as its opposite. Here, though, in stressing mechanism as the name of a constraint, Kant is aiming to highlight what *limits* freedom of spirit rather than what is independent of it. And with limits, in contrast to metaphysical bulkheads, one can attempt to overcome them in interesting ways.

It may seem as if I am overplaying this distinction between mere mechanical nature and mechanism as constraint. After all, several times in the *Critique of Judgment*, Kant identifies the merely mechanical with nature as such, so perhaps nothing special is being said here. However, since mechanism is presented in this passage and others as constraint, there is still a novelty of usage to be explained. More important, as Kant argues elsewhere, the maxim that the production of material things is possible according to mechanical laws is presupposed by judgment, but it does not thereby prevent judgment from presupposing that the production of *some* material things may also be possible according to some special nonmechanical principle (CJ 266–68). In other words, although a mechanism is a process that determines the existence of the thing produced through it, a determining mechanism cannot determine further that it is only through that mechanism itself that the thing can be produced. Reflective judgment, thus, is not mechanically constrained by the fact of mechanism; put differently, it is possible to *imagine* a world perfectly consistent with mechanical laws that nevertheless does not have those laws as its actual and only principle. Mechanism is, in this sense, a constraint on the free spirit but only as the determining source of the things of the world that spirit *could* be the source of. This important implication of Kant's position can be derived only if there is a second sense of mechanism not just as a principle of natural explanation but also as a constraint on the will.

This clarifies immediately why Kant rejects the idea of genius as operating beyond mechanism. For the work of genius to appear, the artist must produce something—the spirit of genius is the opposite of the renunciation of the world—and that thing must be capable of being made according to natural laws. The artist who says, "I will create what nature itself could not produce" is speaking strictly nonsense. *That* artist's genius could never appear. Every artist thus needs constraint, a bit of pedagogy Kant derives from his metaphysics. However, this does not entail that the artist needs to regard the necessarily possible production according to mechanical law as the principle for the production of the work of art. The artist may, indeed does—I would suggest this is Kant's point—seek to make the work come into existence as the product of another principle, the principle of freedom.

How, then, does the alternative principle appear? It cannot appear as an evacuation of mechanism, that is, as an artifact that could not have been produced mechanically. Thus, it must appear as the negation of mechanicity, as the denial that mechanism alone was the originating principle. If mechanism is a regularity binding an effect to its cause, the point may be put thus: the free spirit appears, that is, an artifact is a work of art not when mechanism is absent but when the mechanicity of mechanism, its determinative power, is visibly absent. In more commonsense aesthetic terms, the free spirit appears in the transformation of mechanism from constraint into raw materials for art.

The work of art, then, is an apparent break in the chain of necessity not because the thing made could have been produced only through freedom but because, in negating the mechanical necessity of mechanism, it visibly was. This requires that for artists to produce something visibly nonnecessitated, they must be intimately familiar with, precisely, the mechanical necessitation they must dismantle. Artists' horizon of action, their raw material, is thus the entire domain of necessity—let us call it the world—as that which may constrain them; the break in necessity then appears as the constraint not constraining, the mechanism not being determining. "*That*," the artist says, "will not force my hand." (Incidentally, no other argument would allow us to make sense of Kant's key thesis that the work of art is both original—its appearance could not have been predicted— and exemplary; once it appears, it then establishes a new rule, a new constraint, for later artists [CJ 175].) Hence, the work of genius, the work of the free spirit, can only appear along with what fails to determine it, along with its nonconstraining constraint, as a mutation in mechanism; to put the point in the terms that got this discussion moving, the work of genius appears as a moment of nonreconciliation between spirit and nature.

My interpretation of the Kantian dynamic of constraint and nonreconciliation can be illuminated by a brief analysis of Michelangelo's *Captives*, carved in the early 1530s. These large statues, between 250 and 275 centimeters tall, struggle heroically to escape the marble they are still, in their incompleteness, encased in. The marble is an obvious constraint on the freedom, in this case the freedom to become completely human, of the subjects striving for life. Each figure has Michelangelo's typical hypermasculine physique, as if, were it to achieve its freedom, it could stand strong and unimpeded in the world, a perfect embodiment of self-determination. However, we must not forget that the stuff against which the prisoners struggle for freedom is also the stuff of which they are made. If they are to become free, it will not be in virtue of escaping the marble—were they to escape the marble, they would become mere vapor—but in virtue of having slipped the marble's mere naturalness. Put differently, the statues' struggle to be free is their nonreconciliation with the unavoidable conditions of their own existence. Not escaping from the stone but negating its stoniness, taking that stoniness into themselves until there is no more of it than the extent of their organic bodies, is the aim of these creatures. We are witnessing, as it

Michelangelo, *Awakening Captive*

were, the effort of stone itself to be human. And just in case we might be inclined to miss the artistic nature of this effort and read these figures as mere allegory, Michelangelo leaves the surface of their skin—because it is skin, it is, in a sense, already human—mottled and textured by its marbled origins, as scars that will continue to remind them and us of their unsublated and unsublatable earthly origins.

It is interesting to note in connection with this interpretation of the *Captives* that Michelangelo carved them to be used as architectural supports for sculpture that would rise on their backs above them. This just magnifies the self-reflexive complexity of the struggle. Statues as supports are images of humans reduced to their embodiment, in this case, images of the reducing itself; these beings function merely to fill an empty space that, if not filled, would allow the elevated statue to sink back to earth. So these prisoners are struggling against not just their materiality but also the conscription into the operations of the world to which that materiality renders them prey; were they to escape the marble, they could, one can imagine them thinking in their stony manner, walk away of their own free will. As Michelangelo shows us, though, this is a hopeless chore, for they are perpetually slaves of what they seek to transcend. However, because these incomplete creatures are being used to elevate something else, perhaps *their* bondage is, by way of contrast, the price to be paid for slipping the earthly bounds of the figure they raise literally and, if so, also metaphorically. But there is no escape through this resuscitated allegory either, for these prisoners were to be used as architectural supports in the tortured tomb of Pope Julius II. Any elevated statue that might redeem the lack of reconciliation in the life below would itself be a memorial, which is to say a reminder that only in death can constraint be forgotten. The limits of their struggle is at the same time what gives the *Captives* the possibility of life.

The autonomy of the work of art, I thus want to say, is an achievement of negation, specifically, the negation of mechanical nature's mechanicity and not a transcendence of mechanism. Hence it becomes even less of a wonder that Kant says the artist requires a mechanism without which the work would have no body and the spirit would not be free. Without the constraint of mechanism, there is nothing for the artist to do, and so rather than constraint's being something to be neglected in the name of artistic autonomy, taken as a kind of isolation from nature, it is the very arena in which that autonomy is achieved. The work of art is the visible transformation of mechanical necessitation into incompleteness of determination and so is the manufacturing of freedom. To give this interpretation one final piece of support, let us recall that Kant's ultimate charge against the misguided art pedagogues is that they treat art as play rather than what it is, labor. Kant remembers what many forget, that a work of art is called work for a reason. Art is the labor of remaking the world of mechanism as a world that need not be the realm of necessity.

Insofar as art is a kind of labor, it is the production of artifacts; however, that labor appears as a negation of mechanicity, a break in the determinate productive chain, hence the appearance of genius. Here we are back at the original paradox, but now it is substantially less startling. For Kant, the artwork appears as nature, because it does not appear to have a determinate purpose, that is, it does not appear to be a production through human labor. Thus, the work of art appears as the look of free labor, of labor having freed itself from what makes labor necessary. This appearance is indeed the result of labor but of labor not tethered to any extrinsic goal. The artwork is the appearance of unnecessary work. In being unnecessary, the artwork is the appearance of the absence of external determination; in this way, the artwork appears like nature, which is now to say that, like the system of nature, nothing outside it determines it. Put most simply, then, the work of art is autonomous when it appears as an internally complete system.

III

We can now fruitfully return to the question: what does the look of autonomous art look like? This, as we now see, is the same as the question: what does negation look like? How does negation appear? (This is a question of aesthetics, in contrast to the question "what is negation?" which is a question of metaphysics.) The traditional answer in the post-Kantian tradition of philosophical aesthetics is that it looks like freedom, an answer that has led to the idealist valorizations of aesthetic autonomy in Schiller and the young Nietzsche, Clement

Greenberg at his worst, and Clive Bell at his best. However, despite the bountiful support for this view in Kant's writings, if my interpretation of Kant so far is right, the proper answer is that autonomous art looks like the failure of freedom.

The idealist misinterpretation of the autonomy of art is attributable to the false inference from autonomous art's nonnecessitation by circumstances to its metaphysical isolation from the realm of necessity. That this must be a bad interpretation, even if Kant himself sometimes inclines toward it, is clear both from Kant's metaphysics in general as well as, more important, the claim iterated throughout the *Critique of Judgment* that everything that appears must appear as capable of having been produced mechanically. The inference is false, because it mistakenly takes the claims about the nonnecessitation of autonomous art to be claims about a metaphysically unique monadic object; instead, such claims are about art as working on the external circumstances that might have necessitated it, whose dismantling is the appearance of nonnecessitation. In other words, if autonomy in art is the work's refusal to let anything outside itself determine its form, then the autonomous work is just the appearance of that refusal. The work of art thus appears as nonreconciliation with the world of external determination only by reproducing or representing that world as deprived of its determinative powers. But this of course entails that the work is bound *irredeemably* to what does not determine it; it is constrained to show what does not constrain it. For the work's power of negation to appear, it must visibly negate something and can only appear as the negation of that thing. Thus, for the work of art to be autonomous, it is bound to show what it is not bound by and so reveal itself as incapable of escaping from the world it seeks to transcend.

(It is worth restating that I am discussing the *appearance* of freedom here; I am not making the rather different metaphysical assertion that all negation a priori requires preservation of what it negates. This would certainly be false to Kant and it may well be false overall, but in any case a defense of it would require other arguments than the ones being made now. I am concerned only with how freedom shows itself, and that display, I am arguing, requires the display of mechanism and hence can establish itself only in failure.)

It is precisely this failure of artistic autonomy, this irredeemable connection to circumstance and sensuousness, that will permit Hegel's rehistoricization to get underway. If autonomous art is entangled with what it seeks to disentangle itself from, then the form of the work of art seems to be a function of the factors it most insistently claims are irrelevant to it. Hence, autonomous art's self-understanding is wrong, and the error must be made good by a recontextualization that is itself justified by art's unintentional but unavoidable revelation of its lack of freedom. From the point of view of the contextualizer, art's claim to be the appearance of the free spirit is false, because freedom is incompatible with the kind of constraint art requires; the realm within which this falsity is displayed is history or, more exactly, the historical consciousness that can map the disjunction between art's putative goals and the means its deploys in failing to achieve them.

It is important to note here that this historical perspective that details the connection between the unavoidability of external determination and the appearance of art, in claiming to reveal the nature of the historical dynamic that is invisible to art, claims for itself freedom from art's bind. Art tries to work itself free of external determination and fails, but the more spectacular the failure the clearer the incompatibility of art's goal of freedom and its practices—clearer, that is, but not to the artists who keep struggling. The pathos of art's failure is the revelation that the pursuit of freedom has transcended art and migrated to the consciousness of that pathos, that is, philosophical history. As art dies, the striving to overcome external determination is preserved in the historical knowledge that proclaims art dead, and that knowledge is historically self-conscious in knowing the failed remaking of the world to be the preparation for its own emancipation from downward-dragging entanglements. Philosophical history, in grasping the demands of free spirit ejected from the collapse of art, thus redeems that failure as a necessary stage in the development of its own capacity to escape necessitation. Later but wiser. Whether this justification for historicist contextualism takes its more strictly Hegelian journey through the Protestant liberation of spirit from its inadequate appearance in the form of religious icons or the neo-Hegelian, that is, Dantonian, turn directly from art to philosophy need not be

examined here.[8] What matters to my point is that the pronouncement of the historical death of art in the relocating of its goal from
the activity that makes images to the one that reflects on them draws
its impetus from the failure of autonomous art to be the advent of the
freedom from heteronomy for whose sake it speaks. Art is set back
into historical context in the name of the self-consciousness about
context that, in remaining vigilant about the wiles of external determination, now speaks in the name of freedom.

This Hegelian move, however, is deeply problematic. First, the conception of history it deploys is parasitic on the failed freedom of the
autonomous artwork. Let me briefly retrace some steps to demonstrate this. Kant presents the artwork's autonomy as a struggle against
mechanism, against heteronomous determination. Properly speaking, Kant does not set the free artistic spirit against history but against
nature. This is not surprising; as Kant's political essays reveal, he has
no developed concept of history other than natural history, mechanism in time.[9] The work of art is thus the only evidence of freedom,
of human self-creation in time, in Kant's philosophy. (There is some
legitimate question, though, whether this holds after the French Revolution as well.) Please note again the stress on "evidence" here. The
work of art functions as a sign of the unbridgeable metaphysical abyss
across which freedom has been segregated from nature, a sign that, if
true to the nature of freedom, had better not itself be free; if it were,
it would cease being evidence and take up residence in the realm beyond appearance. Freedom from mechanism rather than the effort
to negate it would make the work of art metaphysically impossible.
For the work of art to intervene in the temporal mechanism, it must
fail to be free, and it is just this nonreconciliation between freedom
and nature in art that is the evidence of freedom.

What this summary of my argument reveals is that a dialectical war
between nature and free spirit, which free spirit cannot win, is set in
motion in the autonomous work of art. It is, however, the failure to
win that keeps art in motion, keeps it unreconciled, thus battling
against the realm of external determination, which itself grows more
obdurate with each failure. Art, far from dying of failure, would die
of success. But what is this perpetual conflict between freedom and
nature? What is this process of the always-renewed nonreconciliation

between the self-determination of spirit and external determination? Because art fails to attain the freedom it strives for, it is impossible to treat it as free spirit, but because it remains unreconciled to that failure, it is also impossible to treat it as a segment of the temporal mechanism. It is instead necessary to treat art's renewal of its commitment to failure as the specifically human story of perpetual self-creation in time through nonreconciliation. It is necessary, in other words, to treat art as historical.

It is crucial to stress that the difference marked here between nature and history, between the fact of mechanism and mechanism as constraint, is that history is the dimension of the unreconciled. To have a history, on this view, is to fail to be free yet to bridle against that failure, which is the same as saying that for some entity to be historical is for it to have a past—*its* past—which also establishes for it a future. That there is this concept of history at all is a conceptual consequence of the perceived intolerability that the free spirit should find itself confronted with a mechanical world that is indifferent to it *and* the further perception that turning away from that intolerability in favor of some chiliastic metaphysical comfort provides no solace. Instead, the intolerability of that world's indifference yields a struggle to negate it. This struggle requires the new maxim that the apparent necessity of the world, from this point of view its inhumanity, is not itself metaphysically necessary; this new maxim thus transforms the mutual indifference of nature and freedom into active nonreconciliation. Thus, the artistic struggle of negation binds itself to a world whose structure produces an enlivening rage both of and at alienation. This self-binding transforms the scope of human action in the world, adding art to the more traditional reflective activities of philosophy, science, and ethics as a specifically human form of self-fashioning; further, insofar as art is an essentially temporal activity, it also transforms the world in which that action is pursued, giving it the shape of something that actively resists human freedom. This latter transformation turns the world into an arena of potential self-determination but *always only potential,* for *this* self-determination is now not moral agency as a metaphysical alternative to heteronomy but a process of, to use Hegel's favorite third term, becoming. In sum, the maxim of autonomous art is to never be reconciled, to treat its necessary failure to be free as the heart of its thrust into what is now open to it as a future, and it is for just this reason that the perspective of history, as opposed to nature, is a consequence of autonomous art's failure to be free.[10]

It is, of course, exactly this concept of the historical dimension, of history as nonreconciliation between nature and freedom, that forms the starting point for Hegel, or perhaps anyone's, thoroughgoing historicist account of human life and institutions. If the essential claim of a historicist philosophy of art is that art is bound to its historical moment and that therefore it is not free, then historicism is not in conflict with my account of art's autonomy; rather, it makes explicit one aspect of the maxim of artistic action that art appear to be free through the negation of its circumstantiality. However, in claiming (1) that art's failure is a sign that it is a dead thing, a thing whose life is in the past, that it has been defeated by precisely the extra-aesthetic factors it remains unreconciled to and claiming (2) that the necessity of that defeat is explicable from the point of view of the self-conscious historian who can explain how art is determined by its historical moment and who thus now claims to speak for freedom as the real possibility of reconciliation—in making this set of claims, the historicist clearly invokes a different sense of history. What is this alternative sense of history such that art's nonreconciliation is a sign of its death, such that failure to be free is the end, rather than the beginning, of a commitment to some future? It is precisely history as a closed domain of entirely external determinations relative to which the only sign of human freedom is the capacity to remain detached from it. If nonreconciliation to external determination is taken as a sign of art's belonging to a past characterized by an internally flawed effort after freedom, then the implicit characterization of the present is as a reconciliation to the impossibility of freedom by means of a philosophical investigation of the history of prior necessitation. Not only is this, in its reconciliation with history, a cynical disposition, it is also a denial of history as a process of temporal self-creation oriented toward a future and so is a retraction of the concept of history it used as a starting point.

This closure of history is not, to be sure, a consequence a Hegelian would reject. Hegel announces the death of art in the birth of the historical-philosophical consciousness to which nothing remains unreconciled; he thus explicitly identifies the history of human self-creation in time as having come to an end. Danto, too, proclaims the end of art, or at least the end of art as a process of historical development, as artistic consciousness becomes philosophy and leaves in its wake the possibility that now, finally, art may make us happy. In both cases, we can hear the sigh of relief: at last, that's over. This closure, though, is the first premise of a *reductionist* historicism, insofar as its fundamental contrast between temporal development and historical consciousness is the renewal of the contrast between nature and freedom. What was regarded from the point of view of the autonomous work as an essentially historical and not merely temporal realm is instead once again represented as a blind play of factors that determine human action, and thus history again becomes nature. The blindness of art, rather than being seen, as Kant saw it, as a negative achievement of imagining open possibility in the face of mechanism, is now seen as art's misrecognition of itself as free of the forces blowing all the more powerfully through it. Art's visible lack of freedom in time is, in short, mistaken for its lack of autonomy. On this basis, of course, art always was reconciled to nature, however vividly it and the philosophers of its autonomy dreamed otherwise.

To sum up these last paragraphs, if the nonreconciliation of art is overcome by history, then history as the process of human self-creation is closed, and thus historicism flips over into a kind of reductive naturalism within which art, in being explained, becomes impossible. I can readily imagine the protests of the historicists to this argument. Surely, invoking extra-aesthetic historical factors in explaining art cannot be wrong. Surely, art, like any human action, is best understood by placing it into its context. But these protests, although making assertions I heartily agree with, miss the point of my critique. The very idea of a historical factor, as opposed to mechanical determination, the very idea of historical context, as opposed to location in nature, presupposes the autonomy, the failed freedom, of the work of art. Historical factors and contexts are what freedom remains unreconciled to, and in this regard any analysis of art at all concerned with how art appears and what artists do must invoke them. It is in this sense that I suggested in my introduction that what art calls for is a history of apparent underdetermination. On the other hand, that art calls for history does not mean it calls for reduction; any historicism that takes art to be dead and thus treats historical factors and contexts as determining art the way a puppeteer determines the motion of a marionette or, to extend the death imagery, the way Victor Frankenstein built a creature he mistakenly thought was alive, is not invoking historical factors and contexts at all. History is that which the striving for self-determination breaks against, and in that sense art stands in objective contradiction to the history, *its* history, to which freedom is not reconciled. Only an art history capable of representing this contradiction has, if I may put it this way, any hope.

IV

I will conclude with a brief comment about the history of art itself. Although I am not the first to observe this, art manifestly did not come to an end in the time of Hegel. Indeed, if a modified Kantian account of autonomous art as standing in objective contradiction to the history to which it remains unreconciled is right, then it would not be melodramatic to say that art only becomes conscious of its commitment to autonomy around that time. But this is not just a historical coincidence with the cute consequence of making Hegel look foolish. Art and Hegel grew historically self-conscious simultaneously because both confronted the same challenge, the first dramatic failure of art to present itself as free and so the first moment when it became thinkable that art might be impossible. I am referring to the failure of romanticism.

The romantic understanding of art and genius was either a direct consequence of a misunderstanding of Kant, as in the case of Schiller, or was at least consistent with that misunderstanding, as in the cases of the young Goethe and Wordsworth. In both cases, a view was adopted according to which artistic activity was to be the refounding of the world in human freedom. However, the romantic project of constructing the artistic symbol that would incorporate its distance from its object into itself by means of representing that distance and so build a bridge across the metaphysical chasm separating the constraints of art from freedom failed (as, I might add, it was bound to). It tended to either fall into allegory, as in the paintings of Friedrich; compress into lyric impressionism, as in the odes of Shelley; or turn aggressively against the means of art making itself, as in late Beethoven. In each of these cases, the turning sour of romanticism's promise is made perceptible.

Explaining the dynamics of romanticism is obviously beyond the scope of this essay, but no topic is more central to understanding the fates of Kantian and Hegelian aesthetics. Hegel was prescient in seeing that the romantic project had to come to grief, that it rested on a metaphysical contradiction such that even the most exquisite self-consciousness could not get around the irreconcilability of freedom and nature. However, since Hegel, too, mistook art's autonomy for freedom from constraint, he took the failure of romanticism to be the moment art finally ceded its goal to philosophy. That is, the end of romanticism would also be the death of art. However, the end of romanticism, the failure of art to refound the world in freedom, also created a problem for art itself: how does it keep the war against external determination alive in the face of, precisely, its own failure?

Art's answer is to begin to tilt against its own history, to begin the dialectical process of attempting to incorporate the failure of art into its own appearance. To pursue the goal of freedom, to maintain its autonomy, art must begin to negate the necessity of its own history of failure, which, on my account, means negating itself. Art thus begins to struggle against not just nature or context as mechanical constraint but also against history itself in the form of the history of art.[11] This is the origin of what Harold Bloom has called the anxiety of influence that appears as the ceaseless striving for the new, anticipated by Kant in his theory of exemplarity, which is a primary characteristic of modernism. I need not get involved here in the various debates about the periodization of modernism, but from the concerns with the materiality of the artwork, in, say, Rimbaud, to concerns about dependence on the audience, in, say, Cézanne, to concerns about cultural valorizations of handiwork, in, say, Duchamp, to concerns about the social isolation of spaces of display, in, say, situationist art, modernist art is impelled to show itself to be unreconciled to what, from the point of view of its self-proclaimed newness, stands revealed as its own past failure to be free. As Adorno says of even the most violent antiart, "The idea of the abolition of art is respectful of art because it takes the truth claim of art seriously" (AT 43). But art's tilting against history in the form of its own history, its explicit compact with what it knows to have failed, is just its autonomy, its refusal to accept the necessity of the external determinations to which its own past failures reveal it to have been prey, and thus is art's historically self-conscious maintenance of the struggle between mechanism and spirit. In this sense, modernism is the Kantian alternative to Hegelian historicism.

The extremes to which art must go to hold open the project of nonreconciliation with the history of its own failure are notorious. But the only way to hold history open is, precisely, to insist ever more furiously on the necessity of the failure of art. The question, though, remains open: what form will this insistence take? No more poignant answer can be found than in Thomas Mann's *Doctor Faustus*. The composer Adrian Leverkühn is grief-stricken over the death of his nephew Nepomuk in whom he had invested all his hope that there could yet be goodness on the earth. In his anguish, Leverkühn curses life itself to his friend Zeitblom, who narrates the tirade:

I was leaving when he stopped me, calling my name, my last name, Zeitblom, which sounded hard too. And when I turned round:

"I find," he said, "that it is not to be."

"What, Adrian, is not to be?"

"The good and the noble," he answered me; "what we call the human, although it is good, and noble. What human beings have fought for and stormed citadels, what the ecstatics exultantly announced—that is not to be. It will be taken back. I will take it back."

"I don't quite understand, dear man. What will you take back?"

"The Ninth Symphony," he replied. And then no more came, though I waited for it.[12]

That the "Ode to Joy" could not save Nepomuk makes its joyfulness a mockery, not a redemption, of human suffering, so to live in a world with it but without the child is to be condemned to a life of being scorned by the unfulfillable promise of liberation from pain and guilt. Hence, the Ninth Symphony failed and so must be repealed. But how can one respond to this failure of art? One could say, with

Hegel, that art is dead. Or one could, as does Leverkühn, write the "Faust Oratorio" to respond to Beethoven's failure with one of one's own, to show that *of course* it had to fail—it was only art. Art's response to its own failure is to seek to negate it by incorporating it. This might yield, as it does for Leverkühn, a lamentation, but that lamentation is nonetheless a roar of protest against false reconciliation. And this antiutopianism, roaring at itself in the realm of the sensuous, both gives the lie to historicism and establishes the project for a critical history of art oriented by the idea of autonomy.

Notes

1. For analyses of this consequence of Hegel's historicism, see E. H. Gombrich, "In Search of Cultural History," in *Ideals and Idols: Essays on Values in History and in Art* (Oxford: Phaidon Press, 1979), pp. 24–59; and "The Father of Art History," in *Tributes: Interpreters of Our Cultural Tradition* (Oxford: Phaidon Press, 1984), pp. 51–69. As noted, nonreductionist conclusions can also be drawn from Hegel, and several recent defenses of Hegel pursue such a tack. See, for example, William Desmond, *Art and the Absolute: A Study of Hegel's Aesthetics* (Albany: State University of New York Press, 1986), pp. 57–76 especially.

2. Hegel writes,

> Art is not, either in content or form, the supreme and absolute mode of bringing the mind's genuine interests into consciousness. The form of art is enough to limit it to a restricted content. Only a certain circle and grade of truth is capable of being represented in the medium of art. Such truth must have in its own nature the capacity to go forth into sensuous form and be adequate to itself therein, if it is to be a genuinely artistic content, as is the case with the gods of Greece. There is, however, a deeper form of truth, in which it is no longer so closely akin and so friendly to sense as to be adequately embraced and expressed by that medium. Of such a kind is the Christian conception of truth; and more especially the spirit of our modern world, or, to come closer, of our religion and our intellectual culture, reveals itself as beyond the stage at which art is the highest mode assumed by man's consciousness of the absolute. The peculiar mode to which artistic production and works of art belong no longer satisfies our supreme need. We are above the level at which works of art can be venerated as divine, and actually worshipped; the impression which they make is of a more considerate kind, and the feelings which they stir within us require a higher test and further confirmation. Thought and reflection have taken their flight above fine art.

G. W. F. Hegel, *Introductory Lectures on Aesthetics,* trans. Bernard Bosanquet (New York: Penguin Books, 1993), pp. 11–12.

3. Hegel writes,

> In all these respects art is, and remains for us, on the side of its highest destiny, a thing of the past. Herein it has further lost for us its genuine truth and life, and

Gregg M. Horowitz

rather is transferred into our ideas than asserts its former necessity, or assumes its former place, in reality. What is now aroused in us by works of art is over and above our immediate enjoyment, and together with it, our judgment; inasmuch as we subject the content and the means of representation of the work of art and the suitability or unsuitability of the two to our intellectual consideration. Therefore, the *science* of art is a much more pressing need in our day than in times in which art, simply as art, was enough to furnish a full satisfaction. Art invites us to consideration of it by means of thought, not to the end of stimulating art production, but in order to ascertain scientifically what art is.

Hegel, *Introductory Lectures on Aesthetics,* p. 13.

4. This formulation sounds sufficiently Hegelian that it serves well to clarify my perhaps paradoxical goal of retrieving the historical dialectic of the autonomy of art against Hegel himself. In stressing the connection between autonomy and the refusal of external determination, rather than between autonomy and full self-determination, I am, of course, working from the form of critique elaborated in *Negative Dialectics*. In particular, I am pursuing in a different context Adorno's arguments from "An Excursion to Hegel" that dialectics and historicity are at war in Hegel's philosophy.

> The unhistoric concept of history, harbored by a falsely resurrected metaphysics in what it calls historicity, would serve to demonstrate the agreement of ontological thought with the naturalistic thought from which the ontological one so eagerly delimits itself. When history becomes the basic ontological structure of things in being, if not indeed the *qualitas occulta* of being itself, it is mutation as immutability, copied from the religion of inescapable nature. This allows us to transpose historic specifics into invariance at will, and to wrap a philosophical cloak around the vulgar view in which historic situations seem as natural in modern times as they once seemed divinely willed. (ND 358)

Historicity as ontology freezes the dialectical dynamism of Hegel's "dynamic of fixed and dynamic elements." See "Skoteinos, or How to Read Hegel," in Theodor W. Adorno, *Hegel: Three Studies,* trans. Shierry Weber Nicholson (Cambridge: MIT Press, 1993), p. 143. In one sense, then, the dialectical critique of historicism can be fairly seen as Hegelian self-criticism. However, because Hegel's aesthetics in particular magnifies the historicist dimension of his philosophy at the expense of the variability of the dialectical, such a self-criticism needs to go beyond the bounds of the Hegelian circle. This much I draw from Adorno. What may prove surprising is that going beyond Hegel may be accomplished most fruitfully by rereading Kant. That it is fruitful is, of course, what this essay must show.

5. Immanuel Kant, *Critique of Judgment,* trans. Werner S. Pluhar (Indianapolis: Hackett Publishing, 1987), pp. 45–46. *Critique of Judgment* will henceforth be referred to as CJ.

6. Friedrich Nietzsche, *The Birth of Tragedy,* trans. Walter Kaufmann (New York: Random House, 1967), p. 37.

7. "A practical precept which presupposes a material and therefore empirical condition must never be reckoned a practical law. For the law of pure will, which is free, puts the will in a sphere entirely different from the empirical." Immanuel Kant, *Critique of Practical Reason,* trans. Lewis White Beck (Indianapolis: Bobbs-Merrill, 1956), p. 34.

8. See Arthur Danto, "The Philosophical Disenfranchisement of Art" and "The End of Art," both in *The Philosophical Disenfranchisement of Art* (New York: Columbia University Press, 1986).

9. This point is exemplified most vividly in Kant's commentary on the ninth proposition of "Idea for a Universal History with a Cosmopolitan Purpose," in Immanuel Kant, *Political Writings*, trans. H. B. Nisbet (Cambridge: Cambridge University Press, 1991), pp. 51–52 especially. The options available for making plausible the project of a specifically human history are to assimilate it either to natural development or to fiction. Kant writes,

> It is admittedly a strange and at first sight absurd proposition to write a *history* according to an idea of how world events must develop if they are to conform to certain rational ends; it would seem that only a *novel* could result from such premises. Yet if it may be assumed that nature does not work without a plan and purposeful end, even amidst the arbitrary play of human freedom, this idea might nevertheless prove useful.

It is, to be sure, a legitimate question whether Kant holds to this point of view after the French Revolution. In the second part of *The Contest of the Faculties,* trans. Mary J. Gregor (Lincoln: University of Nebraska Press, 1992), pp. 140–71, Kant develops a conception of the prophetic history of humanity as philosophically rigorous on condition that the prophet's premonitions themselves be influential in producing the events that make them true, i.e., if the premonitions themselves become reasons for public actions. This position then requires Kant to develop a conception of the essentially public nature of philosophically rigorous prophetic history. Even here, however, Kant insists on seeing the achievement of the prophet's premonitions as a result of natural evolution from an original cause, and thus as consistent with the one systematic totality of nature. In other words, no break in nature is possible, hence no real distinction between human and natural history can be maintained.

10. Adorno writes,

> Whether art becomes politically relevant or indifferent—an idle play or a decorative frill of the system—depends on the extent to which art's constructions and montages are at the same time de-montages, i.e. dismantlements that appropriate elements of reality by destroying them, thus freely shaping them into something else. The unity of the social criterion of art with the aesthetic one hinges on whether art is able to supersede empirical reality while at the same time concretizing its relation to that empirical reality. (AT 362)

11. As Adorno writes, "[n]ow, modern art is different from all previous art in that its mode of negation is different. Previously, styles and artistic practices were negated by new styles and practices. Today, however, modernism negates tradition itself" (AT 31).

12. Thomas Mann, *Doctor Faustus,* trans. H. T. Lowe-Porter (New York: Random House), p. 478.

11

Construction of a Gendered Subject: A Feminist Reading of Adorno's *Aesthetic Theory*

Sabine Wilke and Heidi Schlipphacke

The vanishing of the subject beyond subjective reason is one of the main arguments developed in Adorno's writings. In his last and unfinished book on aesthetics, he describes this dialectic as a dilemma manifest in the work of art whereby the subject in its quasi-logical universality becomes the functionary of an act of aesthetic synthesis. What is more, Adorno claims that it "is through this process of vanishing rather than by deferential assimilation to reality that the work of art goes beyond mere subjective reason, if it does so at all."[1] Adorno's subject therefore becomes the aesthetic subject and, at the same time, is overcome by the aesthetic construction of the work of art. The essays collected in this volume wish to document these intricate dialectical processes and show their relevance to the contemporary discussion of the role of critique in aesthetic theory. In this contribution, we want specifically to address Adorno's construction of subjectivity from a feminist angle and show how this subject is not the neutral category it is frequently considered to be in the literature. Rather, Adorno relies on the typical stereotypes and projections of male and female subjectivity available in patriarchal discourse. Our argument is that a hidden and unacknowledged projection of male and female subjectivity informs his aesthetic judgments in *Aesthetic Theory* and that this may account for some of the most obvious dilemmas presented by the book. We will read Adorno's reflections on subjectivity in *Aesthetic Theory* through a reconstruction of Horkheimer and Adorno's narrative of the entwinement of myth and rationality in *Dialectic of Enlightenment,* which sets the stage for an understanding of the projections of male and female subjectivity and sexuality operative in classical Frankfurt School writings.

It would, in fact, be misleading to claim that scholarly research on the writings of the Critical Theorists of the Frankfurt School has focused on the topic of gender. Quite the contrary is indeed the case. The reception of Horkheimer's and Adorno's texts in the English-speaking world so far has primarily focused on philosophical, literary, and intellectual-historical issues. The discussion of this material in feminist circles is likewise a relatively recent phenomenon, which focuses mainly on a critical understanding of the unfolding of the dialectic of enlightenment. The psychoanalyst Jessica Benjamin first introduced such a feminist critique of the *Dialectic of Enlightenment* in her work about the antinomies of patriarchal thinking. She claims that Horkheimer and Adorno explain rationality from the perspective of a relatively narrow focus on male subjectivity in terms of a polarization between instrumental rationality and nature.[2] Feminist critics who have followed in Benjamin's footsteps have more recently pointed to a rather ambivalent concept of subjectivity and nature in these writings. On the one hand, they acknowledge the great achievement of the authors of *Dialectic of Enlightenment* to include the historicity of human emotions and feelings in their philosophical-historical perspective on modern Western civilization. By understanding the relationship of the subject to its body as an expression of a social structure of reification, Horkheimer and Adorno introduce a line of argument that is close to more-contemporary theories of sexual politics. If we accept this theory about the social and cultural constructedness of the human body as one of the prime locations where reification manifests itself, we find ourselves in the middle of an interesting and important debate within feminist and theoretical circles about the status of the body in society. On the other hand, as we will see, Horkheimer and Adorno's critique of enlightenment nevertheless remains bound to a narrative of Western civilization that dictates an androcentric model of male bourgeois subjectivity.[3]

Let us explain this dilemma in greater detail, by discussing crucial passages. In *Dialectic of Enlightenment,* Horkheimer and Adorno rewrite the history of Western civilization as a history of repression, domination of nature, and instrumentalization of reason. They begin to unfold this dialectic when they claim, in the introduction, that "in the most general sense of progressive thought, the Enlightenment has always aimed at liberating men from fear and establishing their sovereignty. Yet the fully enlightened earth radiates disaster triumphant. The program of the Enlightenment was the disenchantment of the world; the dissolution of myths and the substitution of knowledge for fancy."[4] This dialectical process of myth and enlightenment is reconstructed in the form of a topographical narrative, whose key constellations include Odysseus's journey through the Aegean Sea, transcendental aesthetics in Kant and its critique by Marquis de Sade and Nietzsche, European fascism, and American popular culture. Some of the crucial positions and constellations in this process consist of women figures that are described within a conventional paradigm of images available for women within patriarchal society.

Odysseus's journey is, for Horkheimer and Adorno, the earliest document that displays clearly the dialectic of enlightenment, the dialectical process of myth and enlightenment: myth is enlightenment, and enlightenment becomes myth. "Myth turns into enlightenment, and nature into mere objectivity. Men pay for the increase of their power with alienation from that over which they exercise their power. Enlightenment behaves toward things as a dictator toward men. He knows them insofar as he can manipulate them" (DE 9). Progress turns into regress; enlightenment becomes a tool of domination unless the very conditions of enlightenment are subjected to critical self-reflection. It is this criterion of self-reflection that characterizes the project of Critical Theory and sets it apart from other philosophical traditions. Moreover, it is with the help of this criterion that Horkheimer and Adorno can describe the history of Western civilization as the "dialectic of enlightenment" whose logic they believe they can deconstruct. We will have to see if we can agree with their own assessment of the situation.

Several of the stations Odysseus passes on his return journey to Ithaca are marked by female mythological figures. Horkheimer and Adorno locate him at first before his encounter with the Sirens. Let us quote this passage at length:

Sabine Wilke and Heidi Schlipphacke

The entanglement of myth, domination, and labor is preserved in one of the Homeric narratives. Book XII of the Odyssey tells the encounter with the Sirens. Their allurement is that of losing oneself in the past. But the hero to whom the temptation is offered has reached maturity through suffering. Throughout the many mortal perils he has had to endure, the unity of his own life, the identity of the individual, has been confirmed to him.... But the Sirens' song has not yet been rendered powerless by reduction to the condition of art. They know "everything that ever happened on this so fruitful earth," including the events in which Odysseus himself took part, "all those things that Argos' sons and the Trojans suffered by the will of the gods on the plains of Troy." While they directly evoke the recent past, with the irresistible promise of pleasure as which their song is heard, they threaten the patriarchal order which renders to each man his life only in return for his full measure of time. Whoever falls for their trickery must perish, whereas only perpetual presence of mind forces an existence from nature. (DE 32–33)

As we all know, no man who hears the Sirens' song can escape, yet Odysseus devises an intelligent trick so that he can listen to them, indulge in pleasure, and, at the same time, retain the organization of the—apparently still fragile—male bourgeois self, which he had worked so hard to gain: he plugs his men's ears with wax so that they hear neither the Sirens nor, as it turns out, his orders, as he listens with pleasure while bound to the mast. Horkheimer and Adorno interpret this scenario with the help of Hegel's paradigm of the master/slave dialectic: Odysseus, as the master, may indulge in pleasure but must, ultimately, sublimate his desire, whereas the rowers, as laborers, must ignore the pleasures that lie to the side:

What Odysseus hears is without consequence for him; he is able only to nod his head as a sign to be set free from his bonds; but it is too late; his men, who do not listen, know only the song's danger but nothing of its beauty, and leave him at the mast in order to save him and themselves. They reproduce the oppressor's life together with their own, and the oppressor is no longer able to escape his social role. (DE 34)

Horkheimer and Adorno also interpret the threat of the Sirens as a different—presumably more ancient—organization of time that endangers the patriarchal time sequence. Feminist critic Irmgard Schultz has objected that, by identifying the mechanism of social hierarchization as a temporal relation with nature, the authors remain stuck within stereotypical patterns of thought: although they presumably explain historical progress in terms of exchange and domination of nature, they still posit nature and timelessness as the other of history and subjectivity, thereby reinscribing the dichotomy between (the male active) subject and (female passive) nature.[5] In fact, Horkheimer and Adorno describe the effect of Odysseus's passing by as a process of neutralization: the temptation of the Sirens is effectively neutralized and becomes art: "The prisoner is present at a concert, an inactive eavesdropper like later concertgoers, and his spirited call for liberation fades like applause" (DE 34). For the authors, this scenario serves as an allegory for the dialectic of enlightenment, which neutralizes nature only to sublate it into art and subjectivity.

Horkheimer and Adorno still have to present their argument about the attainment of (male) bourgeois subjectivity. Although Circe had warned Odysseus about the Sirens' powers to cause disintegration, he nevertheless cannot pass by without submitting to their temptation.

The strain of holding the I together adheres to the I in all stages; and the temptation to lose it has always been there with the blind determination to maintain it. The narcotic intoxication which permits the atonement of deathlike sleep for the euphoria in which the self is suspended, is one of the oldest social arrangements which mediate between self-preservation and self-destruction—an attempt of the self to survive itself. The dread of losing the self and of abrogating together with the self the barrier between oneself and other life, the fear of death and destruction, is intimately associated with a promise of happiness which threatened civilization in every moment. (DE 33)

Central to the Homeric tale is that the Sirens sing a song and that this song brings about regression, in this case the destruction of the (male bourgeois) self. Whether or not the Sirens have desire is never the question. The question of desire, in fact, cannot be posed in a context other than the construction of male bourgeois subjectivity. The point is, first of all, the effect of the Sirens' song on the male subject and, second, the association between (archaic female) sensuality and the destruction of the male subject. The (male) bourgeois self has to reject both in order to survive. The promise of happiness contained in this image of the Sirens has to be successfully

Sabine Wilke and Heidi Schlipphacke

banned from bourgeois society for the sake of the male subject's self-preservation.

Horkheimer and Adorno use this scenario in order to formulate their critique of the exclusionary logic of Western civilization and its central feature of the domination of nature and, by extension, the domination of the sensual and the feminine. In this text, they develop the concept of a critique of instrumental reason as critique of the domination of nature in the context of patriarchal society.[6] Yet, as we would argue, this critique mimetically repeats the stereotypes of female sexuality in patriarchal society. In other words, Horkheimer and Adorno use the language and imagery of female sexuality as passive, as lacking in active desire, as the object of male contemplation, and the traditional conception of its proximity to nature in order to criticize this discourse of domination. If we go back to the assertion that the human body, in this case the female body, is the location at which societal structures of reification become manifest, this reading of the *Odyssey* is consistent with the theoretical position about the politics of sexuality developed in the *Dialectic of Enlightenment*. Some feminist critics, however, have pointed out that the exclusive use of such radical language of social politics may, in fact, inhibit a critical understanding of the negative associations between nature and the feminine. It seems as if for Horkheimer and Adorno the Sirens embody a promise of happiness, precisely *because of* their closeness to "nature" and a different organization of time, because of their otherness to Western patriarchal culture. To us, however, it remains unclear whether or not the authors have critically reflected on the possibility, first of all, that this otherness may be a projection of patriarchal culture or, second, that it was utilized time and again as an argument against the full economic and social integration of women in modern society.[7]

Let us study this dilemma of representation through Horkheimer and Adorno's discussion of the mythological characters of the lotus-eaters and Circe. Similar to the threat of the Sirens, the victims of the lotus-eaters are cursed to a life in oblivion and the complete surrender of will, although they are merely condemned to a primitive state without work and struggle. Horkheimer and Adorno's analysis of this allegorical scenario focuses on the illusory character of this promise of happiness:

This kind of idyll, which recalls the happiness of narcotic drug addicts reduced to the lowest level in obdurate social orders, who use their drugs to help them endure the unendurable, is impermissible for the adherents of the rationale of self-preservation. It is actually the mere illusion of happiness, a dull vegetation, as meager as an animal's bare existence, and at best only the absence of the awareness of misfortune. (DE 63)

This particular threat to the rationale of Odysseus's self-preservation comes from regression into an ancient state of mere vegetation, a pre-productive stage, so to speak, which—although closer to "nature"— nevertheless carries a "promise of a state in which the reproduction of life is independent of conscious self-preservation, and the bliss of the fully contented is detached from the advantages of rationally planned nutrition. The fleeting reminiscence of that most distant and most ancient pleasure attached to the sense of taste is still limited by the almost immediate need actually to consume the food. It points back to prehistory" (DE 63–64). The lotus-eaters as well as the patriarchal clan of the cyclops, which comes next in the succession of Odysseus's journey, represent stages in the history of civilization that have to be overcome by the master Odysseus, the *Homo oeconomicus,* on his way to the mastery of language and a stabile, rationally organized self. Horkheimer and Adorno read the Homeric epic allegorically from the perspective of philosophical self-reflection. In this passage, they express a self-criticism of the earlier assessment of the episode, in which the Sirens represented a promise of happiness that has no place in bourgeois society.

Similar to the Sirens and the lotus-eaters, Circe comes from a magical realm and, as such, embodies the threat of dissolution: "Circe tempts Odysseus' men to give themselves up to instinct: therefore the animal form of the tempted men has always been connected with a reversion to basic impulse, and Circe has been made the prototype of the courtesan" (DE 69). Taking their lead from the following passages in the *Odyssey,* the authors discuss the structure of images of female sexuality in Western culture. In Circe, they see an ambiguity that is characteristic of the polarity between corrupter and helper that determines most images of the female in that culture. Circe will take the erotic initiative but, at the same time, she will not injure her guests. In fact, Horkheimer and Adorno argue that the Homeric epos systematically underrepresents the pleasure that is connected to this act of enchanted transformation. They interpret this misrepresentation by the Homeric "authors" as an allegorical scenario for the plight of women in patriarchal society. Again, we cite this crucial passage at length:

Like her, women under the pressure of civilization are above all inclined to adopt the civilized judgment on women and to defame the sex. In the confrontation of enlightenment and myth, the traces of which are preserved in the epic, the powerful temptress is already weak, obsolete and defenseless, and needs the obedient animals as her escorts. As a representative of nature, woman in bourgeois society has become the enigmatic image of irresistibility and powerlessness. In this way she reflects for domination the pure lie that posits the subjection instead of the redemption of nature. (DE 71–72)

Circe rejects those who fall for her, and she desires only those who reject her. Horkheimer and Adorno read this passage in the *Odyssey* as an allegory for the situation of women in bourgeois patriarchal society: in the end, Circe is the one who is dominated and who has to organize her desire along the lines of male pleasure.

Horkheimer and Adorno's interpretation of this figure and her relationship with Odysseus is interspersed with more general reflections on love and marriage: "Marriage is the middle way by which society comes to terms with itself. The woman remains the one without power, for power comes to her only by male mediation" (DE 72). They read the bourgeois institution of marriage in terms of the logic of exchange that governs it: Circe has to subject her will to the one who resists her and thus enacts the prohibition of love, which later in bourgeois society becomes all the more powerful as the ideology of love reconstructs feelings of love. "Circe's power, which subjects men to her and makes them obedient, becomes her obedience to the man who through renunciation refused to submit to her" (DE 73). In the end, Horkheimer and Adorno return to their reflections about gender and sexuality in patriarchal society by extrapolating from this specific scenario to a more general level of societal analysis:

Prostitute and wife are the complements of female self-alienation in the patriarchal world: the wife denotes pleasure in the fixed order of life and property, whereas the prostitute takes what the wife's right of possession leaves
free, and—as the wife's secret collaborator—subjects it again to the order of
possession: she sells pleasure.... If the courtesan makes the patriarchal
world-order her own, the monogamous wife is not herself happy with it and
does not rest until she has made herself equal with the male character. Thus
the marriage partners come to terms. (DE 73/74)

Horkheimer and Adorno read the mythological female figure of
Circe as an allegory of repressed desire, yet a desire that in a society
of exchange is already reconstructed through the patriarchal ideology of love. At no point is it a question of describing *actual* women or
actual female sexuality and desire, but, true to the position of sexual
politics described earlier, they weave their way through these already
reconstructed images of the female that are available in patriarchal
culture and show the extent to which women in this society have always already accepted these images. Both women, the courtesan and
the wife, Circe and Penelope, accept the paradigm of male domination in bourgeois society. Penelope watches over Odysseus's property
while he is gone; Circe gives him pleasure under his conditions. They
accept the patriarchal world order and are thus guilty of supporting
that order.

In these passages, Horkheimer and Adorno reflect on the relationship between men and women from the vantage point of class domination and economic exchange value. So far, they do not problematize
the concept of gender, although they offer valuable insights into the
relationship between the human body and its social construction. Andrew Hewitt has argued that the *Dialectic of Enlightenment* presents an
analysis of political power as a system of representations that, however,
incorporates moments in which a restoration of experience as a form
of escape from the totality of power is attempted: "What is notable,
however, is that where such possibilities are articulated in terms of a
potential agency, it is in and around figures of women—or, perhaps, a
fantasm of the feminine—that they are collected. In fact, the very re-
thinking of power as representation is inextricable from the thematiza-
tion of woman in the *Dialectic of Enlightenment*."[8] According to Hewitt,
Horkheimer and Adorno problematize the exclusion of women from

Sabine Wilke and Heidi Schlipphacke

philosophical discourse by reconstructing a position of potential exemption from this discourse that these female figures occupy: "Women are instrumentalized as the representatives of the possibility of exclusion understood as an *escape* from the all-inclusive system of power. In other words, the initial—and damning—exclusion of women from the philosophical project is reworked as a potential exemption from the totality both of power as ontologized domination and of reason as a system of closure."[9]

Contrary to Hewitt's line of argument, we conclude that precisely through their idealization of female figures as sites of possible exemption from the totality of power Horkheimer and Adorno engage in instrumentalization. We do not share Hewitt's conclusions about the idealization of women as bearers of an unreconstructed notion of experience and promise of happiness. On the contrary, we believe that in *Dialectic of Enlightenment* there is, at best, an ambiguous space for such an unreconstructed notion of experience in the episode of the Sirens. But even there, we do not believe that women are reconstructed from the perspective of patriarchal culture that projects this promise of happiness into such a preproductive, naturelike stage. To substantiate his argument, Hewitt points to the function of magic as alternative mythology and as a point from which representation could be reconstructed in terms of a different motivation of the sign.[10] In magical mimesis, the sign is motivated metonymically, through a relation of relatedness that is different from the relation of domination that characterizes bourgeois semiotics. This system of magical signification has been displaced by exchange logic, which governs all power relationships in bourgeois society. Hewitt claims furthermore that this other system of signification is somehow connected with mythological female figures through their assumed closeness to nature and prehistory, and that Horkheimer and Adorno therefore "cannot break out of that instrumental rationality. Women—as the bearers of specificity—are never considered as a potential social and political collective, and specificity of experience itself becomes a paradoxical panacea—a general solution to the totalizing tendencies of the dominant masculine discourse."[11] Contrary to Hewitt, we do not see the problem so much in the arguable idealization of female figures as the repository of an alternative conception of signification as in the totalization of patriarchal discourse as inhabiting not only its very own sites but also the language of its own critique.[12]

It is primarily the perceived association between women and nature in Horkheimer and Adorno's discourse that has triggered critical responses from feminists, who point to the androcentric nature of their critique of patriarchy. They claim that both authors are blind to patriarchal projections of female subjectivity and sexuality. Christine Kulke, for example, faults Horkheimer and Adorno but also Habermas for the fact that they are not sensitive to patriarchal projections, despite their otherwise critical viewpoint on society: their total generalization of the relationship between power and domination completely determines their judgment of the relationship between the sexes, so that any protest against this universalized structure is no longer conceivable.[13] As a consequence of this universalized logic, the concept of male bourgeois subjectivity is juxtaposed with the nonsubject of woman.[14] Horkheimer and Adorno thus ignore the history of female repression, in the name of nature, biology, and passive sexuality that is inscribed in patriarchal images of women.[15] Although, as we will see, they critically reconstruct the mechanism of projection in other contexts, such as the history of European fascism, in the context of the relationship between the sexes, they mimetically reproduce its core images. Regina Becker-Schmidt also maintains that "although the *Dialectic of Enlightenment*—just like other texts by both authors—radically problematizes the victory of male sexuality, even male claims for supremacy in general, the relationship between the sexes and its forms of organization as the foundation for such usurpation of power remains unreflected on a social-theoretical level."[16] Here the authors follow the classical Marxist tradition of Friedrich Engels and others who can conceive of gender relations only in terms of the division of labor.

This androcentric component of the critique of patriarchy also determines Horkheimer and Adorno's rewriting of classical aesthetics and its critical self-reflection in de Sade and Nietzsche. They attempt a reading of Kant's position on morality and virtue through the criticism of de Sade and Nietzsche, both of whom try to go beyond a traditional understanding of those concepts. They claim that "the work

Sabine Wilke and Heidi Schlipphacke

of de Sade, like that of Nietzsche, constitutes the intransigent critique of practical reason, in contradistinction to which Kant's critique itself seems a revocation of his own thought" (DE 94). This self-correction within philosophical discourse, so to speak, again focuses on a female figure, de Sade's figure of Juliette: "Juliette draws the conclusion that the bourgeoisie wanted to ignore. . . . Juliette embodies (in psychological terms) neither unsublimated nor regressive libido, but intellectual pleasure in regression—*amor intellectualis diaboli,* the pleasure of attacking civilization with its own weapons" (DE 94). In rational and systematic fashion, she manipulates others through the arrangement of dangerous liaisons. Juliette is the quintessential enlightened person who believes in science and despises any form of irrational worship. She takes part in sacrilege and crime, because it amuses her. Horkheimer and Adorno at this point cite the example of another woman, the American murderess Annie Henry, who said "just for fun," when asked about the motivation for her crimes (DE 104).

Faced with these texts by de Sade and Nietzsche, Horkheimer and Adorno continue to rewrite the history of gender relations in modern society as follows:

Juliette tries to retain enjoyment by rejecting the faithful bourgeois love which is characteristic of the bourgeoisie in the last century as a form of resistance to its own cunning. In love enjoyment was coupled with a deification of man, who vouchsafed it; it was the human emotion proper. Finally it was revoked as a sexually conditioned value judgment. . . . Woman appeared voluntarily to accept defeat, and man to concede her the victory. In marriage, Christianity transfigured the hierarchy of the sexes, the yoke that the male organization of property had put on the female character, as a union of hearts, thus assuaging the reminiscence of the better past enjoyed by women in pre-patriarchal times. The decay of middle-class possession, the disappearance of the free economic subject, affects the family: it is no longer the formerly landed cell of society, because it no longer constitutes the basis of the citizen's economic existence. (DE 106–7)

In times of formalistic reason, the utopia of humanity vanishes among mass deception and fascism. For Horkheimer and Adorno, Jews, but also women, become the victims of false projections. It is still unclear, however, to what extent the authors themselves internalize these projected images.

In these selected passages from the *Dialectic of Enlightenment,* we see how the two authors retell the history of civilization as the unfolding of two different gendered subjectivities. The primary focus is on the development of the male bourgeois subject. The female subject serves mainly an instrumentalized function on the male's way to self-actualization. Beyond that, the female subjects in this text are all associated with forbidden, though socially and politically impotent, forms of sensuality and are thus reconstructed out of stereotypical patterns of female images in patriarchal culture.[17] It is our contention that this scenario of gendering also has an unacknowledged and important effect on the construction of the concept of subjectivity in *Aesthetic Theory,* which deals primarily with the notion of aesthetic experience and the phenomenological function of the artwork. We will see how the most important constellations of gender roles, such as the relationship between gender and nature, have a lasting effect on Adorno's later writings as well.

The concepts of subjectivity and the aesthetic subject in Adorno's *Aesthetic Theory* are central problems for this collection of essays, particularly in relation to other conceptions of subjectivity currently debated in philosophical and literary-theoretical circles. We are interested in describing a bifurcation between two different subjects, one potent and one impotent and effeminate, and the ramifications of this process of gendering for a critical-feminist understanding of this major text. Just as in the discussion of *Dialectic of Enlightenment,* we want to pay close attention to the function of the body and its relation to art and society. Indeed, such attention seems to lead us directly into one of the major themes developed in *Aesthetic Theory,* that is, the irrevocable emancipation of art from a bodily determination to aesthetic autonomy. Adorno formulates this process as follows: "The trajectory leading to aesthetic autonomy passes through the stage of disinterestedness; and well it should, for it was during this stage that art emancipated itself from cuisine and pornography, an emancipation that has become irrevocable" (AT 18). Autonomous art, in other words, is opposed to cuisine and pornography in that it has emancipated itself from its very bodily nature, from its materials, so to speak. But that is, of course, only one side of the coin. Adorno is a dialectical thinker through and through and would not leave a concept as undeveloped as we just formulated it. What is left by the

Sabine Wilke and Heidi Schlipphacke

wayside, that is, aesthetic sensuality, is transfigured in modern art into pain and therefore preserved as a moment of pleasure. Let us quote this important passage about the function of aesthetic hedonism at length:

> It is through the moment of sensuous satisfaction that works of art constitute themselves as appearance, which is an essential aspect of art.... In significant works of art the sensuous shines forth as something spiritual, just as, conversely, the spirit of the work may add sensuous brilliance to an individual detail, however indifferent it may be towards appearance.... Dissonance (and its counterparts in visual arts)—the trademark, as it were, of modernism—lets in the beguiling moment of sensuousness by transfiguring it into its antithesis, that is, pain.... The taboo on sensuality in the end spreads even to the opposite of pleasure, i.e., dissonance, because, through its specific negation of the pleasant, dissonance preserves the moment of pleasure, if only as a distant echo. (AT 21–22)

Dissonance can preserve the distant echo of a moment of pleasure as pain, because it mimetically represents most closely the growing power of external reality over the subject. But this subject in its quasi-logical universality vanishes, or rather it becomes an act of aesthetic synthesis. Through this process of vanishing, the work of art can go beyond mere subjective reason and become part of an objective construction.

One example of such a dialectical process is what Adorno calls the ideal of darkness or blackness (*das Dunkle*) in modern art: successful modern artworks assimilate themselves mimetically to the darkness of external social reality: "If works of art are to survive in the context of extremity and darkness, which is social reality, and if they are to avoid being sold as mere comfort, they have to assimilate themselves to that reality. Radical art today is the same as dark art: its background colour is black" (AT 58). But this dark modern art, which is the antithesis of consumer capitalist sensuality, has a sensual appeal, too—precisely because of the dialectical thought articulated above. Adorno calls it "the unfathomable" (AT 73), and he observes its "radiance" (AT 75) and "its own magical moment" (AT 86). Blackness in art serves as a spiritually transfigured moment of sensuality; it leaves its mark as the repressed bodily component in art, what was left behind in the trajectory toward aesthetic autonomy.

Another example of a repressed moment of aesthetic sensuality returning surreptitiously is the image of the circus and Frank Wedekind's ideal of body art. Horkheimer and Adorno first allude to that in the chapter of *Dialectic of Enlightenment* on the culture industry as mass deception. In the skill of circus artists, the culture industry, which otherwise is characterized as a complete system of mass deception, retains one of the very few moments of something better: "The culture industry does retain a trace of something better in those features which bring it close to the circus, in the self-justifying and nonsensical skill of riders, acrobats, and clowns, in the 'defense and justification of physical (*körperliche*) as against intellectual art'" (DE 143). But even the artistry of bodily art is relentlessly destroyed by schematic reason. Adorno returns to this quotation by German playwright Wedekind in *Aesthetic Theory*, where he calls Wedekind's ideal of body art (*Körperkunst*) a revolt against all overly intentional spiritualization in the name of spirit (AT 62). Body art opposes this tendency of spiritualization:

In other words, we can get a handle on what the pre-artistic is by taking a look at phenomena which aesthetic sensibility has left behind. Such a phenomenon is the circus, which is a leftover of low-brow art, justly or unjustly so called, or, as we will say here, anti-artistic art. In France it was the cubist painters, in Germany the playwright Frank Wedekind who turned to the circus. According to Wedekind the circus is body art. This implies both its backwardness as over against the spiritual arts and its role as a model for spiritual art because body art is non-intentional. By its mere existence every work of art as an entity alien to alienation evokes the circus without imitating it; if it does imitate it, it is lost. Art becomes an image not directly *qua* apparition but through the counter-tendency to apparition. The pre-artistic dimension of art is moreover a reminder of art's anti-cultural characteristics—the non-rebellious opposition it mounts to empirical life. (AT 120)

The body art of the circus is one of those phenomena left behind on art's trajectory toward aesthetic autonomy. Its tableaus, however, are "unintentional archetypal images of the very same truth we try to decipher in art" (AT 401). Its constellations, such as the elephants standing on their hind legs carrying a pretty ballerina on their trunk, catch the same truth that art seeks to express through its constructed form. But it also retains the bodily character that successful spiritual art transfigures into pain.

Adorno uses two metaphors to describe the processual essence and character of aesthetic experience. One is the phenomenon of fireworks, which are apparitions that suddenly crystallize into a brilliant appearance only to vanish afterward (AT 119–20). The other example is that of (male) orgasm. Adorno wishes to establish a likeness between sexual and aesthetic experience in the following extraordinary passage: "During orgasm the beloved image changes, combining rigidification with extreme vividness. Orgasm is a bodily prototype of aesthetic experience" (AT 253). He wishes to explain the mechanism of aesthetic experience as process: "Dynamic therefore is reciprocity, a restless antithetical process which never comes to a halt in static being. Works of art exist only *in actu;* their tensions never resolve themselves into pure identity with one or the other extreme.... Their motion must come to a halt and yet remain visible *qua* motion in this standstill" (AT 253). Like his treatment of fireworks, Adorno's description of the process of aesthetic experience is modeled after male orgasm in terms of a dynamic between tension and resolution. In this way, (male) bodily experience is restored to (male) aesthetic experience, after having been repressed by art on its trajectory to aesthetic autonomy, with one important difference: the repressed bodily nature of art (as retained in cuisine and pornography) is marked female. The circus artist in the German text of *Dialectic of Enlightenment* is female. The signification of her tableau rests, for Adorno, in the fact that she mimetically adapts her female body to societal structures of reification. Thus, what we can observe in Adorno's text is a movement to replace the repressed female body (in modern autonomous and spiritual art) with a process of aesthetic experience that is modeled after male sexuality.

Let us return to the concept of subjectivity. We have claimed that Adorno is really dealing with two different notions of subjectivity in his *Aesthetic Theory*. Let us substantiate this claim with a couple of examples. To say that he refers to actual men and women (artists) would be claiming too much. In fact, he mentions almost exclusively men, such as—and we know their names—Ludwig Beethoven, Samuel Beckett, Hugo von Hofmannsthal, Stefan George, Bertolt Brecht, Walter Benjamin, Arnold Schoenberg, and many other major and some minor figures of modern art, literature, and music. He mentions only two women, in passing, in his entire text, a second-rate writer of popular literature (according to the traditional aesthetic judgment that he adopts here), Hedwig Courts-Mahler (1867–1950), and Selma Lagerlöf (1858–1940), the Swedish writer who won the Nobel Prize in literature in 1909. Adorno uses Courts-Mahler as an example to mark quality in artworks: "Bad works of art, like the novels of Hedwig Courts-Mahler, reveal their poor quality as soon as they objectively make the pretence of being art, never mind the fact that their authors may disavow any such intention subjectively (as Courts-Mahler in fact did in a private letter)" (AT 416–17). Although his judgments about what sort of art remains viable under advanced capitalist conditions may have been historically correct, he nevertheless instrumentalizes Courts-Mahler as an example of artistic pretence, without looking further into the sociological and structural aspects that determined her artistic production. Similar to Courts-Mahler, Lagerlöf was a successful writer. She was the first woman to become a member of the Swedish Academy and to achieve economic independence through the sale of her works. Adorno uses her affirmative treatment of utopian aspects merely as a counterexample to the successful banishment of a positive representation of utopia in Beckett (AT 196).

Let us look at some male writers and composers who are also criticized. Examples that come to mind are the Austrian writer Hugo von Hofmannsthal, the German poet Stefan George, the British playwright Oscar Wilde, and the Polish composer Frédéric Chopin. In the beginning paragraph of his second chapter, Adorno plays them out against the art and artistic judgments of Schoenberg and Kafka. The context for this is his wish to argue for the loss of a priori validity of artistic materials themselves:

Hugo von Hofmannsthal's *Letter of Lord Chandos* is known to be the first work that testifies impressively to the existence of such a decomposing trend. Neo-romantic poetry as a whole can be viewed as an endeavor to check this trend and to recover some of the substantiality of language and other materials. The strong aversion to *Jugendstil*, however, stems from the fact that that attempt has failed, appearing retrospectively to have been no more than a lighthearted journey without substance, as Kafka remarked. In an introductory poem to one of the cycles from the *Seventh Ring*, Stefan George put the words "gold" and "karneol" next to each other, confident that the choice would evoke the image of a forest and make poetic sense. Sixty years later we are able to recognize that the choice of these words is merely a decorative arrangement, hardly superior to the crude mass of precious materials piled up in *Dorian Gray* where the interior decorations of Wilde's super-chic aestheticism resemble nothing so much as antique stores, auction rooms, and the whole sphere of commerce Wilde pretends to hate. Along the same lines, Schönberg noted what an easy time Chopin had composing something beautiful because all he needed to do was choose the then little used key of F-sharp major. (AT 23)

In other words, Hofmannsthal, George, Wilde, and Chopin "had an easy time" and presented "merely a decorative arrangement" in their superficial art, which does not live up to the serious aesthetic construction of form in the art of Schoenberg, Kafka, and Beckett. Similarly, the Munich composer Richard Strauss, with whom Hofmannsthal collaborated on several opera libretti, is "a good technician," but his music consists, in the end, of "a number of well calculated effects" (AT 306), whereas Arnold Schoenberg "insisted on logically consistent craftsmanship" (AT 307). The concept of beauty in George and Hofmannsthal is said to be "strangely empty and content-laden" (AT 336).

It is interesting to note that Adorno's distinction between successful spiritual art and calculative artistic production falls in line with traditional attributions to stereotypical representations of gender. This delineation derives from judgments of art formulated in earlier essays, such as those collected in the volume entitled *Prisms*. For example, in the essay "Perennial Fashion—Jazz," written in 1953, Adorno dismisses jazz as the syncopated musical product of the culture industry.[18] "The aim of jazz is the mechanical reproduction of a regressive moment, as castration symbolism. 'Give up your masculinity, let yourself be castrated,' the eunuchlike sound of the jazz band both mocks and proclaims, 'and you will be rewarded, accepted into a fraternity which shares the mystery of impotence with you, a mystery revealed at the moment of the initiation rite'."[19] Adorno's scorn for jazz music comes out in his contempt for the castrated, effeminate individual who performs or listens to jazz. The very same metaphor of sexual impotency is utilized in Adorno's critique of Hofmannsthal, in the 1939–1940 essay "George und Hofmannsthal—Zum Briefwechsel: 1891–1906." Hofmannsthal's syncopated, decorative style in poetry relates him to the jazz musician and marks him as similarly inauthentic. "Its syncopation, the best known of Hofmannsthal's stylistic devices, was taken from the English writers. It is designed by the poet-technician to serve the needs of the actor inherent in the theatrical form" (P 203). Further, Hofmannsthal's ornamental style, which is well suited to the inauthentic theater, is interpreted as a sign of regressive tendencies. Hofmannsthal's poetry tends to childishness and weakness, and it shuns responsibility. "What may prove to endure in Hofmannsthal is his untiring imitation of the childhood gestures which, as it were, reproduce the only stage in which tragic drama can still be experienced. In the hands of his voice every subject is bewitched into childhood, and it is this transformation which enables him to avoid the pitfalls of bearing and responsibility. The magical power to manipulate childhood is the strength of the weak" (P 204). Hofmannsthal's regression to childhood, we suggest, is reminiscent not only of the effeminate jazz musician, but also of the female figures in *Dialectic of Enlightenment,* who are the regressive other of the male bourgeois subject.

The effeminate, impotent, and thereby unsuccessful art of Hofmannsthal and the jazz musician in *Prisms* finds its opposite in the mythically potent music of Arnold Schoenberg. Although Adorno's discussions of Schoenberg are not straightforward endorsements of his music, in the 1953 essay "Arnold Schoenberg: 1874–1951," he successfully avoids the contemptuous, feminizing vocabulary of the Hofmannsthal and jazz essays: "The Orchestral Songs op. 22 conclude with the words, *Und bin ganz allein in dem großen Sturm* [*And am all alone in the great storm*]. At the time, Schoenberg must have experienced the height of his powers. His music expands like a giant, as though the totality, the 'great storm' were about to emerge from self-oblivious subjectivity, 'all alone'" (P 163). In contradistinction to the mindless, repetitive syncopation of Hofmannsthal's poetry and jazz music, Schoenberg's music demands the engagement of its listeners. In other words, the former emasculates/castrates the listener, and the latter returns to him his lost potency. "It [Schoenberg's music] requires the listener spontaneously to compose its inner movement and demands of him not mere contemplation but praxis. In this, however, Schoenberg blasphemes against the expectation, cherished despite all idealistic assurances to the contrary, that music will present the comfortable listener with a series of pleasurable sensations" (P 149–50). Whereas syncopation comforts the consumer, Schoenberg's music refuses to please.

Hofmannsthal and Schoenberg, among others, are evaluated in a similar language in *Aesthetic Theory.* For example, Stefan George "manages only the phoney posturings of a would-be aristocrat" (AT 352), Chopin's (and Wagner's and Brahms's) pieces are characterized by a "'kind-of-aesthetic' quality" (AT 410), and Oscar Wilde, Gabriele d'Annunzio, and Maurice Maeterlinck are all "precursors of the culture industry" (AT 339), whereas Beckett's work radiates an "irresistible attraction" (AT 24), and he commands "an extremely keen and conscious understanding of technique" (AT 40). Beethoven's music goes beyond "some beautiful melody" or "some perfectly expressive music" and represents true hope (AT 398), and Schoenberg is an artist with "integrity," who goes beyond the subjective point (AT 44), just as Beckett's art discards "the illusion of meaning-constitutive subjectivity" (AT 45). Schoenberg's art is superior to many compositions that have imitated it (AT 65), he commands an "ingenious technique" (AT 206), his art is "of the highest calibre" (AT 212), in sum, he is one of the paradigmatic artists of this century (AT 363). The artists who display neoromantic tendencies, such as Hofmannsthal, George, Wilde, and Chopin, are described as impotent, as empty and without content, as relying on superficial material, and as hiding behind mere effects, whereas Schoenberg, Beethoven, and Beckett command the true dialectic technique of artistic form that emerges from content and thereby undermines its own apparent unity. We would like to suggest that a series of unreconstructed stereotypes of genderization have influenced the language Adorno uses in order to set up his schema of successful dialectical modern artworks and bad art that, nonetheless, pretends to be called and treated as art.

For Horkheimer and Adorno, female sexuality, the female body and, with it, the entire realm of the feminine are the location of societal repression in patriarchal culture. They mimetically reconstruct (with critical intention, of course) the discourse of that culture in their scenarios from *Dialectic of Enlightenment.* We saw how some feminist critics reacted quite ambiguously to this text, praising, on the one hand, its clairvoyance with regard to the mechanisms of projection in patriarchal culture and criticizing, on the other, the authors' unreflected repetition of stereotyping in reconstructing the female mythological figures in the *Odyssey*. It is our contention that this mimetic adoption of patriarchal stereotypes also has some bearing on the language of Adorno's aesthetic judgments in his later work. Our reconstruction of female and male bodies in *Aesthetic Theory* has led us to conclude that in Adorno's account the female body as the initial sensuous moment in art is inadvertently repressed during art's emancipation from its material (as opposed to cuisine and pornography), and that Adorno fails to problematize this repression. The opposition between the sexes is instead replaced by a dual concept of artistic subjects in an aesthetic realm modeled after the male sexual experience. Adorno's critique of the affirmative moment in classicism, we suggest, can be held against his own text: "By re-enacting this scenario of repression in the realm of imagination, art turns into a triumphal song (with that it sublimates the circus just as it does with its moment of silliness [with sex]). Art thus stands opposed to the idea of redeeming repressed nature" (AT 230).

Notes

1. Theodor W. Adorno, *Aesthetic Theory*, ed. Gretel Adorno and Rolf Tiedemann, trans. C. Lenhardt (London: Routledge & Kegan Paul, 1984), p. 85; hereafter cited as AT.

2. See Jessica Benjamin, "Authority and the Family: A World without Fathers," *New German Critique* 13 (1978): 35ff.; "The End of Internalization: Adorno's Social Psychology," *Telos* 32 (1977): 42–64.

3. See, for example, Irmgard Schultz, "Julie & Juliette und die Nachtseite der Geschichte Europas: Naturwissen, Aufklärung und pathetische Projektion in der 'Dialektik der Aufklärung' von Adorno und Horkheimer," *Zwielicht der Vernunft: Die Dialektik der Aufklärung aus der Sicht der Frauen*, ed. Christine Kulke and Elvira Scheich (Pfaffenweiler, Germany: Centaurus, 1992), pp. 30ff.

4. Max Horkheimer and Theodor W. Adorno, *Dialectic of Enlightenment*, trans. John Cumming (New York: Seabury Press, 1972), p. 3; hereafter cited as DE.

5. Schultz, "Julie & Juliette und die Nachtseite der Geschichte Europas," p. 33.

6. See in this context the work of feminist political scientist Christine Kulke, "Die Kritik der instrumentellen Rationalität—ein männlicher Mythos," in *Die Aktualität der "Dialektik der Aufklärung". Zwischen Moderne und Postmoderne*, ed. Harry Kunneman and Hent de Vries (Frankfurt, New York: Campus, 1989), p. 133, as well as her essay

Sabine Wilke and Heidi Schlipphacke

"Die Politik instrumenteller Rationalität und die instrumentelle Rationalität von Politik—Eine Dialektik des Geschlechterverhältnisses?" in *Denken der Geschlechterdifferenz: Neue Fragen und Perspektiven der feministischen Philosophie*, ed. Herta Nagl-Docekal and Herlinde Pauer-Studer (Vienna: Wiener Frauenverlag, 1990), p. 82.

7. Irmgard Schultz has argued that Horkheimer and Adorno critically point to this mechanism of projection as a necessary component of human sensuality in patriarchal society; see her "Julie & Juliette und die Nachtseite der Geschichte Europas," p. 37.

8. Andrew Hewitt, "A Feminine Dialectic of Enlightenment? Horkheimer and Adorno Revisited," *New German Critique* 56 (1992): 147.

9. Hewitt, "A Feminine Dialectic of Enlightenment?" p. 147.

10. See Hewitt, "A Feminine Dialectic of Enlightenment?" pp. 161ff.

11. Hewitt, "A Feminine Dialectic of Enlightenment?" p. 170.

12. See here also the critique of Harry Kunnemann and Hent de Vries in the introduction to their collection of essays, *Die Aktualität der "Dialektik der Aufklärung,"* p. 42.

13. See Kulke, "Die Politik instrumenteller Rationalität und die instrumentelle Rationalität von Politik," p. 83.

14. See Kulke, "Die Kritik der instrumentellen Rationalität—ein männlicher Mythos," p. 142. Another line of critique focuses on Horkheimer's association between woman and mother in his writings from the thirties. See, for example, Mechtild Rumpf, *Spuren des Mütterlichen: Die widersprüchliche Bedeutung der Mutterrolle für die männliche Identitätsbildung in kritischer Theorie und feministischer Wissenschaft* (Frankfurt and Hannover: Materialis, 1989), pp. 18ff.

15. See also Cornelia Giese, *Gleichheit und Differenz: Vom dualistischen Denken zur polaren Weltsicht* (Munich: Frauenoffensive, 1989), pp. 66ff.

16. Regina Becker-Schmidt, "Identitätslogik und Gewalt: Zum Verhältnis von Kritischer Theorie und Feminismus," *Beiträge zur feministischen Theorie und Praxis* 12 (1989): 52.

17. Another aspect that would support a gendered reading of *Dialectic of Enlightenment* is the intrinsic nostalgia for a traditional male authority figure, which can be detected in Horkheimer's writings from this period and the chapters on the culture industry and anti-Semitism.

18. Jazz is already named as the emasculating music of late capitalism, in the culture industry chapter of *Dialectic of Enlightenment:* "Life in the late capitalist era is a constant initiation rite. Everyone must show that he wholly identifies himself with the power which is belaboring him. This occurs in the principle of jazz syncopation, which simultaneously derides stumbling and makes it a rule. The eunuchlike voice of the crooner on the radio, the heiress's smooth suitor, who falls into the swimming pool in his dinner jacket, are models for those who must become whatever the system wants" (153).

19. Theodor W. Adorno, *Prisms* (c. 1967), trans. Samuel and Shierry Weber (Cambridge, Mass.: MIT Press, 1981), p. 129; hereafter cited as P.

12

The Philosophy of Dissonance:
Adorno and Schoenberg

Robert Hullot-Kentor

Theodor Adorno and Arnold Schoenberg are two of the most uncompromising figures of this century. Photographs of them in old
age witness the clenched stubbornness of an African fetish reappear-
ing in their faces. The intensity of this spirit shaped and penetrated
every detail of their work. In his *Theory of Harmony,* for example, it
compelled Schoenberg the educator to disclaim the book's massive
pedagogical effort. After four hundred pages of careful and sometimes bombastic instruction, reasons for the book are increasingly
met by counterreasons, until the two sides come to grips in a locked
tangle. At one point, Schoenberg goes so far as to reject craft—the
entire content of the book—as a standard of composition. Authentic
technique is, on the contrary, he says, occult knowledge. He confronts himself with the challenge that this hermetic ideal poses to
what he has written: "Someone will ask why I am writing a textbook
of harmony, if I wish technique to be occult knowledge. I could answer: people want to study, to learn, and I want to teach."[1] Having
driven himself into a cul de sac of his own manufacture, the only escape route he permits himself to imagine is further self-resistance.[2]

This is an eccentric process, but the passage tips the hand on Schoenberg's occult knowledge, which he clearly did not consider unteach-
able. In fact he constantly demonstrated his basic sorcery in
composition class. Once, for instance, having demolished, phrase by
phrase, the blackboard exercise of the precocious teenage composer
Dike Newlin, he turned to the other students to explain the logic of his

Arnold Schoenberg [From the conference brochure for "Constructive Dissonance," see note 2, p. 318.]

coup de grâce, as he wiped out a final measure of eighth notes: Class "do you know why I do not let her use eighth notes?...Why, because she *wants* to use them!"[3] Schoenberg thought this funny, and it is. But the technique he is recommending—which permits giving only under the auspices of taking away and requires that one hand always be ready to undo the work of the other—is keyed to the most rapacious demands of twentieth-century composition. For it is not possible to do justice to the experience of this century without knowing how, in the same instant, to scream and put one's hand over one's mouth. In "A Survivor from Warsaw," German soldiers, before dawn, throw open the sewer where Jews, asleep, are hiding. But even the first moments—the orders shouted, the searchlights—are hard to follow and describe. The narrator provides the only report of the event, which he relives as one of the haggard crowd as it is driven out of hiding and provoked into a stumbling fast march in the street. He does not know what is or is not dream as the soldiers wade into them and he is clubbed down. The chaos and shattering of his perceptions deprive the listener of any objective recourse. Listening becomes the realization that one's head has been grabbed from behind and forced under water. Everyone having been knocked to the ground, the sergeant—maybe to save bullets—orders their heads smashed. In the concussive instant that the rifle butt strikes the narrator's head, however, we do not, and could not possibly, hear a scream. The subjective form of the report prohibits the event being registered externally. Instead, the sound that must have occurred is documented only by a muffled, suddenly slack and hollow peacefulness that suspends the recurrent heart-spasming alarm motif that knits the work together. There is perhaps no other composition, no other artwork, in which fright and hope become comparably identical in the moment that they vanish. The power of the composition depends on this moment. The panicky inconsolableness of history ignites in this stifled, imploded instant, whereas any scream would have provided the rationalization that it might have been heard.

I

Schoenberg's intransigence is easily lost from sight in America, where the edifice of New Music—to estimate its cultural magnitude—would be diminutively tented by the League of Professional Bowling, itself one of the lesser sports. Yet Adorno's work is on this same horizon even more recondite than Schoenberg's, and as a person he was ultimately more self-protective and austere. Compared to the innumerable vignettes that circulate about Schoenberg, funny classroom stories do not seem to exist about Adorno. Likewise, where Schoenberg's letters have been a major source regarding all aspects of his life, Adorno saw to it that the bulk of his correspondence—if it is ever published at all—will not be read by many adults alive today, delaying the moment when, as he feared, it will be used biographically to dilute his work. He spoke by starting at the top of a full inhalation, which he followed down to the last oxygen molecule left in his lungs, and his written style perfected dozen-page paragraphs hardened to a gapless and sometimes glassy density, as if the slightest hesitancy for an inhalation or any break for a new paragraph would have irretrievably relinquished the chance of completing the thought. Every one of his stylistic peculiarities was defined by the effort to maintain a moment of critical, historical self-consciousness in opposition to mass culture. This is why his work currently draws increasing attention as a lightning rod of cultural resentment. For without flinching, he unmasked the substitute gratifications and betrayals of contemporary society. A population that knows perfectly well that it is the service sector of the culture industry will not soon forgive him for putting his finger on what people jockey for as they crowd in line for a new film: "people watch movies with their eyes closed and their mouths open";[4] or for revoking the sensed prerogatives of stardom—mass culture's universal bestowal—by showing that what scintillates in glitter is powerlessness: "he who is never permitted to conquer in life conquers in glamor."[5]

II

Adorno and Schoenberg are related more integrally than comparisons demonstrate. In the *Philosophy of Modern Music*, Adorno marshals the resources of the entire theodicean tradition of German idealism—the Kantian justification of empirical, practical, and aesthetic judgments, the Hegelian expansion of the transcendental deduction to comprehend the rightness of the universe—on behalf of the justification of an irreconcilable music. He shows that this isolated music had, just by the strength of its isolation, become a singular repository of critical historical experience. Adorno does not deduce this position. On the contrary, his thinking originates in this musical experience, and he put his life into its elucidation. What distinguishes Adorno's efforts in this from almost the whole grim genre of aesthetics is that, whereas it generally demands either systematic philosophers who are deaf and blind or effusive admirers of Beethoven's triumph, the *Philosophy of Modern Music* is a defense of Schoenberg's work that presents New Music's own philosophy; the study aims to carry out conceptually the historical reflection implicit in the music and to raise this reflection to the point of the music's self-criticism. Insofar as Schoenberg's music is a dissonant order, Adorno's work is fundamentally the philosophy of dissonance. Only because Adorno was constantly following the traces of his own sensorium through this music was he able to complete this Hegelian project.

III

The central thesis of Adorno's aesthetics is that art becomes the unconscious writing of history through its isolation from society. In the *Philosophy of Modern Music* Adorno details the immediate object of aversion from which modern art and Schoenberg's music withdrew. There he writes that just as abstract art was defensively motivated by its opposition to photography—the mechanical artwork—Schoenberg's music developed in "antithesis to the extension of the culture industry into music's own domain."[6] In that Adorno took the side of this music against the culture industry, it can be assumed that he would hardly have made himself more popular at a rock concert than at a conference, such as this one, on Schoenberg entitled "Constructive Dissonance." His Krausian trained ears would have recognized in this title the intention of providing sounds that literally dug a moat around themselves—music that will never be heard in any hotel elevator—with the requisite positive glow of popular culture. Just as the latter makes sure its monsters turn out cuddly, "Constructive Dissonance" puts a finger out to give a tickle under the chin: "See, those nasty sounds aren't so bad. You don't put them on at bedtime, but they want to help, too." Whatever this conference's intention to hear and think Schoenberg anew, in the *Philosophy of Modern Music*, Adorno writes that the conciliatory gesture—such as is unmistakably lodged in the phrase "Constructive Dissonance"—was the sign that led the historical retreat from Schoenberg's music: "Such conciliation to the listener, masking as humaneness, began to undermine the technical standards attained by progressive composition."[7]

Adorno's criticism would not have stopped at the title. The conference brochure itself documents the formula for the translation of modern art into mass culture: there in the center of a paste-up of famous people meeting famous people, Schoenberg with Kokoschka, a picture of Schoenberg playing table tennis, is a photo of the composer seated in front of a wall of his paintings (see p. 310). Whereas the effort of these well-known paintings is to break from the visible world and present a deposition of isolated subjectivity, the photograph, with its limited powers of focus, contrast, and construction patches over this content with a melodramatic, stereotypical image of Schoenberg's face, half in darkness, half in light. And however much the paintings themselves force their way into the present, the photograph embalms each moment with stasis as a dull sign of an irretrievable past.[8] This irretrievability is a fundamental source of its mass culture appeal, because the past that is shaped is anecdotal and sentimental. Every photograph is somehow equally old—even one snapped a second previously—and calls for the same identical tear to be shed on its behalf. An amnesiac's historiography is created: the need for continuity in time is fulfilled while assuring that the impulses of time remain at a neutral, unshifting distance. If popular music sings of sentimental journeys, the conference brochure promises a sentimental conference. And this promise is made good by the actual conference organization into three parts: contexts, interactions, and reception—which could be deduced from the advertisement. "Contexts and Interactions" are to provide a photograph of Schoenberg in the historicist "back then." This is followed, plausibly enough, by dredging for bodies, that is, with "reception," a concept that, however the phenomenologists doll it up, surfaces on the palate with such enthusiasm and legitimacy only because it derives from the sensorial order of radio and television.

IV

Glossed by mass culture's carefully managed populist eye, the continuous claim throughout Adorno's writings to emphatic musical experience—particularly that of Schoenberg's music—has often been grounds for shrugging off his social criticism as elitist. This is only secondarily because of mass culture's allergy to New Music. More important is that both New Music and Adorno are assumed to be representatives of the world of the symphony hall. Insofar as this is the perception, the rejection is not altogether unjustified. If music becomes important as the voice of the voiceless, its symphony hall performers, sponsors, and auditors occupy almost exclusively social positions that gain from the voiceless remaining so. Symphony hall is not shy about this class allegiance: with its playbill of aperitifs and perfumes; an audience of scions in swagger fashions; opera lovers coasting by like ocean liners wrapped in camel-hair overcoats; and a conductor who, whenever he circles from the orchestra to deliver his bows, reveals his aristocratic bearing to be that of a majordomo. Any doubts as to whom these performances are for is dispersed by the San Francisco Symphony, which each year offers subscribers a selection from the Mercedes Great Performers Series and the opportunity to attend BankAmerica Foundation preconcert talks. Popular music fans correctly recognize that they are not invited to these events. But the resentment felt blocks recognition of how much the two worlds have in common, from the sequined dresses to the fame of powerless dukes, kings, and princes, to the inevitably glossy, repetitive performances. Symphony hall and popular music are not the different substances their audiences are encouraged to believe them to be, but different layers of mass culture.

It is only because so-called classical music has been completely absorbed as one layer of popular culture that it is difficult to realize that Adorno took the side of emphatic music against symphony hall, where he found this music neutralized. He did not, however, consider this neutralization simply adventitious. On the contrary, through its beauty, emphatic music participates in its commercial neutralization, and Adorno wanted to show how the direction of music itself was toward overcoming this neutralization through its internal critique of beautiful semblance. Schoenberg was, in his opinion, the key figure in this transformation of music.

V

A recent San Francisco Symphony performance of Mahler's Sixth Symphony condenses these issues and makes a bridge to Adorno's analysis, in the *Philosophy of Modern Music,* of Schoenberg's achievement.

At a BankAmerica preconcert talk, in fall 1991, the contemporary composer Christopher Rouse—who is a pop music aficionado—introduced Mahler's Sixth Symphony, a work, as Rouse mentioned, of special importance to Schoenberg's group. Rouse's introduction is of interest for what is characteristic in it, much of it owed directly to Mahler's own programmatic comments. Only a condensed sentence of fragments from his introduction, taken up in medias res, needs paraphrasing to bring this familiar genre of music appreciation to mind: In the theme of the third movement, Rouse explained, Mahler announces his towering love for Alma. And in the finale, the hammer blow of fate sounds for the third and last time, presaging the final disaster that would befall the composer the following year.[9] Just as moviegoers watch their stars illustrated by the role performed, this introduction to the Sixth Symphony obeys the constitutive limits of mass culture—simulation and portrayal—and converts the music into a snapshot of the great man's life. It sets the music as an event back behind the white border of that never-never land where fame keeps its trophies.

The music itself, however, is hardly content with the role of portraying Mahler's life. And it is possible that members of the audience sensed something of this as they craned their heads above their seats to see these blows of fate struck. In Mahler's Sixth, these sounds are performed not by the plausible kettle drums but by a sledgehammer. This is, of course, not one of the spiritualized instruments of the symphony orchestra, as the percussionist makes obvious by the struggle to fit the blow of a fifteen-pound hammerhead to the beat. These three blows, however programmatically conceived as three blows of fate, go beyond the programmatic. The hammer blow of fate becomes fate, the hammer blow; no longer the portrayal of fate but the leveling impact itself. And whatever the force delivered to the subjectivity that stirs in the music, this extra-aesthetic sledgehammer delivers a blow to the fictional order of music altogether. If the various introductions of sections of the orchestra seem to occur without reference to actual time, the three hammer blows break through the autonomous temporality of music each with the intention of notching the clock face itself.

VI

This act, in the decades surrounding the symphony's composition, was only one of many similar events that transformed art into modern art. In drama, it has common origins with the untempered shock dealt by August Strindberg's chamber plays; it has affinities with Georges Braque's and Pablo Picasso's *tableaux choses,* with Isadora Duncan's effort directly to objectify the inward, and with Wassily Kandinsky's rejection of illusionistic space. The sculptor and dramatist Ernst Barlach formulated the Platonic antimimetic, antiart direction of modern art: "I do not represent what I for my part see, or how I see it from here or there, but what *is,* the real and the truthful. . . . The world is already there, it would be senseless just to repeat it."[10] Throughout these decades, art moved fundamentally against fiction, against portraying or representing the world, and toward essence.

Adorno shows in his major study of Schoenberg that he carried out this project in the medium of music, extending the anti-illusion intention of Mahler's hammer blows to the total musical structure. This was a radical transformation of musical expression. Whereas music since the seventeenth century had simulated subjectivity and dramatized passions, producing images of expression, Schoenberg's break from tonality achieved a depositional expression, a docket of the historical unconscious that registered impulses of isolation, shock, and collapse.

This depositional capacity depended in the first place on the decline of tonality and the resulting possibility of a free manipulation of the musical material. But, second, for expression to be expression, it must be necessary; what occurs must have the quality of needing to be as it is. And what Schoenberg discovered—according to Adorno—was that the impulses sedimented in the material could be bindingly organized according to a principle of contrast. Dissonance, the bearer of historical suffering, would be the rational order binding together melody and harmony. Harmonic simultaneity would be that of independent contrasting voices. As a result, in Adorno's words, "the subjective drive and the longing for self-proclamation without illusion, became the technical instrument of the objective work."[11] This transformed musical time: whereas the constitutive repetition of traditional forms makes music indifferent to time and susceptible to the background function required of popular music, in Schoenberg's music, the repetition of the *Grundgestalt*—the basic shape—must become new. It answers the dialectical question of how the old can become new at the same time that the music refuses to hold its even distance from the listener. Rather, in the words of Adorno's Kafka description, it races toward the listener like a freight train. Schoenberg emancipated dissonance, but, more important, he made dissonance necessary.

Adorno's understanding of the significance of this technique needs to be understood in the full context of the *Dialectic of Enlightenment*, the companion text to, and written in part contemporaneously with, the *Philosophy of Modern Music*. Whereas, extra-aesthetically, subjectivity translates phenomena into examples of a subordinating concept and thereby consumes the potential of expression, in Schoenberg's music, subjectivity organizes the nonidentity of the universal and the particular; it is an organization that, in its dissonance, constantly surpasses its own organization. The ideal that inheres in this music is a transformed subjectivity that, rather than dominating its object, gives it binding expression. Necessity in this case really is—for once—freedom in that inseparable from the bindingness of this music's historical deposition is the sounding implication that what has transpired historically did not need to have happened, and does not need to continue.

Notes

1. Arnold Schoenberg, *Theory of Harmony*, trans. Roy E. Carter (Berkeley: University of California Press, 1983), p. 415.

2. This paper was first presented at a conference at the Arnold Schoenberg Institute, University of Southern California, in honor of Leonard Stein, entitled "Constructive

Dissonance: Arnold Schoenberg and Transformations of Twentieth-Century Culture," November 16, 1991.

3. Dika Newlin, *Schoenberg Remembered* (New York: Pendragon Press, 1980), p. 30.

4. Theodor W. Adorno, *Minima Moralia,* trans. E. F. N. Jephcott (London: NLB, 1974), p. 164.

5. Theodor W. Adorno, "On Popular Music," in *Zeitschrift für Sozialforschung* 9 (1941): 28.

6. Theodor W. Adorno, *Philosophy of Modern Music,* trans. Anne Mitchell and Wesley Blomster (New York: Seabury Press, 1973), p. 5. "Philosohy of Modern Music" is a mistranslation of the German title; a better translation would be "Philosophy of New Music."

7. Ibid., p. 6.

8. This passage is indebted throughout to Richard Hennessy's brilliant paper "What's All This about Photography," *Artforum* (May 1979): 22–25.

9. These comments are reported from the preconcert talk by Christopher Rouse to the San Francisco Symphony's performance of Mahler's Symphony No. 6 in A Minor, October 11, 1991.

10. In *Theorie des Expressionismus,* ed. Otto F. Best (Stuttgart: Reklam, 1971), p. 86.

11. Adorno, *Philosophy of Modern Music,* p. 162.

Select Bibliography

The works listed below provide an extensive but selective survey of the literature in English and in German. They are an updated version of the first two sections of the bibliography in Lambert Zuidervaart, *Adorno's Aesthetic Theory* (pp. 351–80). In addition to the bibliographic sources mentioned on p. 351 of Zuidervaart's book, readers may wish to consult two lists compiled by Joan Nordquist: *Theodor Adorno: A Bibliography;* and *Theodor Adorno, (2): A Bibliography* (Santa Cruz, Calif.: Reference and Research Services, 1988 and 1994, respectively). The editors thank Matt Beaverson for his assistance in compiling this updated bibliography.

1 Theodor W. Adorno

Section 1.1 lists Adorno's books in the order of their abbreviations, which are derived from the German titles. The list includes works coauthored by Adorno, but it does not contain all of his books. The titles of English translations are given directly after their German originals. Section 1.2 contains complete information on these translations, presenting them in the order of the abbreviations from section 1.1. Books listed without abbreviations were originally published in English. Section 1.3 contains most of Adorno's articles in English, both articles originally published in English and articles translated into English. The title of each translated article is followed by the date of the German original.

1.1 Adorno's Books in German

GS   *Gesammelte Schriften*. 20 vols. Edited by Rolf Tiedemann. Volumes 5, 7, and 13 were coedited by Gretel Adorno. Volume 9 was coedited by Susan Buck-Morss. Frankfurt: Suhrkamp, 1970–86.

NS   *Nachgelassene Schriften*. Approximately thirty volumes are planned as "Editions of the Theodor W. Adorno Archive." Frankfurt: Suhrkamp, 1993–.

AKB   *Theodor W. Adorno und Ernst Krenek: Briefwechsel.* Edited by Wolfgang Rogge. Frankfurt: Suhrkamp, 1974.

Select Bibliography

AT *Ästhetische Theorie* (1970). GS 7. 2d ed. 1972. *Aesthetic Theory* (1984/1996 [forthcoming]).

B   *Berg: Der Meister des kleinsten Übergangs* (1968). GS 13 (1971): 321–494. *Alban Berg: Master of the Smallest Link* (1991).

BPM *Beethoven: Philosophie der Musik.* Fragments and texts. Edited by Rolf Tiedemann. NS, div. I, vol. 1. 1993.

Bw *Briefwechsel 1928–1940.* Theodor W. Adorno/Walter Benjamin. Edited by Henri Lonitz. Frankfurt: Suhrkamp, 1994.

D   *Dissonanzen. Musik in der verwalteten Welt* (1956, 1958, 1963, 1969). GS 14 (1973): 7–167.

DA Horkheimer, Max, and Theodor W. Adorno. *Dialektik der Aufklärung. Philosophische Fragmente* (1947, 1969). GS 3. 1981. *Dialectic of Enlightenment* (1972).

E   *Eingriffe. Neun kritische Modelle* (1963). GS 10.2 (1977): 455–594. In *Interventions and Catchwords,* forthcoming.

EM *Erziehung zur Mündigkeit. Vorträge und Gespräche mit Hellmut Becker, 1959–1969.* Edited by Gerd Kadelbach. Frankfurt: Suhrkamp, 1970.

EMS *Einleitung in die Musiksoziologie. Zwölf theoretische Vorlesungen* (1962, 1968). GS 14 (1973): 169–433. *Introduction to the Sociology of Music* (1976).

H   *Drei Studien zu Hegel* (1963). GS 5 (1970): 247–381. *Hegel: Three Studies* (1993).

I   *Impromptus. Zweite Folge neu gedruckter musikalischer Aufsätze* (1968). GS 17 (1982): 163–344.

JE *Jargon der Eigentlichkeit. Zur deutschen Ideologie* (1964). GS 6 (1973): 413–526. *The Jargon of Authenticity* (1973).

K   *Klangfiguren. Musikalische Schriften 1* (1959). GS 16 (1978): 7–248.

KKA *Kierkegaard. Konstruktion des Ästhetischen* (1933, 1962, 1966). GS 2. 1979. *Kierkegaard: Construction of the Aesthetic* (1989).

M   *Mahler. Eine musikalische Physiognomik* (1960). GS 13 (1971): 149–319. *Mahler: A Musical Physiognomy* (1988).

ME *Zur Metakritik der Erkenntnistheorie. Studien über Husserl und die phänomenologischen Antinomien* (1956). GS 5 (1970): 7–245. *Against Epistemology: A Metacritique* (1982, 1983).

MM *Minima Moralia. Reflexionen aus dem beschädigten Leben* (1951, 1962). GS 4. 1980. *Minima Moralia: Reflections from Damaged Life* (1974).

Mm *Moments musicaux. Neu gedruckte Aufsätze 1928–1962* (1964). GS 17 (1982): 7–161.

ND *Negative Dialektik* (1966, 1967). GS 6 (1973): 7–412. *Negative Dialectics* (1973).

NL *Noten zur Literatur 1* (1958), 2 (1961), 3 (1965), 4 (1974). GS 11. 1974.

OL *Ohne Leitbild. Parva Aesthetica* (1967, 1968). GS 10.1 (1977): 289–453.

P   *Prismen. Kulturkritik und Gesellschaft* (1955, 1963, 1969). GS 10.1 (1977): 9–287. *Prisms* (1967).

Select Bibliography

PM   *Philosophie der neuen Musik* (1949, 1958, 1966, 1972). GS 12. 1975. *Philosophy of Modern Music* (1973).

PS   Adorno, Theodor W., et al. *Der Positivismusstreit in der deutschen Soziologie.* Neuwied, Berlin: Luchterhand, 1969. (Adorno's contributions are reprinted in GS 8.) *The Positivist Dispute in German Sociology* (1976).

PT   *Philosophische Terminologie. Zur Einleitung.* Edited by Rudolf zur Lippe from lectures given in 1962–1963. 2 vols. Frankfurt: Suhrkamp, 1973, 1974.

Q   *Quasi una fantasia. Musikalische Schriften II* (1963). GS 16 (1978): 249–540.

S   *Stichworte. Kritische Modelle 2* (1969). GS 10.2 (1977): 595–782. In *Interventions and Catchwords,* forthcoming.

SE   Institut für Sozialforschung. *Soziologische Exkurse. Nach Vorträgen und Diskussionen.* Frankfurt: Europäische Verlagsanstalt, 1956. *Aspects of Sociology* (1972).

SII   Horkheimer, Max, and Theodor W. Adorno. *Sociologica II. Reden und Vorträge.* Frankfurt: Europäische Verlagsanstalt, 1962. (Adorno's contributions are reprinted in GS 8.)

VA   *Vorlesungen zur Ästhetik 1967–68.* Zurich: H. Mayer Nachfolger, 1973.

VW   *Versuch über Wagner* (1952). GS 13 (1971): 7–148. *In Search of Wagner* (1981).

WB   *Über Walter Benjamin.* Edited, with notes, by Rolf Tiedemann. Frankfurt: Suhrkamp, 1970.

WBB   *Walter Benjamin: Briefe.* 2 vols. Edited by Gershom Scholem and Theodor W. Adorno. C. 1966. Frankfurt: Suhrkamp, 1978.

1.2   Adorno's Books in English

AT   *Aesthetic Theory.* Translated by C. Lenhardt. London: Routledge & Kegan Paul, 1984. *Aesthetic Theory.* Translated, edited, and with an introduction by Robert Hullot-Kentor. Minneapolis: University of Minnesota Press, 1996 (forthcoming).

      The Authoritarian Personality. T. W. Adorno, Else Frenkel-Brunswik, Daniel J. Levinson, and R. Nevitt Sanford, in collaboration with Betty Aron, Maria Hertz Levinson, and William Morrow. *Studies in Prejudice.* Edited by Max Horkheimer and Samuel H. Flowerman. Vol. 1. New York: Harper & Brothers, 1950. Chapters 1, 7, 16, 17, 18, and 19 appear in GS 9.1 (1975): 143–509 under the title *Studies in the Authoritarian Personality.*

B   *Alban Berg: Master of the Smallest Link.* Translated with introduction and annotation by Juliane Brand and Christopher Hailey. New York: Cambridge University Press, 1991.

      Composing for the Films. With Hanns Eisler. New York: Oxford University Press, 1947. The book appeared under only Eisler's name until Adorno published a German version in 1969 titled *Komposition für den Film.* This version and an account of the manuscript's history appear in GS 15 (1976): 7–155.

The Culture Industry: Selected Essays on Mass Culture. Edited with an introduction by J. M. Bernstein. London: Routledge, 1991.

DA *Dialectic of Enlightenment.* Translated by John Cumming. New York: Seabury Press, 1972.

E In *Interventions and Catchwords.* Edited, translated, and with an introduction by Henry W. Pickford. New York: Columbia University Press, forthcoming.

EMS *Introduction to the Sociology of Music.* Translated by E. B. Ashton. New York: Seabury Press, 1976.

H *Hegel: Three Studies.* Translated by Shierry Weber Nicholsen. With an introduction by Shierry Weber Nicholsen and Jeremy J. Shapiro. Cambridge, Mass.: MIT Press, 1993.

JE *The Jargon of Authenticity.* Translated by Knut Tarnowski and Frederic Will. London: Routledge & Kegan Paul, 1973.

KKA *Kierkegaard: Construction of the Aesthetic.* Translated, edited, and with a foreword by Robert Hullot-Kentor. Minneapolis: University of Minnesota Press, 1989.

M *Mahler: A Musical Physiognomy.* Translated by Edmund Jephcott. Chicago: University of Chicago Press, 1988.

ME *Against Epistemology: A Metacritique; Studies in Husserl and the Phenomenological Antinomies.* Translated by Willis Domingo. Oxford: Basil Blackwell, 1982; Cambridge, Mass.: MIT Press, 1983.

MM *Minima Moralia: Reflections from Damaged Life.* Translated by E. F. N. Jephcott. London: NLB, 1974.

ND *Negative Dialectics.* Translated by E. B. Ashton. New York: Seabury Press, 1973.

NL *Notes to Literature.* 2 vols. Translated by Shierry Weber Nicholsen. New York: Columbia University Press, 1991, 1992.

P *Prisms.* Translated by Samuel Weber and Shierry Weber. London: Neville Spearman, 1967; Cambridge, Mass.: MIT Press, 1981.

PM *Philosophy of Modern Music.* Translated by Anne G. Mitchell and Wesley V. Blomster. New York: Seabury Press, 1973.

PS *The Positivist Dispute in German Sociology.* Theodor W. Adorno, et al. Translated by Glyn Adey and David Frisby. London: Heinemann, 1976.

Q *Quasi una fantasia: Essays on Modern Music.* Translated by Rodney Livingstone. New York: Verso, 1992.

The Stars Down to Earth and Other Essays on the Irrational in Culture. Edited with an introduction by Stephen Crook. New York: Routledge, 1994.

S In *Interventions and Catchwords.* Edited, translated, and with an introduction by Henry W. Pickford. New York: Columbia University Press, forthcoming.

SE *Aspects of Sociology.* The Frankfurt Institute for Social Research. Translated by John Viertel. Boston: Beacon Press, 1972.

VW *In Search of Wagner.* Translated by Rodney Livingstone. London: NLB, 1981.

WBB *The Correspondence of Walter Benjamin, 1910–1940.* Edited and annotated by Gershom Scholem and Theodor W. Adorno. Translated by Manfred R. Jacobson and Evelyn M. Jacobson. Chicago: University of Chicago Press, 1994.

1.3   Adorno's Articles in English

"The Actuality of Philosophy" (1931). *Telos,* no. 31 (spring 1977): 120–33.

"The Aging of the New Music" (1955). *Telos,* no. 77 (fall 1988): 95–116.

"Alienated Masterpiece: The *Missa Solemnis*" (1959). *Telos,* no. 28 (summer 1976): 113–24.

"Analytical Study of the NBC Music Appreciation Hour." *Musical Quarterly* 78 (summer 1994): 325–77. (Written between 1938 and 1941.)

"Anti-Semitism and Fascist Propaganda." With Leo Löwenthal and Paul Massing. *Anti-Semitism: A Social Disease,* pp. 125–37. Edited by Ernst Simmel. New York: International Universities, 1946. Reprinted in GS 8: 397–407. Reprinted in Adorno, *The Stars Down to Earth,* pp. 162–71.

"Bibliographical Musings" (1965). *Grand Street* 10 (1991) 3: 135–48.

"Bloch's Traces: The Philosophy of Kitsch" (1960). *New Left Review,* no. 121 (May–June 1980): 49–62.

"Bourgeois Opera" (1959). *Opera through Other Eyes,* pp. 25–43. Edited by David J. Levin. Stanford: Stanford University Press, 1993.

"Commitment" (1962). *New Left Review,* nos. 87–88 (November–December 1974): 75–90. Reprinted in *Aesthetics and Politics,* pp. 177–95; and in *The Essential Frankfurt School Reader,* pp. 300–18.

"Contemporary German Sociology" (1959). *Transactions of the Fourth World Congress of Sociology,* vol. 1, pp. 33–56. London: International Sociological Association, 1959.

"Culture and Administration" (1960). *Telos,* no. 37 (fall 1978): 93–111. Reprinted in Adorno, *The Culture Industry,* pp. 93–113.

"Culture Industry Reconsidered" (1963). *New German Critique,* no. 6 (fall 1975): 12–19. Reprinted in *Critical Theory and Society,* pp. 128–35. Also in Adorno, *The Culture Industry,* pp. 85–92.

"The Curves of the Needle" (1928). *October,* no. 55 (winter 1990): 49–55.

"Education for Autonomy" (1969/1970). With Hellmut Becker. *Telos,* no. 56 (summer 1983): 103–10.

"The Essay as Form" (1958). *New German Critique,* no. 32 (spring–summer 1984): 151–71.

"The Form of the Phonograph Record" (1934). *October,* no. 55 (winter 1990): 56–61.

"Freudian Theory and the Pattern of Fascist Propaganda." In *Psychoanalysis and the Social Sciences,* vol. 3, pp. 279–300. Edited by G. Róheim. New York: International Universities Press, 1951. Reprinted in GS 8: 408–33. Also in *Critical Theory: The Essential Readings,* pp. 84–102; and in Adorno, *The Culture Industry,* pp. 114–35.

"Functionalism Today" (1966). *Oppositions,* no. 17 (summer 1979): 31–41.

"Goldmann and Adorno: To Describe, Understand and Explain" (1968). In Lucien Goldmann, *Cultural Creation in Modern Society* (1971), pp. 129–45. Translated by Bart Grahl. Introduction by William Mayrl. Oxford: Basil Blackwell, 1976.

"How to Look at Television." *Quarterly of Film, Radio and Television* 8 (spring 1954): 213–35. Reprinted as "Television and the Patterns of Mass Culture," in *Mass Culture: The Popular Arts in America,* pp. 474–87. Edited by Bernard Rosenberg and David Manning White. Glencoe, Ill.: Free Press, 1957. Also in *Critical Theory: The Essential Readings,* pp. 69–83; and in Adorno, *The Culture Industry,* pp. 136–53.

"Husserl and the Problem of Idealism" (1940). *The Journal of Philosophy* 37 (1940): 5–18.

"The Idea of Natural History" (1932/1973). *Telos,* no. 60 (summer 1984): 111–24.

Introduction (1969) to *The Positivist Dispute in German Sociology,* pp. 1–67.

"Is Marx Obsolete?" (1968). *Diogenes,* no. 64 (winter 1968): 1–16. The German title is "Spätkapitalismus oder Industriegesellschaft," now in GS 8: 354–70.

"Jazz" (1946). In *Encyclopedia of the Arts,* pp. 511–13. Edited by Dagobert D. Runes and Harry G. Schrickel. New York: Philosophical Library, 1946.

"Late Style in Beethoven" (1937). *Raritan* 13 (summer 1993): 102–7.

"Letters to Walter Benjamin" (1930s). *New Left Review,* no. 81 (September–October 1973): 46–80. See also *Aesthetics and Politics,* pp. 110–33.

"Looking Back on Surrealism" (1956). In *The Idea of the Modern in Literature and the Arts,* pp. 220–24. Edited by Irving Howe. New York: Horizon Press, 1967.

"Lyric Poetry and Society" (1951). *Telos,* no. 20 (summer 1974): 56–71. Reprinted in *Critical Theory and Society,* pp. 155–71.

"Messages in a Bottle" (1951). *New Left Review,* no. 200 (July 1993): 5–14.

"Metacritique of Epistemology." *Telos,* no. 38 (winter 1978–1979): 77–103. Originally published as "Einleitung" in ME, 1956.

"Modern Music Is Growing Old" (1955). *The Score,* no. 18 (December 1956): 18–29. (For a better translation, see "The Aging of the New Music," listed above.)

"Music and Technique" (1958). *Telos,* no. 32 (summer 1977): 79–94.

"Music and the New Music: In Memory of Peter Suhrkamp" (1960). *Telos*, no. 43 (spring 1980): 124–38. New translation in Adorno, *Quasi una fantasia*, pp. 249–68.

"Music, Language, and Composition" (1956). *Musical Quarterly* 77 (fall 1993): 401–14.

"New Music and the Public: Some Problems of Interpretation" (1957). In *Twentieth-Century Music*, pp. 63–74. Edited by Rollo H. Myers. Rev. and enl. ed. London: Calder and Boyors, 1968.

"Odysseus or Myth and Enlightenment." *New German Critique*, no. 56 (spring–summer 1992): 109–41. (New translation from *Dialektik der Aufklärung*, GS 3: 61–99.)

"Of Barricades and Ivory Towers: An Interview with T. W. Adorno." *Encounter* 33 (September 1969) 3: 63–69.

"On Jazz" (1937). *Discourse* 12 (fall–winter 1989–1990): 36–69.

"On Kierkegaard's Doctrine of Love." *Studies in Philosophy and Social Science* 8 (1939–1940): 413–29.

"On Popular Music." With the assistance of George Simpson. *Studies in Philosophy and Social Science* 9 (1941): 17–48.

"On Some Relationships between Music and Painting" (1965). *Musical Quarterly* 79 (spring 1995): 66–79.

"On the Fetish-Character in Music and the Regression of Listening" (1938/1956). In *The Essential Frankfurt School Reader*, pp. 270–99. Reprinted in Adorno, *The Culture Industry*, pp. 26–52.

"On the Historical Adequacy of Consciousness" (1965). With Peter von Haselberg. *Telos*, no. 56 (summer 1983): 97–103.

"On the Logic of the Social Sciences" (1962). In *The Positivist Dispute in German Sociology*, pp. 105–22.

"On the Question: 'What Is German?'" (1965). *New German Critique*, no. 36 (fall 1985): 121–31.

"On the Score of Parsifal" (1956). *Music and Letters* 76 (August 1995): 384–97.

"On the Social Situation of Music" (1932). *Telos*, no. 35 (spring 1978): 128–64. Translation of "Zur gesellschaftlichen Lage der Musik." *Zeitschrift für Sozialforschung* 1 (1932): 104–24, 356–78.

"On Tradition" (1966). *Telos*, no. 94 (winter 1993): 75–81.

"Opera and the Long-Playing Record" (1969). *October*, no. 55 (winter 1990): 62–66.

"Perennial Fashion—Jazz" (1953). In *Prisms*, pp. 119–32. Reprinted in *Critical Theory and Society*, pp. 199–209.

"Progress" (1964). *The Philosophical Forum* 15 (fall–winter 1983–1984): 55–70. New translation in *Interventions and Catchwords*, forthcoming.

"The Psychological Technique of Martin Luther Thomas' Radio Addresses" (1943), in GS 9.1 (1975): 7–141.

"Punctuation Marks" (1956). *Antioch Review* 48 (summer 1990): 300–305.

"The Radio Symphony: An Experiment in Theory." In *Radio Research 1941*, pp. 110–39. Edited by Paul F. Lazarsfeld and Frank N. Stanton. New York: Duell, Sloan and Pearce, 1941.

"Reconciliation under Duress" (1958). In *Aesthetics and Politics*, pp. 151–76.

"Resignation" (1969). *Telos*, no. 35 (spring 1978): 165–68. Reprinted in Adorno, *The Culture Industry*, pp. 171–75.

Review of Jean Wahl, *Études Kierkegaardiennes*; Walter Lowrie, *Kierkegaard*; and *The Journals of Soren Kierkegaard*. In *Studies in Philosophy and Social Science* 8 (1939): 232–35.

Review of Wilder Hobson, *American Jazz Music*; and Winthrop Sargeant, *Jazz Hot and Hybrid*. With the assistance of Eunice Cooper. *Studies in Philosophy and Social Science* 9 (1941): 167–78.

"Richard Strauss at Sixty" (1924). In *Richard Strauss and His World*, pp. 406–15. Edited by Bryan Gilliam. Princeton, N.J.: Princeton University Press, 1992.

"Scientific Experiences of a European Scholar in America." In *The Intellectual Migration: Europe and America, 1930–1960*, pp. 338–70. Edited by Donald Fleming and Bernard Bailyn. Cambridge, Mass.: Belknap Press, Harvard University Press, 1968, 1969).

"A Social Critique of Radio Music." *Kenyon Review* 7 (spring 1945) 2: 208–17.

"Society" (1966). *Salmagundi*, nos. 10–11 (fall 1969–winter 1970): 144–53. Reprinted in *The Legacy of the German Refugee Intellectuals*, pp. 144–53. Edited by Robert Boyers. New York: Schocken Books, 1969. Also in *Critical Theory and Society*, pp. 267–75; and in *Critical Theory: The Essential Readings*, pp. 61–68.

"Sociology and Empirical Research" (1957). In *The Positivist Dispute in German Sociology*, pp. 68–86. An excerpt under the same title is contained in *Critical Sociology: Selected Readings*, pp. 237–57. Edited by Paul Connerton. Harmondsworth, Middlesex: Penguin Books, 1976.

"Sociology and Psychology" (1955). *New Left Review*, no. 46 (November–December 1967): 63–80; no. 47 (January–February 1968): 79–97.

"The Sociology of Knowledge and Its Consciousness" (1937/1953). In *The Essential Frankfurt School Reader*, pp. 452–65.

"Spengler Today." *Studies in Philosophy and Social Science* 9 (1941): 305–25.

"The Stars Down to Earth." *Jahrbuch für Amerikastudien*. Vol. 2, pp. 19–88. Heidelberg: Carl Winter, 1957. Reprinted in GS 9.2: 7–120. An abbreviated German version, published in 1962 as "Aberglaube aus zweiter Hand," is reprinted in GS 8: 147–76. See also "The Stars Down to Earth: The Los Angeles Times Astrology Column," *Telos*, no. 19 (spring 1974): 13–90; reprinted in Adorno, *The Stars Down to Earth*, pp. 34–127.

"'Static' and 'Dynamic' as Sociological Categories" (1956/1961). *Diogenes*, no. 33 (spring 1961): 28–49.

"Subject and Object" (1969). In *The Essential Frankfurt School Reader,* pp. 497–511.

"Theory of Pseudo-Culture" (1959). *Telos*, no. 95 (spring 1993): 15–38.

"Theses against Occultism" (1951). *Telos*, no. 19 (spring 1974): 7–12.

"Theses on the Sociology of Art" (1967). *Working Papers in Cultural Studies*, no. 2 (Birmingham, spring 1972): 121–28.

"Theses upon Art and Religion Today." *Kenyon Review* 7 (autumn 1945) 4: 677–82.

"Transparencies on Film" (1966). *New German Critique*, nos. 24–25 (fall–winter 1981–1982): 199–205. Reprinted in Adorno, *The Culture Industry*, pp. 154–61.

"Trying to Understand *Endgame*" (1961). *New German Critique*, no. 26 (spring–summer 1982): 119–50. Previously published as "Toward an Understanding of Endgame," in *Twentieth Century Interpretations of Endgame*, pp. 82–114. Edited by Gale Chevigny. Englewood Cliffs, N.J.: Prentice-Hall, 1969.

"Veblen's Attack on Culture: Remarks Occasioned by the Theory of the Leisure Class." *Studies in Philosophy and Social Science* 9 (1941): 389–413.

"Wagner, Nietzsche and Hitler" (review). *Kenyon Review* 9 (winter 1947) 1: 165–72.

"Wagner's Relevance for Today" (1964/1965). *Grand Street* 11 (1993) 4: 32–59.

"What Does Coming to Terms with the Past Mean?" (1960). *Bitburg in Moral and Political Perspective*, pp. 114–29. Edited by G. Hartman. Indianapolis: Indiana University Press, 1986.

"What National Socialism Has Done to the Arts" (March 1945). GS 20.2 (1986): 413–29.

"Why Philosophy?" (1962/1963). In *Man and Philosophy*, pp. 11–24. Munich: Hueber, 1964. Reprinted in *Critical Theory: The Essential Readings*, pp. 20–30.

2   Writings on Adorno and Critical Theory

Section 2.1 lists anthologies containing articles by Adorno and articles on Adorno and Critical Theory. It also includes special issues of journals devoted to Adorno. Individual articles in these anthologies and special issues are not listed separately. Section 2.2 contains other secondary sources on Adorno and on Critical Theory, with an emphasis on aesthetics and cultural theory.

2.1 Anthologies and Special Issues of Journals

Adorno-Konferenz 1983. Edited by Ludwig von Friedeburg and Jürgen Habermas. Frankfurt: Suhrkamp, 1983.

Adorno und die Musik. Edited by Otto Kolleritsch. Studien zur Wertungsforschung, no. 12. Graz: Universal Edition, 1979.

Aesthetics and Politics: Debates between Bloch, Lukács, Brecht, Benjamin, Adorno. Edited by Ronald Taylor. Afterword by Fredric Jameson. London: NLB, 1977; Verso, 1980.

The Aesthetics of the Critical Theorists: Studies on Benjamin, Adorno, Marcuse, and Habermas. Edited by Ronald Roblin. Lewiston, N. Y.: Edwin Mellen Press, 1990.

Critical Sociology: Selected Readings. Edited by Paul Connerton. Harmondsworth, Middlesex: Penguin Books, 1976.

Critical Theory and Society: A Reader. Edited and with an introduction by Stephen Eric Bronner and Douglas MacKay Kellner. New York: Routledge, 1989.

Critical Theory: The Essential Readings. Edited by David Ingram and Julia Simon-Ingram. New York: Paragon House, 1991.

Die Aktualität der "Dialektik der Aufklärung": Zwischen Moderne und Postmoderne. Edited by Harry Kunnemann and Hent de Vries. Frankfurt, New York: Campus, 1989.

Die "Frankfurter Schule" im Lichte des Marxismus. Zur Kritik der Philosophie und Soziologie von Horkheimer, Adorno, Marcuse, Habermas. Edited by Johannes Henrich von Heiseler, Robert Steigerwald, and Josef Schleifstein. Frankfurt: Verlag Marxistische Blätter, 1970.

Die Frankfurter Schule und die Folgen. Referate eines Symposiums der Alexander von Humboldt-Stiftung vom 10.–15. Dezember 1984 in Ludwigsburg. Edited by Axel Honneth and Albrecht Wellmer. Berlin: Walter de Gruyter, 1986.

Die neue Linke nach Adorno. Edited by Wilfried F. Schoeller. Munich: Kindler, 1969.

The Essential Frankfurt School Reader. Edited by Andrew Arato and Eike Gebhardt. Introduction by Paul Piccone. New York: Urizen Books, 1978.

Flaschenpost und Postkarte: Korrespondenzen zwischen Kritischer Theorie und Poststrukturalismus. Edited by Sigrid Weigel. Cologne: Bohlau, 1995.

Foundations of the Frankfurt School of Social Research. Edited by Judith Marcus and Zoltan Tar. New Brunswick, N.J.: Transaction Books, 1984.

The Frankfurt School: Critical Assessments. 6 vols. Edited by Jay M. Bernstein. London: Routledge, 1994.

Hamburger Adorno-Symposium. Edited by Michael Löbig and Gerhard Schweppenhäuser. Lüneburg: Dietrich zu Klampen, 1984.

Hermeneutik und Ideologiekritik. With contributions by Karl-Otto Apel, et al. Frankfurt: Suhrkamp, 1971.

Humanities in Society 2 (Los Angeles, fall 1979) 4. This issue contains four articles drawn from an Adorno symposium held in May 1979 at the University of Southern California.

Journal of Comparative Literature and Aesthetics 10 (1988–1989) 1. Special issue on Frankfurt School aesthetics.

Kritik und Interpretation der Kritischen Theorie. Aufsätze über Adorno, Horkheimer, Marcuse, Benjamin, Habermas. Giessen: Andreas Achenbach, 1975.

Materialen zur ästhetischen Theorie Theodor W. Adornos. Konstruktion der Moderne. Edited by Burkhardt Lindner and W. Martin Lüdke. Frankfurt: Suhrkamp, 1979.

Negative Dialektik und die Idee der Versöhnung. Eine Kontroverse über Theodor W. Adorno. Traugott Koch, Klaus-Michael Kodalle, and Hermann Schweppenhäuser. Stuttgart: W. Kohlhammer, 1973.

New German Critique, no. 56 (spring–summer 1992). Special issue on Adorno.

On Critical Theory. Edited by John O'Neill. New York: Seabury Press, 1976.

Praxis International 3 (July 1983) 2. Issue on "The Critique of Critical Theory."

The Problems of Modernity: Adorno and Benjamin. Edited by Andrew Benjamin. New York: Routledge, 1989.

Revue d'Esthétique. Special issue on Adorno. Nouvelle série, no. 8 (Toulouse, 1985).

Sozialforschung als Kritik. Zum sozialwissenschaftlichen Potential der Kritischen Theorie. Edited by Wolfgang Bonss and Axel Honneth. Frankfurt: Suhrkamp, 1982.

Studia Philosophica Gandensia, vol. 9 (Adorno-Heft) (Meppel, 1971).

Theodor W. Adorno (1977). Edited by Heinz Ludwig Arnold. 2d, enl. ed. Munich: Edition Text + Kritik, 1983.

Theodor W. Adorno zum Gedächtnis. Eine Sammlung. Edited by Hermann Schweppenhäuser. Frankfurt: Suhrkamp, 1971.

Über Theodor W. Adorno. With contributions by Kurt Oppens, et al. Frankfurt: Suhrkamp, 1968.

Zeitschrift für Musiktheorie 4 (Adorno-Heft, 1973) 1.

Zeugnisse. Theodor W. Adorno zum sechzigsten Geburtstag. Edited by Max Horkheimer. Frankfurt: Europäische Verlagsanstalt, 1963.

Zwielicht der Vernunft: Die Dialektik der Aufklärung aus der Sicht der Frauen. Edited by Christine Kulke and Elvira Scheich. Pfaffenweiler, Germany: Centaurus, 1992.

2.2 Articles and Books on Adorno and Critical Theory

"Adorno: Love and Cognition." *The Times Literary Supplement*, 9 March 1973, pp. 253–55.

Agger, Ben. *The Discourse of Domination: From the Frankfurt School to Postmodernism*. Evanston, Ill.: Northwestern University Press, 1992.

Alt, Peter Andre. "Das Problem der inneren Form: Zur Hölderlin-Rezeption Benjamins und Adornos." *Deutsche Vierteljahresschrift für Literaturwissenschaft und Geistesgeschichte* 61 (September 1987): 531–62.

Alt, Peter Andre. "Hölderlins Vermittlungen: Der Übergang des Subjekts in die Form." *Germanisch Romanische Monatsschrift* 38 (1988) 1–2: 120–39.

Alway, Joan. *Critical Theory and Political Possibilities: Conceptions of Emancipatory Politics in the Works of Horkheimer, Adorno, Marcuse, and Habermas*. Westport, Conn.: Greenwood Press, 1995.

Anderson, Perry. *Considerations on Western Marxism*. London: NLB, 1976; Verso, 1979.

Anderson, Perry. *In the Tracks of Historical Materialism*. Chicago: University of Chicago Press, 1984.

Antonio, Robert. "The Origin, Development, and Contemporary Status of Critical Theory." *Sociological Quarterly* 24 (summer 1983): 325–51.

Arato, Andrew. "Introduction: The Antinomies of the Neo-Marxian Theory of Culture." *International Journal of Sociology* 7 (spring 1977) 1: 3–24.

Arato, Andrew. "Critical Theory in the United States: Reflections on Four Decades of Reception." In *America and the Germans: An Assessment of a Three-Hundred-Year History*. Vol. 2: *The Relationship in the Twentieth Century*, pp. 279–86. Edited by Frank Trommler and Joseph McVeigh. Philadelphia: University of Pennsylvania Press, 1985.

Arato, Andrew, and Paul Breines. *The Young Lukács and the Origins of Western Marxism*. New York: Seabury Press, 1979.

Bahr, Ehrhard. "Art Desires Non-Art: The Dialectics of Art in Thomas Mann's *Doctor Faustus* in the Light of Theodor W. Adorno's *Aesthetic Theory*." In *Thomas Mann's Doctor Faustus: A Novel at the Margin of Modernism*, pp. 145–66. Edited by Herbert Lehnert and Peter C. Pfeiffer. Columbia, S.C.: Camden House, 1991.

Baugh, Bruce. "Left-Wing Elitism: Adorno on Popular Culture." *Philosophy and Literature* 14 (April 1990): 65–78.

Baum, Klaus. *Die Transzendierung des Mythos: Zur Philosophie und Ästhetik Schellings und Adornos*. Wurzburg: Königshausen & Neumann, 1988.

Baumeister, Thomas, and Jens Kulenkampff. "Geschichtsphilosophie und philosophische Ästhetik. Zu Adornos 'Ästhetischer Theorie.'" *Neue Hefte für Philosophie*, no. 5 (1973): 74–104.

Benhabib, Seyla. *Critique, Norm, and Utopia: A Study of the Foundations of Critical Theory.* New York: Columbia University Press, 1986.

Benjamin, Jessica. "The End of Internalization: Adorno's Social Psychology." *Telos,* no. 32 (1977): 42–64.

Berman. Russell A. "Adorno, Marxism and Art." *Telos,* no. 34 (winter 1977–1978): 157–66.

Berman, Russell A. "Adorno's Radicalism: Two Interviews from the Sixties." *Telos,* no. 56 (summer 1983): 94–97.

Berman, Russell A. *Modern Culture and Critical Theory: Art, Politics, and the Legacy of the Frankfurt School.* Madison: University of Wisconsin Press, 1989.

Bernstein, J. M. "Aesthetic Alienation: Heidegger, Adorno, and Truth at the End of Art." In *Life after Postmodernism: Essays on Value and Culture,* pp. 86–119. Edited by John Fekete. New York: St. Martins Press, 1987.

Bernstein, J. M. "Philosophy's Refuge: Adorno in Beckett." In *Philosophers' Poets,* pp. 177–81. Edited by David Wood. London: Routledge, 1990.

Bernstein, J. M. *The Fate of Art: Aesthetic Alienation from Kant to Derrida and Adorno.* Cambridge, England: Polity Press, 1992.

Bernstein, J. M. *Recovering Ethical Life: Jürgen Habermas and the Future of Critical Theory.* London: Routledge, 1995.

Bernstein, J. M. "The Death of Sensuous Particulars: Adorno and Abstract Expressionism." *Radical Philosophy* 76 (1996): 7–18.

Bernstein, Susan. "Journalism and German Identity: Communiques from Heine, Wagner, and Adorno." *New German Critique* 66 (1995): 65–93.

Birus, Hendrik. "Adornos 'Negative Ästhetik'?" *Deutsche Vierteljahresschrift für Literaturwissenschaft und Geistesgeschichte* 62 (March 1988): 1–23.

Blomster, W. V. "Sociology of Music: Adorno and Beyond." *Telos,* no. 28 (summer 1976): 81–112.

Blumenfeld, Harold. "Ad Vocem Adorno." *Musical Quarterly* 75 (winter 1991): 263–84.

Boehmer, Konrad. "Adorno, Musik, Gesellschaft" (1969). Reprinted in *Texte zur Musiksoziologie,* pp. 227–38. Edited by Tibor Kneif, with an introduction by Carl Dahlhaus. Cologne: Arno Volk, 1975.

Böhme, Gernot. *Natürlich Natur. Über Natur im Zeitalter ihrer technischen Reproduzierbarkeit.* Frankfurt: Surhrkamp, 1992.

Born, Georgina. "Against Negation, for a Politics of Cultural Production: Adorno, Aesthetics, the Social." *Screen* 34 (autumn 1993): 223–42.

Brantlinger, Patrick. *Bread and Circuses: Theories of Mass Culture as Social Decay.* Ithaca, N.Y.: Cornell University Press, 1983.

Bronner, Stephen Eric. *Of Critical Theory and Its Theorists.* Cambridge, Mass.: Blackwell, 1994.

Brown, Lee B. "Adorno's Theory of Popular Music." *Journal of Aesthetic Education* 26 (spring 1992): 17–31.

Brunkhorst, Hauke. "Adorno, Heidegger and Postmodernity." In *Universalism vs. Communitarianism: Contemporary Debates in Ethics,* pp. 183–96. Edited by David Rasmussen. Cambridge, Mass.: MIT Press, 1990.

Brunkhorst, Hauke. *Theodor W. Adorno: Dialektik der Moderne.* Munich and Zurich: Piper, 1990.

Bubner, Rüdiger. "Über einige Bedingungen gegenwärtiger Ästhetik." *Neue Hefte für Philosophie,* no. 5 (1973): 38–73.

Bubner, Rüdiger. *Essays in Hermeneutics and Critical Theory.* Translated by Eric Matthews. New York: Columbia University Press, 1988.

Buck-Morss, Susan. *The Origin of Negative Dialectics: Theodor W. Adorno, Walter Benjamin and the Frankfurt Institute.* New York: Free Press, 1977.

Burgard, Peter J. "Adorno, Goethe, and the Politics of the Essay." *Deutsche Vierteljahresschrift für Literaturwissenschaft und Geistesgeschichte* 66 (March 1992): 160–91.

Bürger, Christa. "Mimesis and Modernity." *Stanford Literature Review* 3 (spring 1986): 63–73.

Bürger, Peter. *Theory of the Avant Garde.* Translated by Michael Shaw. Foreword by Jochen Schulte-Sasse. Minneapolis: University of Minnesota Press, 1984.

Bürger, Peter. "The Decline of the Modern Age." *Telos,* no. 62 (winter 1984–1985): 117–30. Reprinted as chap. 3 in Bürger's *Decline of Modernism.* Translated by Nicholas Walker. University Park: Pennsylvania State University Press, 1992.

Bürger, Peter. "Adorno, Bourdieu und die Literatursoziologie." *Jahrbuch für Internationale Germanistik* 17 (1985) 1: 47–56.

Bürger, Peter. "Adorno's Anti-Avant-Gardism." *Telos,* no. 86 (winter 1990–1991): 49–60.

Butterfield, Bradley. "Enlightenment's Other in Patrick Suskind's *Das Parfüm:* Adorno and the Ineffable Utopia of Modern Art." *Comparative Literature Studies* 32 (1995): 401–18.

Cahn. Michael. "Subversive Mimesis: Theodor W. Adorno and the Modern Impasse of Critique." In *Mimesis in Contemporary Theory: An Interdisciplinary Approach.* Vol. 1: *The Literary and Philosophical Debate,* pp. 27–64. Edited by Mihai Spariosu. Philadelphia: John Benjamins, 1984.

Select Bibliography

Calhoun, Craig. *Critical Social Theory: Culture, History, and the Challenge of Difference.* Oxford: Blackwell, 1995.

Caughie, John. "Adorno's Reproach: Repetition, Difference and Television Genre." *Screen* 32 (summer 1991): 127–53.

Champion, James W. "Tillich and the Frankfurt School: Parallels and Differences in Prophetic Criticism." *Soundings* 69 (1986): 512–30.

Clark, Kevin M. Review essay on Susan Buck-Morss, *The Origin of Negative Dialectics*; and Gillian Rose, *The Melancholy Science. Graduate Faculty Philosophy Journal* 8 (spring 1982): 269–305.

Clark, Michael. "Adorno, Derrida, and the Odyssey: A Critique of Center and Periphery." *Boundary 2* 16 (winter/spring 1989): 109–28.

Cook, Deborah. *The Culture Industry Revisited: Theodor W. Adorno on Mass Culture.* Lanham, Md.: Rowman and Littlefield, 1996.

Cooper, Harry. "On *Über Jazz:* Replaying Adorno with the Grain." *October* 75 (1996): 99–133.

Dahlhaus, Carl. "Adornos Begriff des musikalischen Materials." In *Zur Terminologie der Musik des 20. Jahrhunderts,* pp. 9–21. Edited by Hans Heinrich Eggebrecht. Stuttgart: Musikwissenschaftliche Verlags-Gesellschaft, 1974.

Dahlhaus, Carl. "Soziologische Dechiffrierung von Musik. Zu Theodor W. Adornos Wagner-Kritik." *The International Review of the Aesthetics and Sociology of Music* 1 (1979): 137–47.

Dallmayr, Fred R. "Phenomenology and Critical Theory: Adorno." *Cultural Hermeneutics* 3 (1976): 367–405.

Dallmayr, Fred. *Between Freiburg and Frankfurt: Toward a Critical Ontology.* Amherst: University of Massachusetts Press, 1991.

Davidov, Iu. N. "The Problem of Art in the Social Philosophy of the Frankfurt School." *Soviet Studies in Philosophy* 24 (fall 1985): 62–85.

Demirovic, Alex. "Aspekte der Aktualität Adornos." *Bulletin of the Faculty of Human Sciences* 21 (1995): 25–44.

Demmerling, Christoph. *Sprache und Verdinglichung: Wittgenstein, Adorno und das Projekt einer kritischen Theorie.* Frankfurt: Suhrkamp, 1994.

de Vries, Hent. *Theologie im Pianissimo & zwischen Rationalität und Dekonstruktion: Die Aktualität der Denkfiguren Adornos und Levinas'.* Kampen: J. H. Kok, 1989.

Dews, Peter. *Logics of Disintegration: Post-structuralist Thought and the Claims of Critical Theory.* London, New York: Verso, 1987.

Dews, Peter. *The Limits of Disenchantment: Essays on Contemporary European Philosophy.* London: Verso, 1995.

Dineen, Murray. "Adorno and Schoenberg's Unanswered Question." *The Musical Quarterly* 77 (fall 1993): 415–27.

Donougho, Martin. "The Cunning of Odysseus: A Theme in Hegel, Lukács, and Adorno." *Philosophy and Social Criticism* 8 (spring 1981): 11–43.

Dubiel, Helmut. *Theory and Politics: Studies in the Development of Critical Theory.* Translated by Benjamin Gregg. Cambridge, Mass.: MIT Press, 1985.

Dunn, Allen. "The Man Who Needs Hardness: Irony and Solidarity in the Aesthetics of Theodor Adorno." In *Germany and German Thought in American Literature and Cultural Criticism,* pp. 470–84. Edited by Peter Freese. Essen: Blaue Eule, 1990.

Düttman, Alexander Garcia. *Das Gedächtnis des Denkens. Versuch über Heidegger und Adorno.* Frankfurt: Suhrkamp, 1991.

Eagleton, Terry. *The Ideology of the Aesthetic.* Oxford: Basil Blackwell, 1990.

Edgar, Andrew. "An Introduction to Adorno's Aesthetics." *British Journal of Aesthetics* 30 (January 1990): 46–56.

Engh, Barbara. "Adorno and the Sirens: Tele-phono-graphic Bodies." In *Embodied Voices: Representing Female Vocality in Western Culture,* pp. 120–35. Edited by Leslie C. Dunn and Nancy A. Jones. New York: Cambridge University Press, 1994.

Feenberg, Andrew. *Lukács, Marx and the Sources of Critical Theory.* Totowa, N.J.: Rowman and Littlefield, 1981.

Fehér, Ferenc. "Negative Philosophy of Music—Positive Results." *New German Critique,* no. 4 (winter 1975): 99–111.

Fehér, Ferenc. "Rationalized Music and Its Vicissitudes (Adorno's Philosophy of Music)." *Philosophy and Social Criticism* 9 (spring 1982) 1: 41–65.

Fenves, Peter. "Image and Chatter: Adorno's Construction of Kierkegaard." *Diacritics* 22 (spring 1992): 100–114.

Figal, Günter. *Theodor W. Adorno. Das Naturschöne als spekulative Gedankenfigur. Zur Interpretation der "Ästhetischen Theorie" im Kontext philosophischer Ästhetik.* Bonn: Bouvier Verlag Herbert Grundmann, 1977.

Floyd, Wayne Whitson, Jr. "Transcendence in the Light of Redemption: Adorno and the Legacy of Rosenzweig and Benjamin." *Journal of the American Academy of Religion* 61 (fall 1993): 539–51.

Fluxman, Tony. "Bob Dylan and the Dialectic of Enlightenment: Critical Lyricist in the Age of High Capitalism." *Theoria* 77 (May 1991): 91–111.

Focht, Ivan. "Adornos gnoseologistische Einstellung zur Musik." *International Review of the Aesthetics and Sociology of Music* 5 (1974): 265–76.

Frow, John. "Mediation and Metaphor: Adorno and the Sociology of Art." *Clio* 12 (fall 1982) 1: 57–65.

Früchtl, Josef. *Mimesis: Konstellation eines Zentralbegriffs bei Adorno.* Würzburg: Königshausen & Neumann, 1986.

Früchtl, Josef. "Natur als Projektion und Adornos Modell von Wahrheit." *Philosophisches Jahrbuch der Gorres Gesellschaft* 96 (1989) 2: 371–81.

Früchtl, Josef. "Zeit und Erfahrung: Adornos Revision der Revision Heideggers." In *Martin Heidegger: Innen- und Aussensichten,* pp. 291–312. Edited by Forum für Philosophie, Bad Homburg. Frankfurt: Suhrkamp, 1989.

Gendron, Bernard. "Theodor Adorno Meets the Cadillacs." In *Studies in Entertainment: Critical Approaches to Mass Culture,* pp. 18–36. Edited by Tania Modleski. Bloomington: Indiana University Press, 1986.

Geyer, Carl-Friedrich. *Kritische Theorie: Max Horkheimer und Theodor W. Adorno.* Freiburg: Karl Alber, 1982.

Gillespie, Susan. "Translating Adorno: Language, Music, and Performance." *Musical Quarterly* 79 (spring 1995): 55–65.

Gomez Moriana, Antonio. "The (Relative) Autonomy of Artistic Expression: Bakhtin and Adorno." *Critical Studies* 1 (1989) 2: 95–105.

Gracyk, Theodore A. "Adorno, Jazz and the Aesthetics of Popular Music." *Musical Quarterly* 76 (winter 1982): 526–42.

Gramer, Wolfgang. "Musikalische Utopie: Ein Gespräch zwischen Adornos und Blochs Denken." *Bloch Almanach* 4 (1984): 175–89.

Grenz, Friedemann. "'Die Idee der Naturgeschichte.' Zu eine frühen unbekannten Text Adornos." In *Natur und Geschichte,* pp. 344–50. Deutscher Kongress für Philosophie, Kiel 8.–12. Oktober 1972. Edited by Kurt Hübner und Albert Menne. Hamburg: Felix Meiner, 1973.

Grenz, Friedemann. *Adornos Philosophie in Grundbegriffen. Auflösung einiger Deutungsprobleme.* Frankfurt: Suhrkamp, 1974.

Habermas, Jürgen. *Philosophical-Political Profiles.* Translated by Frederick G. Lawrence. Cambridge, Mass.: MIT Press, 1983.

Habermas, Jürgen. "Questions and Counterquestions." In *Habermas and Modernity,* pp. 192–216. Edited by Richard J. Bernstein. Cambridge, Mass.: MIT Press, 1985.

Habermas, Jürgen. *The Theory of Communicative Action.* Translated by Thomas McCarthy. Vol. 1: *Reason and the Rationalization of Society.* Vol. 2: *Lifeworld and System.* Boston: Beacon Press, 1984, 1987.

Habermas, Jürgen. *The Philosophical Discourse of Modernity: Twelve Lectures* (1985). Translated by Frederick Lawrence. Cambridge, Mass.: MIT Press, 1987.

Haimbockel, Dieter. "Anspruch und Wirklichkeit: Theodor W. Adornos Beitrag zur 'Rettung' Stefan Georges." *Castrum Peregrini* 40 (1991): 70–79.

Hamilton, Carol V. "All That Jazz Again: Adorno's Sociology of Music." *Popular Music and Society* 15 (fall 1991) 3: 31–40.

Hansen, Miriam. "Of Mice and Ducks: Benjamin and Adorno on Disney." *South Atlantic Quarterly* 92 (winter 1993): 27–61.

Harding, James Martin. "Integrating Atomization: Adorno Reading Berg Reading Buchner." *Theater Journal* 44 (March 1992): 1–13.

Harding, James Martin. "Historical Dialectics and the Autonomy of Art in Adorno's *Ästhetische Theorie*." *Journal of Aesthetics and Art Criticism* 50 (summer 1992): 183–95.

Harding, James Martin. "Trying to Understand Godot: Adorno, Beckett, and the Senility of Historical Dialectics." *Clio* 23 (fall 1993): 1–22.

Harding, James Martin. "Adorno, Ellison, and the Critique of Jazz." *Cultural Critique* 31 (1995): 129–58.

Held, David. *Introduction to Critical Theory: Horkheimer to Habermas.* Berkeley: University of California Press, 1980.

Hjort, Ann Mette. "'Quasi una Amicizia': Adorno and Philosophical Postmodernism." *New Orleans Review* 14 (spring 1987): 74–80.

Hohendahl, Peter U. "Autonomy of Art: Looking Back at Adorno's *Ästhetische Theorie*." *German Quarterly* 54 (March 1981): 133–48.

Hohendahl, Peter U. "The Dialectic of Enlightenment Revisited: Habermas' Critique of the Frankfurt School." *New German Critique*, no. 35 (spring–summer 1985): 3–26.

Hohendahl, Peter Uwe. *Reappraisals: Shifting Alignments in Postwar Critical Theory.* Ithaca, N.Y.: Cornell University Press, 1991.

Hohendahl, Peter Uwe. "The Displaced Intellectual? Adorno's American Years Revisited." In *Die Resonanz des Exils: Gelungene und misslungene Rezeption deutschsprachiger Exilautoren*, pp. 110–20. Edited by Dieter Sevin. Amsterdam: Rodopi, 1992.

Hohendahl, Peter Uwe. *Prismatic Thought: Theodor W. Adorno.* Lincoln: University of Nebraska Press, 1995.

Holz, Hans Heinz. "Das theologische Geheimnis der ästhetischen Theorie Th. W. Adornos." *Deutsche Zeitschrift für Philosophie* 38 (1990): 866–73.

Honneth, Axel. "Communication and Reconciliation: Habermas' Critique of Adorno." *Telos*, no. 29 (spring 1979): 45–61. A complete translation is reprinted as "From Adorno to Habermas: On the Transformation of Critical Social Theory," in Honneth, *The Fragmented World of the Social*, pp. 92–120.

Honneth, Axel. *The Critique of Power: Reflective Stages in a Critical Social Theory.* Translated by Kenneth Baynes. Cambridge, Mass.: MIT Press, 1991.

Honneth, Axel. *The Fragmented World of the Social: Essays in Social and Political Philosophy.* Edited by Charles W. Wright. Albany: State University of New York Press, 1995.

Horowitz, Gregg. "Objectivity and Valuation in Contemporary Art History." In *Explanation and Value in Literary and Visual Studies*, pp. 127–45. Edited by Salim Kemal and Ivan Gaskell. Cambridge: Cambridge University Press, 1993.

Horowitz, Gregg. "'Suddenly One Has the Right Eyes': Illusion and Iconoclasm in the Early Gombrich." In *Artifacts, Representations, and Social Practice*, pp. 253–70. Edited by C. C. Gould and R. S. Cohen. Boston: Kluwer Academic Publishers, 1993.

Hrachovec, Herbert. "Was lässt sich von Erlösung Denken? Gedanken von und über Th. W. Adornos Philosophie." *Philosophisches Jahrbuch* 83 (1976): 357–70.

Huhn, Thomas. "Adorno's Aesthetics of Illusion." *Journal of Aesthetics and Art Criticism* 44 (winter 1985): 181–89.

Huhn, Thomas. "The Concept of Sublimation in Adorno's Aesthetics." In *The Aesthetics of the Critical Theorists*, pp. 291–307.

Huhn, Thomas. "Diligence and Industry, Adorno and the Ugly." *Canadian Journal of Political and Social Theory* 12 (1988): 138–46.

Huhn, Thomas. "The Movement of Mimesis: Heidegger's 'Origin of the Work of Art' in Relation to Adorno and Lyotard." *Philosophy & Social Criticism* 22 (1996): 45–69.

Hullot-Kentor, Robert. "Popular Music and Adorno's 'The Aging of the New Music.'" *Telos*, no. 77 (fall 1988): 79–94.

Hullot-Kentor, Robert. "Back to Adorno." *Telos*, no. 81 (fall 1989): 5–29.

Huyssen, Andreas. "Adorno in Reverse: From Hollywood to Richard Wagner." *New German Critique*, no. 29 (spring–summer 1983): 8–38.

Huyssen, Andreas. "Mapping the Postmodern." *New German Critique*, no. 33 (fall 1984): 5–52.

Huyssen, Andreas. *After the Great Divide: Modernism, Mass Culture and Postmodernism*. London: Macmillan, 1993.

Jacoby, Russell. *Dialectic of Defeat: Contours of Western Marxism*. Cambridge: Cambridge University Press, 1981.

Jameson, Fredric. "Introduction to Adorno." *Salmagundi*, nos. 10–11 (fall 1969–winter 1970): 140–43.

Jameson, Fredric. *Marxism and Form: Twentieth-Century Dialectical Theories of Literature*. Princeton: Princeton University Press, 1971.

Jameson, Fredric. *Late Marxism: Adorno, or, The Persistence of the Dialectic*. London, New York: Verso, 1990.

Jauss, Hans Robert. "The Literary Process of Modernism: From Rousseau to Adorno." *Cultural Critique* 11 (winter 1988–1989): 27–61.

Jay, Martin. "Adorno in America." *New German Critique*, no. 31 (winter 1984): 157–82.

Jay, Martin. *Adorno*. Cambridge, Mass.: Harvard University Press, 1984.

Jay, Martin. *Marxism and Totality: The Adventures of a Concept from Lukács to Habermas.* Berkeley: University of California Press, 1984.

Jay, Martin. *Permanent Exiles: Essays on the Intellectual Migration from Germany to America.* New York: Columbia University Press, 1985.

Jay, Martin. *The Dialectical Imagination.* 2d ed. Berkeley: University of California Press, 1996.

Kager, Reinhard. *Herrschaft und Versöhnung: Einführung in das Denken Theodor W. Adornos.* Frankfurt: Campus, 1988.

Kaiser, Gerhard. *Benjamin. Adorno. Zwei Studien.* Frankfurt: Athenäum Fischer Taschenbuch, 1974.

Kappner, Hans-Hartmut. *Die Bildungstheorie Adornos als Theorie der Erfahrung von Kultur und Kunst.* Frankfurt: Suhrkamp, 1984.

Kaufman, Robert. "Legislators of the Post-Everything World: Shelley's Defense of Adorno." *English Literary History* 63:3 (fall 1996).

Kaufman, Robert. "The Sublime as Super-Genre of the Modern, or, *Hamlet* in Revolution: Caleb Williams and His Problem." *Studies in Romanticism,* forthcoming.

Kellner, Douglas. *Critical Theory, Marxism, and Modernity.* Baltimore: Johns Hopkins Press, 1989.

Kellner, Douglas, and Rick Roderick. "Recent Literature on Critical Theory." *New German Critique,* no. 23 (spring–summer 1981): 141–70.

Kemper, Peter. "'Der Rock ist ein Gebrauchswert': Warum Adorno die Beatles verschmähte." *Merkur* 45 (September–October 1991): 890–902.

Kerkhoff, Manfred. "Die Rettung des Nichtidentischen. Zur Philosophie Th. W. Adornos." *Philosophische Rundschau* 20 (1974): 150–78; and 21 (1975): 56–74.

Kistner, Ulrike. "Writing 'after Auschwitz': On the Impossibility of a Postscript." *Acta Germanica: Jahrbuch des Germanistenverbandes im Südlichen Afrika* 21 (1992): 171–83.

Knapp, Gerhard. *Theodor W. Adorno.* Berlin: Colloquium, 1980.

Koch, Gertrude. "Mimesis and *Bilderverbot.*" *Screen* 34 (autumn 1993): 211–22.

Koebner, Thomas. "Warnung vor den Massenmedien: Zu amerikanischen Erfahrungen und zur Nachkriegs-Kulturkritik von Theodor W. Adorno und Gunther Anders." In *Ruckkehr aus dem Exil: Emigranten aus dem Dritten Reich in Deutschland nach 1945: Essays zu Ehren von Ernst Loewy,* pp. 115–27. Edited by Thomas Koebner. Munich: Edition Text + Kritik, 1990.

Kofler, Leo. "Weder 'Wiederspiegelung' noch Abstraktion: Lukács oder Adorno?" In *Zur Theorie der Modernen Literatur: Der Avantgardsismus in soziologischer Sicht,* pp. 160–87. 2d ed. Düsseldorf: Bertelsmann Universitätsverlag, 1974.

Krukowski, Lucian. "Form and Protest in Atonal Music: A Meditation on Adorno." *Bucknell Review* 29 (1984) 1: 105–24.

Kuspit, Donald B. "Critical Notes on Adorno's Sociology of Music and Art." *Journal of Aesthetics and Art Criticism* 33 (spring 1975): 321–27.

Lacoue-Labarthe, Philippe. "The Caesura of Religion." In *Opera Through Other Eyes*, pp. 45–77. Edited by David J. Levin. Stanford: Stanford University Press, 1994.

Lang, Peter Christian. *Hermeneutik, Ideologiekritik, Ästhetik: Über Gadamer und Adorno sowie Fragen einer aktuellen Ästhetik.* Königstein/Ts: Forum Academicum, 1981.

Lehmann, Hans Thies. "Nach Adorno: Zur Rezeption ästhetischer Theorie." *Merkur* 38 (June 1984): 391–98.

Levin, Thomas Y. "For the Record: Adorno on Music in the Age of Its Technological Reproducibility." *October* 55 (winter 1990): 23–47.

Levin, Thomas Y., with Michael von der Linn. "Elements of a Radio Theory: Adorno and the Princeton Radio Research Project." *Musical Quarterly* 78 (summer 1994): 316–24.

Löwenthal, Leo. "Recollections of Theodor W. Adorno." *Telos*, no. 61 (fall 1984): 158–65.

Lüdke, W. Martin. *Anmerkungen zu einer "Logik des Zerfalls": Adorno—Beckett.* Frankfurt: Suhrkamp, 1981.

Lüdke, W. Martin, ed. *"Theorie der Avantgarde": Antworten auf Peter Bürgers Bestimmung von Kunst und bürgerlicher Gesellschaft.* Frankfurt: Suhrkamp, 1976.

Lunn, Eugene. *Marxism and Modernism: An Historical Study of Lukács, Brecht, Benjamin, and Adorno.* Berkeley: University of California Press, 1982.

Lyotard, Jean-François. "Adorno as the Devil." *Telos*, no. 19 (spring 1974): 127–37.

Marcuse, Herbert. *The Aesthetic Dimension: Toward a Critique of Marxist Aesthetics.* Boston: Beacon Press, 1978.

Mayer, Günter. "Zur Dialektik des musikalischen Materials" (1966, 1969). Reprinted in *Texte zur Musiksoziologie*, pp. 200–226. Edited by Tibor Kneif, with an introduction by Carl Dahlhaus. Cologne: Arno Volk, 1975.

McCormack, W. J. "Seeing Darkly: Notes on T. W. Adorno and Samuel Beckett." *Hermathena* 141 (winter 1986): 22–44.

McHugh, Patrick. "Ecstasy and Exile: Cultural Theory between Heidegger and Adorno." *Cultural Critique* 25 (1993): 121–52.

Menke, Christoph. *Die Souveränität der Kunst: Ästhetische Erfahrung nach Adorno und Derrida.* Frankfurt: Suhrkamp, 1991.

Missac, Pierre. *Walter Benjamin's Passages.* Cambridge, Mass.: MIT Press, 1995.

Mörchen, Hermann. *Macht und Herrschaft im Denken von Heidegger und Adorno.* Stuttgart: Klett-Cotta, 1980.

Mörchen, Hermann. *Adorno und Heidegger: Untersuchung einer philosophischen Kommunikationsverweigerung.* Stuttgart: Klett-Cotta, 1981.

Morrison, David E. "Kultur and Culture: The Case of Theodor W. Adorno and Paul F. Lazarsfeld." *Social Research* 45 (summer 1978): 331–55.

Müller, Harro. "Gesellschaftliche Funktion und ästhetische Autonomie: Benjamin, Adorno, Habermas." *Literaturwissenschaft: Grundkurs 2,* pp. 329–40. Edited by Helmut Brackert and Jörn Stückrath. Reinbeck bei Hamburg: Rowohlt, 1981.

Müller, Ulrich. *Erkenntniskritik und negative Metaphysik bei Adorno: Eine Philosophie der dritten Reflektiertheit.* Frankfurt: Athenäum, 1988.

Müller-Strömsdörfer, Ilse. "Die 'helfende Kraft bestimmter Negation.' Zum Werke Th. W. Adornos." *Philosophische Rundschau* 8 (1960): 81–105.

Naeher, Jürgen, ed. *Die Negative Dialektik Adornos: Einführung—Dialog.* Opladen: Leske and Budrich, 1984.

Nägele, Rainer. "The Scene of the Other: Theodor W. Adorno's Negative Dialectic in the Context of Poststructuralism." *Postmodernism and Politics,* pp. 91–111. Edited and introduced by Jonathan Arac. Minneapolis: University of Minnesota Press, 1986.

Narskii, I. S. "Adorno's Negative Philosophy." *Soviet Studies in Philosophy* 24 (summer 1985): 3–45.

Nicholsen, Shierry Weber. "Toward a More Adequate Reception of Adorno's *Aesthetic Theory:* Configurational Form in Adorno's Aesthetic Writings." *Cultural Critique,* no. 18 (spring 1991): 33–64.

Nicholsen, Shierry Weber. "Subjective Aesthetic Experience in Adorno and Its Historical Trajectory." *Theory Culture & Society* 10, no. 2 (May 1993): 89–125.

Nicholsen, Shierry Weber. *Exact Imagination, Late Work: On Adorno's Aesthetics.* Cambridge, Mass.: MIT Press, forthcoming.

Nuyen, A. T. "Habermas, Adorno and the Possibility of Immanent Critique." *American Catholic Philosophical Quarterly* 66 (summer 1992): 331–40.

Nye, William P. "Theodor Adorno on Jazz: A Critique of Critical Theory." *Popular Music and Society* 12 (winter 1988) 4: 69–73.

Osborne, Peter. "Adorno, Theodor W." *A Dictionary of Cultural and Critical Theory,* pp. 13–16. Edited by Michael Payne. Cambridge, Mass.: Blackwell, 1996.

Paddison, Max. "The Critique Criticised: Adorno and Popular Music." *Popular Music* 2 (1982): 201–18.

Paddison, Max. *Adorno's Aesthetics of Music.* New York: Cambridge University Press, 1993.

Paddison, Max. *Adorno, Modernism and Mass Culture: Essays on Critical Theory and Music.* London: Kahn & Averill, 1996.

Paetzold, Heinz. *Neomarxistische Ästhetik.* 2 parts. Part 2: *Adorno, Marcuse.* Düsseldorf: Pädagogischer Verlag Schwann, 1974.

Paetzold, Heinz. *The Discourse of the Postmodern and the Discourse of the Avant-Garde.* Maastricht, The Netherlands: Jan Van Eyck Akademie, 1994.

Pena Aguado, Maria Isabel. *Ästhetik des Erhabenen: Burke, Kant, Adorno, Lyotard.* Vienna: Passagen, 1994.

Pepper, Thomas. "Guilt by (Un)free Association: Adorno on Romance *et al.*" *MLN* 109 (December 1994): 913–37.

Phelan, Shane. "The Jargon of Authenticity: Adorno and Feminist Essentialism." *Philosophy & Social Criticism* 16 (1990): 39–59.

Phelan, Shane. "Interpretation & Domination: Adorno & the Habermas-Lyotard Debate." *Polity* 25 (summer 1993): 597–616.

Pickford, Henry. "Under the Sign of Adorno." *MLN* 108 (April 1993): 564–83.

Pizer, John. "Jameson's Adorno, or, the Persistence of the Utopian." *New German Critique,* no. 58 (winter 1993): 127–51.

Pizer, John. "Ursprung ist das Ziel": Karl Kraus's Concept of Origin." *Modern Austrian Literature* 27 (1994): 1–22.

Plessner, Helmuth. "Adornos Negative Dialektik. Ihr Thema mit Variationen." *Kant-Studien* 61 (1970): 507–19.

Plessner, Helmuth. "Zum Verständnis der ästhetischen Theorie Adornos." *Philosophische Perspektiven,* no. 4 (1972): 126–36.

Pollock, Della. "Aesthetic Negation after WWII: Mediating Bertolt Brecht and Theodor Adorno." *Literature in Performance* 8 (November 1988): 12–20.

Posnock, Ross. "Henry James, Veblen and Adorno: The Crisis of the Modern Self." *Journal of American Studies* 21 (April 1987): 31–54.

Puder, Martin. "Zur 'Ästhetischen Theorie' Adornos." *Neue Rundschau* 82 (1971): 465–77.

Puder, Martin. "Adornos Philosophie und die gegenwärtige Erfahrung." *Neue Deutsche Hefte* 23 (1976): 3–21.

Pütze, Peter. "Nietzsche and Critical Theory" (1974). *Telos,* no. 50 (winter 1981–1982): 103–14.

Raddatz, Fritz J. "Der hölzerne Eisenring. Die moderne Literatur zwischen zweierlei Ästhetik: Lukács und Adorno." *Merkur* 31 (1977): 28–44.

Recki, Birgit. *Aura und Autonomie: Zur Subjektivität der Kunst bei Walter Benjamin und Theodor W. Adorno.* Würzburg: Königshausen & Neumann, 1988.

Recki, Birgit. "Die Metaphysik der Kritik: Zum verhältnis von Metaphysik und Erfahrung bei Max Horkheimer und Theodor Adorno." *Neue Hefte für Philosophie* 30–31 (1991): 139–71.

Rehfus, Wulff. "Theodor W. Adorno. Die Rekonstruktion der Wahrheit aus der Ästhetik." Cologne: Universität zu Köln, Inaugural-Dissertation, 1976.

Ries, Wiebrecht. "'Die Rettung des Hoffnungslosen.' Zur 'theologia occulta' in der Spätphilosophie Horkheimers und Adornos." *Zeitschrift für philosophische Forschung* 30 (1976): 69–81.

Riethmüller, Albrecht. "Adorno musicus." *Archiv für Musikwissenschaft* 47 (1990): 1–26.

Roberts, David. *Art and Enlightenment: Aesthetic Theory after Adorno.* Lincoln: University of Nebraska Press, 1991.

Roberts, David. "Crowds and Power or the Natural History of Modernity: Horkheimer, Adorno, Canetti, Arendt." *Thesis eleven* 45 (1996): 39–68.

Robinson, J. Bradford. "The Jazz Essays of Adorno: Some Thoughts on Jazz Reception in Weimar Germany." *Popular Music* 13 (January 1994): 1–25.

Rochlitz, Rainer. "Language for One, Language for All: Adorno and Modernism." *Perspectives of New Music* 27 (summer 1989): 18–36.

Rose, Gillian. *The Melancholy Science: An Introduction to the Thought of Theodor W. Adorno.* London: Macmillan Press, 1978.

Ryan, Michael. *Marxism and Deconstruction: A Critical Articulation.* Baltimore: Johns Hopkins University Press, 1982.

Sample, Colin. "Adorno on the Musical Language of Beethoven." *Musical Quarterly* 78 (summer 1994): 378–93.

Sauerland, Karol. *Einführung in die Ästhetik Adornos.* Berlin: Walter de Gruyter, 1979.

Savile, Anthony. "Beauty and Truth: The Apotheosis of an Idea." In *Analytic Aesthetics,* pp. 23–46. Edited by Richard Shusterman. Oxford: Basil Blackwell, 1989.

Scheible, Hartmut. "'Dem Wahren Schönen Guten': Adornos Anfänge im Kontext." In *Idee, Gestalt, Geschichte: Festschrift für Klaus von See,* pp. 627–712. Edited by Wolfgang Gerd Weber. Odense: Odense University Press, 1988.

Scheit, Gerhard. "Exil zwischen Philosophie und Musik: Zur Entstehung von Theodor W. Adornos Ästhetik." *Theodor Kramer Gesellschaft* 1 (1990): 213–27.

Schirnding, Albert von. "Ruckkehr zu Büchern: Werner Bergengruen, seine Zeit und Adornos Verdikte." *Merkur* 36 (1982): 698–707.

Schlüter, Carsten. *Adornos Kritik der apologetischen Vernunft.* 2 volumes. Würzburg: Königshausen & Neumann, 1987.

Schmidt, Alfred. *Die Kritische Theorie als Geschichtsphilosophie.* Munich: Carl Hanser, 1976.

Schmucker, Joseph F. *Adorno—Logik des Zerfalls.* Stuttgart: Frommann-Holzboog, 1977.

Schoberth, Wolfgang. *Das Jenseits der Kunst: Beiträge zu einer wissenssoziologischen Rekonstruktion der ästhetischen Theorie Theodor W. Adornos.* Frankfurt: Peter Lang, 1988.

Schonherr, Ulrich. "Adorno, Ritter Gluck, and the Tradition of the Postmodern." *New German Critique,* no. 48 (fall 1989): 135–54.

Schultz, Karla L. *Mimesis on the Move: Theodor W. Adorno's Concept of Imitation.* New York: Peter Lang, 1990.

Schweppenhäuser, Gerhard, and Mirko Wischke (ed.). *Impuls und Negativität: Ethik und Ästhetik bei Adorno.* Hamburg: Argument Verlag, 1995.

Seel, Martin. *Die Kunst der Entzweiung. Zum Begriff der ästhetischen Rationalität.* Frankfurt: Suhrkamp, 1985.

Seel, Martin. *Eine Ästhetik der Natur.* Frankfurt: Suhrkamp, 1991.

Siebert, Rudolf. *The Critical Theory of Religion, the Frankfurt School: From Universal Pragmatic to Political Theology.* Berlin, New York: Mouton, 1985.

Simon, Richard Keller. "Between Capra and Adorno: West's *Day of the Locust* and the Movies of the 1930s." *Modern Language Quarterly* 54 (December 1993): 513–34.

Slater, Phil. *Origin and Significance of the Frankfurt School: A Marxist Perspective.* London: Routledge & Kegan Paul, 1977.

Specht, Silvia. *Erinnerung als Veränderung. Über den Zusammenhang von Kunst und Politik bei Theodor W. Adorno.* Mittenwald: Mäander Kunstverlag, 1981.

Spülbeck, Volker. *Neomarxismus und Theologie. Gesellschaftskritik in Kritischer Theorie und Politischer Theologie.* Freiburg: Herder, 1977.

Steinberg, Michael P. "The Musical Absolute (Adorno's Writings on Music)." *New German Critique* 56 (1992): 17–42.

Steinberg, Michael P. "Introduction: Music, Language, and Culture." *Musical Quarterly* 77 (fall 1993): 397–400.

Subotnik, Rose Rosengard. *Developing Variations: Style and Ideology in Western Music.* Minneapolis: University of Minnesota Press, 1991.

Sullivan, Michael, and John T. Lysaker. "Between Impotence and Illusion: Adorno's Art of Theory and Practice." *New German Critique,* no. 57 (fall 1992): 87–122.

Sunner, Rüdiger. "Tanz der Begriffe: Musikalische Elemente im Sprachstil von Nietzsche und Adorno." In *Neuere Studien zur Aphoristik und Essayistik*, pp. 184–202. Edited by Giulia Cantarutti. Frankfurt: Peter Lang, 1986.

Sziborsky, Lucia. *Adornos Musikphilosophie. Genese—Konstitution—Pädagogische Perspektiven.* Munich: Wilhelm Fink, 1979.

Taussig, Michael. *Mimesis and Alterity: A Particular History of the Senses.* New York: Routledge, 1993.

Therborn, Göran. "The Frankfurt School." *New Left Review*, no. 63 (September–October 1970): 65–96.

Theunissen, Michael. *Gesellschaft und Geschichte. Zur Kritik der kritischen Theorie.* Berlin: Walter de Gruyter, 1969.

Tichy, Matthias. *Theodor W. Adorno. Das Verhältnis von Allgemeinem und Besonderem in seiner Philosophie.* Bonn: Bouvier Verlag Herbert Grundmann, 1977.

Toole, David. "Of Lingering Eyes and Talking Things: Adorno and Deleuze on Philosophy since Auschwitz." *Philosophy Today* 37 (fall 1993): 227–46.

Townsend, Peter. "Adorno on Jazz: Vienna versus the Vernacular." *Prose Studies* 11 (May 1988): 69–88.

Ulle, Dieter. "Bürgerliche Kulturkritik und Ästhetik. Bemerkungen zu Theodor Adornos Schrift 'Ästhetische Theorie.'" *Weimarer Beiträge* 18 (1972) 6: 133–54.

van Reijen, Willem, et al. *Adorno: An Introduction.* Translated by Dieter Engelbrecht. Philadelphia: Pennbridge Books, 1992.

Varadharajan, Asha. *Exotic Parodies: Subjectivity in Adorno, Said, and Spivak.* Minneapolis: University of Minnesota Press, 1995.

Vogel, Steven. *Against Nature: The Concept of Nature in Critical Theory.* Albany: State University of New York Press, 1996.

Waldman, Diane. "Critical Theory and Film: Adorno and 'The Culture Industry' Revisited." *New German Critique*, no. 12 (fall 1977): 39–60.

Walther, B. K. "One God among the Gods. Traces of Hölderlin in Adorno and de Man." *Orbis litterarum* 51 (1996): 1–10.

Weitzman, R. "An Introduction to Adorno's Music and Social Criticism." *Music and Letters* 52 (1971): 287–98.

Wellmer, Albrecht. "Reason, Utopia, and the Dialectic of Enlightenment." *Praxis International* 3 (July 1983): 83–107. Reprinted in *Habermas and Modernity*, pp. 35–66. Edited by Richard J. Bernstein. Cambridge, Mass.: MIT Press, 1985.

Wellmer, Albrecht. "Truth, Semblance, and Reconciliation: Adorno's Aesthetic Redemption of Modernity." *Telos*, no. 62 (winter 1984–1985): 89–115.

Wellmer, Albrecht. *Zur Dialektik von Moderne und Postmoderne: Vernunftkritik nach Adorno.* Frankfurt: Suhrkamp, 1985.

Wellmer, Albrecht. "Metaphysics at the Moment of Its Fall." In *Literary Theory Today,* pp. 35–49. Edited by Peter Collier and Helga Geyer-Ryan. Ithaca, N.Y.: Cornell University Press, 1990.

Wellmer, Albrecht. *The Persistence of Modernity: Essays on Aesthetics, Ethics, and Postmodernism.* Translated by David Midgley. Cambridge, Mass.: MIT Press, 1991.

Wellmer, Albrecht. *Endspiele. Die unversöhnliche Moderne: Essays und Vorträge.* Frankfurt: Suhrkamp, 1993.

Welsch, Wolfgang. "Adornos Ästhetik: Eine implizite Ästhetik des Erhabenen." In *Das Erhabene. Zwischen Grenzerfahrung und Grössenwahn,* pp. 185–213. Edited by Christine Pries. Weinheim: VCH Acta Humaniora, 1989.

Wergin, Ulrich. "Zwischen Strukturalismus und Kritischer Theorie: Das 'Wortwerden des Fleisches' in den Ästhetikkonzeptionen Mukarovskys, Benjamins und Adornos." *Deutsche Vierteljahresschrift für Literaturwissenschaft und Geistesgeschichte* 50 (September 1985): 349–79.

Werkmeister, O. K. "Das Kunstwerk als Negation. Zur geschichtlichen Bestimmung der Kunsttheorie Theodor W. Adornos." In his *Ende der Ästhetik,* pp. 7–32. Frankfurt: S. Fischer, 1971.

Whitebook, Joel. *Perversion and Utopia: A Study of Psychoanalysis and Critical Theory.* Cambridge, Mass.: MIT Press, 1995.

Wiggershaus, Rolf. *Theodor W. Adorno.* Munich: C. H. Beck, 1987.

Wiggershaus, Rolf. *The Frankfurt School: Its History, Theories, and Political Significance.* Translated by Michael Robertson. Cambridge, Mass.: MIT Press, 1994.

Wilke, Sabine. "Kritische und ideologische Momente der Parataxis: eine Lekture von Adorno, Heidegger und Hölderlin." *MLN* 102 (April 1987): 627–47.

Wilke, Sabine. *Zur Dialektik von Exposition und Darstellung: Ansätze zu einer Kritik der Arbeiten Martin Heideggers, Theodor W. Adornos und Jacques Derridas.* New York: Peter Lang, 1988.

Wilke, Sabine. "Adorno and Derrida as Readers of Husserl: Some Reflections on the Historical Context of Modernism and Postmodernism." *Boundary 2* 16 (winter/spring 1989): 77–90.

Wohlfart, Günter. "Anmerkungen zur ästhetischen Theorie Adornos." *Philosophisches Jahrbuch* 83 (1976): 370–91. A revised version appears in *Zeitschrift für Ästhetik und allgemeine Kunstwissensschaft* 22 (1977): 110–34.

Wohlfarth, Irving, "Hibernation: On the Tenth Anniversary of Adorno's Death." *Modern Language Notes* 94 (December 1979): 956–87.

Wolin, Richard. "The De-Aestheticization of Art: On Adorno's *Aesthetische Theorie.*" *Telos*, no. 41 (fall 1979): 105–27.

Wolin, Richard. "Utopia, Mimesis, and Reconciliation: A Redemptive Critique of Adorno's *Aesthetic Theory.*" *Representations* 32 (fall 1990): 33–49.

Wolin, Richard. *The Terms of Cultural Criticism: The Frankfurt School, Existentialism, Poststructuralism.* New York: Columbia University Press, 1992.

Wolin, Richard. *Walter Benjamin: An Aesthetic of Redemption.* 2d ed. Berkeley: University of California Press, 1994.

Wurzer, Wilhelm S. *Filming and Judgment: Between Heidegger and Adorno.* Atlantic Highlands, N.J.: Humanities Press International, 1990.

Zenck, Martin. *Kunst als begriffslose Erkenntnis. Zum Kunstbegriff der ästhetischen Theorie Theodor W. Adornos.* Munich: Wilhelm Fink, 1977.

Zenck, Martin. "Auswirkungen einer 'musique informelle' auf die neue Musik: Zu Theodor W. Adornos Formvorstellung." *International Review of the Aesthetics and Sociology of Music* 10 (1979) 2: 137–65.

Zima, Peter V. "Dialektik zwischen Totalität und Fragment." In *Der Streit mit Georg Lukács*, pp. 124–72. Edited by Hans-Jürgen Schmitt. Frankfurt: Suhrkamp, 1978.

Zimmermann, Norbert. *Der ästhetische Augenblick: Theodor W. Adornos Theorie der Zeitstruktur von Kunst und ästhetischer Erfahrung.* Frankfurt: Peter Lang, 1989.

Zuidervaart, Lambert. "The Artefactuality of Autonomous Art: Kant and Adorno." In *The Reasons of Art: Artworks and the Transformations of Philosophy*, pp. 256–62. Edited by Peter McCormick. Ottawa: University of Ottawa Press, 1986.

Zuidervaart, Lambert. "Methodological Shadowboxing in Marxist Aesthetics: Lukács and Adorno." *Journal of Comparative Literature and Aesthetics* 11 (1988) 1–2: 85–113. Reprinted in *The Aesthetics of the Critical Theorists*, pp. 244–90.

Zuidervaart, Lambert. "The Social Significance of Autonomous Art: Adorno and Bürger." *Journal of Aesthetics and Art Criticism* 48 (winter 1990): 61–77.

Zuidervaart, Lambert. *Adorno's Aesthetic Theory: The Redemption of Illusion.* Cambridge, Mass.: MIT Press, 1991.

Zuidervaart, Lambert. "Contra-Diction: Adorno's Philosophy of Discourse." In *The Philosophy of Discourse: The Rhetorical Turn in Twentieth-Century Thought.* Vol. 1, pp. 103–28. Edited by Chip Sills and George H. Jensen. Portsmouth, N.H.: Heinemann, Boynton/Cook, 1992.

Zuidervaart, Lambert. "History, Art, and Truth: Wellmer's Critique of Adorno." In *Dialectic and Narrative*, pp. 197–212. Edited by Thomas R. Flynn and Dalia Judovitz. Albany: State University of New York Press, 1993.

Contributors

J. M. Bernstein is professor of philosophy and dean of humanities at the University of Essex. His most recent books are *The Fate of Art: Aesthetic Alienation from Kant to Derrida and Adorno* and *Recovering Ethical Life: Jürgen Habermas and the Future of Critical Theory*. He also has edited and introduced *The Culture Industry: Selected Essays on Mass Culture by Theodor W. Adorno* and the six volumes of *Critical Assessments: The Frankfurt School*. He is presently completing a book that reconstructs Adorno's thought in terms of its implied ethics.

Rüdiger Bubner is professor of philosophy at the University of Heidelberg. His books include *Handlung, Sprache und Vernunft* (1975, 1982), *Modern German Philosophy* (1981), *Geschichtsprozesse und Handlungsnormen* (1984), *Essays in Hermeneutics and Critical Theory* (1988), *Ästhetische Erfahrung* (1989), *Dialektik als Topik* (1990), *Antike Themen und ihre moderne Verwandlung* (1992), and *Innovationen des Idealismus* (1995).

Gregg M. Horowitz teaches aesthetics and critical social theory in the Department of Philosophy at Vanderbilt University. He has written on the philosophy of art history, especially the historiography of modernism, as well as on the politics of art and antiutopian elements in late modern art. At present, he is working on a manuscript on loss, trauma, compensation, and memory in modern and contemporary philosophical aesthetics.

Tom Huhn teaches in the Philosophy Department and the College of Letters at Wesleyan University. He is completing a book on the aesthetics of Kant, Adorno, and Paul de Man, and coauthoring a volume on the relation between Arthur Danto's theory of art and his taste.

Robert Hullot-Kentor is editor of the *Collected Writings of T. W. Adorno* (47 volumes) in preparation, Stanford University Press, and has written many essays on Adorno's aesthetics. He is the translator of Adorno's *Aesthetic Theory* and *Kierke-*

gaard: Construction of the Aesthetic. Currently, he is a participating editor of Adorno's *Nachgelassene Schriften* [*Posthumous Writings*] and is preparing an edition of *Current of Music: Elements of a Radio Theory,* Adorno's unpublished writings of the 1930s and 1940s.

Martin Jay is professor of European intellectual history at the University of California, Berkeley. Among his books are *The Dialectical Imagination* (1973, 2d ed., with a new preface 1996), *Marxism and Totality* (1984), *Adorno* (1984), *Permanent Exiles* (1985), *Fin-de-siècle Socialism* (1988), *Force Fields* (1993), and *Downcast Eyes* (1993). He is currently working on the discourse of experience in recent European and American theory.

Shierry Weber Nicholsen is a faculty member in the graduate program on environment and community at Antioch University, in Yellow Springs, Ohio. She has written extensively on Frankfurt School aesthetics and has translated several of Adorno's works, including *Notes to Literature* and *Hegel: Three Studies,* as well as works by and about Jürgen Habermas, Herbert Marcuse, and Walter Benjamin. Her book *Exact Imagination, Late Work: On Adorno's Aesthetics* will be published by the MIT Press in 1997.

Heinz Paetzold teaches philosophy at the University of Hamburg and is head of the Department of Theory at the Jan Van Eyck Akademie, in Maastricht, a postgraduate center for fine arts, design, and theory. His fields of interest include philosophical aesthetics, philosophy of culture, anthropology, and philosophy of language. He is the author of *Neomarxistische Ästhetik* (1974), *Ästhetik des deutschen Idealismus* (1983), *Ästhetik der neueren Moderne* (1990), *Profile der Ästhetik in der Postmoderne* (1990), *Cassirer zur Einführung* (1993), *Die Realität der symbolischen Formen* (1994), *The Discourse of the Postmodern and the Discourse of the Avant-Garde* (1994), and *Ernst Cassirer—Von Marburg nach New York. Eine philosophische Biographie* (1995).

Heidi Schlipphacke is a doctoral student in Germanics at the University of Washington. Her dissertation is on the concept of female masochism in the German tradition from the eighteenth century to the present.

Rolf Tiedemann served as Adorno's assistant from 1959 to 1965, and has been director of the Theodor W. Adorno Archive in Frankfurt since 1985. He is editor of the twenty volumes of Adorno's *Gesammelte Schriften* and the ongoing edition of *Nachgelassene Schriften,* and he is coeditor of the seven volumes of Walter Benjamin's *Gesammelte Schriften.* His own writings include the books *Studien zur Philosophie Walter Benjamins* and *Dialektik im Stillstand.*

Sabine Wilke is associate professor of German at the University of Washington, where she teaches modern German literature, culture, and film. She has written books on critical theory and poststructuralism, the reception of mythology in contemporary German literature, and history and subjectivity in Christa Wolf's writings. Her latest book is on Critical Theory and feminism.

Richard Wolin   is professor of modern European intellectual history at Rice University. He is the author of *Walter Benjamin: An Aesthetic of Redemption* (rev. ed. 1994), *The Politics of Being: The Political Thought of Martin Heidegger* (1990), and *Labyrinths: Explorations in the Critical History of Ideas* (1995).

Lambert Zuidervaart   is professor of philosophy and department chair at Calvin College. He also serves as president of the Urban Institute for Contemporary Arts, in Grand Rapids, Michigan. A specialist in cultural theory and in nineteenth- and twentieth-century philosophy, he is the author of *Adorno's Aesthetic Theory: The Redemption of Illusion* (1991), coauthor of *Dancing in the Dark: Youth, Popular Culture, and the Electronic Media* (1991), and coeditor of *Pledges of Jubilee: Essays on the Arts and Culture* (1995). He is currently completing a book titled *Cultural Politics and Artistic Truth* and coediting and introducing a collection of new essays called *The Arts, Community, and Cultural Democracy*.

Index

Studies in Contemporary German Social Thought
Thomas McCarthy, General Editor

Tom Huhn and Lambert Zuidervaart, editors, *The Semblance of Subjectivity: Essays in Adorno's Aesthetic Theory*

Hans Joas, *G. H. Mead: A Contemporary Re-examination of His Thought*

Michael Kelly, editor, *Critique and Power: Recasting the Foucault/Habermas Debate*

Hans Herbert Kögler, *The Power of Dialogue: Critical Hermeneutics after Gadamer and Foucault*

Reinhart Koselleck, *Critique and Crisis: Enlightenment and the Pathogenesis of Modern Society*

Reinhart Koselleck, *Futures Past: On the Semantics of Historical Time*

Harry Liebersohn, *Fate and Utopia in German Sociology, 1887–1923*

Herbert Marcuse, *Hegel's Ontology and the Theory of Historicity*

Larry May and Jerome Kohn, editors, *Hannah Arendt: Twenty Years Later*

Pierre Missac, *Walter Benjamin's Passages*

Gil G. Noam and Thomas E. Wren, editors, *The Moral Self*

Guy Oakes, *Weber and Rickert: Concept Formation in the Cultural Sciences*

Claus Offe, *Contradictions of the Welfare State*

Claus Offe, *Disorganized Capitalism: Contemporary Transformations of Work and Politics*

Claus Offe, *Modernity and the State: East, West*

Claus Offe, *Varieties of Transition: The East European and East German Experience*

Helmut Peukert, *Science, Action, and Fundamental Theology: Toward a Theology of Communicative Action*

Joachim Ritter, *Hegel and the French Revolution: Essays on the* Philosophy of Right

William E. Scheuerman, *Between the Norm and the Exception: The Frankfurt School and the Rule of Law*

Alfred Schmidt, *History and Structure: An Essay on Hegelian-Marxist and Structuralist Theories of History*

Dennis Schmidt, *The Ubiquity of the Finite: Hegel, Heidegger, and the Entitlements of Philosophy*

Carl Schmitt, *The Crisis of Parliamentary Democracy*

Carl Schmitt, *Political Romanticism*

Carl Schmitt, *Political Theology: Four Chapters on the Concept of Sovereignty*

Gary Smith, editor, *On Walter Benjamin: Critical Essays and Recollections*

Michael Theunissen, *The Other: Studies in the Social Ontology of Husserl, Heidegger, Sartre, and Buber*

Ernst Tugendhat, *Self-Consciousness and Self-Determination*

Georgia Warnke, *Justice and Interpretation*

Mark Warren, *Nietzsche and Political Thought*

Albrecht Wellmer, *The Persistence of Modernity: Essays on Aesthetics, Ethics and Postmodernism*

Joel Whitebook, *Perversion and Utopia: A Study in Psychoanalysis and Critical Theory*

Rolf Wiggershaus, *The Frankfurt School: Its History, Theories, and Political Significance*

Thomas E. Wren, editor, *The Moral Domain: Essays in the Ongoing Discussion between Philosophy and the Social Sciences*

Lambert Zuidervaart, *Adorno's Aesthetic Theory: The Redemption of Illusion*